Nine O'clock in the Morning

with

The Holy Spirit and You

ISBN 0 85476 782 7

Designed and produced by Bookprint Creative Services
P.O. Box 827, BN21 3YJ, England for
KINGSWAY PUBLICATIONS
Lottbridge Drove, Eastbourne, E. Sussex BN23 6NT
Printed in Great Britain.

Reproduced from the original typesetting
of the single-volume editions.

Nine O'clock in the Morning

DENNIS J. BENNETT

KINGSWAY PUBLICATIONS
EASTBOURNE

THIS BOOK IS LOVINGLY DEDICATED
IN MEMORY OF
ELBERTA BENNETT

"One of God's great ones" and
a true soldier of Christ

Acknowledgements

I want to thank all those who have helped in the offering of places of retreat in which to write: Dean and Cordie Barber, Norman and Eleanor Smaha, and Cecil and Lillian Cooper. Special appreciation for typing to Eleanor Smaha, Helen Hitchman, and Cordie Barber; thanks also to Cordie for her capable copy editing on half the book.

My thanks to the clergy, their wives, and the people of St. Luke's Church, Seattle for their love and prayers and for the faithfulness of those who have stood with me in this work through the years.

I am grateful to Christian friends all over the world who have been praying for God's blessing on this book.

Loving appreciation to my wife, Rita, who has been a full partner in this project: typing, revising, editing, and in every way lending her creative ability and encouragement. It is her book, too!

Praise and thanksgiving above all, to God Himself, Father, Son, and Holy Spirit, Who makes all things possible in His love. This is a book about Him, and how He's working through people. I pray that He will bless you in the reading of it.

In the love of Jesus,
DENNIS J. BENNETT

Introduction

How could a successful Rector of a 2,500 strong congregation risk the future of his ministry and the unity of his church by getting involved with the "baptism in the Spirit", "speaking in tongues", and all that?

And how could the same man take over a run-down mission church and see it renewed by the Spirit into one of the most spiritually alive churches in North America?

Dennis Bennett's story, told breezily in a thoroughly human and humourous style, is a powerful illustration of the movement of the Holy Spirit today.

What is this "filling of the Spirit"? What about the gifts that have recently caused such controversy? How can all this affect the lives of Christians and churches today?

This book, with straightforward narrative rather than theological explanations, will answer some urgent questions. It will show that God is just as alive and active as He was 2,000 years ago.

The marks of the Spirit's presence have always been the same: a new reality of God, a love for Jesus Christ, a hunger for the Scriptures, spontaneous joy and praise and witness, generous giving . . .

Dennis Bennett's fascinating account will undoubtedly stimulate faith in the lives of many readers.

DAVID WATSON
St. Michael-le-Belfrey, York

Contents

Nine O'clock in the Morning

I

"Fired-up" People

A day off is a good thing, and I was enjoying mine. Sunday is a busy day for a minister, and the week ahead promised to be even more so; but right now it was Monday, and I had been unwinding, pottering in my shop for most of the morning. Now, still luxuriating in the comfort of old clothes, I relaxed after lunch.

"I tell you, Dennis, there's something strange going on in my congregation!" The earnest young man with the clerical collar paused and looked at me across the kitchen table.

A fairly frequent visitor at our house, Frank was a young Anglican priest, recently come to the United States from the north of Ireland, and now, like myself, pastor of an Episcopal church in the Los Angeles area.

"Tell me about it," I said, pushing my chair back. My wife Elberta stopped clearing away the dishes and sat down to listen.

Frank riffled his hand across his close-cropped hair and shook his head ruefully.

"It's this young couple in my church," he began; "they've really got me going!"

"Whatever are you talking about?" I asked him.

Frank was silent for a moment, then shrugged.

"Well, they come to church *all* the time!" he said.

I chuckled. "What on earth is wrong with that?" I asked.

"Yes, I suppose that does sound funny; but you see, although they actually have belonged to the church for years, they hardly ever came until five months ago. As a matter of fact, I'd never met them although I became vicar of the church well over a year ago. Now they're there every Sunday, and during the week, too, if we have special events. They're just there— looking happy!"

"Looking happy in church?" I cracked. "That *is* suspicious behaviour!"

"Yes, but—well, the thing that bothers me most is that when I asked them how come they turn up all the time and look so happy, they said, 'We've been baptized in the Holy Spirit!'"*

"They've been *what* in the *what*?" I asked.

"That's about what I said when I first heard it," Frank went on. "But stranger yet, they also claim to have 'spoken in tongues,' whatever that is."

"Oh," I said, "now I'm beginning to understand what's bothering you; but why be so worried about it? There are plenty of mixed up people in the world. Expect one or two to show up in your backyard now and then. Why don't you ask them to settle down, or leave?"

"It isn't really like that," my friend replied. "You see, they

---

* The terms "baptized in the Holy Spirit," "baptism in the Holy Spirit," "receive the Holy Spirit" are used throughout this book. We are well aware that there is much discussion among Christians as to whether these terms should be used of the experience we are describing. We have been tempted to speak of it as "Experience X-2" to avoid argument, but that would have been clumsy! Please bear with us, and don't be thrown off the track by terminology.

don't *act* peculiar. They don't shout, or jump, or do anything wild. On the contrary, when you're with them, you just can't deny the fact that they've *got* something. They—they glow, like little light bulbs! And they're so loving and ready to help whenever I ask them. In fact, I don't have to ask them—they volunteer! They've even started tithing—you know, giving ten per cent of their income to the church!"

"W-e-l-l, what you've described doesn't sound like too bad a disease to have spread around, Frank, barring the 'speaking in tongues' bit, of course." I rolled my paper napkin into a ball and pitched it at the wastepaper basket in the corner. My day off was getting far too complicated! Hoping to change the subject, I said brightly: "How are things going with you otherwise?"

Frank, however, was not to be sidetracked: "I know it seems odd to be worried over this business," he mused. "It certainly is strange to be upset because people are getting enthusiastic, but this 'speaking in tongues,' 'baptism in the Holy Spirit' thing bothers me. I feel I can't brush it away—I have to understand what's going on. After all," Frank paused and smiled wryly, "I *am* supposed to be the spiritual leader of the church.

"Look here!" he suddenly challenged me. "What about coming down and meeting them? See what you think?"

"Whoa! Not me, Frank! I don't want to get involved. If there's one thing I don't like, it's high pressure. These fiery parishioners of yours would probably seize me by the coat lapels and ask me if I was 'saved,' or something like that! Sorry, old friend—No! You have your little problems, and I have mine!"

Frank shrugged his shoulders again and grinned at me as he rose from the table and prepared to leave.

"Okay," he said, "I've got to get on my way. Thanks for

lunch," said he, turning to Elberta. "And, uh, see if you can get him to change his mind about coming to meet these people."

The door closed on our departing guest. I paused for a moment: "Wow! That's a wild story!" I said. "It isn't like Frank to get interested in *that* sort of thing!"

"What's the matter with it?"

I looked at my wife with some alarm: "The matter? Why it's obviously some kind of off-beat emotionalism!" I said, a little heatedly.

"But he specifically said they weren't emotional, didn't he?" Elberta queried.

"Y-e-s, but—my heavens, honey! 'Speaking in tongues!' What else could it be?"

Frank's situation left me counting my blessings. There was no "emotionalism" in *our* church! We were Episcopalians, and prided ourselves on our cool, even somewhat ironical approach to our faith. I was not eager to become involved in anything that sounded silly or irrational, and anyway, I didn't have time for it. There were, thank God, no starry-eyed zealots among my congregation—St. Mark's, in the Los Angeles suburb of Van Nuys.

Just twenty-six hundred good Episcopalians!

The Case of the "Fired-up" Parishioners refused to be ignored, though. Frank kept after me, and after a solid month of good-natured heckling on his part, I decided I might as well go and see what it was all about. My curiosity was aroused by Frank's persistence, because I did respect his judgment. Besides, I was beginning to feel a bit of a coward! At any rate, I found myself driving down the freeway with Elberta, to meet these mysterious people. It was a beautiful August evening, but I was not enjoying myself. What on earth were we getting ourselves into? I anticipated an awkward and embarrassing scene, and rather wished that it was all safely over.

I continued to feel this way as we walked up the drive to the house, a typical little California suburban bungalow. Frank was there and made the introductions. As we shook hands and sat down in the living room, I watched these people. When would they "make their move"? Then, as we talked, I began to relax somewhat, for our new acquaintances were indeed very "normal" and pleasant; in their mid-thirties: the young man quiet and straightforward; she what the women's magazines would describe as an "attractive young housewife," her dark hair and eyes contrasting pleasantly with her husband's fair colouring. The happiness and assurance that radiated from them both was unmistakable. I began to see why Frank was so intrigued.

There were the usual polite conversational openings and small talk, and then, unable to contain my curiosity any longer, I dived in:

"What's it all about?" I asked. "What *has* happened to you people?"

Without any hesitation they replied, "Why, we've been baptized in the Holy Spirit!"

"We went to a neighbourhood prayer meeting," explained Joan, her face lighting up even more at the memory, "and we enjoyed it very much." ("Good heavens," I parenthized mentally, "*enjoying* a prayer meeting? Oh, come on!") "But what impressed us most," she continued, "was this fellow named Bud. He seemed to be so happy, and so sure of God, that he made us hungry to know what he had. That's about the only way I can put it; and John felt the same." She looked at her husband, and he picked up the story:

"Yes, that's the way it was. So we asked him: 'What's happened to you?' and he just said, 'Oh, I've been baptized in the

Holy Ghost!' We didn't know what he was talking about. We didn't go to church very often—Easter and Christmas mostly —and we didn't know much about the Bible; but we were so attracted by what we felt and saw in that young man's life that we said, 'We want it, too!'"

"Yes," said Joan, "and he didn't say: 'Let's go and talk to my minister,' although he is a loyal member of a big church downtown. He just said: 'Let's pray about it. You can receive this right now.' So we did—and we *did*!"

"Get 'baptized in the Holy Ghost,' you mean," I said. "But what does *that* mean?"

"Just like in the Bible!"

That was a low blow! As a minister of the gospel—with sixteen years' experience and a graduate degree in theology from a well-known university, I was certainly supposed to know what was in the Bible. Yet as John and Joan talked, I realized that there were some very important things I'd somehow missed.

As we left their home that night, my wife, a practical person and not easily swayed, said, as soon as we were out of earshot:

"I don't know what these people have, but I want it!"

I made no outward response, but had plenty to think about. Those people had talked about God, and about Jesus Christ, with an enthusiasm that most people save for their favourite hobby, or their most deeply held political convictions! I couldn't escape the fact that these two friends of Frank's radiated something that stirred feelings and responses deep within me. They seemed to know God—to be so sure of Him. Was what I was feeling real, or was I just responding emotionally to their obvious happiness? I was rector of a large church in the San Fernando Valley and had a couple of thousand people looking to me for spiritual leadership. I didn't want to lead them down the wrong trail. Still I couldn't escape the idea that those two "fired-up" Episcopalians might have something I needed, and something others might want too, if they found out about it. But what *was* it? What did it mean?

2
Something Missing

"Well, what do you think?" My wife looked inquiringly at me across the breakfast table the morning after our encounter with John and Joan.

"I don't know," I replied, putting down my fork. "Those people sure are excited about God!"

Elberta's brown eyes became very thoughtful. She looked out of the window for a few moments before answering:

"Yes. It must be great to know Him that well."

"You know Him, don't you?" My impression was that my wife knew the Lord a lot better than I did.

"I can't remember a time when I didn't," she said slowly, "but these people seem to be so much closer. He seems especially real to them ... I wonder how?"

I wondered too, and took my thoughts out to my study. Sitting at my desk, looking at the pile of unanswered letters, and the tentative notes that hopefully might become next Sunday's sermon, my mind swung back thirty years to my own earlier days. I *could* remember a time when I didn't know God.

My father, an English minister, brought my mother and me

to the United States when I was nine, and we settled in the little town of Campbell, near San Jose, California. As a minister's son I was brought up in "church"; yet I had not known that one could meet God personally until I was eleven years old. Elberta had been brought up in a little old-fashioned "Bible-believing" church in a northern California mill town; but the denomination in which I was raised was in the forefront of the "modernist" movement, and although I went to Sunday School and Youth Group and learned Bible stories, no one, as far as I could remember, had said anything about "accepting" Jesus Christ. Christ was presented as a great "example," and a great "teacher," but not as the divine Son of God who was also a personal Saviour.* Then one memorable night at a junior young people's meeting at our church, we had a visiting speaker, a friend of my father, an executive of the local Christian Endeavour organization. His name was Howard L. Brown.† I don't remember much about his talk, but do remember that when it ended, he looked at us eleven- and twelve-year-olds and asked:

"Is there anyone who would like to ask Jesus Christ to come into his heart?"

This, to me, was a new way of talking. Up until this time,

---

* My father, the pastor of our church, was a man who knew the Lord. He had been called to the ministry by the audible voice of God. Like many men of his generation, however, he was baffled by the outpourings of unbelief from the Biblical scholars and seminaries. It was difficult for a man of limited training to know how to react when the respected leaders of his denomination were denying the basic beliefs of the Christian faith. As a result, I was a grown man before my father shared his own experience of God with me.

† A part of Howard L. Brown's ministry was song-writing, and his name is still found in gospel song books. Having mentioned him in an article I wrote for *Christian Life Magazine* as the one who had led me to Jesus Christ, I received a wonderful letter from his widow, Margaret W. Brown, expressing her joy at finding one more person who had met the Lord through her husband's ministry.

"religion" was just a part of everyday living, like eating and sleeping. You went to church because that was what you did, that's all. Now this man was telling us that we were supposed to take some kind of step for ourselves—make up our own minds about something.

"If you'd like to ask Jesus into your heart, put your hand up," he said.

There would have been a "fat" chance of my doing any such thing, with my friends Ted C. and Bobby B. looking on, especially Bobby, who was the class humourist at school! But the man said:

"Everyone close your eyes and bow your heads."

That made it possible! Somehow I felt I *wanted* to, so I stuck my hand up. That's all I did, and that's all he asked us to do, but something happened! My heart glowed with a new warmth and happiness, as for the first time I felt the Presence of God. I had invited Jesus to come in and He had accepted the invitation!

My thoughts moved on eight years—when God suddenly broke through to me again with a "second touch." I was sitting in front of the fireplace in my father's study, reading a book I had picked up out of curiosity, which told of great men and women and their experience with God. As I read, a wonderful refreshment and joy swept through me as I recognized again the Presence of God with me.

Then in the early days of my marriage, while I was working in the electronics business, I used to get up early and sit in the morning quiet to feel God's nearness, and I would feel it! The assurance of love, warmth, and well-being that God's Presence brought, I found to be what life was all about. I realized that if I could somehow keep this continually with me, all questions would be answered. The only trouble was, I couldn't. God seemed to be gone almost before He was there. When a flash-bulb is fired, you know there has been a dazzling light because of the spots before your eyes and the latent image on the film, but the light itself is gone almost before it comes. God's Presence seemed something like that. Nevertheless, momentary though they were, these "touches" from God kept me moving in His direction.

I didn't want to be a minister, but I did want somehow to work full-time for God, so at the age of twenty-six I left my job and went back to college and then to graduate school, my purpose being to get a degree in theology, so that I would be ready for whatever field might open to me. The theological school I selected was of the most extreme "liberal humanist" persuasion, and I hadn't been there long before I found that my beliefs were to be challenged. It was, in fact, my very first night in the residence halls that my next-door neighbour, a senior, and a very "ministerial," scholarly looking chap, came by to "cue me in":

"Of course, we no longer believe in the miracles of the Bible, the divinity of Jesus, or the virgin birth," he opined, peering at me through his black-framed spectacles. "Science has shown these to be impossible, also life after death, and other such things. We can no longer accept the supernatural. We must develop a natural, scientifically respectable religion that will be accepted by modern intellectuals!" Well, his argument didn't convince me, because, having met Jesus, I knew He was the divine Son of God, but I was a bit taken aback, just the same, as I was to be many times in the following years of study!

I was to find, for example, that one of our most respected professors, a fine old gentleman and a tremendous scholar, began all of his semester classes in the psychology of religion with the preface:

"I want you to understand that I am an atheist!"

In order to support my family while I was in seminary I found it necessary to become pastor, not of one, but *two* little churches in rural Illinois, and there my family lived while I commuted home on weekends from school in Chicago, eighty miles away.

I became increasingly interested in my studies and in ministering to my churches. Strangely enough, I soon realized that theological study and church work were leading me away from my personal relationship with God. In fact, I "came to" after three years to discover that I had ceased saying any private prayers at all! I had become so concerned about study and church work that my personal life with God had become almost nil. As soon as I realized this, I did begin to say petitionary prayers again, but I was too busy for much more. It was a little like having a personal friend become your employer. You are now so busy working for him that you don't have time to spend enjoying his friendship. Your relationship has become "professional."

In 1951, two years after graduating from seminary, I had come into the Episcopal Church (Anglican), because I was dissatisfied with the vague beliefs of the church of my childhood, which seemed to say:

"A Christian is someone who agrees with the ethics of Jesus of Nazareth," or even, "A Christian is someone who says he is a Christian." I felt that the Christian faith had to be more sharply defined than that!

I soon discovered that in practice the Episcopal Church could be vague, too, but there was the great advantage that whereas the church of my earlier days no longer required its people to subscribe to "creeds and dogmas," the Episcopal Church did, so that no matter how much a layman or a priest might deny the basic truths of the Faith or the Scripture, the Creeds were there to show that he was wrong. Then too, every man ordained to the ministry of the Episcopal Church must take a solemn oath in the presence of his bishop and two other clergy, that he holds the Holy Scripture of the Old and New Testaments to be the Word of God, and to contain all things necessary to salvation.[1]

Like most converts, I went "all the way," and embraced the "high church" or Anglo-Catholic position, with strong emphasis on the sacraments, with God's grace being received objectively through the carrying out of specific actions and words—with the right intention of heart. I was happy in my work, and had plenty to keep me busy, with my growing church and growing family. Inside, however, I went on getting drier and drier. This was pointed out to me from time to time, perhaps every year or so when there would be a momentary sense of God's refreshing Presence, reminding me what it had been like to have a closer personal contact with Him. Still, it wasn't until I rounded my fortieth year, after sixteen years in the ministry, that I had really begun to face my need. I had a wonderful wife and family; I was successful in my work; yet I was dry and hungry deep inside.

In my congregation, too, I saw that while people were being helped, lives were rarely being *changed*. Because I had, for the most part, lost my personal awareness of God in my life, I wasn't able to lead the people of the congregation into that kind of awareness. I was propping them up, counselling them, encouraging them, being a "poor man's psychiatrist," teaching them about God; but something was seriously lacking. God wasn't becoming real enough to them to make any noticeable change in their lives. Their religion was a mild sedative to make their lives more palatable, rather than an experience that would drastically change them. Suppose there was something more, a great deal more, to this whole business of Christianity, and we were missing it?

The reason John and Joan intrigued me so much, I mused, was that what I seemingly had lost, they had found—only more so! I had sensed it in them as soon as we began to talk. There wasn't any getting around the fact that these two were enjoying God's Presence in their hearts *while* they were talking with us. I had never witnessed this before, and it was very exciting!

I picked up the Bible that lay on my desk and began to leaf through it. These "fired-up" people claimed to have had some kind of experience with the Holy Spirit. I had to admit that the Holy Spirit was a vague, "theoretical" Being to me. Oh, "officially," I could give a good lecture on Him; I had often done so to confirmation classes in my church, but I had never stopped to think what He was really like. Could a lack of experience with the Holy Spirit be the reason why Christians today don't show the same joy, power, and assurance that we see in the New Testament?

Maybe I'd better do a little research, I thought. So then and there I began to work my way through the New Testament— the part of the Bible that tells about the life of Jesus and the doings of the early Christians—underlining, as I went, any and all references to the Holy Spirit and His work. It was quite a job, and through the days ahead I found that there were about two hundred and forty references to the Holy Spirit in the New Testament. In his letter to the Romans, chapter 8, Paul mentions the Holy Spirit sixteen times in the first fourteen sentences! These early Christians were continually talking about the Holy Spirit; He certainly wasn't vague to them. They talked as though He told them what to do, and where to go, and what to say. They were specific about the Holy Spirit—they didn't confuse Him with the Father or with Jesus.

Another thing in the Bible that caught my attention was that the early believers had a clear-cut experience of receiving the power of the Holy Spirit. I noted that Jesus had told His first followers to stay in Jerusalem because He was going to send them power. "Pentecost" was when it first happened, but I also saw that this experience of Pentecost—of being empowered by the Holy Spirit—was repeated a number of times. Jesus told His people that they couldn't do the job He had for them until they had the power.

I saw, too, that the mysterious "speaking in tongues" kept cropping up. I counted four times in the Acts of the Apostles when there seemed to be a specific "receiving of the Holy Spirit" on the part of a group of people, and in three of the four cases it says something like:

"They began to speak in new languages . . ." [2]

In the fourth case, I found that the commentators pretty much agreed that there, too, at Samaria, they spoke in tongues.

I began to wonder how anything as definite and important as this could have been overlooked by the church today. Or had it been completely overlooked? There was confirmation.* A couple of times a year, having collected together a number of children and adults who desired to share in this rite, and given them a "cram" course in Christian faith and practice, we duly presented them to the bishop. I knew that the average Episcopalian was not too clear as to what it was all about. I wasn't! ! I knew that the major scholars of our denomination disagreed on the purpose of confirmation. I always liked the service, but didn't quite know why.

I recalled confirmation at our church several weeks previously, and pictured in my mind again the people kneeling at the altar rail, while Bishop Gooden, in his eighties but still going strong, moved quietly along laying hands on each one and praying that he would "increase in the Holy Spirit more and

---

* In the Episcopal, Lutheran, Orthodox, and Roman Catholic churches the term "confirmation" is used for the traditional rite intended to strengthen the Christian for service.

more."[3] In that particular class, Mrs. S., a good Presbyterian who was joining the Episcopal Church because her husband was an Episcopalian, had asked me:

"*Why* do I have to be confirmed? What does it mean?" and I had gone through the usual wheel-spinning:

"Well, er, it's the way we do it. It means you are becoming a 'full-fledged' Episcopalian! It gives us an opportunity to make sure that you know what the Episcopal Church is all about— prepares you to become a full and responsible communicant. It's a sort of solemn 'joining the church.' It's the bishop—he's the chief pastor—officially giving you his blessing." Et cetera! One could say to the youngsters:

"This is your 'coming of age,' you know." (A kind of Episcopalian "Bar Mitzvah"!)

I looked again at the "Offices of Instruction" in the Prayer Book:

"The Church provides the Laying on of Hands, or Confirmation, wherein, after renewing the promises and vows of my Baptism, and declaring my loyalty and devotion to Christ as my Master, I receive the strengthening gifts of the Holy Spirit."[4]

There it was again! Yet why was it that statistics in the Episcopal Church at large showed that fifty per cent of these same confirmands who had been prayed for to receive the "strengthening gifts of the Holy Spirit" drifted away from church altogether? What a difference from the early church where those so empowered by the Holy Spirit turned the world upside down!

One day I was browsing through the book *Doctrine in the Church of England,* which is a survey, instigated by the Archbishops of Canterbury and York, of the beliefs of Anglicans on a worldwide basis, and I came across the following thought-provoking statement:

"Participation in the Holy Spirit is set forth in the New Testament as the distinctive mark of Christians, which separated them off from the surrounding world; in the Christianity of Apostolic* times the experience described as that of 'receiving the Spirit' stands in the forefront of the Christian life, at once as the secret of its transporting joy and power and as the source of that victory of faith which could overcome the world." [5]

"Receive the Holy Spirit!" But that was exactly what Frank's enthusiastic parishioners claimed to have done! Was this then the purpose of the bishop's prayer at confirmation? Were we to expect people to be as evidently filled with the power of God as they were in the New Testament when they received the laying on of hands?

Not only did I re-examine the New Testament and the Book of Common Prayer, but I found also that the early Church Fathers, my theology textbooks, church history books, and even the hymn books now seemed to be full of references to the importance of the Holy Spirit, and a great work He was to do in our lives. How did I miss it before?

* The Episcopal Church teaches that we "continue steadfastly in the Apostles' doctrine and fellowship" which means that the same things the Apostles experienced we should expect to happen in the church today.

3
"It Came with the Package"

"Going out again tonight?" asked my long-suffering wife.

"Yep. Vestry meeting. Then I'm going to go down and visit John and Joan for a while."

"All right, I won't wait up for you."

Her smile said, "When are you going to make up your mind?"

I knew she had already made up her mind: I also knew she would not budge until *I* was ready. So once more, after vestry meeting was over, I set out for the little house in Monterey Park, where I had already spent many evenings. I just couldn't get away from the challenge of these "fired-up" people. I was both attracted and repelled. I was attracted, irresistibly, by the Presence of God that I had felt in them, and the fascinating possibility that I might come to find out for myself how one might have such a sense of His Presence. On the other hand, I was repelled by the fact that these were, after all, "mere laymen," who had a very simplistic and narrow-minded idea of the Bible. Why, they were practically *fundamentalists*, taking the Bible at face value! It was not scholarly. Then, too, they kept on about this "speaking in tongues" thing! I was quite sure I didn't want to "speak in tongues"!

This particular night I had asked a friend of mine, another priest of the diocese, to come with me. He had heard the story, and he, too, was interested.

"These people just might have something," he said, as I parked the car and we walked up to the door. "God knows the Church *needs* something!"

As we talked, and as my friend argued politely with John and Joan, I recognized a simple fact that I hadn't faced before, that in spite of my prejudices—I was on their side!

"But are you trying to tell me that you have something I don't have?" said Father C., with just a little asperity in his voice.

John shrugged slightly and smiled.

"If you didn't think we had, why would you be taking the trouble to be here?" he asked gently.

"I don't think they're really saying that," I said. "I don't think they're trying to tell us we don't have the Holy Spirit— I think they're trying to tell us that maybe the Holy Spirit doesn't 'have' us." I looked at John.

"That sounds pretty good," he said. "You fellows have to remember that we're not theologians. We can only tell you what's happened to us, and try to show it to you in the Scripture."

And this was their strong point. I had been doing my "homework," and I found that again and again as the discussion went on, I was saying:

"They're right, you know. That's what it does say in the Bible."

"But what about this 'speaking in tongues' thing?" asked my guest.

"Well," said John, "when we received the Holy Ghost, we spoke in tongues. Just like in the Bible."

There it went! Whenever we got to talking about these

things, they would drag that "red herring" across the trail!

My fellow minister didn't say anything more about it, but I hoped the "tongues thing" hadn't "turned him off." Driving home that night after dropping him at his apartment, my thoughts still ran on the subject:

Speaking in tongues! We had been told in seminary what this meant. It meant that those early Christians, who were, after all, mostly simple people, in fact, in some ways not even quite nice—got very excited and emotional, and well, you know, they made funny noises! "Ululation" was the word one professor used! Intellectuals like St. Paul were, of course, much offended by this, and told them to cool it, or do it at home if they *had* to! The phenomenon in any case hadn't lasted long, and probably was confined to those awful Corinthians!

Yet, as I had re-read my Scripture, I had seen that this wasn't quite the case. I had found that St. Paul didn't condemn "speaking in tongues," just the *mis*use of it. I found, moreover, that he freely and openly admitted that he himself did it more than the rest of them, and for some reason, considered it to be very important. I still didn't want anything to do with it! I was an Englishman by birth and nurture. I had been firmly schooled never to show my feelings. Besides, most of my courses in graduate training at the University of Chicago had been in psychology and counselling, and I knew something about hysteria, hypnosis, auto-suggestion, and stuff like that! These "tongues of ecstasy" sounded a bit too wild for me, although I had to admit that in the Greek originals of the New Testament writings about speaking in tongues, there was no mention of "ecstasy," or anything else that might indicate some kind of frenzied activity. It just said:

"They began to speak in other languages."

I hadn't yet heard anyone "speak in tongues" and hadn't the

least idea what it was all about. I just assumed it was emotionalistic and probably pathological.

Trouble was, St. Paul dragged this "red herring" around too, and even the Lord Himself had something to say about it. He said:

"This is one of the things that will happen after you believe: you will speak in new tongues." [1] And St. Paul said:

"I want all of you to speak in tongues," [2] and, "I thank God, speaking in tongues, more than any of you." [3]

Of course, with my background I could easily explain away these verses. They were "later additions" to the Scripture. Jesus, although the Son of God, was also a man of His day, and shared in some of the funny ideas they had. St. Paul was catering to the pagan notions of the non-Jewish Christian converts. Neither of them had had the benefit of a modern education, nor had they read Freud or Einstein! Yet I was less and less happy with these explanations. John and Joan were uncomplicated and unsophisticated enough simply to believe the Book, and they seemed to be finding in it the key to happiness and effectiveness in a dimension I had never known. My intellect might be saying:

"You've got it wrong," but my heart was saying:

"What have you got? I want it!"

I was like a starving man circling a table on which a delicious-looking feast is spread, watching the people seated at the table obviously enjoying the food, while trying to make up his mind whether it is really safe.

Naturally I was getting hungrier and hungrier. At one point, I had almost sat down to share the feast. I had been having some conversation with Bud, the young man who had impressed John and Joan at first and had prayed for them to receive the Holy Spirit. Bud, at my invitation, had prayed with me, too, and this was the first time I heard anyone "speaking in tongues." At least, that what I understood Bud to be doing. I would never have guessed, for he was in no way "worked up," but just speaking or praying quietly in a language I had never heard. I certainly didn't do anything like that, and apparently nothing happened as he prayed with me, although I must admit that for a few days I seemed to feel a new closeness to God.

Finally, though, on a Saturday afternoon in November, after three whole months of circling, I said to my enthusiastic friends:

"Look here, I've been reading my Bible, my Prayer Book, my theology books, my church history, and as far as I can see this experience you're talking about is in them all. I want what you've got! How did you get it?"

"That's easy," said Joan, "we asked for it!"

"Okay. I'm ready to ask. Show me how!"

I don't know what I really expected from those people that day. I knew they weren't going to pounce on me—they weren't the "pouncy" kind. There were four of us present: myself, a friend of mine who was also an Episcopal priest in our diocese (not the one who had accompanied me before), and John and Joan. We were sitting in their front room, our host and hostess on the davenport under the window, I in an overstuffed chair across the room, and the other clergyman to my right. The California autumn sun was shining bright and hot outside, and the neighbourhood was fairly quiet for a Saturday, the silence broken only by an occasional car going by. I was self-conscious, and determined not to lose my dignity!

"What do I do?" I asked them again.

"Ask Jesus to baptize you in the Holy Spirit," said John. "We'll pray with you, and you just pray and praise the Lord."

I said: "Now remember, I want this nearness to God you have, that's all; I'm not interested in speaking with tongues!"

"Well," said they, "all we can tell you about *that* is that it came with the package!"

John came across the room and laid his hands first on my head, and then on my friend's. He began to pray, very quietly, and I recognized the same thing as when Bud had prayed with me a few days before: he was speaking a language that I did not understand, and speaking it very fluently. He wasn't a bit "worked up" about it, either. Then he prayed in English, asking Jesus to baptize me in the Holy Spirit.

I began to pray, as he told me, and I prayed very quietly, too. I was not about to get even a little bit excited! I was simply following instructions. I suppose I must have prayed aloud for about twenty minutes—at least it seemed to be a long time—and was just about to give up when a very strange thing happened. My tongue tripped, just as it might when you are trying to recite a tongue twister, and I began to speak in a new language!

Right away I recognized several things: first, it wasn't some kind of psychological trick or compulsion. There was nothing compulsive about it. I was allowing these new words to come to my lips and was speaking them out of my own volition, without in any way being forced to do it. I wasn't "carried away" in any sense of the word, but was fully in possession of my wits and my willpower. I spoke the new language because it was interesting to speak a language I had never learned, even though I didn't know what I was saying. I had taken quite a while to learn a small amount of German and French, but here was a language "for free"! Secondly, it was a real language, not some kind of "baby-talk." It had grammar and syntax; it had inflection and expression—and it was rather beautiful! I went on allowing these new words to come to my lips for about five minutes, then said to my friends:

"Well! That must be what you mean by 'speaking in

tongues'— but what is it all about? I don't *feel* anything!"

They said joyfully:

"Praise the Lord!"

This seemed a bit irrelevant and was a little strong for my constitution. It bordered on the fanatical for such a thing to be said by Episcopalians on a fine Saturday afternoon sitting right in the front room of their own home! With much to think about, I gathered up my friend, and we took our leave. On the way to the car he said:

"I guess you must be holier than I am, because you spoke in tongues and I didn't!"

"Well, Keith," I replied, "if I've received some kind of gift, I don't know what it is. I guess I'll have to go home and unwrap it!"

Actually I felt very lighthearted—not at all embarrassed by the afternoon's events—but did not have any sense that some great spiritual breakthrough had taken place.

I thought it over for four days, not saying much even to Elberta, although I knew she was following my activities with great interest. We were alike in that we were not inclined to talk about our deepest thoughts and concerns with anyone, not even with each other, although we were very close in spirit.

It was quite late, perhaps ten o'clock the following Wednesday night, when I made up my mind to pursue the matter further, and headed my '55 Mercury down the freeway to Monterey Park, and once again knocked at the familiar door.

John and Joan greeted me warmly, but I was a little disturbed to see that Frank, their young minister who had originally introduced me to them, was there also. He was still being very "clinical" about the whole matter, and I felt embarrassed to pray for this mysterious "Baptism in the Holy Spirit" in front of him. I felt he would be watching as if it were some kind of lab experiment! Sensing my embarrassment, John suggested:

"Father Bennett, why don't you and I go in the back room and pray some more about this."

It was okay with me. I was still very much interested, and really intrigued by my experience of Saturday afternoon. We sat down on opposite sides of the room and began to pray. Again there was no attempt to "work me up," no emotionalism or excitement. Once more I prayed very quietly and cautiously, and this time, after only about three or four minutes, words began to come in another language, the same language, I noted, that I had spoken on the previous Saturday—at least it sounded like it. Again, I was in no way compelled to speak this new tongue. It was something that I could do if I chose. I was in no strange state of mind whatsoever, and was in full possession of whatever wits I normally had! The dynamics of the new language were entirely under my control: whether I spoke or not, whether I spoke loudly or softly, fast or slow, high or low. The only thing that was not under my volition was the form of the words and sounds that came when I chose to let them come. After all, how *could* I formulate words in a language I didn't know?

It was like playing the work of a famous composer on the piano. I could play—loudly, softly, fast, or slow; and was free to play the whole thing an octave higher or lower, if I chose; but as long as I was playing, say Bach, or Chopin, I couldn't be playing my own notes. I was playing *their* notes, not because I was compelled to, but because I chose to. So it was with speaking in tongues. I was speaking the Holy Spirit's words, not mine, but I was speaking them because I chose to, and in the manner that I chose.

I still felt nothing out of the ordinary: no great spiritual inspiration, no special inner warmth of God's presence. It was interesting, though, and somehow refreshing, and so I spoke on for several minutes. I was about to stop, but John said:

"Don't stop. Go on. Go on speaking."

It proved to be good advice. I went on, allowing the new words to come to my lips, and after three or four more minutes began to sense something new. This language was being given me from the central place in me where God was, far beyond the realm of my emotions. Speaking on and on, I became more and more aware of God *in* me. The words didn't mean anything to me as language, but God knew exactly what they meant. God living in me was creating the language. I was speaking it—giving it voice, by my volition, and I was speaking it to God Who was above and beyond me. God the Holy Spirit was giving me the words to talk to God the Father, and it was all happening because of God the Son, Jesus Christ. As I spoke on I had a vivid mental picture of Jesus on the Cross.

I didn't have to be told to keep on speaking now, but wanted to go on, and on, and on; and I did for about half-an-hour, just letting this beautiful unknown language come to my lips, pouring my heart out to God the Father with a fluency and eloquence that I had never dreamed possible.

So many times, after praying, I had stopped with the feeling that there was so much more to be said, but I just didn't have the words. One great value of this strange phenomenon of "speaking in tongues" I discovered that night was that I could pray beyond the limitation of the intellect, telling God the things that needed to be expressed, but for which I had no words. The Apostle Paul said: "We know not what we should pray for as we ought, but the Spirit Himself makes intercession for us, with unsayable speech." [4] Again he said: "He that speaks in a 'language' isn't speaking to men at all, because no human being understands him, but mysteriously, in a way we can't really grasp, he is speaking to God." [5]

But as I spoke on, something else began to happen. My heart began to get happier and happier! The Presence of God that I has so clearly seen in earlier days to be the real reason for living suddenly enveloped me again after the many, many years of dryness. Never had I experienced God's presence in such reality as now. It might have frightened me except that I recognized that this was the same Presence of the Lord that I had sensed when I first accepted Jesus, and that I had known when I used to get up early during my years in the business world; only the intensity and reality of my present experience was far greater than anything I had believed possible. If those earlier experiences were like flashbulbs, this was as if someone had suddenly turned on the floodlights! The reality of God was something that I felt all the way through—even with my body. But instead of being fearful, I felt tremendously happy and elated.

John and I went back into the front room where Joan and Frank were waiting. I looked at them and said:

"Do you mean to tell me that a Christian can feel like I do?"

John and Joan nodded, all smiles.

"That's what we've been talking about!"

My heart was rejoicing, but I couldn't quite put my feelings into words. I just said:

"I'm floored! I'll be floored the rest of my life over this!"

What a drive home it was that night! I was still rejoicing inwardly and also overflowing with happiness. I found myself singing. I sang all the way, beginning with the traditional Introit for Pentecost: "The Spirit of the Lord hath filled the whole world, Alleluia . . . !" and ending with some gospel songs from my boyhood I thought I had forgotten.

It was well after midnight when I finally tumbled into bed.

Elated as I was, I half-expected that I would have a hard time going to sleep; instead, I fell into a deep, dreamless slumber as soon as my head touched the pillow. I don't ever remember having had such a refreshing sleep as I had that night. I awoke only once and found to my astonishment, that the wonderful happiness and sense of God's Presence was still with me. I knew that purely emotional excitement could be expected to disappear overnight. Evidently something deeper than emotion had happened to me—but what was it? Anyway, it was good, and I rolled over and went back to sleep.

4
Praise the Lord!

A boisterous mockingbird practising his latest achievements awoke me the next morning. The sun was streaming into the bedroom. My first thought was:

This good feeling of God's presence, is it still with me?

As I opened my eyes the wonderful elation of the night before filled my heart, and I said, for the first time in my life (except when instructed to do so in a formal rite of worship)— "Praise the Lord!"

I bounced out of bed and into my bathrobe and slippers. Early though it was, Elberta was already up, getting things prepared for breakfast. The rest of the family was still asleep, or at least pretending to be! I gave my wife a quick hug and a kiss.

"Guess what happened to me!"

'I wouldn't have to do much guessing, with the big smile on your face," said Elberta, dropping two pieces of bread into the toaster. "Anyway," she said, turning to face me, and smiling herself, "I knew all about it last night."

"What do you mean?" I asked, startled. "You didn't even stir when I came to bed."

"No," she said, "but a funny thing happened. I was fast asleep when you came home, but when you put your hand on the front door, a kind of jolt of power—that's the only way I can describe it—went through the house and woke me up! Somehow I knew right away what it meant, and what had happened to you. I was so sleepy that I fell asleep again waiting for you, but I knew!"

Breakfast over, I went into my study, and began to read the day's Scripture lessons. The discipline of the Church of England requires a priest to read the Prayer Book Services of Morning and Evening Prayer daily. Although the American Episcopal Church did not have such a rule, I had, for many years after my ordination, kept up the practice. Later, busyness had caused me to reduce this simply to reading the appointed Scriptures: one from the Psalms, one from the Old Testament, and one from the New. I can't say that I consciously received much inspiration from this—I was fulfilling my self-imposed obligation. After the Bible reading, I would usually pray for a few minutes. Now and then I would try to expand this prayer time, or to make a meditation, but I hadn't found much success.

On this particular morning, however, two things happened. I opened my Bible to read the Psalm and lessons, and the Word of God literally leaped out to meet me!

"Rejoice in the Lord alway, and again I say, rejoice! Let your moderation be known unto all men, the Lord is at hand! Be careful for nothing, but in everything by prayer and supplication with thanksgiving let your requests be made known unto God, and the peace of God, which passeth all understanding, shall keep your hearts and minds through Christ Jesus." [1] The words were freighted with a meaning and a power I had not felt or perceived for years. Clearly this *is* the Word of God. Then I turned to prayer, and again was amazed. As soon as I turned my attention to Him, I sensed immediately that there was a new openness between me and my Father in Heaven. He was *there* and I knew it! I prayed with assurance and confidence.

Time to go down to the office at the church: I knew that this was the place where I was likely to lose any blessing I had acquired! All kinds of petty irritating problems were bound to face me as I walked in the door.

"Oh, Lord," I prayed as I left the house, "I don't exactly understand all that is happening to me, but I know I feel wonderfully close to You. Don't let me lose it." And then I spoke in my new language. All I had to do was open my mouth, and the words were there. This time I did not get the same dramatic "lift" from it that I had the evening before. (But why should I? I was *living* at the new level.) But I spoke on, and felt refreshed.

The sexton was waiting for me at the door of my office:

"Er, Father Bennett, what do you want us to do about the chairs for tomorrow night—the parish dinner, you know?" I explained patiently how the seating was to be arranged. Thank goodness for an intelligent maintenance man!

My secretary was next:

"Mrs. A. called, and she's mad, Father Bennett!"

"Oh, what about?"

"Well, it seems she was in the hospital for two weeks and no one visited her. She's talking about cutting her pledge to the church."

I sighed. "Did she let anyone know she was ill?"

"Not as far as I can find out. Her friend Mrs. B. knew about it, but she didn't call us. You know how it goes."

"Yes, I'm afraid some people *want* to have something to complain about; or else they think the clergy are mind readers! I wonder if she waited for the doctor to hear that she was ill by hearsay, or whether she got on the phone to call him and tell him?"

My secretary grinned. "That isn't all the hot water you're in," she said cheerfully. "Little Miss C. is pretty unhappy with you, too! She said she's been away from church two weeks, and when you shook hands with her on Sunday, you didn't even say you'd missed her."

I sighed again. An average of fourteen hundred people passed that church door every Sunday, and I was supposed to know exactly who had and hadn't been there! What a public relations job!

I grinned back at my secretary: "Okay, okay. Did anything *good* happen by any chance?"

"Are you kidding? They don't call in to tell that sort of thing—just the gripes!"

The bookkeeper was standing at her office door by this time. "Hi, Father Bennett," she said brightly. "Got a minute?" I had. It was my business to have "minutes"!

"Look at this," she said, holding out a ledger sheet covered with figures.

"I'm looking," I said, peering at the hieroglyphics. "What's it about?"

"Just that we're three weeks behind in our pledged income, that's all, and that means more than $6,000. Scotty is having a fit." (Scotty was the treasurer.)

"Tell him I'll issue an order for all hands to make an impassioned appeal next Sunday," I said sardonically. Why in the world couldn't people do what they said they would for God's work, without a lot of pleading and coaxing? Well, a *lot* of it was God's work anyway!

I went into my own office and sat down, taking stock. I *still* felt good! As I paused to "catch my breath," mentally and spiritually, the joy that had been simmering in my heart came to a quiet bubble, and I rejoiced inwardly in the sweetness of God's love with me. It had never been like this before! Again, for a few minutes, I let praise overflow in the new language— letting the Spirit give me the words.

Still praising God, I began shuffling through the maze of papers on my desk; instead of feeling frustrated by the morning's complaints and the work staring me in the face, I was wishing for someone to come in the office so that I could tell about the wonderful things that were happening.

Almost immediately there came a knock at the door, and in came a little woman I knew well, a hard-working member of the church. She looked just about at the end of her tether.

"Oh, Father Bennett," she said, dropping wearily into a chair, "I just had to talk to you. I don't know what's the matter with me. I just don't seem to get anything out of my religion anymore."

"Just sit right there," I commanded. "I've got something to tell you!" And I proceeded to tell her all about what had been happening to me. Two strange things took place: one was that while I was telling her all about my experience, my own heart began to rejoice just as it had the night before; the other was that as I talked she began to look happier and happier, until finally, when I stopped, she got out of the chair and just kind of floated out of my office! Later, she began to speak in tongues. She was the first of many. I found that my counselling changed completely. Now, after a very brief getting-acquainted session, I would come to the point.

"Do you know God? Have you ever accepted Jesus?"

Often my counselling would end in praying for the person to accept Jesus, and to be filled with the Holy Spirit.

When I left the office shortly before noon I was utterly amazed to find that my joy was still with me, and that I drove my car down the highway with the waves of God's love just pouring over me!

The following night was one of those rare luxuries, an evening at home with the family. I was enjoying playing a game of "Monopoly" with Elberta and the kids, and had just acquired both Boardwalk and Park Place and was ready to build some hotels, when the phone rang:

"Father Bennett, can you come out right away? Grandpa died very suddenly this afternoon!" It was the father in one of the faithful families in the parish. The grandfather had died unexpectedly and without warning. It was a very closely knit family, and all were greatly upset.

I hurriedly set out for their home. I always dreaded this kind of call. What can you say to a family at such a time? I would usually just go and sit and offer my sympathy in silence, rather than be betrayed into banalities. Tonight it was different. As I drove along, I praised the Lord and prayed, in English and "in the Spirit." Arriving at the house, I was confident because of the vivid sense of God's presence with me; and as I sat in the room with that family and began to talk as the Lord gave me the words, I was strongly conscious that I was saying the right things to bring comfort and understanding. Even the young grandchildren were listening with close attention, and when I left the house that night, the father of the family wrung my hand, saying:

"We cannot say thank you enough. You said just the right things."

This new awareness, which amazed and delighted me, seemed to pervade my sleeping as well as my waking life. The great spiritual directors bemoan the fact that though a person may try to please God while awake, when he falls asleep, it often seems the devil has free reign! How can a man be a Christian in his dreams? Up to this time, my dreams had been like most: mixed up, sometimes frightening, never making much sense, except as they might express frustration, fear, or suppressed desire. Now, suddenly and immediately, my dream life changed as sharply as my waking life. I began to think about God in my dreams, and to function as a Christian asleep as well as awake. The same standards of morality began to apply in my dreams as in my waking life! I found that if I had a bad experience in a dream, I would call on Jesus for help. Often I would dream I was praying for the sick, preaching, casting out evil spirits, and most wonderful of all, I would dream I was praising God! Other nights I would awaken just knowing that God had been refreshing me while I slept, without my being able to remember exactly how, but knowing He had been there just the same.

All these things were wonderful beyond description, but very soon something else happened, just as important. Like most Christians, I suppose, I had often tried to surrender my life to God. Somehow it had never seemed to "work." I could say all I wanted about "yielding" and "commitment," but the fact was that my life always seemed to come bouncing back into my own hands very quickly. I was thinking about this early one evening as I drove down Sherman Way past St. Mark's Church. The road, wet with an autumn shower, was gleaming in the last glow of the fading sky, and the reflection of the newly-turned-on street lights. As I approached the big intersection at Van Nuys Boulevard and prepared to turn left, suddenly I said:

"Lord, I do surrender my life to You. I do consecrate myself to You!" Many times before I had said it, but this time something happened! It was as if God had replied immediately:

"All right! I'll accept your offer!"

My reaction was not typical for me, for so vivid was the experience that I started to weep, and had to pull the car over to the side of the road while I regained my composure. In that moment I knew, to my great joy that God *had* accepted my offer and that there was no way to back out of it even if I had wanted to, and I surely didn't! God had freely given me the gifts of Salvation and Pentecost, and now I offered to Him the only thing I had to give—myself.

5
A Glorious Fellowship

Late one evening, about three days after my "Pentecost," Frank called me:

"Dennis, we've found another Episcopal priest who speaks in tongues!" he announced. "He's going to meet with us tonight! Can you come?"

Frank called not only me, he also called all of the people who had recently received the Holy Spirit at his church. It was a group of fourteen Episcopalians who came to a home in Monterey Park to meet a youngish man from Texas whose round collar proclaimed him to be a minister. He told us a little about himself and how he had received the power of the Holy Spirit a number of years before. Of those others present, all but two had been baptized in the Holy Spirit, and ironically enough, one of the two was Frank, the one who had called this whole matter to my attention in the first place. Frank had been saying to the rest of us:

"You go and try it, and see what happens to you!" but had himself been keeping his "objectivity," although getting warmer and warmer! He said to the Texas priest:

"Now don't you pray for me tonight! I'm going to pray *tomorrow* to be baptized in the Holy Spirit, but not tonight!"

As the young Texan talked, Frank became increasingly tense. I could feel it, as if I were seated next to a tightly coiled spring! Occasionally he would whisper some comment in my ear: "This is silly!" he said. Then our visitor began to pray. I had never heard anyone pray quite as he did. He was very informal, almost "chatty" with God. He didn't use Prayer Book language, or "thees" and "thous," and he didn't go through elaborate descriptions: "Almighty God," "Most Gracious Lord," etc. He just said: "Dear Father . . ." as if he really felt that way! As he prayed something began to happen: my spirit began to leap for joy within me. The nearness of the Lord which I had been feeling so much was intensified. It was as though the Glory of God came down and tangibly rested upon that little circle of people. Then I realized that the others were feeling the same way. People—good old-line stuffy Episcopalians, too! —were beginning to chuckle to themselves with joy, or weep quietly, as they felt the amazing reality of God's love. God was so definitely *there* that we felt we could almost reach out and touch Him.

In spite of my own joyous involvement, I could not help but notice the reactions of the two men who had not yet received the Holy Spirit. Frank was getting more and more tense, while the layman who had not yet received (he did shortly afterward), was looking around with a puzzled stare trying to comprehend why his friends were behaving so strangely. It was evident that neither of them was feeling the tremendous joy and love that the rest of us were sensing.

Suddenly the leader began to pray for Frank. He didn't mention him by name, but he prayed for him to be baptized with the Holy Spirit. The effect was almost immediate. After perhaps thirty seconds, Frank leaped to his feet, as in a glorious torrent a new language poured from his lips. I have never heard anyone speak more rapidly! He stood up. He sat down. He began to walk around the room, forward, then backward, and all the time the praises of God were pouring from him in a rush of new and unknown words. He was caught up in the glory of God. The rest of us just plain rejoiced! It was wonderful, it was glorious, and it was funny, too, with a kind of divine humour. We even clapped one another on the back as we said:

"Praise God! Isn't He wonderful!" It was like all the birthday parties in the world rolled up into one!

To look at Frank, one would have thought that he was completely "out of it", in "ecstasy", but as a matter of fact he was nothing of the sort. He was enthralled with God, but he was in full possession of his senses. This fact was demonstrated when suddenly, right in the middle of his outpouring, he stopped and said, in a matter-of-fact way:

"Well, I always said that if ever I spoke in tongues, I had a little poem ready for the occasion!" Frank loved to write humorous verse, and out he came with a parody of the song from "My Fair Lady":

> "I spoke with tongues all night,
> I spoke with tongues all night,
> And praised the Lord all day . . ."

Then he immediately went back to pouring out his love to God in an unknown language, and we could scarcely get another word of English out of him that evening!

If we haven't found just being with God the most enjoyable and all-satisfying experience on earth, whatever will we do in

Heaven? Will we have to play interplanetary golf, get a translunary game of bridge going, or interest ourselves in a heavenly workshop, in order to relieve the boredom of "just" enjoying fellowship with God?

For me up until now, as for most Christians, a prayer meeting had sounded about as exciting as a funeral! I had never belonged to a church that had one! (My parish had a prayer group which met to read long lists of names, and say some set prayers for the sick. It was a sincere effort and not without results, but far from exciting!) Now this new and wonderful fellowship with God and with one another began to take priority in our lives. We met together to pray, not out of a sense of duty, but because it was more wonderful than anything else we had ever experienced. God was with us, and everybody knew it, and shared it.

The first prayer meetings centred around praying for people to receive the Holy Spirit, for we soon discovered that just as Jesus had said, all who asked, received. At first there had been a steady trek down to John and Joan's house, but we soon learned that the Holy Spirit could be received just as nicely at Bob's house, or Don's house, or even at the rectory! Meeting to pray with a new "candidate" would so inspire everyone all over again, that we would go on praising God, and loving Him together, long after the newly baptized-in-the-Holy-Spirit Christian had begun to praise God in a new language. Then we began to get together for the express purpose of fellowship, whether there was anyone to be prayed with for the blessing of Pentecost or not, just because it was so wonderful to experience God's love.

These home meetings would begin very casually. There was no attempt at formal procedure. The first half-hour would be spent just chatting and drinking coffee. The air would be blue with smoke from half-a-dozen cigarettes and a pipe or two—

for Episcopalians at that time saw no connection between smoking and religion, pro or con!*

Singing came very naturally into the picture. I remember the first night I came bringing a gospel songbook. Many of these folks had never heard a gospel hymn. They were raised on "good music"! I have nothing against the beautiful cadences of a Bach chorale, or the good poetry in a beautiful hymn, but these things are "set pieces", fine for the professionals to sing. If you want a group of just plain everyday folks to enjoy singing, give them something they can clap their hands to, something with dotted eighths, and lively rhythm.

"Why should the devil have all the good tunes?" asked General Booth—and we say, "Why indeed?" At any rate, these "high church" Episcopalians discovered gospel music, and they loved it! Then they discovered choruses—little short songs that could be learned quickly and could be picked up and sung at any point in a praise meeting.

As the meeting progressed, someone would strike up a chorus, or a gospel song. Coffee cups and cigarettes would be laid down, and we were on our way. The singing might con-

* I myself had been a light smoker until I received the Baptism with the Holy Spirit. At that point I found it a physical impossibility to smoke! We did not find it necessary to make an issue about it. One by one, people who had received the Holy Spirit would stop smoking—without being told to, until it became rare to see anyone smoke in our fellowship. This has puzzled me a bit. Clearly, many who stopped smoking had far worse habits and problems that needed dealing with: overeating, and other overindulgences of various kinds, to say nothing of gossip, lack of honesty, conceit, and all other sins fallen mankind is heir to! The best explanation I can offer is that such things as overindulgence in smoking, or drinking, bad language, etc., are the outward symptoms of deeper problems. Being outward, they can be dealt with outwardly. It takes much longer to change the inclinations of the heart. It is important that these outward patterns be changed, but it is important not to make the mistake of thinking, as many do, that a change in these outward habits means "holiness." Holiness is a matter of the heart.

tinue for a half-hour or even an hour, and this was a clear sign that something pretty basic had happened. These folks who wouldn't have opened their mouths to sing the national anthem at a ball game, or a graduation ceremony, and whose attempts at hymn-singing on Sunday morning had been the despair, no doubt, of generations of clergy, now didn't want to stop. Chorus would follow chorus, and it was a rare evening in which a new song or two was not learned.

After the singing came another completely new thing, praise. Not thanksgiving, but just plain praise, which not only permeated the meetings but our personal everyday affairs also. The prophet Isaiah wrote:

"In the year the King Uzziah died, I saw also the Lord, sitting upon a throne, high and lifted up, and His train filled the temple. Above it stood the Seraphim: each one had six wings: with two he covered his face, and with two he covered his feet, and with two he did fly. And *one cried unto another* and said:

" 'Holy, Holy, Holy, is the Lord of Hosts! The whole earth is full of His glory!' " [1]

A few weeks after I received the Holy Spirit, a phone call came from my church librarian. She was a well-educated person in the best sense of the word, a gracious and cultured lady, and she had just received the Holy Spirit a day or two before.

She said: "Good morning, Father Bennett. I would like to talk with you about some books."

I replied: "Good morning, Madelyn. Praise the Lord!"

She said: "Amen! Glory to God!"

I said: "Praise God!"

She said: "Blessed be His Name!"

I said: "Amen!"

We went on like that for perhaps five minutes, caught up in

praising and glorifying God back and forth over the telephone! We too were, in a small way, sharing the experience of the seraphim around the throne. At length I said: "Madelyn, we've got to talk about books!" It was only with a real effort that we could wrench ourselves away from that joyous fellowship to give our attention to such mundane things.

This new activity of praising God was seen to be the source of power and freedom in our meetings.

"Father, I love you!" "Jesus, You're wonderul!" "Blessed be God!" "Glory be to God!" "Thank you, Jesus!" "Hallelujah!" Perhaps twenty or thirty persons at a time could be heard spontaneously uttering words of praise. Most eyes would be closed, some faces lifted to heaven, a number of hands raised in this ancient gesture of prayer. The voices blended in a murmur that surely the writer of the book of Revelation might have had in mind when he spoke of the "sound of many waters." Such praise might continue for five minutes, or ten, and be repeated several times during the evening.

In such a setting it was only natural that we would pray, but it was a different kind of prayer. The old formalities might be all right in church—and these people were faithful, every-Sunday churchgoers—but formal prayer didn't somehow fit with the intimate fellowship we felt with God and one another. It just wasn't like that. Paul said that the Spirit of God in us would make us cry out "Abba!"[2] "Ab" is an Aramaic word meaning "Father" in the formal sense, and "Abba" is the child's word for the same thing, more like "Daddy." So our prayers were childlike and simple, conversational—talking with the Father in a new freedom—but strangely enough, far more powerful and effective than anything we had seen before.

It was at such a gathering, about a week after my initial experience with the Baptism in the Holy Spirit, that we prayed with Elberta. She had been quite ready to receive the Holy

Spirit ever since the first evening we spent with John and Joan, and now that I had been baptized in the Spirit, there was nothing holding her back. As we gathered around her and prayed, the Holy Spirit filled her so full that when she tried to get up from the chair she was sitting in, she staggered from the sheer weight of joy and glory of God, but she couldn't break through the "sound barrier" to speaking in a new language!

"Ab, ba, ab, ba . . ." was the best she could manage, but it was a good beginning, for unknown to her intellect, her spirit was crying as a child, "Dear Father!" It was a wonderful and natural way to start, but she couldn't seem to get any further.

"I got a 'D' in Spanish in high school, because I wouldn't open my mouth and say the words," she said. "I guess this is sort of the same thing!" Elberta was filled right up to the brim, but longed for the full freedom of the Spirit, and the overflow of her heavenly language.

In the meantime, many friends in the parish were continuing to receive the Holy Spirit.

"There's the phone!" It was nearly midnight. "I wonder who that could be?"

"Dennis!" the voice at the other end of the line said. "Mary received the Holy Spirit two hours ago and has been speaking in tongues ever since! Boy, is she getting a blessing! We just had to call and tell you!"

"Well?" Elberta looked ot me a little grimly, as I hung up the telephone. "Someone else?"

I nodded.

Elberta sighed. She knew that these people were coming into a freedom and joy in the Lord that she didn't yet have, and she knew it had to do with that tongue of hers that somehow wouldn't loosen up!

It was six weeks later that I came home late one night from a meeting and found Elberta waiting for me.

"You still up, honey?" I asked. "It's after eleven."

I took another look at her. The joy on her face told me the story. I raised my eyebrows questioningly:

"Did you?"

"Yes!" she said happily. "I got my new language tonight!"

"How did it happen?"

"Oh, I just knelt down at the bed to say my prayers, and I said, 'Lord, I'm not going to get up until I speak in tongues.'" She chuckled. "I shouted for a while, and it sounded pretty silly. Then I whispered a while, and that didn't seem to do any good either. Then I fell asleep on my knees, and when I woke up, I was talking to Him in a new language!"

At our weekday meetings there would be a good deal of "speaking in tongues", but most of it would be inaudible, or nearly so, except during times of general praise, when people might speak out in the "unknown tongue" praising God, just as others would be speaking in English. Now and then during such an evening some one or another, not more than the scriptural "two or three," might be moved to speak out in their Holy Spirit language, in which case everyone else would stop and listen, and then wait for the interpretation, which St. Paul says must follow a public message in an unknown tongue. This means that someone, either the speaker in tongues or some other person, would be given by the Holy Spirit the general meaning—not a word-for-word translation necessarily—of what had been said in the unknown language. I have heard an interpretation brought in sections by as many as five people, seated in different parts of the room. One of those interpreting stopped right in the middle of a phrase, and across the room another picked up the sentence without a moment's pause. I knew the speakers did not know each other, and could not possibly have rehearsed what they did; yet it would have seemed impossible to have joined the sentence so smoothly without collaboration!

At another meeting, there was an interpretation following a "speaking in tongues", and after it had been given, another person said:

"Father Bennett, I just wanted you to know that I had that same interpretation too." I then asked:

"How many in the group had similar words given them?" Seven hands went up! It is hard, in the face of such evidence, not to see that this was the Holy Spirit at work.

Besides tongues and interpretation, there would be prophecy, which in the Bible is not "fore-telling" but rather "forth-telling": God speaking to His people supernaturally but in a known language, to encourage and strengthen and bless them, and sometimes sharing His plans for the future with them. The gift of prophecy is not looking into a "crystal ball," or "telling fortunes," but God revealing what He is going to do! Someone would feel led to bring words of encouragement, such as:

"The Lord would say to you, 'My child, your life is like fabric. On the outside it looks smooth, and well made, while on the inside you know too well the knots, snarls, and roughnesses that are there. If you will let Me, I will make your life like Mine, of fine twined linen, like damask—beautiful on the inside as well. Let Me weave My character into the fabric of your life. I will fashion that which pleases Me, and you shall know My hand on your life in a new way. My child, I love you! You shall truly be My workmanship and be made in My likeness.'"

"Praise the Lord!" There would be a ripple of praise throughout the group. Certain people would find such words as these especially meaningful to them. Perhaps they brought home something special God had been speaking to them about that week, or that very day. A joyful chorus or two would usually follow these words of edification. Such meetings might well go on until 1.30 a.m., and then break up only because people *had* to go home. A group of hardy souls might continue further, sometimes until 4.00 o'clock in the morning. Quite a bit different from the old way of life—and other kinds of parties continuing until the wee hours, and maybe a hangover to follow!

All this was very exciting, but perhaps the most impressive thing about it was that the lives of these people began to change. A new love and concern began to be shown among them, and from them to others. They showed the same willingness to help and to be involved that those first people to be baptized in the Holy Spirit had shown in Frank's church. Suddenly, in a very practical way, they were "part of the answer" instead of "part of the problem."

6
More to the Package

One evening a few days after I had received the Holy Spirit, Elberta met me at the door looking concerned and a little exasperated:

"Conrad's got a problem," she said. "You know he was supposed to go to a party tonight. . . ."

"Uh-huh. What's the matter?" Conrad, our youngest child, age twelve, was scheduled for his first "dress up" affair, a supper-birthday party at the home of one of his friends. His first real dark-suit, white-shirt, necktie ensemble was the sensation of the week at our house!

"Well, you know Con. He got into his new suit early, and then had to go out and fool around in the yard, playing with the cat. Duffy got up in the tree. Conrad tried to get her down and in the process got a small piece of bark in his eye. I got the thing out of his eye, all right, but it seems to have scratched his eyeball. I don't think he'll be in any shape for the party; it's hurting him too much."

I murmured something sympathetic and then went down the hall to wash my hands for supper; on the way back I looked in on the unfortunate. He was lying on his bed, very glum, with a pad of witch-hazel-soaked cotton on his eye.

"Too bad, kid," I said. Without thinking too much about it, I put my hand on his head and prayed under my breath, then came into the dining room, and sat down at the supper table.

"Funny thing," commented Elberta a few minutes later, coming to the table herself after a brief stop at Conrad's room, "he's perfectly okay. His eye suddenly stopped hurting him and he's going to the party after all!" To confirm her words Conrad emerged, grinning happily, with a beribboned present under his arm.

I didn't say anything to Elberta about the prayer, but my own eyes came open a little wider. Healing? Was this "part of the package" too?

At our church I suppose we must have prayed for at least a thousand people a year to be healed of one ailment or another. We had a special "healing service" each week on Thursday morning, following the Communion, and from time to time had invited someone or another to conduct a "healing mission". It was only a few months since we had had such a mission with a well-known leader from England. It had been an inspiring week, and the man had given some excellent talks on the healing power of God. Hundreds of people had come to hear him, and many of them had come to the altar rail for prayer. I am sure that many of these were much helped, and undoubtedly there were healings we did not hear about, but on the last night of the mission Elberta put into words the question that had been bothering me:

"It's been wonderful," she said, "and I know a lot of people have been helped and encouraged, but—" She looked at me for a moment. "Where are the healings?"

Then I realized that she, like myself, had been hoping against hope that someone would get up from a wheelchair, or throw away his crutches, or give some definite sign of healing such as we read about in the Bible.

I used to kneel at the altar rail of the church and say:

"Lord, where is the power You promised us?"

My role as a sort of "traffic policeman," determining which people needed more expert help than I was equipped to give, and using my psychological training to play the "poor man's psychiatrist" for those who didn't seem too upset or disturbed, had sometimes bothered me:

"You are too sick for me to help you, Mrs. Smith, so you must go to the doctor."

"You are too disturbed for me to help you, Mrs. Jones, so you must go to the psychiatrist."

"Your family is in too much of a mess for me to help you, Mr. and Mrs. Brown, so you must go to the family counselling board, or to your attorney." That was the way it seemed to go.

I had often asked myself: "If you are a personal representative of Jesus Christ, why are you just a 'referral bureau' for hard cases?"

When Jesus met a sick man, He did not say to him:

"Here is my card. I know an excellent doctor in Jerusalem who specializes in your kind of problem. Tell him I sent you!" When He met the wild man of Gadara, He didn't say:

"My friend, you need to see a good psychiatrist. I recommend Dr. White down in Jericho. He will not charge you too much for group therapy sessions!" No. He dealt with these problems by the immediate power of God, and He told His followers they were supposed to do the same.

"Go on out," He said. "Heal the sick . . . raise the dead, throw out evil spirits . . ." [1]

Yet there had been times when we saw that power. Now and then, every year or two, an unmistakable healing would take place. I well recall the time one of our vestrymen was told by his doctor, a good friend of mine, that he had a carcinoma of the throat. The doctor asked me for help in preparing the man psychologically and spiritually for surgery to remove his pharynx. We tried to counsel him, but we also anointed him with oil and laid hands on him for healing. I shall not forget the excitement and baffled delight of the doctor when he called me to say:

"I don't know how to account for it. I *know* this man had a cancer of the throat, but now he doesn't!" (I find, by the way, that many times doctors are quicker to acknowledge God's healing power than ministers are!) That was a great day, but such days were all too infrequent.

Was the little incident of Conrad's eye an indication of what would follow? I wondered to myself. Could it be that this "Baptism in the Holy Spirit" had something to do with the release of that kind of power? It seemed so.

One day, shortly after this, Dorothy, a faithful church member, hobbled to the altar rail and asked for prayer. She had broken her hip in an automobile accident; it had healed imperfectly, and the doctor told her she would never walk normally again, or without pain. When we laid hands on her and prayed, the hip was instantly healed. That afternoon, her husband, a devout sceptic, called me:

"Dennis, I don't know what's going on over there, but Dorothy's hip is completely normal. She can move her leg in any direction, and without pain!"

About the same time another of our members presented herself for prayer. She had an ugly eczema or psoriasis covering her hands. We prayed; and I wish I had not looked away for a moment, for when I looked back, the unsightly lesions were all gone. The skin was as clear as a baby's.

Sometimes it seemed that nearly everyone who asked was healed, and why not? Jesus had said:

"These signs *shall* follow them that believe, they *shall* lay hands on the sick, and they *shall* recover." [2] No "ifs," "ands," or "buts" about it! And the power to heal the sick was not confined to a special group of people such as the ordained ministry, but was to be exercised by "those who believe."

It was very understandable, with such things happening, that in addition to prayer and praise, a good deal of our time at our meetings should be taken to tell what God had been doing in people's lives: "testimony," to use the old-fashioned word. Such sharing might go on for an hour or more:

"I prayed for my daughter's sore throat, and it was healed!"

"I burned my hand on the stove, and my husband prayed for it. I don't even have a blister—look!" And the hand was held up for inspection to the glory of God!

It wasn't just God's healing that people were discovering, but also His guidance and help in other areas:

"I was out of a job, but God found me a better one! Praise His Name!"

"We had been having real problems in our marriage, but God has just cleared it all away, and it's like we were on our second honeymoon!"

Less dramatic, and yet in a subtle way more so, was the testimony of the person who just stood up, and with the joy of heaven on his face would say:

"I just want to thank God for being so close and so real to me!"

Jesus-said we would be witnesses after we received the Holy Spirit, and sure enough that's what began to happen. God was becoming so real and so wonderful that we wanted to tell others about the joy that had come to us, and the Holy Spirit had set our tongues free to do the telling! So we would have testimonies like this:

"The girl that works at the desk next to mine at the office had a terrible headache. I asked if I could pray with her, and she looked at me funny, but said: 'Yes, it couldn't do any harm,' so I prayed for her and the headache went away. She said: 'How come?' and I told her about Jesus. Now she's accepted Him and she's happy as a clam! She and her husband were fighting all the time and were on the verge of divorce, but she told him about Jesus, and he's interested. They're coming to our house tomorrow night to talk about it some more. Pray for us, will you?"

Sometimes nearly everyone in the room had some kind of a report to give: not what God did years ago, or even last year, but what He did last week, yesterday, today! Since the Bible had come alive to them in a new way, some would share a Psalm or other Scripture that had been significant to them. Then, with faith built higher by this sharing, the group would plunge back into prayer, singing, and praise.

7
Clouds Roll In

"Hey, Bob! How are you?" a vestryman greeted a friend at the coffee hour following the service at St. Mark's Church one Sunday morning late in 1959.

The answer rang out only too clearly across the ranks of loyal churchmen sipping their coffee:

"I'm fine. Praise the Lord!"

And then, as if to add insult to injury, came the response from the other.

"Praise God!"

Most of the company ignored the speakers: here and there glances of amusement or mild surprise were exchanged—this wasn't the usual kind of greeting heard on a Sunday morning! But the closer observer might have seen some brows furrowed with real irritation.

"What's going on in this church? Fanaticism!"

It was the first distant rumble of a storm that was to gather with astonishing rapidity and break about my head. To have "trouble" at St. Mark's would have been incredible to me. When I accepted the "call" in 1953, St. Mark's had been a church of some five hundred members, just recovering from serious difficulties. During my seven years as pastor, the Van Nuys area had undergone tremendous growth, as the sprawling City of Los Angeles overflowed into the San Fernando Valley. The church had grown with the population.

I had three assistant ministers on my staff, capable and trusted men, one of whom had been with me throughout my pastorate; in fact, he predated me, having been interim pastor before I came. One day, as was our weekly custom, the four of us were meeting at lunch to discuss the parish and its work. Toward the end of the meal, my senior assistant suddenly said:

"I understand people in our church are now speaking in tongues!"

My "number two" man grinned. "That's what I hear," he said. "What next?"

My heart flipped. "Wait a minute," I said. "I just want you fellows to know that I take this very seriously."

The older priest dropped the subject, but "Number Two" looked at me sharply. After lunch he walked with me back to my car.

"Do you speak in tongues, Dennis?" he asked seriously.

I nodded.

"I'd like to talk to you about it sometime," he said.

Inwardly, I heaved a sigh of relief. I had hesitated broaching the subject to these two fellow workers of mine. They were men of experience in the ministry, men whose earnestness and sincerity I respected. Now that the subject had been brought up, I felt I could relax; for my third assistant, a young fellow just out of seminary, and his wife had recently been baptized with the Holy Spirit and were eagerly sharing in the fellowship.

Things seemed to be moving along very nicely, which suited me just fine, for I was by preference a compromiser, not a fighter. However, I was underestimating the enemy. Most Christians are half-inclined to think of Satan as a legendary figure, but the Bible says that immediately after the Lord Jesus Christ received the power of the Holy Spirit, just following His baptism in Jordan by John the Baptist, the Spirit drove Him into the wilderness where He was tempted by Satan. All you need to do to be convinced of Satan's reality is start getting Christians empowered with the Holy Spirit. I soon was to discover this for myself.

As word began to spread that some people at St. Mark's were "speaking in tongues," fear and prejudice was stirred in the hearts of a small group of well-meaning but poorly informed folk, who determined to set themselves flatly against this experience. It wasn't long before all the standard rumours were flying: St. Markans were holding secret conclaves in the dead of night, at which there were all kinds of strange goings-on. It sounded like pretty exciting stuff, and there is in fallen human nature a perverse love of scandal which feeds on such talk. Actually nothing untoward or out-of-hand was happening; it was just that Christians were discovering how wonderful the fellowship of the Holy Spirit could be. The people who were the targets of the gossip were among the most faithful members of the congregation. After about sixty people had received the Spirit, we had taken a little census and found that these few persons were supporting ten per cent of the budget of the entire church. They included the junior warden of the parish; another member of the twelve-man vestry or official board; several of our most active and faithful laymen who for years had been turning out at six o'clock every Saturday morning to share communion and study their faith in order to be better witnesses for Christ; the directress of the Altar Guild, and her assistant; the president of our most active Women's Guild; and the church librarian. But position and reliability made little difference. As soon as a person, no matter how respected, was known to be involved, he or she was on the "list." "Look out! They've got it, too!"

Once I asked one of my associates who was very antagonistic to the Baptism with the Holy Spirit:

"What do you think of Mrs. C.?" I had named a very charming and intelligent younger woman of the parish.

"Why, I think she's a fine person, of course."

"Well, then. why don't you have a talk with her?" I asked. "She speaks in tongues."

He looked at me indignantly. "Then I don't *want* to talk to her!" he declared.

It was ironical that while clergymen were reacting in this manner, men of other professions, perhaps even better equipped to judge human mental and physical health, were reacting quite differently. It was too bad that my assistant could not or would not talk with the husband of my Altar Guild directress.

He was a well-known neuro-surgeon in the San Fernando Valley, and after his wife received the Holy Spirit, I anticipated a strong reaction from him. One day I called him to discuss a person in the parish who seemed to be having a neurological problem. When we were through talking about the patient, the doctor said:

"Oh, by the way, I see what's happening to my wife, and I like it!"

I did a "double-take": "You *do*?"

"Yes," he replied. "You're going to have a hard time explaining this 'speaking in tongues' to some people, though." He paused a moment and then added casually:

"Of course, I understand it."

I was so surprised that I simply said again: "You do?"

"Sure! You see, the speech centres dominate the brain. If they were yielded to God, then every other area would be

affected, too. Besides," he continued, "I think about God sometimes, and I run out of words. I don't see why He shouldn't give
me some additional words to use."

Much is being said today about the "generation gap." Ten
years ago the cliché hadn't been invented, but parents were
already pretty well sold on the idea that their children were
potential delinquents who might become unmanageable at any
time. The cult of the "terrible teenager" was thriving, and
Satan used it to further his purposes.

One Sunday night my youngest assistant called me:

"I'm sorry, Father Bennett. I didn't mean to cause any
trouble."

"What are you talking about, Jim?" My heart sank. I was
growing tired of crises.

"Well, I stopped by the drugstore after the young people's
meeting and Susan and Walter were there. They asked me,
'Father Jim, what is all this about the Holy Spirit?' All I did
was to tell them what God had done in my life, that's all. But
something has happened to *them* both. They're just sitting there
as if they're overwhelmed by the whole thing. What'll I do?"

So here it comes! I thought. People had already been
whispering, "Supposing the kids should get hold of this 'speaking in tongues' stuff? It's just like a drug, you know. That's why
these folks get together so often. They have to have this whatever it is."

Even I and others who had received the Holy Spirit had
felt a little apprehensive about our kids finding out about it. It
seemed that they would be sure to misuse this wonderful experience in some way: they wouldn't understand it; they'd
play around with it; they'd go off the beam with it! We know
now that of all the groups in the church, it is the young people

who are most wonderfully helped and blessed by the Baptism in the Holy Spirit, but we didn't know that *then*.

"Whatever you do," I had said to Jim, "don't talk to the teenagers about this." But now the word was out. Could we squelch it? Perhaps all was not lost. Susan was the daughter of my librarian, and her mother would understand. No problem there. Walter, I could probably keep under control. He worked at the church part-time, and I could keep an eye on him.

"That's okay, Jim," I said, thinking fast. "You send Sue home to her mother. I'll talk to Walter."

Sure enough, Susan's mother prayed with her, and she was joyfully baptized in the Holy Spirit. Walter—well, Walter was an example of someone who is filled with the Holy Ghost but not yet *baptized* in Him. He had an infilling all right! Did he ever! He floated around St. Mark's for a week in a happy cloud, "so heavenly-minded that he was no earthly good!" I knew he needed to "come through" completely to the Baptism in the Holy Spirit; the fullness of God that was in him had to find an outlet before it could be expressed effectively. So I invited him to the rectory.

"Come tonight at eight, and we'll pray. But don't tell any of the other kids!"

At eight o'clock, Walter was there, and we slipped into my study. It didn't take long to encourage him to begin praising God in new freedom. In the meantime, another drama was taking place. The first I knew of it was when Elberta showed up at the door of the study.

"You might just as well come up to the front room," she announced happily. "He's *there*, too!"

My wife had not been sharing in the fear I had felt about the young people, or about anything else, for that matter! She wasn't the kind to be too worried about what folks thought. She had found something wonderful from God, and she was enjoying it. Elberta had written a little about our experience to our daughter Margie, at college, and Margie told us later:

"When I got Mum's letter, Ellen and I (Ellen was her roommate, a Jewish girl) sat in bed and shook with excitement. Right away I wrote to my boyfriend and told him about it, too. He wrote back and said:

"When I got your letter, Margie, I was lying in bed in my dormitory just hating another guy in my class, and planning how I would like to get even with him; but as I read your letter, the hatred drained out of me, and I was filled instead with love. I jumped out of bed, and rushed downstairs into the common room to tell the other fellows!"

As I now followed Elberta into the living room, with Walter in my wake, I was stunned by what I saw. Over on the couch, laughing with joy, sat Margie and that same boyfriend. My daughter's chin was trembling as she was beginning to speak in tongues. The boyfriend had a a beatifically happy smile on his face. My older son, Stephen, was slumped down in a chair with his fist stuck in his mouth because, as he explained:

"I felt the new language coming up into my throat, but I was afraid I wouldn't get it right, so I didn't want to speak it out."

Conrad was sitting cross-legged on a hassock in the corner, laughing and crying at the same time. I looked at this little group and thought at first the kids were making fun. I said, rather angrily:

"This isn't a game!"

My wife replied:

"You're right, this is not a game: this is the Holy Spirit. Margie just asked me to tell them some more about the Baptism with the Holy Spirit," she continued, "and this is what happened."

The Spirit had fallen spontaneously on that little group of

young people, just as He had overwhelmed Susan and Walter with His love and power a few days earlier.

That night our daughter and her boyfriend and our younger son received the Holy Spirit, but our older son did not, for the simple reason that he wouldn't speak the language the Holy Spirit was providing. He held out that night and continued to hold out for several weeks; then one morning he came out of his bedroom with the announcement:

"Mum, I had a funny dream last night. I dreamed I had God locked up in my closet, and He was saying through the door, 'When are you going to let me out, Steve?'"

Very shortly after this, he "let God out," and began to speak in the Spirit. It was as though he had suddenly joined the family. We now had something in common that bridged the "generation gap." My fears about teenagers being too immature to be filled with God vanished.

How could something like this be kept from spreading among the other youngsters? It was obvious that something had happened to our kids. They were different. Their friends could see the change, and they asked questions. Susan and Walter tried to keep their counsel, but it was very difficult. There were other parents who had received the Holy Spirit, and wanted their teenagers to be blessed. Soon it was openly known that the young people were "catching it" too! Sadly enough, to the "opposition," the participation of the youth was regarded as further reason to try to put out the fire. The clouds had rolled in, and the storm was ready to break.

I believe that even at this point had I gone into the pulpit and told the people clearly what was happening, the rising tempest might well have died down. Unfortunately, I was, for the first time in my professional life, experiencing unpopularity. I had always avoided open argument and had been the great compromiser, and now I made the wrong move. I decided that if I was very quiet about it all, and if the people involved were very quiet, too, those who were disturbed would calm down and the whole row would blow over.

Alas, I had reckoned without human nature! My silence on the subject and the quietness of the whole group simply darkened the suspicion that this was a dangerous, secret movement that would undermine the church and damage souls. I had also underestimated the irrepressible spread of the fire of the Holy Spirit, once it has been kindled. You can't keep Pentecost under wraps—it burns through!

8
The Storm Breaks

In spite of threatenings and rumours at home, the blessing continued to spread abroad. I had been enjoying the new freedom in the Lord for about three weeks when a call came from the Episcopal chaplain at one of the large universities in the Los Angeles area:

"I just have to talk to you, Dennis," he said. "I hardly know you, but I had an experience last night that's really shaken me up!" He proceeded to describe, almost point for point, an encounter with the Holy Spirit exactly like my own, including the fact that as he began to praise the Lord in the new language, he saw a vivid picture of Jesus on the Cross.

Another minister's life was touched, this time as a result of the Holy Spirit working through a child. Don and Shirley were among the first to be baptized in the Holy Spirit at St. Mark's. One day Shirley said to me:

"I've got something to tell you, Father Bennett. You know Chris, our six-year-old?"

I nodded.

"Well, the first part of this year we were baffled at what to do about him. He was the terror of the first grade! Not a day went by, it seemed, without our getting a call from the school that Chris had been sent to the office, or was in hot water of some kind. The teacher said he was just uncontrollable." She paused, and then looked at me with a twinkle in her eye. "Don and I had an idea what to do about it," she continued. "The Baptism in the Holy Spirit had helped us so tremendously, why shouldn't this experience help Chris?" Shirley saw the concern on my face and went on: "Now, don't get excited, Father Bennett. It's all right, honest it is! We sat Chris down and told him what had happened to us, and asked if he would like to have Jesus baptize him in the Holy Spirit. He said he would, so we prayed, and he began to speak in tongues almost immediately! He laughed happily and then ran off to play."

"Really, Shirley," I remonstrated, "this isn't a toy for children!"

"Listen to the rest of the story," she said firmly. "Several school days later, I got a phone call from Chris's teacher.

"'What in the world has come over Chris?' she asked me. 'This week he's been my best pupil. He hasn't made any trouble at all, and he's so happy it's amazing!' I told her what had happened, and she said:

"'I'll be right over. I need that too!' And do you know, Father Bennett, *she* came over and received the Holy Spirit!"

I was speechless as Shirley finished her story.

"And do you know who *she* is?" she asked me.

I shook my head.

"She's the wife of the assistant minister at one of the Lutheran churches! He's coming over to find out what it's all about too! We want you to be there to help us explain it all to him!"

The young minister was interested in his wife's experience. She had been a doubting Christian, almost an agnostic; so much so that the senior pastor and the leaders of the church had been questioning her fitness to be a pastor's wife. Her sudden acquisition of a truly radiant faith could not fail to impress them—and it all came about because of the change in one small child.*

While many such good things were taking place, the gulf of misunderstanding at the church continued to widen. My policy of "keep quiet and hope for the best" was definitely not working. The opposition was not directed at me personally, but the very small group of people who were stirring up the trouble were convinced that I had gone off the track, and that their mission was to bring me to my senses. For several months I tried to hold the church together by the compromise of silence on my part, but this simply gave the dissidents opportunity to work at sowing the seeds of discontent.

It was a strange time. I was upset by the growing attacks; yet I was enjoying God's blessings in a new dimension. Quite early in the game I had learned something of the peace of the Holy Spirit, and I learned it in a traffic jam! Our daughter was scheduled to come home from college in San Jose, California, for the Thanksgiving holiday, and the rest of the family was en route to the Los Angeles International Airport to meet her. It was a hot, sticky, and smoggy afternoon as we parked the car and walked toward the "Flight Arrivals" of the little local airline. I realized that ocean fog was rolling in to join forces with the smog, and that the airport was rapidly getting "socked in." An announcement over the public address system soon confirmed my fears; the flight had overflown Los Angeles because of the weather, and was on its way to Burbank.

We trudged back to the car. This time as we drove north the boulevard was jammed. The industrial plants that cluster

---

* This same Lutheran Church is now open to the charismatic renewal. The present pastor has received the baptism in the Holy Spirit, together with a number of members of the congregation.

around the airport were disgorging their workers, and traffic was bumper-to-bumper. The air was hotter than ever, with plenty of fresh exhaust fumes to add a little extra fillip to the smog, and it would be a good hour-and-a-half to Burbank! At the airport, I had elbowed my way to the ticket counter and pleaded with the harried attendant to ask that my daughter be paged when she arrived at Burbank and told to wait there for us. The airline clerk's preoccupied manner had not convinced me that he would remember to do it! Yet as we inched our way along, I was not tense. I wasn't gripping the wheel with sweaty palms, muttering exclamations of impatience under my breath, or giving opinions about the slowness and stupidity of the other drivers. I was singing—I caught myself at it!—singing a hymn! And I felt cool and calm, way down inside. I thought to myself:

I feel peaceful. I don't understand why.

Quick as a flash, the Holy Spirit said in my heart:

"Of course you don't. This is the peace that *passes* understanding!"

The next time I saw John and Joan, I said:

"You didn't tell me about 'the peace that passes understanding.' "

"Oh, did you just discover it?" John replied. He was as objective as if he and I had bought identical automobiles, and I had said to him:

"I didn't realize that the car would come equipped with air conditioning," and he had replied:

"Oh, did you just discover that on yours, too?"

We retrieved Margie safely from the Lockheed Air Terminal in Burbank and on the next day, Thanksgiving Day, I had the rare experience of sitting with my family in the congregation of my own church. One of my assisting ministers was conducting the service. As I listened to the familiar words of the Book of Common Prayer, and the reading of the Scripture lesson, I was suddenly overwhelmed by the beauty and significance of it. For the first time in my life, to my remembrance, I was moved to tears by a church service!

The Holy Spirit did not just enhance for me the worship of my own denomination, but He showed me the significance of others. A short time later I had my first experience of speaking to a group of Pentecostal ministers. (Six months earlier, I would have hesitated to address an assembly of Methodist or Presbyterians lest I compromise my Anglo-Catholic position!) I didn't know what to expect, although I had already found out that Pentecostals were very different from the "holy roller" caricature. I respected them because I knew from my research that these were the Christians who had preserved the understanding of the Baptism in the Holy Spirit, sometimes in the face of real persecution, and I owed them gratitude for the blessing that had come into my own life.

The setting of the meeting was unfamiliar, the form of worship was totally different from that used in the Episcopal Church, and the people were strangers to me; yet as they began to sing, and praise, and pray, I knew these were my brothers in the Lord, not because of any official connection, for we had none, but because I felt the wonderful thing the Scripture calls "the fellowship of the Holy Spirit."

My talk to the ministers was well-accepted, and I was amazed at the strength of the bond between us in the Lord. Few of these good men had what my church would consider adequate theological training, but I had more than an inkling that they were my superiors in the training that matters: knowing the Lord, and His ways.

After my testimony, one of the men on the platform asked permission to speak. As I listened, in my spirit I knew that the speaker was not sharing his own thoughts with us, but wisdom that God was giving:

"Father Bennett, we would love to have you join us, and there will always be a welcome for you in our churches, but we know that this is not the thing for you to do. You should stay in your own denomination so they can receive word of the Baptism in the Holy Spirit; for they will listen to you where they would not listen to us."

These words confirmed what I had already known in my heart, but it was surely the wisdom of God to underline the fact so well that day. Had He not, on the following day I might not have been quite so sure. That night as I knelt to say my prayers, my thoughts turned to the situation at the parish, which had been growing steadily more unbearable. I was burdened with a heavy load af anxiety and fear. I felt like a drinking glass into which had been poured two different liquids—light and heavy. The fire and joy of the Holy Spirit were there, undiminished, down in my heart, but they were overlaid and oppressed by fear and anxiety. My experience with the Pentecostal ministers, free, and rejoicing in the Holy Spirit, had stirred *my* spirit; and as I began my prayers, the joy of the Holy Spirit in me suddenly gained power and bubbled over in my new language. I could not stop praising God! I praised Him, and praised Him, and as I did so, I had an inner vision of the Almighty on His heavenly Throne, surrounded by hosts of creatures, earthly and heavenly, praising Him and glorifying Him! I could hardly stop praising! What was even more glorious was that the praise went on through my dreams, all night long.

God had prepared me well for what was coming the next day, Sunday, April 3. On that Passion Sunday, 1960, I did what I should have done five months before. The Holy Spirit had at last got the point through to me:

"I'm not asking you to hold this church together; I'm asking you to tell what has happened to you! This isn't your church anyway, it belongs to Jesus!"

I set aside the preaching schedule for the day, and went into the pulpit at the three morning services and simply shared what had happened to me. I appealed to the people to dismiss the ridiculous rumours.

The general reaction was open and tender—until the end of the second service. At that point my second assistant snatched off his vestments, threw them on the altar, and stalked out of the church crying:

"I can no longer work with this man!"

That "blew the lid off!" After the service concluded, outside on the patio, those who had set themselves to get rid of the movement of the Holy Spirit began to harangue the arriving and departing parishioners. One man stood on a chair shouting:

"Throw out the damn tongue-speakers!"

(Fortunately, even the most distressing events can have their humorous side. That morning, in the midst of the "tumult and the shouting," one little lady, at least, was blissfully unaware. As she shook hands with the greeter at the door she murmured: "It was a lovely service!")

The contrast was amazing: on the one hand was the unreasoning fury of the "opposition," while the people who had received the Baptism in the Holy Spirit were quietly moving around telling their story, faces shining with the love of God, and pleased somehow, in spite of the confusion, that at last they were free to witness openly.

As for me, I was appalled! This unexpected crisis was one too many! When one of my vestrymen, a leader of the "opposition," came to me and said bluntly: "You should resign!" I was ready to do so.

I am often asked the question: "Why didn't you hang on

and fight it out?" It is true, I didn't *have* to leave, for there is no way to force an Episcopal rector to resign against his will as long as he is not guilty of any moral or canonical offence, and even then he is entitled to a trial, but I was tired of being on the spot. I knew that the little group that had arrayed themselves against me would fight me to the death; that it could easily turn into a court battle, with much unfortunate publicity. It didn't seem to be the best way to proclaim the Good News!

Then, too, I had a strong need to "think it over." A lot had happened to me in a fairly short space of time, and I did not feel that I completely understood it all. If I had the knowledge and background on the whole matter that I have now, things might have been different, but I didn't. I wanted to take inventory, to sit down quietly somewhere and think, and pray about it.

So it was with relief that I said to the vestryman:

"Okay, I'll resign. Right away." At the 11.00 a.m. service, I announced my resignation to an astonished and distressed congregation and walked away from the parish that I had served for seven years.

When I came home that memorable Passion Sunday I found my wife waiting for me, her eyes shining!

"Dennis," she said, "it was wonderful! We got to tell so many people what was really happening!" I didn't at that moment share her enthusiasm; I was still too shocked by the morning's events, but later I began to realize the truth of her words. The phone and the doorbell began to ring, as people came by to ask the question:

"What is it all about?"

We suddenly found ourselves free to talk.

That night there was a real air of impending victory when seventy-five enthusiastic Christians met for prayer and praise. They felt that if enough people at the church received the power of the Holy Spirit, and found how beneficial it is, the parish might yet be united. Many people from St. Mark's and elsewhere came, and many were baptized in the Holy Spirit.

Contrary to popular report, there was no "split" at St. Mark's. The "opposition" group was actually very small. The majority of the church had no idea "what had hit them." My only dispute with those who created the furor at St. Mark's was that they really did not investigate carefully, but rather acted from prejudice and hearsay—a very human thing to do, indeed!

I didn't know what to do next, but just tried to follow the Lord one step at a time. God continued to do great things.

Louise, who was eighty-three years old, for ten years had been suffering from a painful arthritis of the spine, and angina of the heart. She was forced to keep to her bed most of the time, and I had often called at her little home.

Louise had friends who had received the Holy Spirit, and one day, shortly after the blow-up at St. Mark's she said to me:

"I believe all this that is happening is real, and I know, too, that if you lay your hands on me, Father Bennett, I will be healed!"

Accordingly I laid my hands on her head, and asked God to heal her. I do not remember that I personally felt much confidence, in fact I left the room after praying for her without even asking if she felt any better! About a week later when I saw her at a prayer meeting, I said:

"How are you, Louise?"

She replied: "I'm fine, *of course!*"

Later that week she came to our house and *skipped* around the front room.

"See what I can do!" she chortled.

A year after her healing she wrote me a note saying that she was still feeling just fine. She added that one evening her neighbour, seventy-two years of age, had locked herself out of her house.

"She's a bit crippled up," Louise said, "so *I* climbed in the window and let her in! I do get a bit tired sometimes," she added.

Three weeks after my resignation, on April 25, the traditional feast of St. Mark, it seemed fitting that those of us who had been meeting together regularly for prayer should fast and pray for the parish and its future. At the end of the day we all met at the rectory and began by reading the evening lessons from the Prayer Book.

"Oh," I said, as I looked in the lectionary (the list of daily Bible readings in the front of the Prayer Book), "the Old Testament lesson is from the Apocrypha.* I don't have a copy of the Apocrypha here, so I'll pick another reading instead."

"Can't you get an Apocrypha from your office?" inquired one of the women. "I think we ought to read the lessons as they are appointed. It seems important somehow."

I found an Apocrypha and turned to the evening lesson. It was from Ecclesiasticus 51 : 13–22. Everyone listened dutifully as I read the first part of the lesson which was a typical piece

* The Apocrypha is a collection of fourteen books, written in the time between the Old and New Testaments. Some of them are historical, some are prophetic, some collections of proverbs and wisdom, one or two illustrative stories, and one very beautiful long psalm. Much of the Apocrypha is very helpful, and any Christian would benefit from reading it. The books were not accepted as a part of the Canonical Scripture in the early days. Rome made them a part of her official Scriptures at the Council of Trent between 1545 and 1563. The Episcopal Church, following the custom of the Church of England, reads them: "For example of life and instruction of manner; but yet doth it not apply them to establish any doctrine . . ." (Article of Religion VI)). Nevertheless, selections from the Apocrypha are appointed to be read on certain days at Morning and Evening Prayer.

of "wisdom" literature, poetic, but not too exciting. I read the twenty-first verse:

"My heart was troubled in seeking her (wisdom): therefore have I got a good possession." Then as I read the twenty-second verse there was sensation:

"The Lord hath given me a tongue for my reward, and I will praise Him therewith!"

How could the Holy Spirit have known and guided the compilers of that lectionary, many years before, to select a lesson for St. Mark's Day that would come through with such meaning to this little group of Christians? Marvellous are the ways of God! In amazement we began to praise Him.

Many spiritually hungry people came to talk about and pray for the power of the Holy Spirit which would enable them to live more effective Christian lives. We met in private homes. Since I was no longer rector of the parish, as an Episcopal priest I would have been violating canon law had I held public meetings; the authorities interpreted our actions as uncanonical anyway. It was soon clear that if I continued, I might not be able to remain in the Episcopal ministry. I could not forget the words of wisdom from the minister at the Pentecostal rally, that I was needed in my own denomination.

We wrestled with various thoughts of what to do next. I began to investigate what other leaders of the Episcopal Church thought about this renewing experience of our faith. Madelyn, the church librarian, was an old friend of the then presiding bishop of the Episcopol Church, the late Bishop Lichtenberger. At her urging, he invited me to come and talk with him. I flew to San Antonio, Texas, and unfolded my story. I must have talked for more than an hour while he listened patiently and attentively and with obvious interest. When I finished he said:

"Dennis, there's nothing wrong with this. It's wonderful,

but you know I don't have any authority to help you with your local situation."

Even so, his interest and kindness encouraged me to carry my investigation further. Later in the month a priest of the diocese, a friend of mine who had been quite interested in what was going on in my life, returned from a conference in the San Francisco area and said to me:

"You know, Dennis, I shared your story with the bishops from Seattle and Portland, and they are not closed to your experience. Why don't you go and see them?"

I determined to do just that. I had had some contact with both of these men before and when I wrote them, each said he would be happy to talk with me.

9
Fire Moves North

It was a lovely June day when the 720 Boeing jet in which I was a passenger taxied out to the end of Los Angeles International's runway 25-R and swung into her take-off roll. It was not quite so nice as she touched down on runway 16 at Seattle-Tacoma, after a tolerably "hairy" approach through a low overcast. The son of a good friend in Van Nuys, stationed in Seattle in the Army, met me at the airport and took me into town. As we rode along Highway 99 in Jon's little Corvette, through the congested Boeing plant traffic (the freeway has relieved this picture since then), I had my introduction to the "Queen City" of Seattle. Especially in those days, the visitor coming from the airport did not get the best impression at first view.

"It's a beautiful city, but you'd sure never know it on a day like this, or in this part of town," said Jon; and indeed, as we drove through the grimy industrial area and on into town under lowering skies, my own feelings were more than a little clouded.

However, the next day dawned bright and cheerful, and my spirit was much higher as I walked into the diocesan house to keep a ten o'clock appointment with the bishop. I was ushered into a sunny, high-windowed room, which commanded a wonderful view of the city and its environs to the west. Right below lay Lake Union, busy with small boats and variegated shipping, including four old clipper ships riding at anchor. In the middle distance, beyond the town, Puget Sound sparkled blue and inviting, dotted with green islands, while on the horizon the snowy Olympics were rifting through into the sunshine. It was indeed a beautiful day, and as Jon had said, a beautiful place.

"Why, good morning, Dennis!"

My eyes and thoughts returned to the office, as I stood to greet the man I had come so far to see. The Rt. Rev. William Fisher Lewis, Bishop of Olympia, was an old acquaintance. He beamed at me happily and motioned me to sit down.

"Tell me about it," he invited, leaning back in his chair, "I've heard a little. I was in Los Angeles when the excitement took place at St. Mark's. What's it all about?"

As simply as I could, I told him my story.

"There's nothing wrong with that," he stated firmly, as I concluded. "Look, Dennis, what about coming up to this diocese? Bring the fire with you! I don't have a big church to offer you, but I do have a little mission out in the Ballard area, St. Luke's. It's never quite got "off the ground" in the last sixty years. I've got to do something or close it up. Would you like to go out and look over the situation?"

I was interested in his offer and I knew I'd like to work under the leadership of this man. I was even more sure of it when he said:

"First, let's pray," and suiting the action to the word, he knelt. I joined him and together we asked the guidance of God. I was to learn that I would never leave Bishop Lewis's office without kneeling and praying with him.

Today, the Ballard district of Seattle has undergone a "face-lifting". Sharp-looking new apartments and business houses have sprung up. A large marina, with its associated restaurants and concessions, has brought new life to the area, while the Seattle World's Fair occasioned the making of the rough Shilshole Waterfront into a park; but ten years ago, and especially for a person used to the bright artificiality of Los Angeles, Ballard seemed a gloomy place.

The outside of the little church building was shabby, and the surrounding residences were quite old and some were run-down. This wasn't the kind of thing I had been used to for the last seven years! However, when I went inside, my feelings changed. It was warm and attractive, neat and clean, and had that feeling of having been "prayed in". Obviously, *somebody* cared about "St. Luke's, Ballard". I turned to the archdeacon of the diocese who had brought me.

He smiled: "It's not bad, is it?" I nodded my agreement as we walked down the steps to his car.

"Not bad at all."

Heading southward and homeward, I stopped at Portland, Oregon, for a chat with Bishop Carman. Again I was received most cordially and again I told my story to an interested listener. When I finished, the Bishop made one terse comment:

"This is where the Pentecostals get their fire, isn't it?"

He, too, invited me to come to his diocese, but somehow I felt that my new direction would be that little run-down church in Seattle, Washington.

Back in Van Nuys, Elberta and I talked and prayed, and arrived at our decision: we would go to St. Luke's in Seattle. I know that my decision was made for mixed reasons: first, God did seem to be opening the way; second, I was eager to see what would happen if the Baptism in the Holy Spirit was openly accepted and taught in a local congregation; third, I did not want to leave the security of my own denomination; and last but not least, I was tired of being "on the spot," and wanted to get away! How gracious God is to use a mixed bag of motives like that!

The next week, the Assemblies of God of Southern California were holding their annual men's fellowship retreat in the mountains at Pinecrest, and I was invited to be the speaker. I was growing quite accustomed to my Pentecostal brothers and their ways and I knew I could expect an inspiring time. Naturally, one thought was uppermost in my mind: had I done the right thing in deciding to go to Seattle? As I sat on the platform looking out at five hundred or more men worshipping and praising God, I said a prayer in my heart:

"Oh, Lord, I need confirmation that my decision was the right one." I had hardly formed the prayer in my thoughts before a man whom I had never seen before stood up and began to speak in a language given by the Holy Spirit. As soon as he stopped, another man I had never seen began to interpret, and this was the essence of it:

"If you will go with Me and not deny the work of My Holy Spirit, I will prosper your ministry!"

I said quietly: "Thank You, Lord!"

In the meantime, publicity guns were firing; I found myself both famous and notorious. I didn't mind being considered a hero, but didn't care too much for the role of villain! After all, up until the explosion of St. Mark's, I had always been the "fair-haired boy" who got along with everyone. A "successful" minister is usually a "hail-fellow-well met": a "nice guy," everyone's friend. Now I suddenly found myself a controversial figure, and didn't quite like it! Hearing that *Newsweek* *

* *Newsweek,* July 4, 1960, page 77.

magazine was preparing an article scheduled to appear the first of July, I said to Elberta:

"Will you stay here and pack up the house? I'm going to head for Seattle right away. I can't stand any more phone calls, and when that magazine article comes out, it'll be insufferable!"

I meant it too, and my wife, quietly enduring my cowardice, would have done it, but I had no more than declared my intention when the telephone rang. With a gesture of impatience I reached for the instrument:

"Father Bennett?"

"Speaking."

"This is ———." The caller gave the name of a well-known commentator in the Los Angeles area. "I want to do a story on the things that are happening at St. Mark's; you know, speaking in tongues, and all that."

"I'm sorry," I said, "but I'm just getting ready to leave for Seattle, and won't have time."

"Well, okay," the commentator said, "but I'm going to do the broadcast whether to co-operate or not." His voice rather indicated he thought he was dealing with a bunch of happy "kooks" and was anticipating some laughs. I felt that I had to stay in town after all, if only to defend myself! We set up an appointment for the next day. Thank heavens it was radio and not *television*!

The next morning we were in the midst of packing when the doorbell rang.

"Oh, that must be the radio interviewer now," I said to Don and Shirley, two friends from St. Mark's whom we had asked to take part in the programme with us.

Don looked out the window and exclaimed, "Oh, no! Cameramen!" It *was* TV!

My wife and I glanced at one another aghast over the stacks

of cartons that nearly filled our front room. In came the well-known commentator, a breezy little man with an unmistakable air of "show biz" about him and of wanting to get the whole silly thing over with as soon as possible. He was visibly surprised as he met the four of us. Apparently we weren't as "kooky" as he had expected. His manner changed as we talked together. He asked many questions and became increasingly interested, more and more showing that he realized that this was not just a game, but very serious business. He seemed sincere, and when he sat down with me to decide how the interview should be set up, he asked: "About this 'speaking in tongues'—would you be willing to do it for me now?" I agreed and prayed briefly "in the Spirit."

He was visibly moved as he remarked: "Father Bennett, you've got to do this on the programme as part of the interview! If you don't, the audience will still think it's something crazy, but if they hear you speak, they'll know that it's for real."

Before the interviewer had arrived, the others and I had resolved not to speak in tongues over the air; we were sure that this would be asked of us. Nevertheless, I knew that he was right, and so it came about that I did pray in the Spirit, speaking in tongues on TV in the sight and sound of what may well have been a milion Los Angelenes. The programme was sensitively handled, and an effective witness was made to God's work. The *Newsweek* article came out, and we survived that, too. The next week found us on our way to Seattle, and on Sunday, July 15, I conducted my first service in St. Luke's, Ballard.

A good-sized group of people had turned out to meet and to hear the new minister. My first sermon was simply aimed at letting them know that I was "normal"! I liked them, and they seemed to respond to me, although I myself was in much fear and trepidation. I had just had a church blow up in my face, and the experience was not one I wanted to repeat.

But I soon began to discover the real discouragement that there was at St Luke's. The very first week, Wally, a young businessman, came to me:

"I hate to do this to you when you've just arrived, Father Bennett," he said, "but I'm going to have to resign as Sunday School Superintendent. I just don't have anything left to give. I seem to have lost whatever faith I had, after all that we have been through around here." With this, he handed me his keys and books.

Ballard, lovingly nicknamed "herring-bone hill," had originally been a Scandinavian fishing village on the shores of Puget Sound, and it is not hard to understand the struggles of an Episcopal Church to get started, as the early religious colour of the community was almost entirely Lutheran. However, in recent years the population of the district had increased to around 100,000, only a minority of whom were Scandinavian, and yet St. Luke's, the only Episcopal Church in the area, had never managed to get on its feet.

Like so many struggling missions, St. Luke's had run the gamut in leadership: young men on the way up, willing to stay until economic pressure or ambition forced them to accept what one of my seminary professors called a "louder call"; older men nearing retirement, bringing the ripeness and wisdom of years, but looking for a lighter work load, and unable or unwilling to meet the challenge; and, most difficult of all, men who were hampered by some personal problem in their lives, or in their families. St. Luke's had enjoyed some very good leadership from time to time, and some good foundations had been laid, especially by one young man whom they had liked very much and who had stayed five years. But by the time I came, the bishop was ready to close the church—he had the padlock in his hand. I was the last chance! Some of the people told me later:

"Boy, when we heard the bishop was sending *you*, we wondered what kind of last chance we were being given! We had read about you in the papers!"

The first few weeks in Seattle were uneventful. The sheer natural magnificence of the country took my breath away. We had arrived during one of those spells of clear summer weather which northwesterners sometimes enjoy, and which, when they come, more than make up for a lot of rainy days! On every hand there were snow-clad mountains: to the west the beautiful line of the Olympics, and to the east the alpine ruggedness of the Cascades. There was blue water and green forests and —fresh air! In these surroundings, I began to enjoy the idea of settling down to a routine pastorate for a while. I wanted to be once again a nicely accepted, quiet, respectable parish priest! On the other hand, I had seen God's power in action among His people, and I knew very well I could not long be content to lead a congregation without telling them about receiving the Holy Spirit.

Nevertheless, I was mighty hesitant about beginning, but just as I was making myself comfortable, there came another blast. In August, *Time* magazine devoted a full page to the Van Nuys incident and finished by saying that I had come to St. Luke's, Seattle.* The people came that Sunday literally waving the magazine over their heads:

"We're internationally famous!" they cried. "But *what* is it all about?"

That morning, again smoked out of hiding, I told my story. I concluded:

* *Time*, August 15, 1960, pp. 53–55.

"I'm not going to push this on you at all. If you want to know more about it, you'll have to ask me; then I'll be perfectly happy to talk to you about it—I'll talk all night, if necessary!"

10
Off the Runway

"Whew! Thank goodness we're finally getting settled!" said Elberta, plunking herself down on the settee in the front room of our new home in Seattle.

It was a nice little house: big enough for our family, yet small enough to be cared for easily. Its one dramatic feature was that out of the south living-room window one had a perfectly framed view of Mt. Rainier when he had a mind to be seen! (Rainier broods over Seattle like an American Fujiyama, all 14,410 feet of him, showing that fascinating characteristic of mountains to look close or far away, huge or quite insignificant, according to the location of the viewer. I have seen Rainier when he seemed to fall back and become just a distant peak on a far skyline, much farther away than his actual distance of sixty miles.)

A knock came at the door, and we welcomed two of our new parishioners.

"Just thought we'd stop by to see how you were doing, and if we could help you," said Alice.

We chatted about this and that, but eventually they came to the point:

"What you were talking about on Sunday in your sermon," said Jack, "—we're interested. Would you consider coming to our house on Friday night? We have one or two others who are interested, too."

When Friday evening came, Elberta and I were surprised to see nine people waiting for us. Four men and five women looked at us expectantly as we took our seats in the living room. As we sat and talked, and imbibed tea and cake, I sized up the group. Most I had met before, or seen in church; one or two I did not recall. Their occupations, it turned out, were various. One was a pharmacist, another a personnel man for Boeing aviation. There were two in insurance work, and our host worked in the shipping room of the Seattle *Times*. Of the women, two were employed: one as a secretary, and the other as a research technician at the University of Washington Medical School.

They were all "old-timers" at St. Luke's. This was emphatically not a group of new disciples gathered from among the "fringe"; this was part of the little nucleus who had worked and struggled through the years to keep the church alive. Most of them had held, or were holding, positions of responsibility in the congregation. Several were, or had been, on the vestry, the official board of the church. I was surprised and delighted to see among them the young man, Wally, who had just resigned as Sunday School Superintendent because he was so discouraged. It was interesting too, as they told me later, that these people had not been close friends. Each seemed to have been moved separately to come that night; they had not urged one another, and each couple seemed somewhat surprised to see the others there.

"Start at the beginning," said our host, Jack. "What happened down there in Southern California?"

I talked for nearly two hours while my listeners sat in rapt attention. When I stopped, there was a moment or two of silence, broken by one of the men:

"So there is more to this Christianity than we've realized!"

"We ought to go on and talk about this all night!" said someone else. We agreed to meet the following Friday at the home of one of the other couples, and the next week all were on hand, including the husband who had been working and unable to attend the first gathering. As we took our places, someone said:

"Tonight we don't want to talk, we want to pray!"

This comment shook me a little, for these people were not the "prayer-group" type, nor did they come from "prayer-meeting" backgrounds. They were, rather, typical Episcopalians: earnest, down-to-earth people who felt the need of religious observance, but who had been taught not to get too excited about it. Religion was a "department" of their lives, wonderful in its place, but not too much related to their other activities.

Why didn't I, then and there, pray for these open and eager people to be baptized in the Holy Spirit? Simple enough—I was afraid to! I knew what was likely to happen as soon as folks began to get "fired-up." I remembered, only too well, that vestryman's "Praise the Lord" at the coffee hour at St. Mark's the year before!

The prayer meeting that night would have seemed undramatic enough to anyone who did not know how unusual it was for it to happen at all! Everyone agreed with enthusiasm that we should meet again on the following Friday, and we also concurred that we should move to the church parish hall. This move would forestall any foolish rumours that might get started if we kept on meeting in private homes. At the church, we would be in a public place where all the world was free to come and see, if it chose.

A somewhat expanded group met on that third Friday night. With us was our pretty, twenty-year-old daughter, Margaret, who had joined us in Seattle that week. (She had remained in California when we left, in order to finish her year at college.) Also present was Jim, the man who had been my youngest assistant at Van Nuys, who, with his wife Sharon, was visiting in the area. Jim and Sharon were an engaging young couple and gladly shared with our Seattle-ites something of their own experience in the Holy Spirit. So did Margie. We prayed around the room that night and as we prayed, the Presence of the Lord was so strong that several of the group were moved to tears.

It was the custom of the Bishop of Olympia to call together the clergy of his diocese for a conference once a year, and the following week was the time of this conference. As I and my fellow ministers arrived at the little Oregon seacoast resort where we were to spend three days, there was a holiday spirit of good fellowship. The programme for the first evening got under way: evening prayer, supper, a lecture by the guest—a very austere and scholarly English bishop!—and the session closed with the nightly prayer office of compline. We fragmented off in various directions: some to bed, some for a late stroll on the beach, but most to get together in various rooms for talk—reminiscences, anecdotes, and some good solid gossip about church matters and personalities, especially bishops! Five or six of my new acquaintances among the clergy centred in on me and said:

"We want to hear about your experience."

One fellow offered his room, and we were soon deep into the story. I don't know what they were expecting to hear, but all of them listened most intently to everything that I had to say, questioning me until well after midnight. I looked at my watch and exclaimed:

"Say, you guys, it's nearly one o'clock! We've got to go to bed!"

There was a pause. Nobody made a move to go. Then from one crewcut young priest, sitting on the floor, came:

"We ought to pray."

This suggestion startled me. Episcopal clergy certainly pray, but their praying tends to be either a private matter, or liturgical "common" prayer. It was quite unusual for this young man to suggest an informal group prayer, and even more unusual when in a very relaxed way these men proceeded to pray —good prayers, spontaneous prayers.

Another day went by, with lectures, discussion, prayer, and fellowship, and the next night after compline again a group came to me with the request:

"Let's go and talk about your experience, Dennis."

Some of the men were repeaters from the night before, but most were new. Again we talked, and again, in the wee small hours of the morning, somebody who had not been present the night before said:

"We ought to pray!" And we prayed.

The third night it was the archdeacon of the diocese, the man who had taken me out to see St. Luke's Church on my first visit to Seattle, who said:

"Dennis, I haven't heard your whole story. Won't you come to my room tonight?"

The archdeacon was much beloved and respected, and when I entered his room, there were fourteen men waiting. Again I talked of what had happened to me, and again when I finished there were many questions. Then came the pause I was almost expecting by now, and someone said:

"Let's pray!"

What followed was really very strange. As those men prayed, they sounded like a Pentecostal meeting! One said: "Praise the Lord!"; another, "Hallelujah!" Suddenly one of the priests, a man I did not know, jumped to his feet and began to recite the "Sanctus":

"Holy, Holy, Holy, Lord God of Sabaoth; heaven and earth are full of the majesty of Thy Glory." His face was radiant, and his hands lifted. Suddenly he began to prophesy. Beautiful words of promise and blessing came from his lips. There was no missing the fact that these words were inspired of God. He ended, and fell into his chair, a look of sheer amazement on his face.

"Where in the world did *that* come from?" he gasped.

On the final morning of the conference, as I was preparing to leave, someone behind me asked:

"Would you like to ride home with us?"

I turned around and was scarcely sure I recognized the young minister who had spoken to me. I had met him and conversed with him when he had first arrived at the conference. He had told me how frustrated and empty his life had become, and how he was thinking very seriously of leaving the ministry. Certainly I had rarely seen anyone look more unhappy. Subsequently, he had been present at all three of the informal, late-night meetings. Plainly something had already happened to him, for his face was as happy and smiling now as it had been sad and gloomy before. I accepted his invitation with pleasure. As we drove back to Seattle, every few miles he slapped his knee exclaiming:

"Praise God!"

When we arrived at my home, Elberta was waiting with interesting news:

"Dennis, guess what! Father W. is in town—you know, the man who wrote you from Illinois! He has some free time, and would like to come over and visit us!"

I was delighted. Father W. was the Rector of a good-sized

parish in the Chicago area. Right in the midst of my troubles in Van Nuys, he had written to me to tell me that they had been experiencing the Baptism in the Holy Spirit in his parish for the past five years.

"Most of my key people have received, and it's wonderful the way God's love and joy is being shown in their lives," he wrote. And he proceeded to encourage me to stand my ground. I was very pleased, of course, for up until this time, as an Episcopal priest, I had felt very alone in my experience. I had telephoned him and we had had much exchange of correspondence. Now here he was in Seattle!

I called him immediately and he agreed to meet with us that evening. I quickly telephoned all the little Friday group. Would they like to meet another Episcopal priest who believed in the Baptism with the Holy Spirit? Would they? Can a fish swim?! They were all at our home in very short order, plus some old friends from Van Nuys who were visiting—the neuro-surgeon, "Duke", and his wife, Claire—and the once depressed and now joyful young minister, who had brought me home from the conference and stayed to see what further blessing God had in store for *him*!

Father W. from Chicago turned out to be a personable man in early middle-life. His pleasant manner and openness quickly broke the ice, and he was soon telling of his own experience and how people in his congregation had been blessed. Then he looked at those present:

"Is there anyone here who would like to receive the Holy Spirit?" he asked.

This was the question I had been avoiding, or postponing. I was sitting on the couch, but I felt much as I did when I was about to solo an airplane for the first time. Sitting securely on the runway, you have no problems, but neither are you getting anywhere! You must apply full power to take off, and *then* you have your hands full! This man was about to push in the throttle for me! I knew that the minute we invited God to apply His power to this group of Christians we would "take off" and begin to go places, but I was the pilot—could I fly the ship without mishap this time? That had been a wild ride down in Van Nuys! Was I ready for another?

In the last nine years I have had many church leaders say to me in one way or another, "Dennis, we know that the church organization is dying and that we need something to help us. What you are talking about might be what we need, but, oh, Dennis, we just can't afford to have any *trouble*!" I, as an administrator, knew what they meant. If the boat is floating, even though it is gunwale deep in the water, and the waves are sloshing over the decks, for heaven's sake don't rock it! What I failed to realize was that St. Luke's was already resting quietly on the bottom of the lake, and there was no fear of rocking the boat. Rather, the attitude was, "If you think you can raise her—go ahead and try!"

Father W. looked at his watch:

"Don't have to leave for the airport for an hour-and-a-half," he smiled happily. "That will be plenty of time for everyone here to be baptized with the Holy Spirit."

I sat firmly on the couch—*This I've got to see!*

The little contingent of Episcopalians needed no urging: they were ready. So was the young priest who had brought me home. I watched as my friend from Chicago laid hands on these people. One after another they were prayed for, and repeatedly and simply we saw and heard the miracle of Pentecost reenacted. "They were all filled with the Holy Ghost, and began to speak in new languages, as the Spirit gave them utterance." [1]

Father W. quietly and simply encouraged them to open their mouths and begin to speak "as the Spirit gave them utterance." No such encouragement was needed for the young priest from the clergy conference! Before Father W. came anywhere near him, he threw back his head and began to speak fluently in a new language, while a glorious radiance overspread his already glowing countenance. With some of the others, it was almost as spontaneous, while some needed a little help to overcome their shyness. These good folk who had struggled so many years to do something for God in Ballard were suddenly aware of His power and glory in them in a new way.

It was impossible to miss the change that was visibly taking place. Joy, freedom, and spiritual understanding came as the new language poured from their lips. Though our visitor had to leave, the work had begun. Father W. had not imparted the Power, nor would the Power leave when he left. He had simply showed these people how to accept and express That which was already in them because they were in Christ. They were fulfilling the prayer which had been said for them at confirmation —that they might "increase in Thy Holy Spirit more and more . . ."* We were off the runway and "climbing out"—but what next? I was braced!

There was one interesting sidelight on this evening's experience: Jack, the member of the group in whose home we had first met, was an ardent bowler and had had to bowl in a tournament, so arrived late at the vicarage. He told us:

"When I came up the road, I saw the light outside your house, Father Bennett, and it was shining many times brighter than a one-hundred watt light *could* shine! I knew that I must hurry when I saw that because surely something wonderful was going on!"

* Not that the Holy Spirit would increase in *them*, which is the way we tend to think of the situation, but that *they* would increase in the Holy Spirit, that is, make more of themselves available to Him.

II
Airborne

The next afternoon I received a telephone call.

It was Pat, one of the group who had received the Holy Spirit the night before.

"I don't understand all that happened to me at the meeting last night," she said, hesitantly, "but I've been getting some words all day long, and I think they're for you. Can I have an appointment to tell you about them sometime?"

"If you've got some words from the Lord," I said, "I know better than to keep *Him* waiting. Come on over!"

She arrived at the office.

"The Lord seems to want me to say this," she began, seating herself across the room: "'You are afraid. You are afraid that this church will blow up like the church in Van Nuys! But don't be afraid. You'll never have any trouble here that you can't handle, and you'll have strong support from the top down!'"

As she spoke, I could have no doubt whatever that the Lord was using her as His messenger on that day. She could not possibly have known how much those words were true, and were needed. I had indeed been living with fear much of the time since the explosion in Van Nuys. I had not realized how oppressed I was until suddenly the oppression was broken. It seemed that I could feel the hot wind of the Holy Spirit blowing in my face, and that a silver rain of joy was visibly coming down from heaven! My heart began to leap with joy—I laughed, I shouted, I praised God! I am afraid I startled the newly-baptized-in-the-Holy Spirit Christian whom God had used as His emissary.

With this kind of assurance from the Holy Spirit, I plunged into the new work with enthusiasm. "The most important thing is to get started visiting people," I had said to Florence, the church secretary who had been heroically holding things together at St. Luke's while they were without a minister. "I'm going to divide the community into areas, and appoint a 'key family' over each area. We've got to get *organized*!"

In the very first St. Luke's newsletter after our arrival, I was all set to get "churchy."

"Just as soon as we are settled and moved in, I intend to begin an intensive round of visiting," I had written. Brave words! I thought *I* knew what to do about St. Luke's. I had revived a couple of other dead little churches in my time, and calling or visiting was basic. Ministers are trained to pay calls on people, in the hopes that people will come and "pay a call" on God! But clearly, God had other ideas. *He* was going to revive this church. St. Luke's was going to be different; it wasn't going to be a group of dependent souls being "taken care of" by a minister. These people were going to be equipped to help each other, and those around them, too. I was never permitted to carry out my "calling programme." God did allow me to care for the people who were in real need—sick or in trouble—but He never let me organize a round of home visiting for public relations purposes.

I have often been told:

"The reason for the revival at St. Luke's Church is that you are a clever organizer who knows just how to go about the business of building up a congregation!" The fact is that my "cleverness," if any, was not allowed to be used. All the little tricks of the trade that I had acquired in sixteen years of ministry were never put to use, because God kept me too busy to use them!

It had been only our second week in Seattle when the pastor of a nearby Assembly of God Church came to see me.

"Would you come and tell us of your experience, Dennis?" he said. That was the first of many invitations, so many that I soon saw that I would have to limit my acceptances. During the first four months as vicar of St. Luke's, I travelled to Denver, Spokane, Portland, and Vancouver, B.C., as well as to many nearby communities and local churches to tell the story. I began to be asked to speak to groups of ministers and lay people of many denominations: Methodist, Baptist, Quaker, and Lutheran were some of the first invitations. Lay people and pastors of all these groups, and many others, began to receive the Holy Spirit. My own bishop asked me to speak at the Clericus, the meeting of the local clergy of the Episcopal Church, where I was received with courtesy and interest. Several more Episcopal priests were at this time baptized in the Holy Spirit.

In the newsletter from January 8, 1961, appears the first of many similar statements:

"I am trying to hold these outside engagements to a minimum!"

It soon became evident to me, and to the people of St. Luke's that these "outside engagements" were to be a large part of my ministry, for I was one of the few ministers from an "old-line" denomination who was "willing and able" to talk about my experience of the Baptism in the Holy Spirit. Moreover, my background and academic training equipped me to explain the work of the Holy Spirit in a manner acceptable to the "intellectuals" and to fellow ministers. As for the people of St. Luke's Church, from the beginning they accepted my dual role with patience and understanding, and in doing so, felt that they had a part in an outreach ministry.

I was able to be away from the parish frequently because the laypeople were taking their rightful place as ministers and priests to God and to one another. When I was away, "business" continued as usual, for the newly-empowered-by-the-Holy-Spirit people, because of their new desire to serve, were only too willing to lead meetings, pray with people, conduct services, and even preach sermons in church on Sunday, and do it all very effectively! When I returned from an outside engagement they would often say to me:

"We had a wonderful time while you were away, Father Bennett!"

I found, too, that the finances of the church did not falter when I was away. I was becoming a commanding officer leading an army made up of soldiers who were capable of doing their own fighting, rather than a purveyor of spiritual remedies to a lot of dependent customers! It was great!

The first "fired-up" St. Lukans of course were telling their experiences to their friends. We began to meet regularly on Friday nights at the church, and there, as I gave my witness, I was joined by others with a story to tell.

"Guess what happened last night?" Amy's face was positively shining with joy. "We had some old friends over to our house and they accepted Jesus!"

I would hardly have known it was the same person that I had spotted in the congregation one Sunday morning shortly after my arrival in Seattle.

Good heavens, that woman looks depressed! I had thought. I learned that the woman's name was Amy, and that she had a husband, Ed, who occasionally came to church—when he wasn't fishing! Somewhat to my surprise, Amy had stopped me after church one fine Sunday morning:

"I hear you are having some prayer meetings in people's homes," she said. "Why don't you come and have one in ours?" Accordingly, several evenings later we did. As people were assembling, Amy said:

"I have a bad sore throat. Would you pray for me, Father Bennett?" Calling a man to help who had already been remarkably used in praying for the sick, we laid hands on Amy's head and the soreness immediately left her throat. But that wasn't all! The Lord also baptized her in the Holy Spirit, and she began to speak in tongues!

How things changed for that couple! When Ed saw what happened to Amy, he said:

"I want that, too!" We prayed for him. He had a hard time beginning to speak in tongues, because he was a bit shy and inhibited. Obviously, the Holy Spirit was at work in him, and as at so many other times I was tempted to say:

"Oh, well, that's all right. Never mind about the 'tongues.' They'll probably come later." But God again made Himself clear on the subject. It wasn't long before Ed reported:

"I'm beginning to speak in tongues in my dreams at night!" After that, it was just a matter of time until he was speaking fluently in his waking hours, and at will. (Since then we have known of many cases in which "speaking in tongues" came first in a dream.) Once again I had opportunity to see how completely the blessing of Pentecost could change two people. Both Ed and Amy had "church" backgrounds. Ed had given up on expecting anything important to happen at "church." Amy was hanging on, as women in a family often do. When Ed saw his wife healed and suddenly brought to a glowing life in the Holy Spirit, he immediately wanted to share in something so obviously good.

Now instead of Amy being in church looking bored, with Ed away fishing, Amy and Ed were in church not only every Sunday, but several times on Sunday, and also at meetings several times during the week. They had "come alive" in the Spirit.

They said: "You know, before we were baptized in the Holy Spirit our only concern was to get through the weekend! We would have some friends over for a visit, but it was usually pretty dull. A few drinks would help to liven things up, but not much. Now we get our friends over and tell them about Jesus! It's much more exciting."

It wasn't just what was said that moved people. "The happy faces of those Episcopalians is what convinced me," said one man. "I knew it had to be real!"

Within a short time, many more members of the congregation received the Holy Spirit. Just as at Van Nuys, these were established members of the church who had been struggling to keep the church open. One woman had been at St. Luke's for over thirty years; most of the rest had belonged for ten, fifteen, or twenty years. The average age of these newly baptized Christians was probably fortyish, although one lady in her seventies was among the first to receive the Holy Spirit.

One of the stalwart old-timers was Monty, a man with a rich background in business and professional life. He was my bishop's warden (the minister's "right hand man" in the Episcopal polity) the first year at St. Luke's, and also the treasurer —which office he had held for ten years past. He had seen the little church go through its ups and downs, and finally settle into the downhill trend. Now all of a sudden he saw the trend sharply reversed, and he determined to find out why! For several weeks he sat in our meetings and observed us as objectively as he could—and he was a sociologist by profession!

"He makes me nervous!" commented one person. "He's just sitting there watching us, like a-a- watch-bird!" But one night after vestry meeting the "watch-bird" took me aside.

"My counselling technique is changing because of these Friday nights!" he said. He was at that time a probation officer working with troubled youngsters, in whom he took a deep interest. Now he found his compassion somehow deepening and his attitude subtly changing. The next week in the meeting, as we were all praying together, Monty gestured to me.

"Come here and give me a hand," he said. He was already beginning to speak in tongues!

After this I had a different kind of treasurer.

"Don't spend any extra money this month!" he would warn us, with a harried look, "we're way behind!" Then he would add with a grin:

"I'm not really worried—praise the Lord!"

And Monty was typical of the moving of God at St. Luke's. Very, very few of the people who were active members of the church were in any way distressed or offended by the new experience their friends were claiming. Those who did not see it as something for themselves said:

"Well, we aren't interested in this Holy Spirit Baptism, but we can see that the church is coming alive, and we're happy about it."

There was no division. Occasionally in the early days I would receive a complaint:

"These 'Holy Spirit' people are getting cliquish!"

All it would take would be a word:

"Break it up, people! Don't clump together at the coffee hour and talk about your experiences—get out among the flock and spread the word!" And they would do it. The little church had been torn by internal strife, but now it was obvious that the Love of God was actively at work—healing the wounds, bringing people together into real appreciation of one another.

As people began visiting St. Luke's from other denominations, we saw God's forethought in choosing a tolerably "high" Episcopal Church for a centre of witness, since the unfamiliar liturgical worship discouraged people from leaving their own churches and clustering together at St. Luke's. When members of other churches received the Holy Spirit we told them:

"Your own church is your mission field. You are welcome to come back here for fellowship and for teaching, but we want you to go and tell the good news to your own pastor and your own friends."

One of our people put it this way:

"St. Luke's is like a pilot light. We light the other burners!"

Again, as in Van Nuys, these people discovered the joy of praying together. They, too, began to meet on any possible occasion or with any excuse. The big difference was that there was no opposition, no wild rumours, no fear, and no secrecy. This church honoured the work of the Holy Spirit, and everyone knew it.

Another very clear sign of the fullness of the Holy Spirit in people's lives is their interest in the Holy Scriptures. I had been brought up to look at the Bible as a collection of religious literature—some of it wonderful, some not so wonderful, some valid, some invalid, but the whole thing a mixture from which the scholars could select and tell us what was authentic. To accept the Scriptures in their entirety as the work of the Holy Spirit was foreign to anything I had been taught, and yet that is exactly what I found myself being pressed to do as I continued in the life of the Spirit. It was not an intellectual decision; it was just that I could not be spiritually comfortable taking any patronizing or critical attitude toward that Book!

Other Episcopalians began to experience the same thing. It wasn't so difficult for the layman who had been exposed to the arguments of "higher criticism," but for a minister, seminary trained, it was very hard. It's easy to get complicated, but it's awfully hard to return to simplicity! The people at St. Luke's simply began to rejoice in their newfound love for the Bible and to study it. I struggled with my intellect! One night at a study class a man from another parish expressed the usual "higher-critical" opinion of the Scripture. I tried to challenge him, but failed to be definite and convincing. I found myself spinning my wheels. Suddenly a woman in the class began to speak in tongues. I thought she was out of line in doing so, especially since she was a visitor from another church—a Presbyterian! No one had spoken aloud in tongues at the class before, and I didn't know how people would take it. This lady went on and on, and when at the end she began to repeat one phrase over and over, louder and louder, I decided it was time to do something! I looked at her, but her eyes were closed as she spoke—one hand lifted in praise. I started toward her, intending gently to ask her to stop, when she stopped of her own accord, and without a moment's pause, a man in the back of the class began to interpret. It was Toby. Toby was a big Norseman with a big voice; moreover he was a respected member of our Christian family, who had several times been impressively used to interpret when someone had spoken in tongues at a meeting.

"This is My Book! This is My Book! You read My Book! Don't criticise My Book! Just read My Book! For I am the Lord! I am the Lord! I am the Lord!" Toby's voice, like that of the speaker in tongues, got louder and louder until at the end he was nearly shouting. "I am the Lord! I am the Lord!"

What could one say? That class left greatly chastened and I never forgot the simplest way to define the Bible:

"This is My Book! I am the Lord!"

As I saw the people reading the Bible with great delight and seizing every opportunity to find out more about it, I thought of the years I had spent trying unsuccessfully to get people to read that Book, and I realized again how important is the Baptism in the Holy Spirit.

Although our membership did not increase with great rapidity, our church attendance did, because people who had been casual members, coming to church occasionally, when they felt like it, now were in church every Sunday, often two, three, and four times! What caused the change? Why did they come to church more than once on a Sunday and also pray together two or three times during the week? Not from a sense of duty, nor to show off devotion, but simply because they could not get enough of the fellowship of the Holy Spirit, which is a most tangible thing! For example, one Sunday morning at St. Luke's I turned from the altar to pronounce the ritual absolution to the people. As I did so, something I can only describe as a "wave of fellowship" hit me, coming up from the congregation, where over a hundred Christians were enjoying the Lord. I felt I had to shout "Hallelujah!" or do something to express the tremendous joy and love that engulfed me! I controlled myself, and continued with the liturgy, but I thought I was going to faint on the spot from sheer delight! The thing that led the early Christians to meet together even at the very risk of their lives was the tremendous joy of fellowship with Jesus and with one another through the Holy Spirit.

The profound test of spiritual experience, as the Bible points out quite often, is how people treat one another. The Apostle John said: "If any one says 'I love God,' and hates his brother, he is a liar . . ." [1] And the Apostle James says that there isn't much point in telling the beggar man who comes to you for help: "Go in peace, be warmed and filled!"[2] if you don't do anything to warm his body, and fill his stomach! The people at St. Luke's began to love one another and they began to be concerned about helping people. The first thing they wanted to do was to tell people about Jesus, but the Holy Spirit showed them that along with this they had to help in other ways.

A young man showed up in Seattle shortly after the initial receiving of the Holy Spirit at St. Luke's. Bill had a real concern for the "skid road" derelicts, especially the young ones. Quite on his own he started a sort of halfway house for men. Bill's idea was to deal with these men beyond the usual "skid-road" mission—helpful though it is. He wanted to bring his men away from the "road" into normal society where they could begin to regain their self-respect, and where they could receive real counsel and help.

St. Lukans began to have a new experience in that distasteful and unsavoury characters began to show up in the pews on Sunday morning or evening and in the prayer meetings. Many of these were just out of jail on a variety of charges: theft, alcoholism, drug-pushing, perversion, male prostitution, etc. They were received with real love. Our people took these men into their homes and sometimes would sit up nearly all night counselling with them. Many were led to Jesus, and real changes were made in their lives.

Members of minority groups began to visit and fellowship at St. Luke's, and they too were greeted, not with patronizing kindness, but with real brotherly and sisterly love; lines of colour and nationality melted away as thoroughly as had the walls of denominationalism.

The words of encouragement from the Lord at the beginning of my work at St. Luke's began to come true. At no time did we receive opposition from those in authority, either in the diocese or in the parish. The bishop was as good as his word and gave every kind of support he could. God had planted a tree of blessing at St. Mark's, Van Nuys, but it had been uprooted while just barely sprouting. Now it was transplanted at St. Luke's, Seattle, where in a climate of acceptance and understanding it began to flourish.

12
Every Need Supplied

Life in the Holy Spirit is different! Paul of Tarsus put it simply to his friends at Philippi: "My God will fill up all your needs in proportion to His riches in glory in Christ Jesus." [1] When we decided to go to Seattle, it was evident that we were going to be in a financial "bind." I was making a fairly decent income, for a minister, yet we had not saved any money, or even replaced our "early rummage sale" style furniture! Three teenagers make a dent in the budget! We didn't live extravagantly in any sense of the word, and yet every penny found its destination. I looked at Elberta.

"We're going to take a $4,000 cut in salary," I said. "Wonder what we're going to live on?"

"We've lived on a lot less," my wife replied. "Remember when you were in school we had a net income of $1,100 a year?"

"Uh-huh," I grunted, "I remember. We lived on that, and what the neighbours brought in! We used up, made do, wore out. I don't want to go back to *that*!"

"Well," said Elberta, "there's $3,000 in stock we inherited from Mum. We could always dip into that." Neither one of us had at this time quite realized what a good financial provider God is for His children.

When we left Van Nuys, we didn't bring our living-room furniture with us to Seattle—we took it to the dump! However, when we arrived in the Northwest we went straight to Sears and exercised our faith by picking out a new living-room ensemble and a carpet. Not only that, but it soon became evident, with three teenagers in the family, that we would have to have a second car, and so a little orange 1956 VW joined the family at the end of the year! Yet in spite of these expenses, and the reduction in income, we did not touch our little nest egg. God took care of us—in detail. It wasn't long before Elberta said:

"Let's not use that $3,000 on ourselves; let's save it for the kids—their education, or whatever."

I agreed, and our decision was immediately challenged. It was time to purchase new licence plates for our cars. The first car was already taken care of, but I needed $25 more to equip the "bug." What to do? I was just plain "out of money" until payday, still a week distant, and we needed that car. I took the matter to the Lord.

"Lord," I said, "I need $25 to licence that VW. As a matter of fact, I'm out of spending money and I could use $50!"

The next morning when I opened the mail there was a check for $43.72—an insurance dividend I wasn't expecting! But $43.72—why that amount? It seemed the Lord was saying to me:

"Dennis, if you want $25, ask for $25; if you want $50, ask for $50; but if you say '$25, or maybe $50,' I'll just split the difference!"

I remember another occasion that demonstrated His definiteness, and also the wonderful sense of humour—that's all you can call it—that our Lord displays with His children. I had purchased a typewriter, which was much needed at the church, but knowing that we were still limited in the budget, and yet wanting a good machine, I decided to pay for it out of my ministerial "discretionary fund." * This fund did not amount to very much, and it wasn't long before the first payment on the typewriter came due, and I didn't have the money! What now? Take the machine back? Maybe I had got ahead of the Lord in buying it. That night at the prayer meeting I found an envelope addressed to "Father Bennett" sitting on the piano. I opened it, and there was an anonymous gift of $50! I said:

"Thank you, Lord, but—the payment is $60 you know!" As the prayer meeting was breaking up, a young lady who was doing some volunteer stenographic work for me came up.

"Father Bennett," she said, "I haven't forgotten about that money you lent me from your discretionary fund, and I'll have it for you in the morning." Praise the Lord! I had forgotten that this young lady had borrowed $10 from my fund. This made up the $60!

"Thank you, Lord!" I said again. "That does it." But, alas, when I arrived home and looked at the bill, it was for $70! "Lord," I remonstrated, "I thought the monthly payment was for $60 and so that's what I asked for, but *You* knew it was for $70 all the time!"

But the next morning, Shirley handed me *$20*, not $10! I looked at her with surprise:

"That's right," she said. "Don't you remember I borrowed another $10 from you last month? I hadn't paid it back! I owe you $20." God does provide, and on time too!

It was the same with church finances. When I became vicar of St. Luke's, this little mission church was about $3,500 "in the red" in their operating budget, to say nothing of many

---

* A fund provided for the minister for miscellaneous expenses, especially charitable gifts—not for his personal use.

mortgages and loans they were attempting to pay off. It was a great pleasure to see God meet the financial needs, and as usual, He used interesting ways to do it! The income of the church was rising rapidly, because the Holy Spirit was urging people to tithe, but still some extra boosts were needed. After our fellowship and prayer meeting one night, one of my vestrymen found two one-dollar bills lying in the offering plate. He picked them up, and to his considerable surprise found a $100 bill lying beneath them. Upon retrieving the $100, to his astonishment he found nine more $100 bills with it! Someone—and we never found out who it was—had dropped $1,000 cash in that offering plate!

It was evident that we were going to be obliged to build a new meeting hall. Three hundred and more people were beginning to crowd into the little parish hall under the old church on Friday nights, so great was the interest in hearing about the blessing of Pentecost. But how could we build without capital?

"Lord," I said, "I'm just *not* going to have a capital funds drive. If you want us to have that new building, you'll have to send us the money!" I didn't even formulate in my mind what we would need to finance such a project. In the bank we had about $15,000 that had been given several years before in a building drive that had almost totally failed. (They were trying to raise $90,000.) Since it had been given for a new building it could not be used for any other purpose. I was sitting at my desk one afternoon, when in walked one of the faithful who had been at St. Luke's many years and had recently received the Holy Spirit. She put an envelope on my desk, saying:

"The Lord told me to give you this for the church." She turned quickly and walked away and was almost out of the building by the time I had opened the envelope. In it was a cheque for $10,000! I caught up with her at the street door.

"You can't do this!" I expostulated. "I know you don't have this kind of money!"

"I said the *Lord* told me to," she replied. "I sold some property, and He told me to give you that!" Nothing I could say would shake her resolve. $10,000 plus $15,000 made up the necessary capital to begin the new building! And so it went. As our budgeted income increased year by year, I watched the Lord meet every need.

One day I came into the office to find my treasurer looking a bit glum.

"What's the problem?" I asked him.

"The R's," Monty said sadly. "They're moving away, and taking over $1,000 a year pledge with them! *That'll* leave a hole!"

Next morning, in walked another good layman who had just completed a deal in real estate. Smiling broadly, he said, "Here's my tithe! "and he laid a cheque for $1,000 on the desk! He knew nothing about the other family moving away, but God knew—and filled the hole immediately!

We know that when money was needed on one occasion, to pay the temple tax, Jesus produced it miraculously through the coin found in a fish's mouth. Most people remember the time that the Lord found Himself faced with five thousand hungry people out in the desert.

"It'd cost a lot of money to feed this crowd," said Philip, one of His disciples. "What can we do?" In this case Jesus did not supernaturally produce the money to buy the food, but asked:

"What do you have on hand?"

Andrew answered, "There's a youngster here with some bread and fish he's brought with him for lunch, but what is the good of that for a crowd like this?"

And then Jesus proceeded to feed the five thousand from

the little fellow's lunch-box! I believe that happened because the Bible says it did, but I also believe it because Jesus did something similar in my own house! It was the day our daughter was married. Husbands can be thoughtless people, and I'm no different from the average. That day I brought sixteen people home to lunch without even warning my wife! She told me later what had happened.

"I stood in the kitchen and said, 'Lord, Dennis has brought these folks home with him, and You know I don't have food for this many. This casserole is large enough to feed only five or six, and I haven't time to go to the store. I don't want to say anything about this, so I'm going to put the food on the table and trust You to do the rest!'" She did just that, and said to me later:

"You know, I just watched that food go round and round. They kept digging in, and digging in, and everyone seemed to get enough to satisfy him and there was enough left over to feed two more who arrived later in the afternoon!"

"My God shall fill up all your needs!"

I hadn't been at St. Luke's more than a week or two when another kind of need was presented.

"What's the matter, Al?" someone asked at the vestry meeting. "You look worried."

"It's my daughter-in-law," Al said. "She's in the Swedish Hospital waiting for surgery. Ulcerative colitis."

I learned that this young wife was hemorrhaging so badly and was in such critical condition that her doctor was urging immediate surgery to remove her colon—not a good operation for anyone, but especially not for an attractive young woman in her early twenties. I called on Karen in the hospital, and after a little time of getting acquainted, I said:

"Ever think about praying to be healed?"

Her answer was diffident—obviously she hadn't.

"Do you mind if I pray for you?" No, she didn't, so I prayed. I called again later in the week. She seemed not unpleased to see me. Yes, the hemorrhaging was still going on, and, yes, the doctor was still fingering his scalpel impatiently!

"D'you mind if I pray again?" I queried. This time it seemed to me that her response was a little more interested, and again I prayed for her.

On my third visit she said:

"I still have the hemorrhage, and my doctor says I've got to have the surgery." But this time *she* asked *me*, "Would you pray for me again?" We prayed—and the hemorrhage stopped! For five months, week by week, we prayed for Karen —one jump ahead of the good doctor all the time.

"I'm scheduled for surgery next week," she would say.

"Does the doctor say you are in immediate danger so that you *must* have the surgery next week?" I would ask.

"No."

"Can you ask him to give you another week of grace?"

She did, he would consent, and we would pray some more. The doctor became a little more hopeful each time, and a little less eager to do the operation. Then came the victorious day when he said:

"Karen, I didn't expect it, but this thing has gone into complete remission. We'll postpone the surgery indefinitely!"

It must have been several months later that I met Rupe, a big, friendly man whom it would have been hard not to like. He was a teacher of reading skills and was establishing a reading institute nearby in the university district. We met Rupe through a mutual friend and parishioner, a commercial artist, who did much beautiful work for the church's printing department. She had solicited the resources of our print shop to help produce a brochure to publicize Rupe's new venture, thereby saving him quite a little money.

We all had dinner together at our house one evening, and Rupe, after we were well acquainted, shared with us his physical problem. Some time ago he had been hospitalized with severe pain which the doctor diagnosed as kidney stones. Whether this was correct or not, the pain masked the fact that Rupe had a seriously infected appendix, and while he was being treated for the kidney problem, the appendix ruptured. Before the condition was caught, peritonitis was raging through his abdomen. The infection had virtually destroyed his diaphragm, the big muscular wall that separates the abdominal cavity from the chest cavity and serves as the main breathing muscle. One lung was partly collapsed and Rupe's heart was displaced so far that it was on the wrong side of his chest.

"My diaphragm is like a limp rag, the doctors tell me," Rupe said. "It's not only paralysed, but it's full of holes! In fact," he went on, "they are intrigued that I am able to breathe at all. It seems I have learned to use my rib muscles for breathing, but they tell me I'll be in a respirator soon, and probably won't live too long. Right now my voice is weakened by this of course, and it is too high in pitch, which is a serious handicap in my profession."

"Do you believe in Jesus?" I asked.

"No," he replied frankly, "I can find no contemporary records of His ever having existed." Rupe was the son of a minister, but had lost his faith.

"Would you come to our prayer meeting tonight?" I pursued.

Rupe said later: "I had to say 'yes'; you'd just saved me about two hundred dollars!"

Rupe sat and listened that night at the meeting while one person after another stood up and testified to God's healing power. It seemed as though there were more healing testimonies than usual.

"I burned my finger badly last night while I was cooking the dinner," one woman said, "but my husband prayed for it, and look, it isn't even red!"

"I smashed my thumb working in my shop. It was all black and blue, but I prayed for it myself, and when I got up this morning there wasn't a sign of a bruise! Look! My doctor says it's impossible; isn't that great?"

Another person told of laying aside her glasses. "I had to take my glasses off," she said, "because as God began to heal my eyes, soon I couldn't see with my glasses *on*!"

Even more impressive was the story brought by one of our young people. It had happened the summer before while she was at the church youth camp. She slipped on the rocks while hiking up the creek bed the first day at camp, and cracked her ankle. The foot swelled up and became a beautiful black-and-blue.

"They took me to the doctor in Everett," Chris said. "He X-rayed it, and said: "Yes, it's broken all right!" The orders were to stay on crutches and put no weight on it at all. As soon as the swelling had gone down, the doctor said he would put a cast on it. It didn't sound like much fun to be spending the week at camp on crutches, so I said to two of my girl friends: 'At home the folks would pray for this ankle to be healed.' So we all went into the chapel, and Rochelle and the other girl laid their hands on my foot, and we asked *Jesus* to heal it. It stopped hurting right away! I didn't need the crutches anymore, so I put them down and went out and joined a baseball game! By that night all the swelling had gone, and by the next morning the black-and-blue colour was all gone too! The camp nurse and the clergy were pretty unhappy with me because I wouldn't use my crutches. In fact, they wrote a letter to my mother saying that they couldn't be responsible, and the insurance wouldn't cover my injury because I was refusing to co-operate in the treatment!'"

I saw Rupe get up and leave a little before the meeting was over. I slipped out and caught up to him just as he got into his little Ford Anglia. I climbed into the seat beside him. He was obviously moved.

"I don't believe the things those people were saying in there are possible! I don't believe in that sort of thing!" he protested.

Then turning to me he said:

"But why did I weep while they were saying them?" He paused, then, almost fiercely, he blurted:

"Can you heal my diaphragm?"

"No, *I* can't," I responded, "but *God* can!" And so I put my hand on his shoulder and prayed.

"Dear Lord," I said, "we sure could use a miracle right about now!" Nothing visible happened and as Rupe drove away, I thought:

"Well, that will probably confirm him in his unbelief. Too bad."

A week went by. I had almost forgotten about Rupe, but was brought sharply and uncomfortably aware of him when I saw him again as he walked into our prayer meeting on Tuesday night, a big broad smile on his face!

Perhaps he's come to laugh at us, I thought to myself, but I was very wrong. As soon as the time came to share, Rupe was on his feet. He told about the prayer we had said in the car the week before and then he went on:

"Nothing seemed to happen that night, but yesterday my son and I were crossing the sound on the ferry when suddenly a terrific pain hit me in the diaphragm. I felt it tighten up, and I've been breathing normally ever since!"

Rupe went back to the doctor, whose curiosity was completely aroused by this man who was breathing normally without a diaphragm! So interested were the doctors that they scheduled an X-ray moving picture to be made of Rupe's abdomen.

"Your diaphragm is still full of holes—it's still a mess," said one of the doctors, "but it's *working*!"

That first wonderful experience with the power of God threw Rupe into a rather amazing state of mind! He still could not accept Jesus intellectually, yet he clearly saw God's power. He began to have other prayers answered, and it wasn't long before his intellect had to capitulate to his spirit. He received Jesus and was baptized in the Holy Spirit.

It would have been miracle enough if the story had ended there, but it didn't! Nearly two years later, Rupe was praying at home with two friends, after attending a prayer meeting at St. Luke's.

"We'd had a wonderful evening," Rupe said. "One woman's eyes had been healed and several other miracles had happened. We came back to my apartment, and were kneeling around the big hassock in my living room—Bill, Ellee his wife, and me. Suddenly Bill said: 'My hands are on fire! They're hurting me!' I said: 'Put 'em on me!' I shuffled around the hassock on my knees to where Bill and his wife were kneeling, and he laid his hands on my chest. I felt as though all my insides had fallen out! I sprang to my feet, and literally had to grab at my trousers to keep them from falling off; they were suddenly too loose. I had to struggle to get my coat unbuttoned, it was now so tight. The whole outward configuration of my body was changing as my internal organs were renewed and went back into their proper positions. My heart was thumping like a hammer, of course, and I felt it move three or four inches, back into its normal place under my breast-bone. Not only was my diaphragm restored, but my physical body was changed so much that I had to get all new suits!"

But there are needs for more than money, food, or healing. We hadn't been at our new church very long before my wife and I began to discover how important it was that we get away once in a while to rest and relax. One Monday morning— and Monday was the day we hopefully called our "day off" —we looked unhappily at the cloudy skies.

"Well, we didn't pick a very good day for a picnic, dear," I said to Elberta. "Looks like it's going to be pouring after a while. What'll we do?"

"Pray?"

! ! ! ! There it was again! Pray about the weather? Wasn't that carrying things a bit *too* far? Still—Jesus prayed about the weather, and He got results! He said, "The works that I do shall you do also, and greater things than these shall you do . . ." [2]

"Okay." So we prayed; but the clouds did not roll away, and the sun did not blaze forth!

"What do we do now?" I asked my wife.

"Let's start out," she replied, so we put the picnic basket into the car and headed for the mountains, I, personally, feeling very silly. If the weather was bad in Seattle, one thing was sure; it was worse up in the hills. As we rolled along, we talked about it.

"We prayed for good weather—I think we're supposed to keep on driving until we get to the good weather," said my wife. And that's just what we did. We had clouds all the way up into the mountains until we began to approach the area where we had wanted to picnic, and, lo and behold, the sun began to break through!

"Keep driving!" said my woman of faith, and in a few

miles we emerged into full sunshine, right at a beautiful little picnic spot where we had a lovely warm day by the river. When we had eaten and basked in the sunshine for a while, we packed our things and headed back for town. We hadn't driven twenty minutes before we were in rain! Coincidence? Well, as a certain bishop of our acquaintance puts it: "All I know is that when I stop praying, the coincidences stop happening!"

Our next experience with "weather prayers" took place the following year. I had been invited to speak at several places in the San Francisco area. We had decided to drive to San Francisco and make our return journey up the Oregon coast as neither of us had ever seen the famous and beautiful Oregon coastline. The day before we were to make this journey, I flew to Eugene, Oregon, to make an address, and had ample opportunity to observe that all of Northern California and Oregon was under a solid deck of clouds. The weather on the ground in Oregon was rainy, and the airplane was almost refused permission to land because of marginal visibilities. I said to my wife:

"We aren't going to see the Oregon coast in very good weather. I've seen what it looks like from above!" Nevertheless, the next day we set out. When we got about one hundred miles north of San Francisco, sure enough, we started to go under the solid bank of clouds that I had flown over the day before. It hadn't changed much! We stopped that night at a little motel along the way, and in the morning, looking at the still threatening skies, I said to Elberta:

"Let's pray for sunshine on the Oregon coast!"

And so we did. We agreed for good weather on the Oregon coast, and then continued to drive through Northern California under increasingly gloomy clouds.

When it is raining in Northern California, you do not expect it to be sunshiny in Oregon, and besides that, we who live in the Northwest know that the weather normally becomes worse, not better, as we go out toward the coast! Everything was working against our prayer, and yet as we approached the Oregon border, the skies suddenly began to lighten! Exactly as we crossed the border, the sun came out. By the time we had driven a mile into Oregon, the last of the scattered clouds had disappeared and we were driving in beautiful warm sunshine! All the way from there to Tillamook we saw the Oregon coast in the most beautifully clear weather imaginable. We stopped several times along the way during the day, and people would say:

"It's funny; this set out to be such a gloomy day, and then all of a sudden it changed!"

Arriving at Tillamook, we turned inland, and in twenty minutes we were driving in the pouring rain! God had answered our prayer with His accustomed exactness—we had asked for "sunshine on the Oregon coast," and that is exactly what He provided!

People ask, when you talk about "weather prayers":

"But what if you are praying for sunshine, and someone else is praying for rain?" The answer is simple: It'll rain on him, and the sun will shine on you!

It was while on the trip that culminated in the "sunshine-on-the-Oregon-coast" experience that I had underlined for me another aspect of "my God shall supply all your need." One of my assignments had been to spend a week on the Stanford University campus, and to preach at the Stanford Chapel on Sunday morning. I remembered my preaching classes in theological school.

"Now," our professor would say, "you gentlemen must remember that you should put in at least thirty hours of preparation each week on your sermon!" This was the way the "great preachers" did it, we were given to understand, and who didn't want to be a "great preacher"? Alas, we overlooked the fact that the "great preachers" had "great secretaries" to keep files of information, and to read, type, correct, etc., and that most of *us* would be going out to undermanned, underpaid, under-equipped situations, where we would be working twelve hours a day just to keep up with the administrative and pastoral needs of the people, and probably cranking a mimeograph and licking stamps, too; to say nothing of sweeping floors and stoking furnaces! It didn't take us long to realize that three hours a week for the sermon would be hard enough to find, let alone thirty!

I enjoyed preaching and seemed to do it pretty well, but I never went into the pulpit without a prepared manuscript. I didn't always follow it exactly, but it was there. After receiving the Holy Spirit, however, I found that I was unable to feed the people on Sunday with food I had prepared the previous Wednesday! Instead I found myself laying my manuscript aside and beginning to speak the words which the Spirit gave me on the spot. Before, when I had tried to preach extemporaneously I had simply rambled, but now after the service people would say:

"How did you know that I needed to hear *that* this morning? You answered the exact question that has been troubling me!"

I discovered that a sermon does not have to be a literary masterpiece, but it should be more like "scratch feed," with something for everyone! From then on, and since coming to St. Luke's in Seattle, I had been preaching without a manuscript, my only preparation being that I had been working with people during the week, praying, and reading the Scripture. The raw material was there, and I trusted the Holy Spirit to put it together. Indeed, it was fortunate for me that I could work this way, for sometimes I was called upon to speak or preach anywhere from six to ten times in a week, and it would have been impossible to prepare all those addresses beforehand, and deadly to the work of the Holy Spirit to deliver a "canned" speech, even one I had prepared myself. But here was an invitation to preach at the Stanford Chapel—the "Harvard of the West". The Tempter was quick to point out to me:

"Think of the students and faculty in the congregation. You'd better write out *this* sermon for sure! This is no time for the 'off-the-cuff' sort of thing!"

I had the grace to reply: "If the Holy Spirit can give me the words for the people of Seattle, He can give them for the people here. Get lost, Satan! In Jesus' Name!"

And when I stood up to speak on that Sunday morning, sure enough the words were there; and that week, in that great academic centre, a number of young men and women were filled with the power of God.

13
God's-Incidents

"Anne?" The voice on the telephone was trembling with anxiety.

"Yes? What's the matter, Peggy?"

"Oh, Anne, I'm so worried. Chuck left on a sales trip yesterday and gave me a $300 cheque to deposit in the bank. He's going to be depending on it, and I've mislaid it. I can't find it anywhere!" Peggy was on the verge of tears. "Will you call some of the others and ask them to pray, too, please!"

"Of course I will!" Anne hung up on the phone and went to work on it. Anne and Peggy and "the others", members of a nearby Episcopal church, had received the Baptism in the Holy Spirit at St. Luke's in that first year. Typically, they did not leave their own church, but were trying in every way to get their own parish to see the importance of what had happened to them.

Peggy began cleaning up the breakfast dishes, but her mind was still very much on the missing cheque when after a bare half-hour, the phone rang. It was Anne.

"Peg, the cheque is in the laundry, under a pile of clothes." Peggy looked hastily and, sure enough, there it was!

Clairvoyance? No! God forbids that sort of thing. Anne was not exercising some kind of ability in "extrasensory perception"; instead, God simply gave her a Gift of Knowledge and showed her where the cheque was as she prayed.

Shift the scene to winter of that same year. It's snowing—hard. The vicar of St. Luke's has just been asked to make a call at King County Hospital, Unit II, on Queen Anne Hill. Queen Anne Hill is one of the more confusing parts of Seattle and I was not even aware that there was a hospital of any kind in that vicinity! Nevertheless, I climbed into the car and took off. I was perhaps halfway to my destination when suddenly I realized that in all my rush I had forgotten to look up the address and to figure out the location of the hospital! Bother! Now I would have to stop along the way to get information. It was snowing harder than ever, and there were several inches of wet slush on the sidewalks. Suddenly, I thought:

Look here, I'm a Christian, filled with the Holy Spirit. The Holy Spirit knows where that hospital is, and if He can guide me to speak in a language I've never learned, He can guide this car as I drive it! So I went on, determining to drive the car as I felt led, trusting the Lord. I had no special feelings about it, and saw no guardian angel leading me down the road! I just simply drove on, and coming to Mercer Avenue, I was inclined to turn left, which I did. Then left again on to Queen Anne and up the steep hill. When I got to Boston Avenue, a street I did not even know existed, I was again inclined to turn, this time to the right. After driving a few more blocks, there, to my admitted amazement, I saw the hospital for which I was looking!

On another occasion it was Christmas Eve, and I had to make a last-minute shopping foray into the heart of one of Seattle's busiest areas. Before I arrived at my destination I prayed, and had assurance that there would be a parking place awaiting me! Sure enough, there it was as I pulled up in front of the store—right by the crosswalk a car was pulling out, leaving time on the meter! Coincidence? Well, about two weeks later, again at the very busiest time of day, I had to go to the same store. Again I prayed, and the very same parking place was waiting for me! After this sort of thing happens repeatedly, one ceases to say "coincidence", but says instead "God's-incidents"!

One of our church members lived for a time on Bainbridge Island and had to cross on the ferry daily to come to work. His was a later ferry than most, and when he arrived at the terminal each morning the parking lots were already jammed, except for one parking place, right by the entrance to the boarding ramp. That one was always waiting for him!

"What about speaking in tongues? Surely this, too, played a part in the experience of the early years at St. Luke's?" Yes, it certainly did!

One St. Lukan felt led to go once a week to the County Hospital to visit the wards where there were lonely and aged folk who didn't have anyone to care. Here she was like an angel of mercy, and many were helped and brought to Jesus by her "unofficial" ministrations. One day she stopped to to speak with a little man who was sitting on the side of his bed looking sad.

"May I pray with you?" she asked.

He looked at her even more sadly, and replied:

"I no spik! I no spik!" But this did not frustrate the Holy Spirit, ᴏʳ her. She felt that God wanted her to talk to this little man, and if he did not understand her language she would have to trust God to give her words to say, so she opened her mouth and began to speak just as "the Spirit gave utterance." She did not understand the words she said, but to her delight the little man opened his eyes wide in amazement as he leaned over and with trembling hands drew a little book, obviously a New Testament, out of his bedside table drawer.

"Canary Island Spanish!! Canary Island Spanish!!" he said, tapping the little book with his forefinger, while his eyes shone with excitement and joy. His visitor bowed her head and began to pray for him, still accepting the words that the Spirit gave her, and the little man spoke every syllable right with her. She was speaking his language, and although she did not understand a word she was saying, she knew from his actions that she was reaching his heart with comfort from the Lord!

The husband of another of the "faithful women" received the Baptism in the Holy Spirit. He had been a consistent scoffer for many years, but when his wife received the Holy Spirit and he began to see miracles happening in his own family, he became interested and asked for and received this experience himself. His "tongue" was strikingly oriental, so much so that one day, while on his delivery route—he drove a delivery van—he encountered a Chinese customer, and boldy spoke some words in his "tongue"! The Chinese man answered him in the same dialect. Bob spoke again, and the Chinese person again responded, then asked in English:

"Where did you learn to speak my language?"

"What language is it?" Bob inquired.

"Why it's Mandarin, of course," the other replied, "and you speak it perfectly!"

"What did I say?"

"You greeted me, and I returned your greeting. Then I suggested that since you spoke my language, you should take a trip to the Orient with me next year and meet my family. You replied:

" 'I can't go now, but I will go later.' "

Sometime later, this man was at a prayer meeting and in the course of the evening spoke in his new tongue. There was an interpretation in English expressing praise to God. Present at the meeting was a Chinese woman, the wife of a medical doctor, and an exchange student at the University of Washington. She spoke up:

"How can this man speak Mandarin so perfectly? Where did he learn such beautiful Mandarin?"

Where indeed—?

One day, at about ten o'clock in the morning, my wife Elberta felt a strong impression:

"Pray for Steve!"

Steve, our older son, was in his senior year in high school. His mother was given no indication of why she should pray, or what for—just "Pray!" She prayed as the Holy Spirit gave her the words. How else could she pray? The New Testament says: "We know not what to pray for as we ought, but the Spirit Himself makes intercession for us, with unsayable utterances." [1] Elberta let the Spirit make intercession for Steve by giving her the words. After praying for a few minutes in a language unknown to her, she felt that the job was done, so she stopped. At four o'clock that afternoon Steve walked into the house.

"You prayed for me at 10 o'clock this morning, Mum!" he said. She never found out what it was that she was praying for —he didn't tell her, but he had known and felt the power of her prayer when he needed it.

A similar, although more dramatic example of the same thing took place near this time. A Presbyterian family—father, mother, and two sons—had received the Holy Spirit, and become part of an interdenominational prayer group meeting in the neighbourhood. Another member of the group, a Lutheran, was a jet captain for a major airline. One night, Earl, the captain, was on a trip overseas. Betty, the mother of the first-mentioned family, was awakened with a strong urge from the Holy Spirit:

"Pray for Earl!" No data, just the urge to pray. Again, what choice did she have? She prayed as the "Spirit gave the utterance," in an unknown tongue, until the burden of prayer was lifted. She fell back to sleep, and did not think too much more about it until Earl returned to the neighbourhood meeting from his flight.

"We had a rather hair-raising experience at our destination this trip," he said. "We were holding in solid instrument weather, awaiting landing clearance from the tower. When the permission came, due to an error, two airliners were cleared on the same approach, and as we broke out of the clouds we were frighteningly close together, and for a few moments it looked as though we were going to collide. My co-pilot was at the controls. To my surprise he made no effort to manoeuvre us away from the other ship, but just held his course and allowed the other aircraft to get out of our way. After we had successfully and safely rolled out, and turned off on to the taxi-way, my co-pilot said:

"Captain, that was a very strange thing. You know, when I saw the spot we were in, I naturally felt that I should make some effort to get out of there, but my hands and feet were just frozen to the controls. I couldn't move them at all! Now I realize that if I had tried to change the attitude of the airplane in some way, we might have been in serious trouble. The safest thing I could have done was just hold the course."

When Earl said this, Betty of course spoke up and told of her prayer during the night, and when times were compared they found that her prayer "in the Spirit" was offered exactly at the moment of the danger over that distant city!

"These signs shall follow them that believe . . ." said Jesus, and sure enough they do! But just as wonderful as these gifts of the Holy Spirit are the fruits of the Holy Spirit—the love, joy, and peace that begin to show in the lives of people who are truly beginning to trust Jesus.

One night, at about 10.30, my wife and I were just about ready to turn in when suddenly the front door burst open and in came our two sons, faces flushed with excitement.

"Mum, Dad! Do you know what just happened?" Steve flung himself into a chair, and Conrad followed suit.

"We were taking the girls home after the ball game, and we stopped at the drive-in in Ballard to get a hamburger and a coke. Con and I were waiting at the counter, when suddenly two fellows came up and just pushed their way in ahead of us. Well, we didn't like that very well, so we shoved back into our place."

"Yeah," broke in Conrad, the younger. "Then they yelled, and grabbed us from behind. I really thought we were going to have to let 'em have it!"

"What happened then?" I asked apprehensively. The boys didn't seem to be damaged in any way—I knew they were both very capable of taking care of themselves.

"It was the funniest thing," said Steve. "Both of us swung around. I know my fists were ready, and I'm pretty sure Conrad's were too." He looked at his brother, who nodded.

"I was going to 'deck' my guy, I know that. But as I swung around, my hands just sort of fell to my sides, and my fists came open, and I found myself saying:

'I can't hit you. I'm a Christian!' "

"And exactly the same thing happened to me," his brother said.

"Yeah. But even funnier, when I said that, those two tough characters literally turned pale, and ran for their lives!"

One Sunday morning after the 11 o'clock service, as I greeted a pleasant-looking young fellow and his petite wife, he said:

"We were kind of disappointed."

"What do you mean, sir?" I inquired, as I shook his hand.

"Well, my wife and I, we're Roman Catholics, you see, and we'd heard about this church. So we came to see what was going on. And—well, nobody *did* anything. I mean, it was a real nice service, but we thought somebody would, er, speak in tongues or—or something," he ended, a little lamely.

I laughed. "Oh, I see what you mean! Well, that doesn't usually happen on Sunday morning. There are people visiting who might not understand, you know. Why don't you come to our prayer meeting on Tuesday evening? It is very informal, and you are likely to hear the gift of tongues and interpretation."

"Oh, but it was wonderful just the same!" his wife broke in, her eyes positively sparkling with enthusiasm. "Why, those people certainly love God, don't they? I mean, you can feel it! I've never been to a mass where the people were so intent on the Lord!"

They went on down the steps and I turned to greet another stranger, who was somewhat shabbily dressed.

"I just want to tell you, Father Bennett," he said squeezing my hand earnestly, "that two of your men prayed with me for nearly three hours last Friday night, and they got me straightened out, too!" The man's voice shook just slightly as he added:

"I never dreamed anyone would care enough to take that much time with me and my problems."

"'Lo, how these Christians love one another!'" Well—yes, more and more! And this is the greatest of all manifestations of the Holy Spirit! "The greatest of these is love." Not human love, but God's love in people: drawing them together, bringing them to forgive one another, and reaching out to others in need of love and forgiveness—this, as Paul said, is the greatest. But, as Paul also said, we need the other too—the miraculous manifestations of God's power. It isn't "gifts *or* fruits," but "gifts *and* fruits" of the Spirit that we need, and at St. Luke's we began to see them both.

14
The Valley of Baca

"The way I've got it figured, Dennis, it's all downhill from now on!" Bob grinned at me happily. He had received the Baptism with the Holy Spirit two days before, and like most of us at that point, felt that he "had it made"! I well remember the first week after my own receiving the Holy Spirit. Amazing! What were those old-time saints having such a struggle about, anyway? It was all very simple! When I arose in the morning—there was God! Who could help but praise Him? At night, I fell asleep listening to the Holy Spirit in my heart saying:

"Praise the Lord!"

All day long I felt His Presence with me. When I had to speak, He provided the words. When we prayed, things happened. What was all the problem? Yes, I knew what Bob meant. I don't remember exactly how long this "free ride" lasted for him, but for me it had been about one week!

What happened then? I lost my temper! Parents of teenage children will have sympathy when I explain that I got angry with one of our sons! He hadn't done anything so awful; in fact, I don't even remember the cause of my anger, but I was furious beyond all reason. I had considered myself a good-natured fellow, rather mild—certainly not bad-tempered in any sense of the word, except that now and then, you know, one had to give vent to one's irritation! Oh, there was the mark on the breakfast-nook wallpaper where I had hurled a tuna sandwich one lunchtime in a fit of frustration, and the hole in the masonite picnic table I had put my fist through while emphasizing a point with one of our children! It was a kind of family joke that now and then, as my kids phrased it, "Daddy blew his top!" Those same children could calculate pretty accurately just about how far I could be pushed without detonating! If they went too far, they took the consequences with philosophical aplomb!

But, you see, Satan had this weak spot all picked out. He had been nurturing it for years. I had a temper—I was sometimes impatient and irritable—and this was the means by which he tripped me up. As a result, when my son got into trouble one night, I lost my temper. I yelled, I swore, I stamped my foot; *in fine* I made a complete fool of myself, and when I was through with my tantrum, the devil whispered to me:

"Filled with the Holy Spirit, eh?"

My anger drained away as quickly as it had come. I was crushed. I apologized to my son, who had of course taken my pyrotechnics in his stride as a "to-be-expected" reaction. I went to bed that night a sad and discouraged person. All my joy was gone. There was no spontaneous praise in my heart as I addressed myself to sleep; instead, the words of the Bible came to me: "They crucify to themselves the Son of God afresh, and put Him to an open shame."[1] For the first time in my life, I *wept* for my sins.

When I awoke the next morning, my heart was still very heavy. I had lost the blessing—would I ever get it back? I thought back over the events of the past week, and I said:

"Praise the Lord anyway!" And as I did so, joy flooded back into me, and again tears came to my eyes as I realized how much God puts up with, and how ready He is to forgive.

It was the beginning of a long time of getting up and falling down. I was disappointed to find that I hadn't suddenly been made perfect! But I did begin to understand that the Holy Spirit, Who had come to live in me when I'd first accepted Jesus so many years before, was now, through my baptism in the Holy Spirit, at work in my soul in a tremendous new way. At salvation my *spirit* had been made perfect, but I was to find that even after my Pentecost, my soul or psychological nature was not perfect, and would take time and effort to be brought into line. The *soul* and not the spirit was where the "hangups" were: the bad temper, the emotional upsets and complexes, the wrong thinking, the mixed up reactions—and some of them were very firmly entrenched. Now in receiving the Holy Spirit,* I had opened my psychological being—mind, will, and emotions—to be inundated or "baptized" in Him, so that He could really clean up the mess in my soul—but it wouldn't happen overnight!

It was only a few weeks after Elberta and I had both received the Baptism in the Holy Spirit that we received warning of a coming time of trial that would be the most severe we had yet experienced. Our doctor had expressed concern about Elberta. He felt that he should operate and remove what he hoped and expected would be a benign growth. She had had a similar surgery several years before without problem, and for this reason was not over concerned, although she did consent to be prayed for at the altar before the operation. The

---

* Receiving the Holy Spirit, or being "baptized in the Holy Spirit," does not mean "getting the Holy Spirit," but "receiving" or "making welcome," permitting the Holy Spirit to fill more areas of our lives, and to flow out through us to the world.

doctor had explained to us that if the growth was malignant, they would proceed without delay to perform a radical mastectomy (removal of the breast), so that the patient would not know the extent of the surgery until she came out of the anesthetic.

I had tried to share Elberta's optimism, but it was an anxious time in the waiting room of the Valley Presbyterian Hospital the next morning. When, after three hours, the surgeon came out to talk with me, my heart sank as I saw his serious face. The biopsy showed malignant tissue, and they would have to continue into radical surgery. Later that day, while my wife was still in the recovery room, our doctor tried to explain to me what a shattering blow this would be to her, both physiologically and psychologically, and how long it would take her to adjust. I was, of course, terribly shaken by it all, and dreaded my first visit with Elberta after the surgery. How would I find the strength and conviction to give her the courage she needed?

Both the doctor and I had under-estimated Elberta—and the Lord! I found her smiling—"glowing" would be a better word, seemingly unperturbed at the catastrophe which had overtaken her. Elberta had a firm hold on her victory in the Spirit even though physically she was in deadly combat. She proceeded to leave the hospital in half the time the doctor had predicted. Within two weeks she was able to be in church. There were over five hundred people at the family Eucharist that morning, yet Elberta seemed to me to stand out like a gentle beacon.

But we weren't through the woods yet! The doctor prescribed a course of cobalt radiation for her, just to be sure. Some who had been through it said the effect of this treatment was worse than the surgery! Radiation sickness was inevitable —nausea, weakness, lowered blood count. And sure enough, as she started through the treatment, Elberta began to have all the expected reactions, plus one more—the radiation began to thicken her oesophagus, and she developed a distressing lump in her throat that troubled her a great deal.

Some weeks after Elberta's surgery, we had a guest speaker at our evening service, a well-known leader of the healing movement in the Episcopal Church. After the service she came to our home, and met with a number of people who were interested in the work of the Holy Spirit. In the course of the evening, without having time to say anything to our guest about the nature of the problem, we asked her to pray for Elberta. We all joined with her in prayer, of course.

From then on, the lump-in-the-throat symptoms disappeared, and not only that, my wife went through the entire series of cobalt radiation treatments with no further symptoms of radiation sickness at all. She confounded the doctors and nurses in attendance each time she walked into the treatment room, submitted to the therapy, and then simply walked out again as if nothing had happened, while other patients were temporarily exhausted and debilitated. Not only did she have no nausea or weakness, but her blood count went up instead of down ! She had suffered from serious anaemia all her life, but now she discontinued using an iron supplement she had needed for years. She began to enjoy a physical vigour she had never known—even her need for sleep was sharply reduced. The surgeon said that if there were no further trouble within five years, Elberta would be in the clear.

Then, shortly after our coming to Seattle in 1960, just about a year after the first surgery, the enemy struck again. The malignancy was recurring ! There were new tumours in the breast area. As far as the doctors were concerned this was a death sentence. There was nothing more to be done, except to try by various means to slow down the growth of the disease. In a basic attempt to do this, the surgeon urged an operation to remove the ovaries, and Elberta consented to it. Again came the doctor's warnings of the results of this procedure: there would be a premature menopause, with attendant symptoms, depression, and other side effects. None of these things took place! Elberta had no lasting symptoms from the surgery, and continued to enjoy her newfound vigour—but the tumours continued to grow.

At the time of the first surgery, in Van Nuys, Elberta had said to me:

"You know, Dennis, while I was under the anesthetic, the Lord said to me: "Will you take all this out of Satan's hands and give it to me?" I said, 'Yes, Lord.' I know He has His hand on this whole situation. I'm not worried about it at all."

Now she said:

"I'm not going back to the doctor or the hospital. They have done all they can. I've put this thing in God's hands, and He has everything under control." Elberta did not take this stand because she was ungrateful to the doctors—she had accepted and had appreciated their ministrations, but now she had given the case to God completely, and there it was to stay.

The next two years were the happiest and most fruitful my wife had ever known. She once confessed to me:

"Before I received the Holy Spirit, at times I used to get so bored and depressed with the prospect of years and years of church bazaars, rummage sales, ladies' guilds, fashion shows, etc., that I felt I just couldn't go on!"

Now things were different for her. She still hardly ever opened her mouth in a meeting. Once she commented about her role in this way: "I just occupy a chair!" But quietly and effectively she counselled and helped many people, and earned their respect and love.

Our family all depended on her strength, and no one leaned on her more than I did. Elberta wasn't a highly trained theologian. She had never attended Bible school or seminary, but she read the Scriptures almost continuously since being baptized with the Holy Spirit, and she was equipped with that wonderful and blessed characteristic known as common sense. She felt that her place was at home, keeping an eye on our maturing family, although she did occasionally make a "missionary journey" with me. She disliked "making speeches," but when needful could give a good account of herself. Things like clothes and fashion were of little interest to her; yet she always looked neat and pretty.

The weeks went by, and the months. Still she enjoyed physical vitality, but the malignant sores in her body ate away, and gave no sign of abating. Every night I would anoint her and pray. Her friends were praying. The church was praying. Yet although we had intercessions as a part of the church service, so surely did she feel that the whole matter was in God's hands, that for a long time she did not want public prayer to be made for herself. Finally one night, I said:

"Honey, I just can't go to that altar and pray for everyone else, and not pray for you." So she consented.

Early in 1963, she began to have difficulty in breathing if she exerted herself beyond an ordinary pace. It was evident that the disease was working in her lungs. Her trust in God was unshaken. I commented to her one day on her faithfulness in praying and reading the Scriptures. She said:

"When you are facing the possibility of death daily, it makes a difference!" Death was one thing she did not fear at all.

She wanted to keep her mind on God all the time. If I would thoughtlessly sit down at the piano and play light opera or sing some popular song, she would say:

"That's the wrong tune!" This wasn't because she was being puritanical. She explained:

"I want to have the right kind of music running in my mind. If I listen to 'Oklahoma,' or 'South Pacific,' I'll wake up in the morning humming the words to 'I'm Going to Wash that Man,' or 'The Surrey with the Fringe on Top'! I want to have songs about God running in my mind, and wake up singing *them*!"

In June of that year I was asked to go to Alaska for several days to speak for Episcopalian and Full Gospel* groups in Anchorage and Fairbanks. I didn't want to leave Elberta. She was beginning to have real difficulty in breathing if she put forth more than minimal effort, but she insisted that I carry out the mission, and so, reluctantly, I went. She was in no pain, and was able to function quite normally in every way. No one would have known by talking ot her that there was anything physically wrong with her. When I returned from Alaska, she said:

"You know, Dennis, while you were away, my lungs began to fill with fluid. I knew that the doctor would drain that fluid if I asked, but I had determined not to turn to man for help. I went to the altar at the church and just said: 'Lord, you'll have to help me because my whole trust is in You,' and He immediately took care of it, and I was fine!"

By the middle of July, however, she was having to sit up in a chair to sleep at night, to help her breathing. Still, during the day she was able to lead a comparatively normal life. By the last of the month she was forced to remain seated on the couch in the front room day and night, and she began to have real pain. Still she was adamant. She would not have a doctor, nor would she go into hospital. She would not accept any painkiller or drug, not even so much as an aspirin tablet. Hers was not a sickroom, but a battleground.

* "Full Gospel" is one of the terms used for those Christian groups that teach not only salvation through Jesus Christ, and other essentials of the Christian Faith, but also the Baptism in the Holy Spirit.

The combat became fiercer. At night I slept on the floor in the front room. The one thing she wanted me to do was to play and sing gospel songs. They helped her to sleep at night; they helped her to get through the day. Good friends assisted me in nursing her. Two wonderful doctors were hovering in the background. One of them said to me:

"Dennis, she's choosing the right way. There's nothing we could do." But they were afraid for what might be yet to come. I knew what they feared.

She continued to get worse. For a week she ate nothing, beyond a few sips of bouillon; yet there was not any visible loss of weight or pallor. At this time one of our sons said:

"Dad, I've never seen Mum look so beautiful!"

The pain was very bad, and yet it was never more than she could handle. She fought it out with the enemy toe-to-toe—her mind clear, and unfogged by drugs. Being unable to persuade her to take any kind of medicine, I said:

"Honey, won't you accept at least a little oxygen to make your breathing easier?" She did so, for my benefit I think, because she must have known how helpless I felt. Throughout that day, off and on, she took some oxygen. Then after a while Elberta said softly:

"Take it away."

It was evident that she was growing weaker, but she was peaceful and seemed in a lot less pain. As evening drew on, while our three children and I were there with her, I said:

"I love you."

She said: "I love you."

I said: "Praise the Lord!"

She said: "Praise Him!" And very simply, with no struggle, she died.

One of our doctor friends said a short time later: "Her death is a miracle!" He was fearing hemorrhages and nausea, and all the horrors that can accompany a cancer death, but Satan's hand was limited.

Elberta's death was surrounded by victory. It was more like a soldier's death—a martyr's death. Half-an-hour after she died, my older son came to me and said:

"Dad, I saw Mum go into heaven!"

"What do you mean, Steve?" Stephen at twenty was a very practical young man, very much like his mother in an apparent lack of sentimentality; he was certainly not given to romanticizing.

"Why," he said, "about ten minutes after she died, the whole room faded away, and I found myself standing on the bank of a great river. A little boat was there, and I saw Mum get into the boat and go across the river. Jesus met her on the other side, and I saw them go up the grassy bank, laughing and talking together. I could see the beautiful city in the background; and before she left, she turned and waved at me! I know she saw me, too!"

At the same time, a mile across town, some friends had heard of Elberta's death and were weeping about it. Suddenly Claudia, one of the teenage girls in the family, started to laugh:

"Why," she said, "I see Elberta! She's going across a green field, laughing and talking with Jesus!"

The Lord did not cease to give signs of His blessings, even during the funeral and burial. When we went to select the coffin, I feared this would be a terrible ordeal. I looked at the various elaborately decked-out caskets, none of which seemed to be right. The mortician, a personal friend of mine, and characteristically helpful and understanding, was trying his best. Suddenly I turned and saw it! A bronze casket, simple and handsome; on each of the handle plates there was a portrayal of the Last Supper, and at each corner there was the figure of an angel! It was as if it suddenly dropped from heaven.

"This is the one!" I said. Though I'd officiated at hundreds of funeral services, I had never seen another like it.

The funeral was an affirmation of her victory in Christ. Bishop Lewis, who had stood with us so firmly in our coming to Seattle, celebrated the Lord's Supper, while the people of St. Luke's crowded into the little church with feelings of mingled joy and sorrow.

As we stood around her grave, we began to sing spontaneously, "Praise God from Whom all blessings flow!" We knew that although the mortal body was laid away with honour, Elberta was not there, but with Jesus in His Kingdom, where one day we too would rejoice with her when our course was run.

15
A Crown of Life

For some time after Elberta's death I seemed spiritually to be in a kind of limbo. There was no doubt that she had won through to victory, but it was a victory that left her on the other side of that great river Stephen had seen in the vision. She had gone on into the City of God, and she was with Jesus, but she had gone. She wasn't with me anymore, and I missed her very much.

There was much misunderstanding and bitterness in my soul. What could I now say about answers to prayer, especially prayer for healing? Had not God failed or refused to heal just when healing was most needed, when the one human being dearest to me had not been healed?

The Baptism in the Holy Spirit had opened my eyes, and I had come to see, all the way through the Bible, how God was ready to help His people even in their simplest physical needs. He was involved in every detail of their lives. I had come to see that God was the same for this present day, and to trust Him to heal a cold, a burned finger, or to guide in the seeming little things of life—like jobs, and parking places! This wasn't because one wanted to get things from God, as much as because one wanted to experience God's reality and closeness and love. Before receiving the Holy Spirit I had known God's leadings and answers to prayer in what seemed like a far too infrequent kind of way. Now I had had a taste of what it was like to live in a new relationship, in which God did, as the Scripture said, "supply all your need." [1] Was I going to have to return to that uncertain world where God sometimes did and sometimes didn't? A place where you couldn't really depend on Him? Where every prayer had to be ended with what has been called the "faith-destroying phrase": "If it be Thy will . . ."?

The evening of Elberta's death, after everyone had either gone home or gone to bed, I sat down and opened the Bible, looking at random for something that might speak to me. My eyes fell on these words in the Book of the Prophet Ezekiel:

"Also the word of the Lord came unto me, saying: Son of man, behold, I take away from thee the desire of thine eyes with a stroke . . . and at evening my wife died . . ." [2]

It was too pointed a reference to be a coincidence, but what did it mean?

Again the next evening I opened the Bible, and this time a verse in the Book of Isaiah presented itself to me at once:

"The righteous perisheth, and no man layeth it to heart . . . none considering that the righteous is taken away from the evil to come." [3]

Since Elberta had been gone I had taken to walking around the neighbourhood first thing in the morning. It seemed to help somehow. There were still some flowers blooming, and as I walked and admired the gardens which are so much a part of the crisp beauty of Seattle, I had a feeling that Elberta was walking in the gardens of God's Kingdom, enjoying their beauty. It wasn't that I sensed her presence with me. I knew that any kind of imagined contact with the departed was utterly forbidden by God and that Elberta was in no sense still in or even adjacent to this world; but it was as if there were a parallel experience and it gave me comfort. As I walked along on this particular autumn morning, I asked God:

"How come Elberta died?"

His response was immediate, in that "still, small voice," not an answer to my question, but a statement:

"She was one of my great ones!"

"I know that, Lord," I replied. He brought Scripture to my mind, vividly and unmistakably:

"That I may know Him, and the power of His resurrection, and the fellowship of His sufferings, being made conformable unto His death, if that by any means I might attain unto the resurrection of the dead."

I tried to work it out.

"*That I may know Him* . . ." Yes, I knew that Elberta had not only come to know God, but that during the last three years of her life she had pressed closer and closer to know Him better. Her whole life had been taken up into the effort to know Him better.

"*The power of His resurrection* . . ." We had all been aware of this in a tremendous new way since the renewing experience of the Holy Spirit. Elberta had experienced the resurrection power even in her physical body, in greatly increased vigour, less need of sleep, and increased blood count, just as the Apostle Paul said:

"If the same Spirit Who raised Christ from the dead dwells in you, He . . . will give new life to your dying bodies . . ." [4]

"*The fellowship of His sufferings* . . ." Ah, there was the sticking-point! Did anyone truly want that? What was the real meaning of these words?

One thing I knew—when the word "suffering" was used in

the New Testament it didn't mean what we mean by the word today. When we say we "suffer," we usually signify that we are hurt, or have pain, but the Bible word always means: "To put up with something voluntarily." If you *have* to do it, it isn't really a "suffering." I knew that the Apostle Paul was saying something like:

"I willingly put up with all kinds of hardship, even death itself, rather than stop telling about Jesus." And even more profoundly, "rather than stop trusting Jesus implicitly for every need of my life," for to the world this is the deepest offence of the gospel, that we trust God instead of man.

I turned a corner in my walking. The sun, which had been hiding his morning face behind a long roll of clouds concealing the eastern mountains, now began to glint through. It looked as though it would be a fine day. I pursued my thoughts as I pushed on

"The fellowship of His sufferings" then, was something that God's people were supposed to live day by day, and Elberta had certainly done this. She, together with the rest of us, had endured scorn for the sake of Jesus, and had left her home and moved to a faraway city she had never seen. She had gone along with me without flinching when I had resigned my prosperous church, and had expressed no fear at the prospect that my career might come to an end suddenly in the middle of what should have been my most productive years. Elberta had met God in a new fullness; she knew what she had, and what it was worth. She was a faithful witness and, in her quiet way, a strong one.

Yet it was difficult to see how her sickness could be called a part of the "*fellowship* of His sufferings," for Jesus was never sick, and it is impossible to think of Him as being sick. Then, too, sickness is involuntary. The sick person does not take his sickness willingly, and it would be wrong if he did. Rather he attempts to get rid of it: by doctors and medicine; by change of climate or diet; by prayer. No one really questions but that sickness comes from the devil, for if it came from God, how would we dare to seek to be cured?

Elberta did not accept her sickness. She never stopped praying for and expecting healing. When she had put the situation in God's hands at the time of her first surgery, this did not mean that she accepted the sickness, it just meant that she was going to trust God implicitly for her healing. When she decided after her second surgery to accept no more medical treatment, and then refused to take painkillers or drugs, she was not surrendering to the disease, but putting her whole trust in God.

"Why did she died prematurely? Did God refuse to heal her?" Impossible. I knew that if Jesus had come into her room, she would have asked Him, and He would have healed her instantly and completely. As for death, I recall that someone once said:

"Jesus Christ was the world's worst funeral director! He broke up every funeral He ever attended, including His own!" And I know that Jesus was the perfect image of His Father, and did only the things He saw His Father do. All these things about Jesus had to be of the Father, too.

"But God is all-powerful; why did He not heal? God can do anything." We forget that God has limited Himself in one way as far as man is concerned; He has given man free will, and will not overrule our decisions. We are the ones who unconsciously put up blocks to God's power. I have little idea what such blocks might have been in Elberta's case—to speculate would be fruitless—but one thing I do know is that it was not a lack of trust in God on her part. All I know is that for some reason or reasons, the enemy was able to press in and attempt to bring about her death by disease which he and he alone causes, but in this he failed utterly and totally; for God, after letting her fight a brief battle and gain her victory, "took her away . . . by a stroke" as the Scriptures had told me—that is, "in a moment." God did not "take her away" by means of the illness, nor by death—for death, too, is Satan's thing—He took her away *from* illness, from pain, from death, into the glory of His Kingdom. Since her healing was blocked by causes unknown to us, God did what was for her a greater thing, although far harder for us to take: He brought her home! He saw that her life had reached a peak of love and grace, and that there was much "evil to come" for the world, and said:

"The next series of battles is not for you. You have done your work and I'm bringing you home."

As I went up the walk to our little white house on Jones Avenue, the sun was much higher now and comfortingly warm on my back; I felt that some things in this puzzle were fitting into place. It would be a while before I could come to terms all the way, but it was no longer a complete riddle to me.

I went into the house, and sitting down in my study, rested my eyes on Elberta's picture. God's words were certainly true. Yes, she was great in His Kingdom because she walked faithfully in life and in death. The ache in my heart was diminished by the knowledge that God had given her the "crown of life" which He promises to all those who are "faithful unto death."

16
Missionary Rector

Though I was struggling to understand the sorrowful happening in my own life, God did not stop opening doors and giving me assignments. I discovered what many others who had been baptized in the Holy Spirit have discovered, and that is, no matter what doubts and reservations were in my mind, when I stood up to testify to what the Lord was doing, I found myself speaking out with a conviction that I did not know was there! Indeed, sometimes I would feel like a hypocrite; yet it was not hypocrisy, but was the truth in my spirit overriding the doubt in my soul.

It was a chilly autumn Sunday later that year. I had just completed the celebration of the Lord's Supper at our family service. My assistant minister had been "serving" for me, and was standing at the end of the altar with water and wine, assisting me with the "ablutions," the ceremonial cleansing of the communion vessels.

"Ed," I whispered, as he poured the water over my fingers into the chalice, "isn't that the Bishop of Alaska out there?"

Ed looked round quickly. "Yes," he said, "I believe it is!"

The bishop had come, in non-clerical garb, to see for himself what went on at St. Luke's! After the service we renewed our acquaintance at the coffee hour.

"Dennis," he said, putting down his cup, "I'd like to invite you to come to Alaska again so more of my clergy can meet you."

So it was that in January 1964 I went back to Fairbanks, only this time, at 38° below, it was a fairyland completely sheathed in sparkling frost: the midwinter days very short, but very beautiful. It was a contrast to my last visit, which had been in midsummer, when the sun had dipped only briefly below the horizon and one could take snapshots even at midnight!

I went out to the Arctic coast, to Kotzebue, a large village situated on a sand-spit separating the frozen ocean from a frozen lagoon, 7° below, with a brisk 20-knot gale blowing! Here I met my first Eskimos—a people that I quickly came to love and appreciate. Here too I began to experience some of the rigours of missionary life, as I shared with the vicar and his wife, Bobby and Judy, their three-room vicarage, a little bigger, it is true, than most of the Eskimo one-room huts, but utterly devoid of such everyday conveniences as plumbing (of any kind whatever, indoor or outdoor!), running water, or even safe drinking water. I went with Bobby out to the ice lakes behind the town on the dog sled, where chunks of frozen lake water are cut out, brought back, thawed, and the water boiled before it is safe for drinking. I found that for nine months of the year, a bath was a well-nigh unheard-of luxury, unless one was fortunate enough to be invited to the home of a government or school employee who luxuriated in indoor plumbing and hot running water. In the Arctic, an invitation to "dinner and a shower," is perfectly valid, and highly prized!

The night I was to give my testimony, the little Pentecostal Church of God across town closed its own prayer meeting and came to share with us, and I felt far from home in the little corrugated iron building (since replaced with a handsome wooden church) that housed the congregation of "St. George's-in-the-Arctic," my homesickness was tempered as I looked out over a sea of Eskimo faces and saw the familiar glow of those who had been baptized in the Holy Spirit.

That week, too, I met Charlie, a vigorous man in his early seventies, and a much respected leader in the Eskimo community and in the church. Charlie's wife, Lucy, had been quite ill, and Vicar Bob and I went to call and to pray. Another new experience faced me as we walked into their little home, for there was a seal thawing out in the kitchen area, ready for skinning and butchering! After we had prayed with Lucy, I turned to her husband. His love for the Lord seemed obvious.

"Do you know about the Holy Spirit?" I inquired.

"Oh, yes!" he replied, with an infectious smile. "I go down beach. I see seal. I kill seal. I very happy! Holy Spirit fill me!" He gestured expressively.

"Have you ever spoken in tongues?" I inquired.

Charlie shrugged. "I get tongue caught in teeth," he said, seriously. "Talk funny!"

I came back to Anchorage, which looked like a very big city indeed, and then out to amazing Kodiak Island, and back again to Anchorage and on to Seldovia, Juneau, Petersburg, Wrangell, Ketchikan.

The bishop did everything possible to put me in touch with as many of his missionaries as he could—actually I met twenty-three out of thirty-one and a number of these received the Holy Spirit. I also found several who had been speaking in tongues for some time without fully realizing what it meant.

"Dennis," said the pastor of one church, as we came into his house after a meeting, "I think I've been doing something like what you're talking about."

"What do you mean?" I inquired, pulling off my huge fur-lined mitts, and beginning to struggle out of my parka. (Boy, it was cold outside, and good to be in the house!)

"Well, I've a kind of special language that I've used in my prayers for years. I'd never said anything to anyone about it. I guess I thought it was kind of silly, but it always seemed to help me somehow." He sat down on the arm of a chair, and was silent for a second. "Do you think it could be 'speaking in tongues'?"

I was smiling—I had heard this sort of thing before and thought I knew the answer.

"Let's pray," I said, sitting down across the room, "and you pray in this language of yours."

My friend hesitated, then closed his eyes, and after a few halting syllables, began to speak fluently in a beautiful dialect.

"There's no doubt about that!" I said, as he stopped. "Praise God!" It wasn't only the beautiful language that convinced me, it was the refreshing presence of the Holy Spirit which I know we both felt.

This was my longest "missionary journey" thus far. It seemed strange as I returned to Seattle to realize that I had made some good friends in that remote outpost separated from me by thousands of miles of icy water, and frozen tundra.

That same year of 1964 was saddened for us all by the death of the Rt. Rev. William Fisher Lewis, D.D., the man who had originally opened the door to my coming to Seattle and St. Luke's. Bishop Lewis had never wavered in his support of our work, indeed he had shown deep personal interest.

"When are some more churches going to begin doing what yours is doing?" he asked me, on one occasion. He attended a Tuesday night "prayer and praise" meeting back in 1962.

"How did you like it?" I asked him, in a little trepidation.

"It was fine!" he grinned at me. "You rather wore me out,

though. I don't attend many prayer meetings that last three hours!"

During the last few months of his life, he visited meetings at St. Luke's on three occasions. In his last illness, few were allowed to visit him, but he said to me:

"We've been through a lot together, Dennis, and you're not going to be shut out now." He gave orders that I should be allowed to call on him and bring him Holy Communion. His victory in Christ was so evident during this time, that his doctor said to me one day:

"I've never seen anything like it. Every time this man is awake, he has this broad and happy smile on his face!" And Bishop Lewis himself said:

"Dennis, I'm so filled with joy, I hardly know what to do!"

His death brought a new bishop into office, the Rt. Rev. Ivol I. Curtis, who had been assistant Suffragan Bishop of Los Angeles during the crisis at St. Mark's. There were many in the Diocese who wondered what the attitude of the new bishop would be towards the "Charismatic Episcopalians." Bishop Curtis was an old friend—we had been fellow-Rectors in the Diocese of Los Angeles, before his election to the Episcopate —and very shortly after his arrival in Seattle, he took me to lunch, and told me:

"I have found Bishop Lewis to be one of the most wonderful people I have worked with, and I just want you to know, Dennis, that my attitude toward you and your work will be just the same as his." Bishop Curtis, too, has been as good as his word, and not only has given us encouragement at St. Luke's in many ways, but has often given me recommendation to other Bishops, when in my travels I needed such.

But my next adventure was to take me yet further afield than my last. I had been hearing about the "Fountain Trust," a group of ministers and laymen in England who had banded together to give responsible leadership to what was now being called throughout the world the "Charismatic renewal."* The Rev. Michael Harper, a priest of the Church of England, was on the staff of All Soul's, Langham Place, a London Church which with its Rector, The Rev. John R. W. Stott, has long been a focus of evangelical zeal. Michael had felt called to leave parish work and spend full time with the Fountain Trust as its executive secretary. Under his Spirit-led guidance, this work had already achieved a good deal toward getting English Christians, and especially Anglicans, to understand the revival. Michael and his wife Jeanne visited us early in 1965, and quickly endeared themselves to the Christian fellowship at St. Luke's. They extended to me an invitation to come to England that very summer, and I accepted. This would be my first visit to the land of my birth since I had left it as a boy of nine.

Although I had travelled to the four corners of the United States, this was my first flight overseas, and I was excited as I checked in at the international area at Kennedy Airport, clutching my passport.

"Pan American Flight Two," came the announcement, "London, Frankfurt, Beirut, Teheran!" Even though I was deplaning at the first stop, I felt a vicarious thrill in knowing the big jet on which I was to ride was going to other exotic ports of call—Bangkok, Hong Kong, Tokyo—right around the world and back to the U.S.A. via Honolulu! Minutes later I was walking on board the aircraft. The door to the pilot's cabin was open, and my feeling of adventure quickened at the sight of the sextant mounted in the roof, and the realization that we

---

* "Charismatic" comes from the Greek *charismata,* which means "gifts of love." It is used in the New Testament of the gifts of the Holy Spirit. "Charismatic renewal" means a renewal of these gifts in the Church.

would be travelling where it might be needed, far from the ordinary land facilities of air navigation.

It didn't seem very long before we were landing at London's Heathrow Airport, and I saw Michael and Jeanne waiting to convey me to their interesting flat at the corner of Harley and New Cavendish Streets.

"Why do you call it a flat?" I asked breathlessly of Michael, as we were struggling my suitcases up the fourth flight of stairs to the Harper's apartment.

Michael chuckled. "I suppose it is a little 'vertical' for a flat," he admitted. "A marriage counselling service has the two floors below, while we occupy the three above!"

I found that it was indeed so. One ascended from the street by three flights of winding stairs to the kitchen and living room, while the bedrooms were distributed between the two floors above that! There was little need for jogging to keep exercised in those quarters! I was soon ensconced in a cosy little bedroom at the top of this castle, which was to be my headquarters while I was in England.

I had no sooner established this base of operations than I was whisked off to Cambridge University, where I was to spend a week, and introduced to the Rev. Simon Barrington-Ward, at that time Dean of Chapel of Magdalen College.* I was feeling a little travel weary as we brought my things into the guest room at Magdalen, where I was to stay, and was not particularly cheered by the visage of old Samuel Pepys looking at me darkly from the mantelpiece! I didn't have much time to be concerned about that famous diarist, however; in fact I didn't even have time to inspect his diary, which is a part of the treasures of the library at Magdalen. I found myself busy day and night. I spoke to many faculty and student groups, ad-

---

* "Magdalen," for reasons known to the English, is pronounced "Maudlin"—American readers, please note!

dressed the chaplains of the University, and preached in several of the Anglican churches in Cambridge.

The Rector of Great St. Mary's, the University Church of Cambridge, had written asking if I would speak at the Sunday 11 o'clock service on October 24, and take as my topic:

"Is it decent to speak in tongues?"

I suspect that his own tongue was tucked in his cheek when he wrote this to me! A very short time before my departure for England, however, I had received a second and hasty note from the Rector, saying that he had just realized that October the 24th was designated a "United Nations Sunday," and moreover that the Mayor and Corporation of the City of Cambridge were to make an official visit to the church on that day, and would I please change my topic to:

"Pentecost and the United Nations"?!!

So on that Sunday I looked out at a packed church over a sea of gold maces, scarlet gowns, wigs and cocked hats, where the Mayor and his *entourage* were seated immediately in front of the pulpit. I tried to show that peace among the nations could not come until we had begun to take Jesus' offer seriously that He would give us His peace, and that this, like other gifts of God, came only through a personal acceptance of that same Jesus, and through the work of the Holy Spirit.

The Provost of Southwark Cathedral (pronounced "sutherk"), the Very Rev. Ernest Southcott, was an old friend. When he heard I was to be in England, he invited me to preach at the Cathedral. It was a moving and impressive service. A freestanding altar had been placed at the crossing of the stately old Gothic building, and there the Holy Communion was offered by five concelebrating ministers, assisted by laymen, who brought the bread and the wine down the aisle at offertory time. I spoke on the power of God, and asked the question:

"We have been marching up and down the aisles of this

ancient church building with great enthusiasm, carrying crosses, torches, banners, and singing the militant hymns of the faith. It's grand and inspiring! Outside the doors of this cathedral is the forbidding griminess of this part of London's industrial area on the South Bank of the Thames, the docks, the slums. Are we going to march out of this church into the city outside with the same kind of confidence with which we march around in the church? Where are the people of God going to get the power to show the rescuing love of God in the world outside?" I tried to give the answer to my question. "By the acceptance of Jesus the Saviour and by the release of the Holy Spirit in and through our lives—by a renewal of the experience of Pentecost!"

I spoke at four of the major theological colleges of the Church of England—Westcott, Ridley, Cuddesdon, and the London College of Divinity. In each I was courteously received, and in all but one, virtually the entire faculty and student body was there to hear what I had to say. My testimony was received with real and deep interest. I came to realize that one of my main tasks on this trip was to help "unhook" some of the "hang-ups" which hamper theologians in their understanding of the Baptism in the Holy Spirit.

The Bishops of Bedford, Southwark, and Coventry all invited me to address them and their clergy, and I was really delighted with the openness that I found there, too. Neither in the theological schools nor from the clergy did I receive any unfriendly or ungracious challenges, although there were, of course, urgent questions.

The chapter meeting of the Coventry clergy was held in the little village of Offchurch, in the old rectory, which had been made into a chapter house. We met in the morning with thirty or so of the clergy who were working in "high-density" areas of the diocese. The Rev. Stephen Verney, well-known for his book, *Fire in Coventry*, a story of the spiritual revival centre-ing around the building of the new cathedral after the old one had been almost totally destroyed in World War II, chaired the meeting, and I told once again of the great things God was doing in my own country and other parts of the world. After luncheon the bishop arrived, the Rt. Rev. Cuthbert Bardsley, prepared to lead a business session, but the men said to him:

"My Lord Bishop, we would like to have more dialogue with our visitor about the work of the Holy Spirit. Would that be in order?"

And the Bishop replied with a beaming smile:

"That's exactly what I would like to do!" So we had another couple of hours of good sharing. The bishop wrote later to Michael:

"I would like to thank you and Father Bennett very warmly indeed for your great kindness in coming to Offchurch last week. It was exactly what we all needed, and I came away tremendously encouraged and grateful for your contribution . . ."

I was also invited to speak at the Ecumenical House at Ox-ford University, where the well-known Russian scholar and churchman, Dr. Nicholas Zernov, was chairman of the meet-ing; then, returning to London, David DuPleiss and I found ourselves as luncheon guests of a group of the leading evangeli-cals of England, both Anglican and Non-conformist. I was delighted with their openness and freedom from prejudice, especially that peculiarly American doctrine of extreme "dis-pensationalism"—"These things are not for today!"—which is so often the defence of the stateside evangelical. Another contact with the heart of English evangelical Christianity came when I spoke at Westminster Chapel, where Dr. Martyn Lloyd-Jones has pastored for many years. The meeting was sponsored by the Fountain Trust, but Dr. Lloyd-Jones attended, and afterwards I enjoyed a warm and encouraging conversation with him. The Dean of Wesminster Abbey, the Very Rev. Eric Abbott, asked Michael Harper and me to come and see him, and we spent a good hour in his study adjoining the Abbey. He, too, was genuinely interested. All in all, it was a fruitful and action-packed time.

Although my main ministry on this trip was teaching, many received the Holy Spirit, and some were delivered from sickness or other oppressions of the enemy. I won't soon forget two striking things that happened at an interchurch meeting in a London suburb. We had met in the social hall of the Methodist Church, and after the main session, a small group had gathered in an upstairs classroom to hear more about the Baptism in the Holy Spirit. Michael Harper was with me. After making sure that all present had personally accepted Jesus Christ as their Saviour, I began to pray for those who asked—a few for healing, or other needs, but mostly praying for them to receive the Holy Spirit. Once again the miracle began to happen, as Christians, already indwelt by the Holy Spirit, began to trust Jesus to inundate them with His power and freedom, so that the riches stored in them could break forth to the world. One after another, some hesitantly, some fluently, they began to speak in new languages.

I came to a young lady with bright red hair sitting expectantly on the edge of her chair, eyes closed in prayer. As I laid my hands on her head and asked Jesus to baptize her in the Holy Spirit, she began to speak. It was obvious from her general appearance that she was not a well educated person, probably a worker in one of the nearby factories. She began immediately and effortlessly to speak in a beautiful and flowing language that was obviously not her own. Everyone stopped and listened. She began very softly, with her head bowed, then lifted her head and her voice. We all knew she was praying and praising God, and the sense of His Presence was very real and sweet. After a few more moments she again dropped her head, began to speak more softly—then stopped. Her hands were lying open in her lap, and her eyes were still closed in prayer. Prompted, I am sure, by the Holy Spirit, I said to her:

"My dear, you can interpret what you have just said!" Ordinarily I would not have encouraged such interpretation, for the kind of "speaking in tongues" that takes place at the time of receiving the baptism in the Holy Spirit is the beginning of the "prayer tongue" which is going to be used in private devotion, and needs no interpretation. It is "speaking to God in a mystery," as Paul says. In this case, however, I felt that God wanted this girl to interpret her speaking, so that we could all share in the blessing.

Without a moment's hesitation, she began to interpret, that is, to bring in English the meaning of her speaking. I cannot remember her words to quote them in detail, except that they were a beautiful and childlike prayer to God. As she interpreted, she began softly with her head bowed, then raised her head and her voice, just as she had done while speaking in tongues, and concluded again by dropping her head and her tone. It was utterly artless, and utterly convincing. Several people in the room were openly wiping tears from their eyes.

I moved on round the room, and in my praying came to a young man whose face was drawn and white; he looked completely depressed and distressed. I put forward my hand to pray for him, but before I could touch him, he was literally thrown from his chair on to the floor. I realized he was being tormented by demonic power, so I rebuked the evil spirit at once, bound it under the Blood of Jesus, and cast it out in the Name of Jesus, never to return. The young man immediately calmed down and climbed back into his chair, but I could see that he was still very agitated. It startled me to see that the whites of his eyes were blood-red from the violence of his ordeal! I said to my companion:

"Would you take this man into the next room and pray for him further?"

Those who went with him told me later that the whole performance was repeated, and another tormenting spirit cast out. After that, the young man happily received the Holy Spirit!

I felt that it was God's wisdom that led the young lady to give such an undoubted manifestation of the beauty and validity of the gift of tongues in order to prepare those in the room for the second, rather shattering, experience. As it was, no one was disturbed, and a number of others also received their Pentecost, but none looked more radiant than the young man who had been so dramatically set free from bondage.

17
A New Chapter

Nearly three years had gone by since Elberta's home-going. During those years I had had no problem keeping busy. I had given my testimony over and over again, not only at home in our Friday night meeting, but throughout the United States and overseas, telling of the release of God's life in people as they received the Baptism in the Holy Spirit. For me on a personal level though, they had been dry and lonely years. I was having difficulty keeping any kind of spiritual joy and freedom, and there were times when, as I told again of my experience, it seemed I was only talking of a memory. It was not surprising that I should feel this way, although I certainly did not understand it at the time. Here I was, entertaining all kinds of doubts and fears and even resentment toward God, because of my great personal loss—behaving with the exact opposite of faith —and yet expecting to be able to enjoy His fellowship at the same time. He hadn't left me, of course, but how could He possibly show Himself to me, when I had my back turned toward Him? Friendship is a two-way street; you cannot at the same time be questioning the goodness of a friend, and also enjoying his love and fellowship, and it isn't any different if that Friend happens to be the Lord! Not fully understanding these things, I almost felt that I had come to the end of my story, and all the while God was waiting for me to trust him, so that He could begin a new chapter.

One Friday night in mid-March of 1966, as I opened the "instruction" meeting at St. Luke's and prepared for the many-hundredth time to give my testimony to the waiting people, my eyes spied an unexpected visitor in the congregation—Rita Reed.

I had known Rita casually for some five years off and on. We had met briefly in the summer of 1961 at the Full Gospel Businessmen's Fellowship International Convention in Miami. Her brother, William Standish Reed, a well-known Christian surgeon, widely hailed in charismatic circles, had introduced us. Both Dr. Bill and I were to be speakers at the convention. On a Sunday morning a group of us went to an Episcopal Church for an early morning communion service, had a pleasant visit over breakfast, and then went to a Full Gospel church service—a truly ecumenical morning! I remembered Rita as an attractive and pleasant young lady, some years younger than I, who obviously loved the Lord Jesus very much.

I had seen her again in 1965 at a convention in Spokane. Mutual friends invited us individually to visit with them in their hotel suite one afternoon, and each of us was surprised to find the other there. It was pleasant to renew the acquaintance and to continue conversation further over dinner. After that visit she sent me a copy of a little book she had prepared for her Bible classes on the gifts of the Holy Spirit, asking me to cast a critical theological eye over it. I found it to be sound, and said so. I had an inclination to get better acquainted with her, but Spokane was three hundred difficult miles away, and I just never found time to make the journey. Now here she was sitting in the parish hall at St. Luke's. I was very pleased to see her.

"Rita!" I greeted her, taking her hand. "How good to see you again!"

"It's nice to see you, too, Father Bennett," she replied with a smile.

"What brings you over Seattle way?"

'Oh," she said, "I was invited to speak for several of the Christian women's clubs in this area, and for some prayer groups, too. Being so close to St. Luke's, I didn't want to miss attending a meeting here."

"Where are you staying?" I inquired.

"With some of your parishioners as a matter of fact, Verle and Chloris," she responded.

It was time for me to open the meeting. "What about coming to speak to the college group tomorrow night? I'll come and get you." I wanted Rita to tell our college people something of the work she was doing with young people in Spokane.

The next night she did come to the meeting, and afterward I took her home. She had never been in Seattle before, and it seemed very logical to give her a little tour of the city—it's especially beautiful at night. As we drove, I asked her about her brother Bill, and others of our mutual friends. Then after a little time of silence, much to my own surprise, I came out flatly with the question:

"Rita, how old are you?"

She looked at me a little surprised, but answered pleasantly enough: "Me? Oh, I'm thirty-two."

Embarrassed by my own impertinence, I lapsed into silence again, but my mind was very busy. *Thirty-two, eh? She's older than I thought she was. Now why should I be thinking like that?*

We stopped at a restaurant for a bite to eat, and then I delivered my guest to the door of the spacious home on Queen Anne Hill. I resisted a strange impulse to kiss her good-night!

I gave myself a "talking-to" on the way home. "Now look here, this young lady is just a friend. Cut out the nonsense! You're going to make a fool of yourself for sure if you don't look out!"

The next day was Sunday, and Rita came to the family church service bringing with her a curly-headed seventeen-year-old by the name of Sibley. I had heard something of this young man. He was from Spokane, and a number of months before he had been run over by a car and terribly injured. Rita had heard of his condition at a home prayer meeting: Fractured skull, brain damage, paralysed on one side, a broken leg which could not be set because of his precarious balance between life and death, gangrene in both feet, in a state of semi-consciousness for a month— It would take a miracle indeed to remedy this young man's condition, but Rita felt led to go and pray with him. At the nursing home, she met Sibley's mother for the first time. Together they, and another friend, went into a room where the boy was lying. He was not a hopeful sight, this once nice-looking teenager: most of his hair had fallen out, his body was mere skin and bones, with tubes carrying out the basic functions of life. His eyes were blank and staring.

The mother broke the silence:

"The doctors tell me that my son cannot communicate with anyone—there has been too much brain damage. I can't quite believe this, though, because when I talk to him, I am sure that he moves his eyebrows in a kind of response."

Rita knew something of this kind of situation. She remembered her brother Bill's experience with a young girl, Karen Emmott, several years before. Karen, too, had been given up as a hopeless case, until God intervened.* She knew her brother believed that even in a coma, a patient could often know and

* Catherine Marshall, *Beyond Ourselves* (McGraw-Hill, 1961), pp. 221–228.

understand everything that was said to him or her, even though unable to respond. She had a sudden inspiration, and taking Sibley by the hand, spoke to him:

"If Jesus heals you, Sibley, will you live for Him? If your answer is 'yes,' squeeze my hand three times."

What was her excitement to feel one—two—three definite squeezes of her hand! Without doubt Sibley had heard and understood every word! With this sign that a miracle of healing was already beginning, Rita now with even greater confidence prayed with the prayer of faith, the others agreeing in prayer with her:

"Father, I thank You for what You have already done, and in Jesus' Name I ask You to restore Your child and make him whole again."

Next day the nurse noticed Sibley moving his head, and seeming more alert. He then proceeded to pull out the tube through which he was being fed directly into his stomach. His nurse decided to try giving him some Jello, and he gobbled it down avidly! She tried a cookie, and that disappeared just as quickly! It wasn't long before the nurse realized she was trying to fill the void in a teenager who hadn't eaten for a solid month! Soon the boy was talking, recognizing people, and eating quite normally. The doctors, being told of Sibley's sudden improvement, brought him back from the nursing home to the hospital to see what they might do further to help him. It was during this time that Rita, arrayed in a sterilized hospital gown, prayed with Sibley to receive the Holy Spirit! Soon this young man, who a few short weeks previously had been considered a hopeless case, unable to communicate at all, was praising God in a new language, given by the Holy Ghost! Not long after this, he was back at home, and on the way to an amazing recovery.

It was a real joy to see Sibley in church that morning, and to realize again the power of God—the power which we limit so pitifully. On the way out of church, I greeted them and asked Rita:

"How much longer will you be in the Seattle area?"

"A few more days," she replied. "By the way, Father Bennett, do you have anyone in the parish who could help me counsel with a woman who is deeply depressed?"

I gave her the name of a long-time Bible teacher, known as Aunt Ada to more than one generation of Christians! Ada, brought up as a Lutheran in Sweden, and later as a good fundamental Baptist, had received the Baptism in the Holy Spirit. To my great delight she had joined our congregation, bringing her strong teaching ministry into our fellowship. Although getting on in years physically, she was young in spirit, and many St. Lukans profited by her teaching and wisdom.

They made contact, and Rita was invited to dinner the next day, but when she arrived at Ada's pleasant little home on Phinney Ridge, her hostess said with a motherly twinkle:

"I hope you won't mind, but I've invited Father Bennett to join us for dinner at the 'Windjammer'!"

That evening as we sat together across the table from Ada, more than once during the meal I found myself glancing at the young lady by my side. How nice to have her there!

18
"Two are Better than One"

When I returned from my second journey to Alaska, I had found my older son waiting to talk to me. He was very excited.

'Hey Dad, I've found out what I want to be!" he said. "I want to be an airline pilot. We've been down to the airport while you were gone, and found out that it'll cost only about $3,000 to get the training I'll need!"

I looked quizzically at my son. "Only $3,000, eh?" I said. "And where are you going to get *that* kind of money?" Steve was at the in-between stage of not yet settling on what he wanted to do with his life, and I thought that this might be a "flash in the pan"—but I was wrong. Steve did manage to finance his project, and before long was on his way to becoming a very fine light plane pilot.

I had been flying on big aircraft for a long time and loved every minute of it. While I was in Alaska, a friend had taken me for my first trip in a small plane. We had flown in his Cherokee 160 over the Kenai Peninsula, and into Seldovia. On the way back he had let me "steer" for a while! Now my son said to me:

"Dad, why don't you come on down and take a lesson? You'll like it, I'm sure."

I did, and I was "hooked"! By the end of 1965 I had my private licence, and early in 1966 took the doubtful step of becoming part-owner of "N-8191-Bravo," an elderly Cessna 172, a gentle old girl with a chequered history. I found this new avocation to be not only intriguing and challenging, but also healing. It was a lot of fun, although I didn't know what use it would be in my life; now I began to get a clue.

By the spring of 1966, I had become a fairly proficient pilot, but I had never made the cross-country journey eastward to Spokane. Here was a good excuse for a visit with Rita! On the 2nd of April I wrote to her and said that, weather permitting, I would be flying "91-Bravo" over the Cascades, and what about lunch?

Rita told me later:

"I realized by your decision to fly over to see me, that you were beginning to show more than a brotherly interest! I was flattered; yet I was happy being single, free to go wherever and whenever God directed. I had had opportunities to marry several times in my life, but somehow had never done so. Suppose you wanted to get serious! I had turned my life over to the Lord, and was not at all sure marriage was in His plan for me, even if it was to someone as nice as Dennis Bennett!"

Since it was my first trip east of the mountains in the little plane, I examined my charts carefully and filed my flight plan. Rita had just moved out to a retreat centre called "Living Springs Ranch," so my destination was the Deer Park Airport, fifteen miles northwest of Spokane. I noticed from the chart that although it was quite a small town, it boasted a good-sized airfield, a relic of World War II.

It was a beautiful day. The flight through the Cascades was without incident, and the scenery magnificent. I crossed the

Columbia and then the long dry plain between the Cascades and the Spokane area. As I came over the last range of hills and eased back on the throttle to begin a long glide down from my cruising altitude, I saw the airport dead ahead—looking just as the chart showed it. There were three big runways arranged in a triangle. No sweat! Just a matter of finding out which way the wind was blowing. Setting my radio to the Spokane tower frequency, I picked up the mike:

"Spokane tower, this is Cessna Eight-one-niner-one Bravo. Please close my V.F.R. flight plan to Deer Park, and give me the wind numbers. Over." The controller's response made the rest very simple. The wind was right down runway 22—but one thing puzzled me as I circled over the field: all the tyre marks were at one end of the runway, the *opposite* end from the one I wished to land on! Gave me a kind of funny feeling. According to those skid marks, or rather the lack of them, nobody had landed on that runway in the direction I wanted to land for a long time! Why not? I flew low over the area several times, but could not see any obstacles—could not see any reason why my 172 should not settle down nicely on that piece of concrete. Finally, with more daring than good sense, I swung into a downwind, base, and final approach, and touched the wheels down in a "greaser" that warmed my pilot's heart! No problem yet—but as I taxied to the far end, I discovered it. There was a fence—a good heavy one, too—stretched right across the airstrip, but invisible from the air. And the black tyre marks all at one end? Very simple. This runway had been converted into an automobile "drag strip"!

I taxied over to tie down the airplane and saw Rita waiting for me. After the ship was secured, she came out to greet me.

"You sure had me concerned for a while!" she said. "I didn't know anything about this airport until arriving to wait for you. A man drove by, noticed I was waiting, and said it was quite rare for anyone to land here since two of the runways had become drag strips. 'Drag strip!' I echoed. He drove away and left me wondering: *How in the world can I warn Dennis?* The only answer was to pray, and pray hard!"

"Sure glad you did!" I said, as we walked to her little white Rambler. "*Someone* was looking out for me. If the wind had been from the other direction I would certainly have bent the airplane, to say nothing of myself!"

We drove through the town and down the country road to the retreat centre where Rita was staying, and greeted her good friends and hosts, Dean and Cordie. The picnic lunch on Mt. Zion, as the nearby wooded hill had been christened, was pleasant but brief, for I had to return to Seattle the same afternoon.

It wasn't long before I found another excuse to visit her. This time I flew "commercial," the Cascade weather not being friendly to small aircraft. We took a stroll in the woods in quest of wild flowers and conversation. I offered Rita my arm as we walked—and it was fortunate I did, for on the way down a steep slope she tripped, and would have fallen had she not been able to steady herself.

"Oh," she apologized, a little embarrassed. "That's me! I tend to stumble when I'm going downhill."

It was only about five minutes later that the trail began to climb, and suddenly it was my turn to stumble. This time I was glad that Rita could help me keep on my feet!

"Well," I said, "you may stumble going downhill, but *I* trip over my feet going *up!*" We laughed about it, not thinking it might have meaning for us later on.

"Why don't we sit down here awhile," I said, indicating an inviting patch of green grass.

"Fine," my companion said, suiting the action to the word, as I seated myself beside her.

"Tell me more of your story, Rita."

"I've known Jesus ever since I can remember," she replied thoughtfully, "but I made a personal acceptance of Him at the age of nine, and shortly after this I was baptized with the Holy Spirit. It was quite a dramatic experience. I spoke in tongues for about two hours and prophesied!"

"Now, that's great!" I said. "Wish I'd received the Holy Spirit that early in life!"

"Yes, it should have been great," Rita went on, "only for me it didn't turn out that way. If someone had just told me what to do next, that the Baptism with the Holy Spirit was a *continuing* experience and that I should pray "in the Spirit" —in tongues—every day, it would have been wonderful. As it was, the memory of my experience faded, and as I entered my teens all I recalled was that something embarrassingly "different" had happened to me. I tried to put it out of my mind. At the same time I was chafing at the "thou shalt nots" and began looking for a church that would make fewer demands on me. I tried a variety, and in my senior year at the University of Florida I began to look at the Episcopal Church. Those Episcopalians didn't say much about 'thou shalt nots'; they quoted St. Augustine instead, who said: 'Love God, and do what you please!' It sounded pretty good to me at the time! Later, of course, I was to find that as you love God more and more, you will soon be doing what pleases Him."

I nodded, and she went on:

"I even spent a month, shortly after my graduation, studying in the Episcopal training programme for educators and church workers at Newport, Rhode Island. While there I was offered a job at a church agency in New Jersey, working with needy children.

"My big brother, whom I much admired, had become an Episcopalian some time before. When he heard I was to be confirmed, he wrote reminding me that at the time of confirmation I was supposed to receive the 'strengthening gifts of the Holy Spirit.' [1] Not understanding my childhood experience, I didn't actually know what the 'gifts of the Holy Spirit' [2] were, or if I had ever received any of them. Following confirmation I didn't see any definite change in my life right away, but the bishop's prayer was to be answered in a remarkable way nearly two years later."

Rita interrupted her story. "It's getting a bit chilly," she said, clambering to her feet and offering me her hand. "Let's walk on a little further."

"Seems a lot of us have to be shaken up before we are ready to come to terms with the Lord," she continued. "It was after I had moved back to my hometown of Tampa, Florida, and had gone into social work that I was shaken out of my complacency. I had a dear and close friend who roomed with me, named Gaye Miller. She confided in me one day that she 'spoke in tongues.' This baffled me. The only time I recalled hearing people 'speak in tongues' was in a public meeting, and they seemed extremely emotional and 'worked up.' On the other hand, as I well knew, Gaye had a quietly beautiful life in which the power and presence of God was very evident.

" 'You speak in tongues?' I asked incredulously.

"And Gaye nodded: 'Every day!' she said.

" 'Every day? But how? Where?' Gaye and I had shared the same apartment for over a year. How could she possibly have been 'speaking in tongues' daily without my knowing it? She explained that speaking in tongues need not be loud or demonstrative at all, but that one could have the benefit of praying in the Spirit quietly during his private prayers and often through the day. I was impressed, but still hesitant about getting involved. Shortly after this Gaye had moved to another state, and I did not discuss it with her further.

"Then came the blow. Gaye, while on her lunch hour, was

suddenly stricken with a cerebral haemorrhage. She just had time to give her name and address before dropping into an unconsciousness from which her physical body never returned. She died eight hours later. When I received the news, I was horribly shocked. For several nights I hardly slept. I knew Gaye was in good standing with the Lord, but I had no such confidence about myself. What if I should die suddenly without any chance to make things right with God? I went, still in great distress, to the funeral, and there met for the first time John and Bertha, the couple in whose home Gaye had met with others for prayer each Friday night.

"The next week Bertha phoned me:

" 'While I was praying today,' she said, 'the Lord suddenly began talking to me about *you*!'

"I said nothing for several moments. This was a new way of speaking which I wasn't quite used to, but the wheels were turning in my mind, rapidly. I answered, 'He did?' Then I thought to myself: *I didn't know for sure whether God still knew I was around!*

"My caller said: 'If you'd be interested to know more about it why don't you drop over to my house today?'

"As I hung up the phone I decided to go right over and see what this was all about.

"I was amazed when my new acquaintance shared with me things that she could not have known unless God had told her. (I know now that this is what the Bible calls the gift of knowledge.) As Bertha told what she felt God had said to her, there was a definite response in my own heart. One statement in particular seemed to stick in my mind:

" 'The gifts are at your feet, where you left them!'

"I was planning that Friday night to audition to sing at a club on the Gulf beach near Tampa, but decided, somewhat to my own amazement, to give up this coveted ambition and go to the weekly prayer meeting instead!

"At that meeting I came into contact again with the experience I had left behind in my youth—the Baptism in the Holy Spirit—only this time in a very different setting. Here were members of 'old-line' churches, yet with an obvious new excitement and involvement which they said had come from receiving the Holy Spirit.

"After a time of enthusiastic singing, intercessory prayer, and inspiring testimonies the leader asked: 'Rita, would you like us to pray for you?'

"I thought, *Prayer wouldn't hurt me, I suppose, but—in front of sixty or seventy strangers?! Now if only there were an Episcopal priest here, I would be sure that everything would be conducted in a dignified manner!*

"I consented to be prayed for, however, and the leader called: 'Father Sherry! Come over here, won't you?'

"Could it be? Yes, here came a little man, an Episcopal priest, lovingly known to his many friends as Father Sherry, to pray for me! Seeing the kindly face and twinkling eyes of the elderly minister, I felt more confident. Then I was in for another surprise: when Father Sherry laid his hands on my head and prayed, he didn't speak English, he spoke fluently in a foreign language! As he prayed, the presence of God broke through so greatly that tears began to pour from my eyes, and I suddenly recognized that this Episcopal priest was praying in tongues, in a language given by the Holy Spirit. Almost before I realized it, I too began to praise God in a new language just as I had done sixteen years before. Truly the gifts were at my feet where I'd left them. From that evening on, my life was utterly transformed. Having known what it was like to walk *without* the conscious awareness of God's presence all those years, I now gave my life completely to Him.

"I worked for a while with my brother Bill, who, in addition to practising medicine, travelled and spoke widely to Christian endeavours. Later I spent two years on the staff of *Trinity*."

"That magazine helped a lot of people understand the charismatic renewal, didn't it?" I commented.

Rita nodded. In our walking we had come to a little glen, brimming with black-eyed Susans.

"What brought you to the Northwest?" I asked, as we stopped for a few moments to enjoy the sight.

"I felt the need to spend some time in prayer seeking God's further will for my life," Rita said. "And I was invited to come to Deer Park, where Dean and Cordie were in the initial stages of developing this retreat centre. I had planned to stay two weeks, but they stretched into two years. I was not only able to make my retreat as I'd planned, but also found myself being put to work by the Lord, teaching classes and study groups, and working with young people in the Spokane area. I was also able to receive some excellent instruction myself."

We didn't say much more as we walked the remaining distance to the little white chalet guesthouse at the heart of Living Springs Ranch.

Our friendship grew during our visits back and forth across the state of Washington. Although neither Rita nor I "fell in love at first sight," we both realized more and more that God was drawing us together. On occasion we talked frankly about the possibility of marriage, yet neither of us wanted to make a decision without being certain that it was what God wanted.

In July, Rita was again invited to the coastal area to speak to some women's clubs, and I came to visit at the home in Olympia where she was staying. As soon as we could find a quiet place, I said:

"Rita, I found a most interesting passage of Scripture this

morning. Seems to me it has something to say to us!" Picking up a Bible and opening it, I continued. "Ecclesiastes 4:9-12 goes like this:

" 'Two are better than one.' " I paused and glanced at Rita. " 'For they have a good reward for their labour. For if they *fall,* the one will lift up his fellow: but woe to him that is alone when he *falleth;* for he hath not another to help him up.' " I paused again, and Rita looked at me and smiled, remembering our hikes in the woods! The reference became more pointed: " '. . . But how can one be warm alone? And if one prevail against him, two shall withstand him, and a threefold cord is not quickly broken.' "

"A threefold cord?" she said. "Sounds like a Christian marriage . . . husband, wife, and Jesus."

"Rita," I said, "I do believe God wants us to walk together, and that He wants us to be married. I know it's what I want. What do you say?"

She looked at me for a moment and then said: "Yes, Dennis, I do want to marry you, but I need to hear from God myself. I'll go home and pray about it for the next three days; then I'll let you know for sure and finally. Okay?"

Those were three long days for me, and I did a lot of tugging at God's sleeve! On the evening of the third day I called Rita:

"Dennis," she said, and my heart skipped a beat, "I just want to tell you that you now have a double 'yes'—once from me, and once from the Lord!"

Before too many days I was again winging my way over the Cascades in Nine-One-Bravo, only this time it was not just to visit, but to bring my bride-to-be back to Seattle.

My secretary and good friend, Florence, had opened her home to Rita while we began the happy process of getting her better acquainted with my family and friends. One day Rita said:

"Dennis, I would like to go to the cemetery with some flowers for Elberta's grave." She added: "You know, I don't want or expect you to forget Elberta. Her memory is a part of you. I want you to feel free to talk about her so I can grow to love her too!"

If there were any reservations left in my heart about the rightness of remarrying, they were at this time put to rest.

When was the wedding to take place? I had been invited to go to New Zealand for three weeks in September.

"Sounds like a good idea for a honeymoon!" I suggested to Rita.

She looked doubtful. "Uh, how many speaking engagements do you have in those three weeks?" she inquired.

"Oh, let's see—fifty-seven at the last count, I think."

Rita smiled sweetly. "I think, Dennis," she said slowly, "that it wouldn't be such a good idea for a honeymoon! Tell you what—" she continued, "I'd love to see New Zealand, but this doesn't seem to be the time. I want to spend a few weeks with my family, so why don't you go to New Zealand, while I go to Tampa and get things ready for the wedding?"

It did make sense, although I hated to part for what I knew would seem much longer than three weeks. Reluctantly, I put Rita on the plane for Florida; then a few days later, I left on my journey to the South Pacific.

19

"Signs Following"

I climbed aboard a Boeing 720 around supper time, flying from Seattle to San Francisco, and then, with a change of planes, on to Honolulu. A brief stopover at 10 p.m. in the Paradise of the Pacific, and on to Nandi, in the Fiji Islands. A few more hours in the stratosphere—with as little sensation of travel as one might have sitting in the living room at home—and it was dawn; we were approaching Auckland, New Zealand. It didn't take long for me to see that it was a very beautiful country, somehow magically blending the rugged beauty of the Pacific Northwest with the tropical softness of the Caribbean.

I learned that the Polynesian discoverers of New Zealand named it "Aotearoa," the "Land of the Long White Cloud," because their first indication of the islands as they voyaged in their canoes were the long stratus clouds hovering over them. When I first arrived at Auckland, however, and for several days thereafter, it seemed rather to be the "land of the long black cloud," for I had arrived in the midst of the spring rains! It reminded me of home!

I was met at the Auckland Airport by the rector of St. Paul's parish, The Venerable Kenneth R. Prebble, a gracious

Englishman who is also archdeacon of Hauraki. On our way to his home where I was to stay during my first weekend in his country, he said:

"I don't know whether I can accept this 'Baptism with the Holy Spirit' you're talking about, Dennis."

"How did you come to be interested in it at all?" I inquired.

"That's a long story," the archdeacon replied. "A number of months ago a young man, a successful clothing manufacturer in Auckland, said he was led by the Holy Spirit to come into my church, St. Paul's, one day during the week—he didn't exactly know why. He approached me and opened a conversation in what struck me as being rather a brash manner. As I recall, he asked me why I had no tracts about salvation in the tract rack!"

I chuckled. "Not the smoothest approach in the world," I commented.

"No," agreed the archdeacon dryly, "it wasn't. As a matter of fact, I was really quite nasty to the young man. Tried to get rid of him, you know! But he wouldn't go—followed me into my office. I had no choice but to offer him a cup of coffee, and we somehow got into conversation about this business of 'receiving the Holy Spirit' and 'speaking in tongues.' I probably wouldn't have listened at all, except that my curiosity had already been aroused. A short time before this I had come into the church one day and found a woman quietly praying out loud in a foreign language. I asked her:

" 'Were you speaking in tongues a moment ago?'

"She said, 'Yes, I was, as a matter of fact.'

"She seemed very normal and well-balanced. Then of course, I'd been hearing some other reports from here and there.

"Anyway, my bold young friend went on to tell me of a prayer meeting that was being held weekly in a private home, and invited me to attend. To my own amazement, and I'm sure to his also, I went!"

I whistled softly. "What happened then?"

"One part of me was shocked to the core, of course," he confided, in his clipped, quiet English manner. "But the other part was tremendously moved. I'd never been where people were praying and sharing so freely. The informality of it backed me off a bit, but on the other hand, I knew immediately that there was genuine holiness there—God was there! I went back the next week, and took my wife with me. She liked it right away!"

The archdeacon brought his little car to a halt outside a white porticoed house that proclaimed by a small signboard: St. Paul's Rectory. Across the street was the church—quite a large building in a rather elaborate Victorian Gothic style. I cast an apprehensive eye at the weather—it was pouring rain. Before we got out of the car, my new acquaintance finished his story.

"We've been to this meeting now a number of times. I've never seemed fully able to take part, though. Seems as though there is a part of me that is still frozen solid! But I do benefit from going.

"Then," he concluded, "a few weeks ago two very junior clergy of this area called on me. 'We hear you are going to this charismatic prayer meeting,' they said, with happy candour. I thought to myself: *The cat's out of the bag, for sure!* but I admitted yes, I had. 'Well,' they said, 'if you're interested in this matter of the Baptism in the Holy Spirit, we thought you'd like to know that Dennis Bennett is coming to New Zealand very soon.'

"I was quite surprised about your coming and wanted to know who was sponsoring you. I had heard a tape of your testimony a few weeks before, and rather liked it, but invitations to overseas' clergy visitors usually come down through accepted channels, and neither the bishop nor I had heard anything about your coming. The young men named the assistant minister at a parish in one of the smaller cities as the person who was setting up the tour. Then they asked if I would sponsor you in Auckland and clear you with the Bishop here! I thought it was a clear case of the tail wagging the dog, but I consented. The Bishop wasn't too pleased at first, but when he received a fine letter from your Bishop Curtis telling us some good things about you, affirming that you were in 'good and regular' standing, he gave his consent."

My friend unbuckled his seat belt and opened the car door. I followed suit. He paused and looked at me with a grin:

"So that's how I found myself sponsoring this questionable character from the U.S.A.!" he said. We both ran for the house through the pelting rain.

I was still sleeping soundly the next morning when the archdeacon arose, as was his custom, and went across the street to say his morning prayers in the church. Again the miracle happened: while he was praying, his words suddenly changed, and he began to pray strongly in a new language. He was overwhelmed with the joy and power of the Spirit!

I was scheduled to spend the day at Gisborne, a little town on the eastern coast of the North Island, about one hundred miles away, and to return that night to make my first public address at St. Matthew's Church in downtown Auckland, so it was with considerable anxiety that I found, when I arrived at the airport for my return plane, that the flight was indefinitely delayed due to weather. I sat in the Gisborne airport and watched the time of the meeting in Auckland approach, and then pass by: 7.30, 8.00, 8.30—and finally the airplane arrived. I felt in my spirit that the Lord had a purpose in this delay—but did not guess what!

I walked into the meeting at St. Matthew's at 9.30 p.m. to find a tremendously enthusiastic group of people. Obviously they hadn't been waiting for me! What had happened? The archdeacon told me about it later.

"We were very distressed when we discovered that we had a crowd of some two hundred people, and no speaker," he said. "And the other committee members just didn't know what to do! When I spoke in tongues this morning, I thought, *Well now, I'd better keep this quiet, I'd better not tell anyone about it for a while, as they might not understand.* But tonight, when I realized that you were not going to get here in time for the meeting, I knew that I was supposed to get up and tell what happened to me. So I did!"

And what a sensation it made in the Anglican Church, not just in Auckland, but the length and breadth of the country!

Later that first week I had a meeting with the Bishop of Auckland and members of the clergy. Hearing of the archdeacon's experience had certainly brought the clergy out in full force. In introducing me, he said:

"My Lord Bishop and brethren, I just want to say to you that I am in full agreement with this man in what he is saying."

In the meantime, I had been thoroughly enjoying my stay at the rectory. The rector's wife, Mary, had been most hospitable, but what did she think about it? She hadn't said a word, pro or con. Was she glad about what had happened to her husband? Later that first week we had taken a day off and gone to Manley Beach, where my friends had a little cottage. The weather was not conducive to bathing or beaching, so we had just been taking it easy in the house in front of a cheerful fire, chatting about many things. Mary had been listening to our talk, dropping a remark here and there; but suddenly she stood up, excused herself, and went outside. She was gone for some little time, then returned, with a broad smile on her face.

"Well," she reported, "I can do it all right! The only problem is that I don't want to stop!" She had gone out into the garden, asked Jesus to baptize her in the Holy Spirit, and after a few moments of prayer, had begun to speak fluently in a new language!

I left Auckland at the end of the week, and travelled pretty much the length and breadth of New Zealand. I spoke to bishops and clergy in the dioceses of Christchurch, Dunedin, and Wellington. I addressed faculty and students at the two Anglican theological colleges, and spoke also to a big gathering of students at Massey University in Palmerston North, where about five per cent of the entire student body had received the Baptism in the Holy Spirit as a result of the witness of the Anglican chaplain, who was the man who had set up my trip in the first place.

As always, there were interesting contacts and "signs following." In a beautiful little seacoast town on the South Island, the Anglican vicar had planned a meeting, and a goodly number turned out to hear the visiting American. As we sat waiting for the evening to begin, my host seemed a little uneasy. Finally he turned and whispered in my ear:

"The local psychiatrist is sitting right in the front row!" I looked, expecting from the concern the vicar was showing to see a Mephistophelian figure, perhaps with a little black goatee and thick-lensed spectacles! Instead I saw a very pleasant-faced little man, waiting in obvious expectancy for my address. Afterwards, the doctor was one of the first to come to me and introduce himself.

"Doctor N.," I said, "tell me—what did you think of what I had to say?"

The psychiatrist broke into a happy smile:

"Oh," he said, "I think it's wonderful to hear the tremendous things God is doing today!"

"What do you think of *me*?" I asked, knowing as a counsellor myself that he must have been sizing me up as I talked.

He pursed his lips and raised his eyebrows. "Well," he said, happily, "you remind me rather of the man who taught me psychiatry!"*

At the time that I was touring New Zealand telling of the work of the Spirit, two Anglican monks from a well-known order in England were also travelling through the country, conducting retreats. I encountered one of them quite early in my stay.

"I'm so glad to meet you, Father Bennett," he said. "You see, I believe in the Baptism in the Holy Spirit, and I want to receive it. I feel that I have a strong work of the Holy Spirit in my life, but I can't seem to speak in tongues!"

We talked awhile, and I tried to point out to him what might be inhibiting him from entering into full freedom in the Spirit. We prayed together, but he just couldn't seem to "let go." As we parted, he said, with a gentle smile:

"I'll just keep praying about it, Dennis!"

"That's wonderful, Father W.," I replied, "but don't forget to keep *trying*, too!"

I pointed out to him that speaking in tongues was something that *he* was going to do—that no amount of praying or seeking was going to help him very much until he could get up his nerve to open his mouth, and trust the Holy Spirit to give him words as *he* spoke.

"You've got to begin speaking and trust the Lord to do the guiding," I said.

It was as I completed my circuit of the country and was

---

* A number of believing psychologists and psychiatrists have received the Baptism in the Holy Spirit; also many members of these professions who are not Christians themselves tend to be friendly toward the Pentecost experience because of its stabilizing and integrating effect on the lives of people.

returning to Auckland by way of Hamilton that one of the priests I was with said:

"Did you know that Father W. is in Huntley? He's laid up with a bad back—can't get out of bed. He wants some of us to come and pray with him!"

Three of us made the short journey to the little town of Huntley. We were admitted to the vicarage, and to the bedroom where Father W. was. I could tell at once that there was something about him which was not quite the same.

"Hello, Dennis!" he said, "I'm glad to see you again. You know," he went on, "I'm beginning to speak in tongues! I do when I first wake up in the morning. I can't seem to keep going, but at least I start!"

There was a change in this man of God. The same quiet graciousness was there, but it was different. There was a freedom—a relaxed look about him that hadn't been there before he had begun to speak in tongues. We laid hands on him, prayed for him, and anointed him with oil in the Name of the Lord. Then we three ministers, we "men of faith," said our goodbyes and left the room to spend a few moments visiting with the vicar and his wife before going back to Hamilton. We were standing with our backs to the hall door. I remember that I had squatted down on the floor to talk with one of the younger members of the vicar's family, a little boy of some three years. Suddenly we were startled by a greeting from the hall:

"Hello in there!"

We looked round—it was Father W. He chuckled at our surprise.

"You prayed for me, and I got healed!" he said. "Didn't you expect me to?"

I returned to Auckland after nearly three weeks, and again

found myself in the home of the archdeacon for a last visit before leaving the country.

"I just can't tell you what's been going on since you left, Dennis," he said. "There has been a steady stream of people coming to our door—sick people, sad people, mixed up people. We have been praying for them, counselling them, even now and then asking deliverance for people who were obviously demon-possessed! We've been busy almost continuously—and we have seen results, too!"

The Holy Spirit had got them *involved*.

20

"Two by Two"

"Great Scott!" I clapped my hand to my forehead. "I've forgotten to bring my suits!" We were standing, Rita and I, in the baggage-claiming area of the Miami International Airport.

I had come back with a high heart, the ten thousand miles from New Zealand to Florida, to marry Rita. Three weeks spent on the other side of the world had brought home only the more clearly how much Rita had come to mean to me. All those long-distance calls reaching my fiancee at the strangest hours were most enjoyable, but not really satisfactory. (I never did get the time differential straight. Was it seven or eight hours? Was it yesterday or tomorrow?) But now we were together.

The wedding had been beautiful. All of Rita's immediate family had been there; even her mother, although she had been very weak and ill for some time, was given special strength. Her parents were actually the last guests to depart from the reception! My older son, stationed at a nearby Air Force Base, had served as best man, and his wife as bridesmaid. We'd been married October 15, 1966, in the little House of Prayer Episcopal Church in Tampa, and I had not thought of myself as a nervous bridegroom until this moment! We were on our way to Nassau, and my suits, except the one I was wearing, were hanging in their travelling bag in a closet in Tampa—with no reasonable way to secure them!

The informality of the Bahamas being what it is, this proved to be no great emergency after all. It was prophetic of our future together, that we returned to the mainland after just a few days to conclude our honeymoon at a conference on the work of the Holy Spirit at Ft. Lauderdale. And this has been our life ever since: telling people about Jesus, and about the full and wonderful life in His Holy Spirit.

"Hey, here's an invitation that looks interesting!"

I was opening the mail in the kitchen one afternoon shortly after our return to Seattle. Rita was standing at the stove stirring something that smelled very appetizing. It was good, after three years of fending for myself, to have good companionship—and good cooking! Rita put down her spoon.

"What is it?" she asked.

"The Full Gospel Business Men's Fellowship up in Calgary, Canada, wants me to come to some meetings. There's an invitation from the Anglicans, too; in fact, the Bishop himself has agreed to speak at the FGBMFI breakfast!"

"That sounds wonderful!" she responded, wiping her hands on her apron.

I looked at her. "Yes," I said, suddenly doubtful, "but you know something? I don't want to take off for Canada without you. I've been going places by myself for a long time, and I'm kind of tired of it."

I had never really enjoyed myself travelling alone, although it had been unavoidable in the past. Now with all the children grown and married, what was there to stop Rita from going with me? Besides, she had had an active ministry of her own before we were married. Did God intend her to give this up? Couldn't we share together in the work? I put these questions to Rita.

"It's a good idea," she said. "You know I'd love to go with you; but Dennis, that means travel fares for two—do you think it would be practical?" She hesitated a moment, then added: "Well, if the Lord wants it that way, He'll provide the funds, won't He?"

And He did just that. When one of our good friends heard of my invitation to Calgary, she said:

"Now you're not going up there without your bride!" and she gave us a good-sized cheque to go towards Rita's expenses.

This first journey settled the question, for we found that we were able to accomplish much more together than we could working separately. We were reminded that Jesus did send His disciples out "two by two." Rita could be talking to one group while I spoke to another. She could address a women's group while I was with the men. After I had given my testimony we could divide the meeting, and while I answered questions, Rita could immediately move into another room and begin to instruct through the Scripture those who were desiring to receive the Holy Spirit. The harvest of people receiving the Baptism in the Holy Spirit increased, and our own spiritual morale was higher than if we had not been together.

Due to our greater usefulness and effectiveness working together, the Lord was able to bless us more fully, and there was no financial problem; in fact, we finished further "in the black" than I had ever done when by myself! Since that first trip to Calgary, Rita and I have made most of the "missionary journeys" together.

In Calgary, I had just concluded my talk one evening in St.

Michael-and-All-Angels Anglican Church, and was answering questions. As always, there was much interest in "speaking in tongues." What is it? What does it mean? A woman raised her hand.

"Father Bennett," she said, "I have always thought of "speaking in tongues" as a very emotional and excitable experience, and I've always been afraid of it. You talk as though it wasn't like that at all, and as if you could speak in tongues at will any time you chose. Would you be willing to do that right here?"

The questioner was obviously very much in earnest. I said: "I'll speak 'in the Spirit' as we close the meeting; then I'll give a blessing in English." So, as I closed the meeting, I spoke briefly, accepting the words that came to my lips as guided by the Holy Spirit. As I began to speak, I felt a quickening of excitement, as though something unusual was about to happen. The language that came to my lips was different from any I had ever heard before, but as soon as I had concluded this prayer "in tongues" and had given a brief blessing, another hand was raised.

"But—but—" stammered a little lady sitting in the front row, "you surely know the language you were speaking, don't you?"

"No, I do not," I answered. "I have never heard it before."

"Why," she said, "that was Nepali!"

Nepali? I had to think for several minutes before realizing that this would of course be the language of Nepal, a country bordering Tibet on the south side of the Himalayas. The woman continued:

"My brother is a Jesuit missionary in Nepal. I am very fond of him, and I've been much concerned about his safety. It's a 'hot spot' for Christians, you know. He sent me a tape recording recently on which he read the Epistle for 'Gaudete'* Sunday, from the fourth chapter of Philippians, in the Nepali language. I have listened to it over and over, and you have just repeated it word for word!"

Faced with this major miracle of speech, this Roman Catholic woman received the Baptism with the Holy Spirit that night, and she too began to rejoice in a heavenly language far beyond the limitations of man's earthbound intellect. So, incidentally, did the woman who had first asked the question!

Rita and I didn't do much more long-distance travelling through the first year of our marriage. There was too much to keep us busy at home. I had been carrying on a multiple ministry ever since receiving the Holy Spirit in 1959, and especially since coming to St. Luke's. There was a continuous stream of people, including ministers and priests, coming to counsel with me. Also there was a fairly steady stream of visitors dropping in from just about everywhere imaginable to see what was going on. One of these, a Roman Catholic, a man whose business took him all over the world, said:

"I have heard of this church in London, England; Cape Town, South Africa; Buenos Aires, Mexico City, and Tokyo, and always from people in my own church! I had to come here to see what was happening!"

The normal work schedule of a minister in an average-size church is from sixty to seventy hours per week. I was ridicu-

---

* "Gaudete" Sunday means "Rejoice Sunday" and is the Roman Catholic name for what other liturgical churches would call the "Fourth Sunday in Advent." The name is taken from the first word of the Epistle: "Rejoice in the Lord alway: and again I say, rejoice. Let your moderation be known unto all men. The Lord is at hand. Be careful for nothing; but in every thing by prayer and supplication with thanksgiving let your requests be made known unto God. And the peace of God, which passeth all understanding, shall keep your hearts and minds through Christ Jesus." (Philippians 4:4-7)

lously busy, single-handedly trying to direct a large parish, while having many other demands. In fact, that year, my senior warden, a man skilled in personnel planning, said to me:

"Dennis, have you ever stopped to figure out how many hours you are trying to put in per week?"

"No, as a matter of fact, I haven't," I replied. "But I know that many times I feel frustrated in this never-ending job!"

He urged me to make a little survey, which showed that in order to accomplish the very minimum of what I wanted to do, I would have to put in two hundred and thirty hours weekly! There aren't even that number of hours *in* a week!

As for Rita, ever since coming to St. Luke's she had been receiving invitations to conduct Bible studies in Seattle and the surrounding cities. She had also found important work to do among the teen- and college-age people at the church. In addition to this, a radio ministry was opening for us. I had for several years given a half-hour radio talk each Sunday in Seattle. Now Rita and I together made this a question and answer programme which was so well received that it expanded to an hour. It was soon suggested that we should have the same type of programme in the Los Angeles area. After a trial period, an effective Christian radio station* offered us a half-hour slot five evenings a week on a noncommercial basis, which we accepted.

Invitations to speak continued to come, and I did not like to have to refuse so many of them, at home and abroad, because I knew how desperately the witness of the work of the Holy Spirit in the Church today was needed. Numerous ministers had shared with me the many concerns over their languishing churches. I also knew that doors which were opening might not be open indefinitely.

In the fall of 1967 God began to bring the answer. The Rev.

* KHOF-FM 99.5 mhz Glendale, Calif.

Richard Driscoll joined the staff of St. Luke's. I had known Father Dick and his wonderful family for several years, and now he felt led to come and be my associate. As soon as it was reasonable to do so after his arrival, I approached my vestry.

"Brethren," I said, "I want your backing in a decision. I've got to face the fact that I can't continue indefinitely trying to do three or four things at once. I don't want to leave St. Luke's, but I know that I must be free to carry on the outreach ministry God has given me, in good conscience—without feeling that I am neglecting one task to do another. You have always been very helpful and open-minded about this, because you know there's a big job to be done, but I am under a good deal of tension trying to be fair to all concerned. Now that I have a capable associate, I want you to approve a kind of semi-sabbatical year for me. Until June of next year I want to spend half of my time at St. Luke's, and the other half of my time travelling, speaking, writing, and generally carrying on an outreach ministry." My vestry concurred with this suggestion, not only without dissent, but without even a discussion!

Feeling a new freedom to do so, right after the first of the year I accepted an invitation to go to Jamaica. This came through an interdenominational group of Christians in Ft. Lauderdale, Florida, who had formed themselves into a "Committee of Forty" to sponsor conferences on the work of the Holy Spirit. Several of the members of this group had been going down to Montego Bay, proclaiming the good news of the full gospel. Already their ministry had resulted in the conversion of two of the leading communists in Jamaica! One of these, a woman of great talent, had been trained in several communist countries of Europe, and in Russia and China, for the proposed Communist take-over of the Caribbean. Now all of her ability and training was on the side of the Lord Jesus Christ!

For two nights I conducted meeting at St. James Anglican Church in Montego Bay, and then we left for the "back country."

We had been asked to spend a few days in St. Elizabeth's Parish in Southfield, a collection of some six Anglican congregations headed by a young English vicar and his wife. As we ministered to these people we noticed again that the hunger was the same, and the Lord's response to that hunger was the same! Nothing could be more diverse that the native Jamaican; there are strains of many nations and races mingled together in these people, but the effect of salvation through Jesus Christ and the Baptism in the Holy Spirit was exactly the same as in New York City, England, Alaska, or New Zealand. We were surprised at the freedom with which we were allowed to testify, not only in churches and church schools, but also in the public schools. At the Hampton School, a government-sponsored school for girls in Southfield, we talked to the whole student assembly. We told them what Jesus Christ had been doing in our lives, and in the lives of young people in the U.S. At the end of the meeting, we asked those who were interested in receiving Jesus Christ and being baptized in the Holy Spirit to stay behind. The entire student body stayed! Thinking that they did not understand what I was talking about, I tried to explain again that this was just for those who really meant business. Most of them still sat tight! Accordingly, we went round that auditorium and prayed with about seventy-five girls. Some needed to accept Christ as Saviour, and twenty-five of them were baptized in the Holy Spirit.

From the warmth of the Caribbean we found ourselves, several weeks later, heading to the far and frozen north! The Episcopal archdeacon of the Arctic had been interested in my ministry ever since my second visit to that largest state, and now wanted us to come to Kotzebue and Point Hope for a week in each place. Kotzebue is the largest Eskimo village in the area, and boasts all kinds of modern conveniences—seven stores and a fine electric power and lighting system. It's truly "downtown" by Arctic standards! Hunters come there from many places to stalk the polar bear, which is done nowadays, somewhat unfairly, by airplane! For me it was a renewal of acquaintances with some of the folk who had made me welcome in '64. We stayed at the home of the vicar and his wife and enjoyed it all thoroughly. Everything was new to Rita, since this was her first visit to Alaska: muktuk, caribou, seal— the only thing that stopped us was Eskimo ice-cream, a concoction of creamed seal-oil and fruit. We couldn't quite acquire the taste! The local people had an Eskimo dance in our honour, and we wondered at the amazing vigour of some of our older Eskimo friends in their seventies, entering into the symbolic and energetic dancing with the vitality of youth!

The most far-flung portion of our trip was Point Hope. This tiny Eskimo village is the farthest north and west you can go in the United States! It is located on a sand-spit projecting into the Chukchi Sea, about 150 miles north and east of Siberia! It is reached only by sea, by air, or by dog team! (Nowadays many Eskimo have gasoline-powered sleds which they use for short hauls, but it would be foolhardy to trust one's life on a long journey on one of these. The dog team is slower, but it is more reliable.) The ocean was frozen solid, we didn't have the time to go by dog sled, so we went by air. The Pilatus-Porter is an awkward-looking aircraft. Originally built to be powered with a reciprocating engine but later equipped with the much lighter turbine, which necessitated lengthening the nose, the plane looks much like a large praying mantis. Somehow the resemblance is heightened when the Porter takes off, lurching into the air at some ridiculously slow speed, after what seems to be only a few yards of take-off roll! It is, however, an intensely practical airplane for difficult conditions; it was built for mountain work in the Alps.

We climbed into the plane, together with the only other passenger, a pleasant-faced Eskimo lady, and the pilot. Baggage and freight were piled high behind us with no protecting barrier—it was evident that no one was counting on any sudden stops! We took off into beautiful clear air and began our hour-and-a-half flight. Mile upon mile of frozen, snow-covered tundra unrolled beneath us, broken only once by a tiny collection of houses between the mountains and the frozen shore.

"Kivalina," our pilot explained. Then he said:

"There's Point Hope!"

I looked ahead, and all I could see was a bank of low stratus clouds completely obscuring the site where the village lay. I waited for our captain to say: "We'll go back to Kotzebue and try again tomorrow!" but he didn't, he just flew on—over the top of the fog, around and around. The nose of our craft was cocked high in the air, our airspeed minimal. My own pilot's sensibilities told me that we were skirting a stall.

"Wonder what he's doing?" I whispered to Rita. She had done enough flying to be a little apprehensive of his manoeuvres.

"I don't know," she whispered back; "looks like we could stall any minute." Just then our pilot saw what he wanted—a break in the clouds below us that revealed, for a moment, the brief stretch of ice and snow that was the runway. Down through that rift we went like a shot partridge; down went all the flaps we had, which was plenty! The airplane shuddered and seemed to stop in mid air as we sank on to the runway. I fully believed that that pilot had his prop in reverse pitch before we were on the ground. What flying! Our skis touched the runway, and we slid about fifty yards and came to a gentle stop in front of what seemed to be the whole village. The arrival of what was hopefully called the "daily" airplane—it sometimes could not get in or out for as much as ten days at a time—was an event, and everyone was there to celebrate it, and to welcome the strangers from the South 48! The zero temperature and blowing fog encrusted everything in icy rime, but the human atmosphere was jovial. Our Eskimo travelling companion was welcomed into the bosom of her family, while Rita and I were whisked off by the Hannums to their cosy little house on the edge of the village, overlooking the frozen sea. It was hard to keep our footing as we walked over the little hills and valleys of snow covering the ground to a depth of many feet. My mukluks were made with uguruk skin, the hide of the big seal, and were actually intended for wet rather than dry snow; as we returned home from the meeting each evening, I always seemed to manage to fall and slide down the snowbank right outside the rectory!

Point Hope is a town of some four hundred Eskimo, and about eight Caucasians—three church leaders, and about five schoolteachers. The village lives by hunting and fishing, whaling being the big thing.

"Like to take a walk this morning?" Walter grinned at me across the breakfast table. I swallowed my last spoonful of cereal, wiped my mouth on my napkin, and said, "Sure! What's up?"

"Let's go over to the cemetery," Walter said. " 'Bout a half-mile over that way," he gestured. "Put on your parka, and muffle up good—you'll need it!"

He was right. When we went outside we found the temperature hovering a little above zero. Walter tucked his hunting rifle under his arm and we left the house.

"Might meet a bear or a wolf," he said encouragingly! A brisk breeze with a sprinkling of snow in it stung our faces as we stumped along over the drifts in the direction of what looked like bent sticks projecting from the snow about a half-mile to the north. As we got a little closer I saw that these curved sticks made a fence surrounding a rectangular area, with other sticklike objects, only much taller, standing on the inside.

"Whalebones," my guide explained. "They don't have any wood hereabouts, so this is what they use."

When we arrived at the little graveyard I saw that the grave markers were similarly fashioned—some of them eighteen feet and more high, the jawbones of gigantic whales inscribed with a cross, and the name of the person. Looking over the snowy tundra I saw another collection of huge whalebones, marking off a smaller area about a quarter of a mile from where we were standing.

"What are those?" I inquired.

"That's where one of the old chiefs is buried," the arch-deacon explained. They claim he was a powerful witch doctor who gained great influence over the village nearly a hundred years ago. Among other evils, he encouraged the villagers to make distilled liquor. It's very dangerous to them in the winter-time. If a man gets a little drunk, he feels warm, and is likely to go out into the cold without proper protection. Many have been frozen to death in that way."

I nodded. "I saw the warning in the post office," I said.

"Yes. Well, they have to keep reminding folk about it. Any-way, the coast guard was finding so many frozen corpses that they actually appealed for a Christian missionary to be sent to the village. That's how the Episcopal Church comes to be here. The first missionary came about three-quarters of a century ago, and built the little church on the outskirts of the village. Today about eighty per cent of the population is Episcopalian."

Each afternoon, during most of our stay, we met in the church with the young people of the village. About thirty came

—all ages and sizes from ages nine or ten, to maturing young adults of eighteen and nineteen. We soon found ourselves not looking forward to this session, for the youngsters were restless after a long day at school, and not inclined to take us too seriously!

According to the tradition of the village, whenever a whaling captain finished the yearly re-covering of his boat with fresh sealskin, he was to treat all the children of the village to candy. At this time of the year, the only "candy" the small general store had was bubble gum, so one day the kids all showed up chewing massive quantities of gum and popping bubbles every so often! Knowing that she was going to be the victim the next day, Rita asked for help. In closing the meeting Archdeacon Hannum said:

"Tomorrow, please park your bubble gum on the snow outside before you come into the church!"

It helped a little, but as Rita told the story of how the Lord had worked in her own life when she was a young person, a number of the boys were squirming and giggling, although some of the girls were attentive. The general effect was still pretty unruly, and I was quite fed up with them. Just before the meeting ended Rita consulted with me:

"Dennis, I think we should invite those that want to, to come to the altar for a blessing." I felt she was thinking in terms of our experience with the young people in Jamaica, the month before. I failed to see the similarity. Those Jamaican kids had been well-behaved, courteous, and interested, but these seemed to be just the opposite. However, I couldn't very well say:

"I don't want to pray for God's blessing on them." But I certainly had my doubts as to whether it would "take"! I consented, rather unwillingly, to invite those who wanted to, to come forward, and dismissed the others. Almost the entire crew came forward and knelt at the altar rail, and around the choir stalls. Still, as they came, some dragged their feet and banged their heels, but as we began to pray with them, a new spirit of sincerity settled on them. Rita and Archdeacon Hannum were praying down one side of the chancel, while the Rev. Donald Oktollik was helping me. Donald, a much respected member of the community, had been the head of one of the two whaling lodges into which the village was divided; he had recently been ordained deacon, and was currently preparing for the priesthood. We asked each youngster whether he had accepted Jesus into his life. Most of them knew definitely that they had done this, but there were six or seven who had not. These we encouraged to receive the Lord, and as they did, one after another began to weep. The whole atmosphere became sweet with the presence of the Lord. The situation had changed so drastically, that after we had gone round once, we decided to go around again, and pray for them to be baptized in the Holy Spirit. This we did, and a very large percentage of those once-unruly children began to speak in other tongues!

The difference in the attitude of these teenagers was amazing! Whereas up to now they had been friendly enough, but in a "smart-aleck" kind of way, showing little respect, now they followed us around like little puppy dogs, wanting to go with us everywhere. As we were walking along over the snowdrifts down the middle of the village, one of a group of girls called to Rita:

"Mrs. Bennett, Mary is singing in the Spirit!" * Rita didn't

---

* St. Paul, in I Corinthians 14:15 refers to "singing with the spirit." This means allowing the Holy Spirit to inspire our spirit not only to speak, but to sing as He gives the words and the tune. Some who are unable to sing at all "in the natural," find that they can sing in the Spirit beautifully, if they trust the Holy Spirit to guide their voices. Sometimes during a prayer and praise time the entire group will join in "singing in the Spirit," allowing the Holy Spirit not only to guide individual voices, but to blend them and produce harmonies that sometimes sound like the angelic choir itself!

hear at first, because she was swallowed up in the big hood of the parka trying to keep her face protected from the blowing wind and snow, but when she finally understood she realized that this young girl, with no instruction from us—as we had not at this time mentioned the possibility—had begun to sing in the Spirit!

During our mission in Point Hope, the older generation met each morning for Bible study with Rita, with the Eskimo deacon, Donald Oktollik, as interpreter, and I spoke to a full church each evening. Having an interpreter also came in handy when praying with many of these older folk to receive the Baptism in the Holy Spirit. Donald helped us to determine whether they were speaking in Eskimo or in tongues! Donald, and his gentle wife, Lily, had both prayed to receive the Holy Spirit early in the beginnings of our meetings. Lily had "come through," but Donald, more inhibited, had not yet spoken in tongues. One evening though, as he helped us pray with some of his friends, forgetting his own self-consciousness in his eagerness to help the others, he too began to speak in the new language that God had for him!

It was so amazing to look at the happy faces of these dear people.

"Taiku!" they would say—the Eskimo version of our English "thank you"—or: "Kuyanak!" their own word. Then, in hesitant English: "This what we look for!" Many of these had met Jesus a long time before, but they knew there was more for them. Now they had it, and they knew it!

At the closing church service in Point Hope, as I looked out at the faces of these good friends in Jesus, I could not miss the fact that in spite of ethnic and cultural differences, these faces looked just like the faces of the Seattle-ites who had been baptized in the Holy Spirit. The same open happy shine was there, the same joy in their eyes. The same Spirit of grace was working in them. It was impossible to miss the literal truth of the Gospel that when we accept Jesus we are born again into a new family, and all become brothers and sisters in the Spirit. "You shall be witnesses of Me, after that the Holy Ghost has come upon you . . ." means far more than witnesses in speech alone.

Our other long journey in 1968 was a return to England. As before, it was the Rev. Michael Harper and the Fountain Trust who sponsored the tour, and we visited London, Bournemouth, Bristol, Birmingham, Liverpool, Teesside, Hull, Normanton, Bradford, Coventry, and many other places. Again we visited many schools and churches, mostly, but by no means all, Anglican. I spoke at Birmingham Cathedral and had many fruitful contacts with the clergy and bishops of the Church of England. We had opportunity to see how effectively the charismatic renewal is continuing to move forward in the British Isles.

At an Anglican Church near London, a woman came forward for healing prayer. She had had arthritis in both knees for many years, and was in much pain. We will not forget how she literally jumped for joy when the Lord Jesus, through prayer and the laying on of hands, took away the pain and crippling, and she was able to walk normally!

We had long been admirers of the rugged saint of the Pentecostal movement, Smith Wigglesworth. What delight to find ourselves in his hometown of Bradford, Yorks! Here we conducted an evening meeting, and when it ended, I remained in the auditorium with those who had theological questions to ask, while Rita retired to an adjoining room to instruct fifty people who wished to receive the Holy Spirit. As a teenage girl started to speak in the Spirit, in a language unknown to her, a young woman nearby expressed great surprise.

"Why," she exclaimed, "that girl is speaking perfect

French! And I should know, for I *teach* French in a local high school!"

We also attended an interesting conference at High Leigh, but perhaps the high point in the tour was the conference held in London at the very heart of the Church of England, "Church House," right next-door to Westminster Abbey! It was here, in the very auditorium we occupied, that one month later the bishops of the Anglican Communion from all over the world would meet for the Lambeth Conference. Indeed, I remarked to Rita:

"The speaker's chair which I sat in this evening is the very same one that the Archbishop of Canterbury will occupy next month as he presides at this worldwide conference!" On both nights of our charismatic conference many received Jesus into their lives, and on the second night seventy people received the Holy Spirit simultaneously, and all together began to speak "in new languages as the Spirit gave the utterance"!

21
A New Thrust

Before returning home from England, we spent a few days in Germany. I had been invited to take part in a conference of Roman Catholics, Lutherans, Reformed, Baptists, Orthodox, Anglicans, and others, all of whom had two things in common —a new freedom in the Holy Spirit, and the manifestation of His charismatic gifts. As a result, these leaders from various denominations were seeing God's love and power beginning to revive churches and communities. That conference brought me two new experiences: it was my first time of witnessing in a non-English-speaking country, and in a language other than English. I gave my testimony in German, a language with which I had some familiarity. One picture which remains indelibly fixed in my memory from this *Oekumenische Dienst* is the figure of "Bruder E.," a vigorous and scholarly Franciscan friar, who had just begun to "speak in tongues." This sturdy follower of the blessed Francis of Assisi, who himself spoke in tongues and whose followers were originally known for their childlike faith, was rather offended at the simplicity of his new experience, and declaimed with emphasis as we discussed the whole matter in his room one evening:

"Dies ist die Demütigkeit von meinem Intellekt!" (This is the humiliation of my intellect!)

We spent two refreshing days with the Mary-Sisters, the *Marienschwesternschaft* in Darmstadt. This Lutheran religious community for women began in the closing days of World War II, when Allied bombers were totally destroying city after city as Hitler's fall became imminent. A group of young women had been meeting for Bible study. Many of them had lost husbands and sweethearts in the tragedy of the war, and when one night they saw their home city transformed in a few hours into a smoking ruin, they determined to band together in a monastic life. The leaders took the names Mother Basileia and Mother Martyria and thus was launched a most amazing work of the Lord. With little worldly goods or support, but with tremendous faith in God and in the power of prayer, the community, in the face of almost impossible odds, established a retreat-centre and convent on a fifty-acre tract of land in the heart of the city of Darmstadt, which they christened *Kanaan-Land*. The first buildings were constructed with their own hands. They had no water, so they prayed for it, and now have fifty times as much as their neighbours!

Today the community includes a well-operated farm, an elaborately equipped printing shop, much beautiful landscaping, and many buildings, including a magnificent chapel. Many acts of charity and service are being performed by these women, not the least of which is the providing of a place of refreshment and retreat for any who wish to go there, without charge. A guest at the Mary-Sisters retreat houses only contributes anonymously as he feels led. One of their specific outreach works is with young people. When Dave Wilkerson *

---

* Dave Wilkerson is the young minister internationally known for work with New York gangs, set forth so admirably in the book, *The Cross and the Switchblade* (Bernard Geis Associates, 1962—Pyramid Books, 1964).

was in Darmstadt, he spoke and ministered to a crowd of several thousand teenagers in their church, while the sisters assisted in counselling the youngsters afterwards.

A most interesting thing about the Mary-Sisters is that shortly after their order was formed, they experienced a Pentecostal outpouring, with the manifestations of speaking in tongues, interpretation, prophesy, etc. This was almost unheard of among non-Pentecostals in the late forties, and they were not made popular by their experience! They "stuck to their guns" however, and today the Gifts of the Holy Spirit are a firmly established part of the devotional life of the community. Rita and I had the privilege of being invited to the private "prayer and praise" meeting of the sisters. We sat on the platform in the prayer chapel, with the superiors, the Lutheran chaplain of the order, and his wife, and listened and shared as the sisters sang folk-type choruses. Many of their songs were originals, given by the Holy Spirit during these meetings. Looking at the bright-faced women, most of them quite young, in their beige-and-white habits, raising their hands in praise, sometimes waving banners they had made with Scripture texts on them (they are strong on banners of all kinds!)—or at one point in the service, waving leafy branches in time to the music as they sang "in the Spirit"—we were again struck by the strangeness, and yet the familiarity of the scene. Eight thousand miles from home, in a foreign city and country, among people of another language and culture, behind the walls of a convent, we saw the Lord, the Holy Spirit, unfailingly at work in God's people. We knew that these girls would be instantly at home in a meeting at St. Luke's, Seattle. More than that, we knew that if we could have gathered together in one place these sisters, the friends who had received the Holy Spirit in Alaska, in Jamaica, in England, and in numerous different far-flung parts of the U.S.A., they would have required no introduction or explanation, but would have immediately been able to enjoy such a meeting as this together. I began to see more clearly what the Apostles' Creed means by the "Communion of Saints."

Arriving home, I found it hard to imagine that just a year before I had thought things were slowing down, or reaching a plateau!

"We seem to be coming to a saturation point," I had remarked to my wife. "During these last eight years, we've probably reached most of the people in Seattle who are interested." How wrong we were! Under Father Driscoll's capable leadership, the church had been booming in my absence; not only that, but it was evident that if my semisabbatical was to continue, Father Dick was going to have to have more help. He was beginning to get the same harried look that I had when he arrived to lift the load off my shoulders! We talked about it to the vestry, and they agreed to provide the salary to retain the services of another man, if we could find the right one. It wasn't long before my associate called me to tell me that a friend of his was interested in joining our staff, and after a brief time of getting acquainted, I formally invited the Rev. Thomas Bigelow to become my second associate. Several weeks after he had arrived and settled in, I listened to him telling his story at the Friday night meeting. To my great surprise, I found that I played a part in the story of his receiving the Holy Spirit! Then I remembered: we had prayed with this young man in our home in Van Nuys nearly nine years ago! At that time he was in business—although he had spent two years in seminary—but he had later gone back to complete seminary training, and had gone into the ministry.

With adequate leadership the parish began to grow even more rapidly. It became almost an embarrassment to discuss the state of the Church with other clergy, for their usual talk was one of woe—of shrinking budgets, shrinking church attendance, diminishing interest, loss of confidence, ministers leaving the ministry to enter lay professions—while all we could say about the condition of the Church was "Praise the Lord! God is moving, drawing many people, and changing lives!" So much did things continue to flourish that six months later we found ourselves retaining the services of a fourth man, a newly graduated seminarian, the Rev. Daniel Stewart. This kind of leadership set me free to do more speaking, writing, travelling, and general outreach and missionary activity, both at home and abroad.

We were on a United Super DC-8 jet returning home from the east coast. For the first two hours of our flight we had been over an unbroken deck of clouds, but now I could see the stratus layers beginning to break apart, and glimpses of the ground beneath. I studied the map.

"Hm-m-m!" I said. "According to my navigation, we should be somewhere off the tip of Lake Michigan." The words had hardly left my mouth before our airplane flew into clear sky, and sure enough, there was Lake Michigan in the distance, sparkling and beautiful in the mid-afternoon sun, while just below us was a good-sized city.

"South Bend!" I hazarded. "It's too far from the lake to be Gary!"

Rita didn't pay too much attention to my navigational exploits, but she murmured, half to herself: "South Bend—oh, that's where Notre Dame University is! Just think, Dennis, they're going to have another conference there this year for 'Catholic Pentecostals' as they call themselves. They had around six hundred in attendance last year, and they expect more than a thousand this time."

I nodded. "That's great, isn't it?" As I leaned back into my seat, my thoughts flew on ahead of our airplane. I saw again the recent meeting in Missoula, Montana, when I addressed seven hundred people before the high altar of St. Anthony's Catholic Church, and later prayed with some forty-five who remained to receive the Baptism in the Holy Spirit.

In retrospect I realized that in all my years of being in the ministry I had had almost no contact with the Roman Catholic Church; in fact, I had been more than a little afraid of Roman Catholic clergy! Then one morning the vicar of our Episcopal Mission in a small town in eastern Washington took me to breakfast with the Roman Catholic rector and his assistant. He listened very carefully, and then put up a careful theological fence. When he saw that I had no intention of knocking it down, he said:

"Actually, there's nothing in this that is contrary to the teachings of the Catholic Church!"

I was surprised at his openness, but did not think much more about it until a year or two later. I was in Boston for a series of meetings, and returned very late one night to the home of the man who was co-ordinating my schedule to find three people waiting to see me: one was a pleasant-faced young man in a clerical collar, the other two, from their happy looks, and from the "Praise the Lord!" with which I was greeted, I took to be members of my friend's Assembly of God Church. It turned out that the first young man was a Roman Catholic priest who was eagerly seeking the Baptism in the Holy Spirit, and the two laymen, also Roman Catholic, had both already received the Holy Spirit. We had a good visit far into the wee, small hours of the morning, and I began to get an inkling of how the walls were crumbling.

Then came a full-scale encounter. It was in England in 1965.

Thanks to that wonderful servant of God, David DuPlessis,*
whom God had used to open doors in many unexpected places
to the witness of the Baptism in the Holy Spirit, I had been
invited to speak to the Jesuit Training College at Chipping
Norton, near Oxford. It was with some trepidation that I
entered upon this assignment. I shall not soon forget our entrance into that huge building that night, with its echoing
corridors, and massive and forbidding appearance. But as soon
as we (Michael Harper was with me) were met at the door, we
were enveloped in warmth and love, and felt immediately at
home. Our hosts were the Principal of the College, the Rev.
Father Murray, S.J., and the well-known Jesuit scholar and
Oxford don, the Rev. Dr. Bernard Leeming, S.J. That night,
as I faced some hundred or more young men, my trepidation
returned. Of these fellows, a good proportion had degrees in
philosophy from Oxford or Cambridge, and they were going
on to intensive graduate study. What was I to say to them? I
knew I didn't want to cross scholarly swords with them! The
answer was simple enough—I told them my story: told them
how I had accepted the Lord Jesus, and how I had been baptized in the Holy Spirit. In no way was I challenged. A great
proportion of those young men stayed for an hour afterward,
and asked me all the same questions that young Methodists, or
young Episcopalians, ask. Their interest was deep and genuine,
and they had no quarrel, it seemed, with my theology! Even
after that, a dozen of them stayed on to talk over tea, and then
the Principal and I talked on far into the night.

I had a foretaste through these experiences of what perhaps
is currently the most unexpected aspect of this charismatic
renewal, and that is the great and deep interest and participation on the part of the Roman Catholics. In 1967 we were all

* *The Spirit Bade Me Go*, by David DuPlessis, distributed by
Logos International, Plainfield, N.J.

surprised to hear of a strong movement of the Holy Spirit at Notre Dame University. That story has been well told in Kevin and Dorothy Ranaghan's book *Catholic Pentecostals*. Later, I was asked to speak to a group of the theological faculty and students at Gonzaga University in Spokane, and was again pleased at the acceptance I received, not only of my person and my testimony, but of my doctrine. A young Jesuit member of the faculty came up to me at the end of my talk and said:

"Father Bennett, I have just completed a book on the Holy Spirit, and I want you to know that I agree with everything you have said here today!"

My thoughts were re-called to the present by a few quivers of turbulence, and glancing up, saw that our captain had lighted the "Fasten Seat Belt" warning. I dutifully tightened my belt, and returned to my thoughts.

Early in 1968 we had met Father Fulton, the rector of one of the largest Roman Catholic churches in our part of Seattle. He had become acquainted with Ron, a young man from St. Luke's who had been marvellously healed by Jesus Christ, both physically and psychologically. Ron and his wife Sally invited us to dinner to meet their friend. We had found Father Fulton to be a kindly and humble person who certainly knew and loved the Lord Jesus. In fact it was he who suggested that we each tell how we met Christ. He heard with great interest our experience of the Holy Spirit and His gifts, but that was as far as the matter went at that time. Then, a month or two later, I received a call from Father Fulton.

"Dennis," he said, "can you come over to St. Thomas Seminary tomorrow? We are having a series of lectures on communications and preaching, and the instructor is a young man from the Midwest, Father McNutt. He is a Dominican monk, and claims to have this same experience that you have, the

Baptism in the Holy Spirit. He speaks in tongues! And he wants to meet you—can you come over?"

You bet I could! At the seminary the next day I met Father McNutt and found he had been praying with some of the local clergy, and that several of them had already received the Holy Spirit. After lunch a few priests joined Father McNutt and myself for further discussion.

"I'm so depressed," one of them said. "I've got to find something to help me, or I don't know what I'm going to do." As I looked at the distressed face of the young priest who had spoken, I was reminded of the priest of my own denomination at the clergy conference eight years before who had received the Holy Spirit along with the first St. Lukan's. Was history about to repeat itself? We prayed with him, and as he began to speak in tongues we saw the miracle happen again. His countenance cleared—he relaxed visibly as he lifted his voice to God in words unknown to him, words given by the Holy Spirit. At the same time, something else was happening. Father Fulton, the man who had invited me to visit the seminary that day, had been sitting back in a corner listening to all that was going on, and he, too, quietly began to speak in tongues!

Then the doors seemed to fly open. The next night I was invited to a prayer meeting with twenty Roman Catholic priests. Since that night they have been meeting weekly! It became not at all unusual to have twelve or so Roman Catholic sisters sitting in our prayer meeting at St. Luke's, often with their hands upraised in prayer and praise. Rita and I began to be asked to address convents in Seattle, Tacoma, and Spokane, and these invitations have continued to come. On our last journey to the eastern part of the country, we were asked to stop off in Odessa, Texas, to conduct a two-day mission at a Roman Catholic Church. We spent a wonderful time ministering to a basically Mexican-American congregation, where both the priests and the parish worker are Catholic Pentecostals, together with an increasing number of the congregation. In our two days at this church, nothing was said or done that would have seemed strange to any other "Full Gospel" group of Christians. The literature displayed on the book tables was derived largely from evangelical and Pentecostal sources. Again we saw the Holy Spirit breaking down the walls of denominationalism, and bringing Christians into unity of heart.

On a trip to Berkeley, California, early in 1970, in one interdenominational meeting alone five Roman Catholic priests received the Baptism in the Holy Spirit. It seems that the late Pope John's prayer that Roman Catholics would experience a new Pentecost is being vividly answered!

My reverie was broken as the young man in the seat ahead of me stood up. He was tall—well over six feet—and very thin. His blond hair, rather obviously unwashed, reached to his shoulders. He was wearing a grimy buckskin shirt and faded jeans. As he turned toward me, my glance travelled upward, from the peace cross that hung from the string of beads around his neck, to his face. It was an intelligent-looking face, although mostly concealed by the scraggly and unkempt growth of beard, and by ridiculously oversized blue spectacles. Slung across one shoulder was a small guitar which the stewardess had vainly tried to persuade him to leave in the coat compartment. The general effect was climaxed by a wide-brimmed black hat. I recalled a comment I had recently heard: "Hippies are lost sheep masquerading as shepherds!" As my hippie neighbour disappeared down the block-long aisle of the airplane, I looked at Rita.

"Look familiar?" I asked.

She smiled, and bobbed her head. "Uh-huh. Reminds me of home on Friday night!"

By now at St. Luke's we were thoroughly accustomed to the hippie type. Our city had been having a serious time with drug use among young people, and our U district was replete with the kind of long-haired youth we had just seen; but a wonderful thing was happening. These lost sheep were beginning to turn to Jesus for some real answers.

It is strange now to look back at the youth group during my first weeks at St. Luke's. On that first Sunday night in July 1960 I discovered they were having a rock and roll dance in the church basement with the lights turned off! Typically, the patient people who were sponsoring the group had given up trying to do any more than entertain the kids and keep them out of mischief as much as possible, or at least trying to keep the mischief where it could be somewhat controlled! The picture began to change when some of the young people received the Holy Spirit along with their parents.

One night a leading layman in the church sought me out.

"Father Bennett, something terrible has happened!"

"What's bothering you, Wally?"

"Oh, those daughters of mine! You know both of them have been baptized in the Holy Spirit. Well, last night they got their neighbour friend over in the basement, and told her about their experience, laid hands on her, and she received the Holy Spirit!"

I roared with laughter! I couldn't help it, for the news was so far from being terrible! But Wally's expression remained very solemn.

"You don't understand, Father B.," he said. "Their dad is very much upset about all that is going on in the church!"

"Well," I said, "we can't expect the young people *not* to tell their friends about something as exciting as the Good News that Jesus is alive and real. Cheer up! It'll come out all right." And it did!

As time went by, more of the teenagers received the Holy Spirit, some through their parents' prayers, and some by talking and praying with one another. We soon had a sizable group of young people. It was great to see them taking part in the prayer meetings along with older people—for the Holy Spirit ignores differences in age, too.

As more and more adults came into the fellowship in the Holy Spirit, however, the younger people began to pull away into their own group again, and to our frustration we found ourselves once more confronted with the "youth group" problem—what to do with them, how to keep them "fired up," how to help them defend themselves in the mounting temptations of modern school life. In 1962 the Full Gospel Business Men had an international convention at Seattle with some very effective youth meetings. A lot more of our kids received the Lord and the Baptism in the Holy Spirit, and those who were already "with it" were revived and strengthened. That summer there was real freedom and joy among them.

"Just wait," they said, "till school starts! We'll really take over those ol' high schools for Jesus!" But alas, when school started and our young spiritual Don Quixotes mounted their chargers, all that ensued was a sickening thud! They found themselves not strong or effective enough to cope with the unbelief and evil they met, and whereas they did not desert their own faith, they did not move ahead with a victorious witness in their schools. Through the next few years the adults continued to move ahead, but the youth work rather languished. It had become a "line-holding" operation. In 1965 and '66 things began to pull together under the direction of a capable young couple, Jack and Sybil, and early in 1967 there began to be real freedom again. About this time our youth leaders asked my wife, Rita, to work with them and to help the young people learn how to enter into free worship and praise, expecting the gifts of the Spirit to be seen in their meetings. As they allowed the Holy Spirit to minister through them, they began to experience healings and miracles, to share exciting testimonies of what God was doing in their lives, of answered prayer and daily guidance. Many teenagers began to receive salvation and the Baptism in the Holy Spirit, and told their friends at school.

"What's happened to you? You look so darn happy!"

"Oh, I was at a prayer meeting last night. I found out how real God is, and asked Jesus to run my life from now on. Boy, do I feel good!"

"You what?"

"I accepted Jesus. Got healed, too. I had a bad cold, and the symptoms just disappeared when I was prayed for!"

"Wha-a-a-t? Well, if you've got anything like that, I want it, 'cause I'm messed up, man! Where do you go to church anyway?"

"St. Luke's Episcopal. But don't worry, you don't have to be an Episcopalian! No one will try to get you to join our church; they couldn't care less about what church you belong to. The important thing is for you to meet God!"

It wasn't long before the little meeting room under the church was crowded with teenagers the way it had been with adults before we built the new parish hall.

"Dennis," Rita said one evening as we were riding along in the car, "we need to have a meeting on Friday night for the teens like the one you have for adults. We need a meeting just for testimony, and to pray with kids to receive the Holy Spirit. Sunday night needs to be a 'believer's meeting' where the young people can be free to pray and praise the Lord, and to get into some good Bible study. If there are too many newcomers it kind of stiffens things up!"

"Fine with me," I said. "Why don't you youth sponsors talk it over, and come up with a plan."

They did, and before long we started to have as many as two hundred young people in the church basement in addition to the crowd of adults in the parish hall. Two more workers, John and Denny, came to fill in for the other youth leaders as duties called them elsewhere. Then, one night, for a special speaker, we rented the Rainier Room at the Seattle Centre to accommodate over eight hundred teenagers for our Friday night meeting!

I glanced out of the window, and saw the patchwork of the Mid West countryside rolling away beneath us. Rita had her eyes closed and seemed to be catching "forty winks." The Lord had certainly used her with the young people.

One high school in particular began to be greatly influenced by this move of God. In this one school alone, fifty kids had been baptized in the Holy Spirit. School teachers were saying:

"What's come over these young people? Virtue is stalking the halls unchecked!" Pretty soon many of these youngsters began to meet together every morning before class to pray for their school, among other things. It wasn't long before answers to prayer became evident. From time to time in the course of the last ten years, our young people have formed singing groups, and have gone out to reach others through music. Now a college-age group calling themselves the "New Men" had formed, and had been having real success in witnessing to young people by singing modern-style Gospel music, interspersed with their own testimonies of what Jesus has done for them. In '68 this group asked the principal of the aforementioned high school if they could sing for an assembly. He listened to them as they auditioned for him privately and said: "Yes. I think our students would enjoy hearing you, but there's one thing that I'll have to ask you to refrain from doing; you can't talk about church!"

"Oh, no sir," responded the leader of the group, with a grin.

"We wouldn't want to talk about church—that could be dull! But we would like to talk about Jesus. Is that okay?"

"Hm-m-m!" the principal said, no doubt thinking about Supreme Court decisions . . . "That's all right. He certainly was a good man: you can talk about Him."

For one solid hour this group held two thousand high-school kids spellbound as they played and sang, and told how Jesus had delivered them from drugs, from hopelessness and emptiness. At the end of the programme there was a standing ovation. The teachers said:

"We haven't had a standing ovation for an assembly programme for ten years!" The principal told the New Men:

"I'd like to see you get into every high school in Seattle!"

To date they have performed in nearly one-hundred high schools not only in Seattle but in other cities, with similar results. A second group, calling themselves the "Fishers of Men" have now formed, and are having a fine ministry, more especially to church groups. It's good to know that similar work is going on, not only in the North West, but all over the country, and that through these ministries tens of thousands of young people are accepting Jesus Christ and being empowered by the Holy Spirit.

Every Friday night for the past three years, from seventy-five to two hundred teenagers gather at our church for a time of singing and inspiring testimonies—paralleling the meeting for adults—and every Saturday night some one hundred or more college-age youth meet to spend several hours in the same way. Some of the young adults still keep their uniform of long hair and strange, old-fashioned dress in order to "catch" others of their friends who need the same deliverance they have experienced.

I thought again about a Saturday night two years before, when this group was still meeting at our house. We had crowded over a hundred young people into our front and dining rooms, by dint of sitting them on the floor, so that we had "wall-to-wall people"! Out in the kitchen were ten or twelve "hip" kids who had come to see what was going on. They would not come into the main meeting, but watched and listened through the doorway, as one after another of the group told how Jesus had rescued them from drugs, or met other needs in their lives.

"I got into my father's liquor closet when I was just a little kid," said one young man. A good-looking, blond-haired fellow with a little moustache, he had kept a "semi-hippie" look, explaining, "If I look too 'straight,' the kids with problems won't come around, so I leave my hair a little long, and keep the gold-rimmed spectacles.

"I was soon on my way to becoming an alcoholic. Then as I got older I tried drugs—pot, LSD, and then speed. That speed is bad stuff. It caused my heart to beat so fast that I finally wound up with a heart attack, but that didn't stop me from taking some more. I was a mean one, too. I wanted to smash and blow things up! Then Jesus got hold of me! Wow, what a wonderful change! What a wonderful life! Now I want to live for God, and help people!" The young man's face was glowing as he told his story.

Pretty soon, the whole group broke into spontaneous praise. Someone started a chorus, and soon they were happily clapping and singing. The general feeling was that of a jolly party, and yet one knew that there was much more to it than that. God's presence and love was felt in that room, and the kids responded to it. One of the hippies turned to his friend standing near him in the kitchen.

"Hey, man, it's a good trip," he said eagerly, "it's a *good* trip!"

The ministry to the youth goes beyond just having meetings

at the church. Faced with the deadly challenge of drugs and psychedelic philosophy attempting to destroy the younger generation, a young couple who joined our congregation had felt directed by God to sell their business and rent a home in the university district just a few blocks away from the "Avenue" where the centre of the drug involvement was to be found. They then took in up to twenty-five drug addicts, young people who were willing to turn their lives over to Jesus, and attempt to break Satan's bondage. This work was all done strictly by faith—no appeals for funds at all. They carried on this work for about two years. St. Luke's people support them, pray for them, help them, but in no way sponsor them or try to tell them what to do—the Lord does that! In 1970 they closed the House of Zaccheus and opened Zacc's Place, a coffeehouse in the basement of one of the nearby churches in the U district. Many chapters could be written about the exciting and productive ministry that they have been carrying out among needy young people.

One night two of the girls from the House of Z. were crossing the Montlake Bridge, when they saw a young boy about to throw himself into the canal. They dragged him to safety and literally sat on him until help could arrive! One of the girls said:

"It's lucky we were bigger than him!" John, the director of the house, arrived with reinforcements, and they took the youngster by main force to the House of Zacchaeus. All the way there he screamed and kicked and struggled, crying out that "God" had told him to jump off the bridge! At the home, John and his wife Diana tried to get the boy to listen to reason, but he still fought. At one point he broke away, rushed up the stairs, and was halfway out the window before he could be stopped.

John could see that the youngster needed prayer for deliverance, so he proceeded to cast out the spirit of suicide, in the

Name of Jesus. The boy calmed down immediately. Then John said:

"In thirty seconds, son, if you wish it to be so, you can be through with all this fear and darkness, and be filled with joy and happiness! All you have to do is ask Jesus to rescue you from all your misery, and come into your heart!"

He did just that. Jesus came into his life, and hell went out. Two weeks later John said:

"He's still smiling. Hasn't stopped since that first night!"

They discovered that the boy was from California, and had virtually been kidnapped by a drug-pushing gang and brought to Seattle. Shortly after this our friends had the great satisfaction of putting the young man on the bus and sending him home to his parents. They have since this time received good letters from him.

Again, like the other wonderful things that are happening, this new life among young people is worldwide in scope. In Palmerston North, New Zealand, the entire family of the treasurer of the local Anglican Parish had received the Holy Spirit. One of their children, a young boy, age nine, entirely on his own initiative started a prayer and praise session among his elementary schoolmates. Every morning before school, some twenty-five of them met at the school for this purpose. There was no adult leadership, and the teachers were especially impressed because the youngsters would come down to have their meeting even though it was a school holiday!

Another interesting encounter concerning youth took place in Christchurch, New Zealand. I had given my testimony that night in the little Anglican Church in Aranui. After the meeting a woman came up to me somewhat agitated.

"Mr. Bennett! I just want to say that I'm worried about my daughter. She's become involved with this movement you're talking about. It just isn't normal! She stays out until eleven o'clock going to these prayer meetings!"

"How old is your daughter?" I inquired.

"She's twenty."

"Hm-m. At twenty she could probably be trusted out till eleven o'clock, even at a prayer meeting!" I commented.

The woman nodded. "Yes, of course," she said, "but she doesn't go to parties, or dances, or anything—well, *normal*. It just isn't *normal* to be going to these religious things all the time!"

I didn't say anything. After a brief pause, my new acquaintance continued:

"Of course, she's really a very nice girl!"

"I'm sure she is," I agreed.

"And," said the mother a little more thoughtfully, "her brother goes out and stays very late, and sometimes comes home drunk." After a pause she added, laughing a little: "I guess I like the way she is acting better than the way he is!"

Then in England, in several widely separated places we found parish churches literally teeming with young people who had received the Lord Jesus and been baptized in the Holy Spirit. Many were children of agnostic or atheistic parents, some of whom were very worried about their "way-out" off-spring! It was quite a switch to see teenagers meeting at church before the main meeting specifically for the purpose of praying for the conversion of their parents!

"You know," I said to Rita, "if I had been told ten years ago of all that is happening today, I would not have believed it *at all*!"

"These last ten years have been amazing for me too," replied Rita. "I want everyone to know how wonderful this life in the Spirit is!"

The soft drone of the jets was restful, and I was sleepy. The next thing I knew I was awakened by a sudden change of sound. Our pilot had reduced power for our descent as we emerged from the mountains to swing out over the coastal plain to the Seattle area. The last part of a jet flight is always fascinating to me, when the engines are cut back to a whisper, and the great bird is gliding along, seemingly without effort. The first twinkling lights were appearing throughout the city as we crossed Lake Washington. The traffic was jammed on the floating bridges and the freeways far below us. Up came the starboard wing as we turned "final." I looked across at the western sky. The sun was setting behind the snow-clad Olympics, throwing them into full relief.

My mind flashed to Indonesia, where what may well be the greatest spiritual breakthrough of our time has been taking place for several years now. I thought of the amazing manifestations of New Testament power being experienced there—the well-documented stories, carried by impartial observers, of people being raised from the dead, of thousands healed, and of even more startling miracles: walking on water, water being turned into wine, as God's people, very often humble and uneducated, see fulfilled the Biblical promise: "He that believes on me, the works that I do shall he do also; and greater works than these shall he do . . ."[1] I remembered hearing of the thousands of Mohammedans and Communists being won to Jesus Christ. Tired of killing one another, and disillusioned with the unsatisfactory answers of both of their religions, many are coming to Jesus and finding Him to be the answer. A missionary friend recently returned from Indonesia said to me:

"I tramped seventy miles into the interior—it was seventy miles to get a glimpse of heaven, as I heard these ex-Communists and ex-Mohammedans singing all day long the praises of the true God for the joy He has brought them." This same man, the head of a strong interdenominational missionary fellowship said also:

"I was a missionary to Indonesia many years ago. We would work for a year to get one convert from Mohammedanism to Christ, and then half the time he would recant. Now the Christians who used to be Mohammedans are organizing evangelistic teams to go to Pakistan to win other Mohammedans to Christ! It is incredible!"

My mind travelled on to South America from where reports come continually, telling of thousands upon thousands who are coming to know Jesus Christ. One leading evangelist—not himself a part of the charismatic movement—pointed out that some eighty per cent of the Christians in South America have the Pentecostal experience.

The flaps whined into full position, and the airframe shuddered as the pilot lowered the landing gear. As I looked to the east, windows caught the red glare of the western sky, as if many little fires were blazing. "Will there be blazes of riot and destruction in the coming years?" I asked myself. "Or fires of the Holy Spirit?" I looked at the city stretched out below, and realized the very small impact that had been made on this mass of humanity. I thought of the tensions, and the sorrows, the spiritual sickness, the hatred, the lostness, the misery spread out there.

We were nearly down now, and in a few moments I felt the familiar bump and squeal of the tyres on macadam, and then the roar of reversed engines. As we slowed and turned off the active runway on to the blue-lighted taxiway, I remembered the invitations and letters on my desk at home, from Sweden, Australia, India, Korea, Africa. So many other cities like this one, so many millions of people. I knew it would not be very long before we would be taking off again from this very runway. I thought of the many new opportunities for outreach that were opening, and the great need to tell of the power of Jesus Christ to change lives—filling them with His love—the need at home and abroad. I thanked God that the Holy Spirit is raising up more and more men and women everywhere to share in this vast work—the only eternally important work—that of telling the world that God is real, and God is available.

22
Acts Twenty-eight

The book of the Acts of the Apostles in the Bible, which could just as well be called the "Acts of the Holy Spirit," has no conclusion. So it is in writing about any follower of Jesus, or any group of His people: we can never find a stopping place. The last chapter of this book, too, like Acts 28, must finish open-ended. I wish I could tell all the things that have happened, and are happening, to the people who have appeared in the pages of this book, but that would be impossible. We can only take a quick glance at one group of Christians after a decade of teaching openly and experiencing freely the blessings of Pentecost.

Most of the Book of the Acts is about the Apostle Paul, and in the last chapter he is still going strong! He has in no sense "cooled off," or settled down! In Acts 28 we are told how, after being shipwrecked, Paul and his shipmates are on the island of Melita. In the process of gathering wood for the fire, Paul picks up a venomous snake and is bitten; but instead of falling down dead, he simply shakes the creature off into the fire and pays no further attention. Hearing that the governor's father is sick, Paul goes and heals him; whereupon many other sick people are brought to him, and he heals them.

There is no sign, after ten years, that the Gifts and Fruit of the Holy Spirit are diminishing in the lives of those who come to St. Luke's. There has been, of course, a continual renewing as people, week by week, come and receive the Holy Spirit, and begin their new life of freedom and power in the Spirit; but those who have been walking in the Spirit for ten years, if they have continued faithfully to trust Jesus, have attained a greater maturity in their lives, and also have not seen any diminishing of God's miracle-working and prayer-answering power.

On two occasions recently, at St. Luke's, broken wrists have been healed by prayer, and in both cases X-ray tests were taken by doctors before and after, leaving no doubt about the healings. One of these is of particular interest because it happened to Frances, a gracious lady who has been a member of the parish for some forty years. Like a number of "old-timers," she received the Holy Spirit shortly after I came, and has been growing steadily in the Lord ever since. She had the misfortune to fall and injure her wrist. Thinking it was just sprained, she treated it at home for several weeks, but when the pain and swelling did not subside, she went to her doctor, who X-rayed the affected part.

"Why, Frances," he said, with concern, "why didn't you come to me before this? This wrist is broken, and you've let it go so long that I can't set it. You'll have to go to a bone surgeon!" And he made the necessary arrangements. Before the appointment with the specialist, however, Frances came to Christian friends and asked them to pray for her wrist. The bone surgeon looked at the arm and said:

"We'll have to have another X-ray."

When the picture was developed he shook his head wonderingly. "Why, my dear," he said, "there's nothing wrong with your wrist!" Jesus had done the work. Frances went straight home and mowed the lawn!

Even more startling was another recent healing. Eleanor came to join the church in 1962. She received Christ as her Saviour, and shortly afterward was baptized in the Holy Spirit. She had had a damaged heart for a long time, and soon after joining our fellowship submitted to open-heart surgery to replace a damaged valve with a plastic one. The results were not satisfactory, and she soon had to have a second open-heart operation, this time to have the plastic unit replaced by a human tissue transplant. In 1968, the heart specialist said to her:

"Eleanor, I'm sorry to have to tell you this, but you're going to have to have another operation on your heart. The valve is becoming defective again."

The night before she was to check in to the hospital for this third surgery, Eleanor was at a meeeting where she heard the testimony of a businessman visiting us from Texas. He had been used by God to bring back to life a man who had been dead for forty-five minutes.* He told of several wonderful healings which had occurred since, due, no doubt, to the tremendous increase of his own faith. At the end of the meeting, this visitor, one of our own laymen, and I prayed for Eleanor with the laying on of hands. The next evening, after she had been in the hospital for her pre-surgical tests, Eleanor telephoned me. She was so excited she could hardly talk, but she managed to say:

"Father Bennett! Praise the Lord! Do you know what happened to me? I checked in to the hospital today, and had all kinds of tests: X-rays, cardiograms, catheterizations, and so forth. Then the doctors on the heart team came in, one by one,

* See "In Time for God's Appointment," by Sherwin McCurdy as told to Jamie Buckingham, *Christian Life*, Oct. 1969, p. 40.

and said: 'Eleanor, we don't know what's happened, but there's nothing wrong with you!' Then the chief specialist came in and said: 'Eleanor, I don't understand it, but your heart has returned to normal. You can go to work eight hours a day if you so desire!' " This she proceeded to do, and has been doing so ever since, in vigorous health!

There is obviously *something* different about St. Luke's Church, for not long ago the local morning newspaper, the *Seattle Post-Intelligencer,* devoted most of the front page of their Saturday night final to a report on St. Luke's! Yet St. Luke's is an Episcopal Church in good standing, its church services in keeping with the "doctrine, discipline, and worship of the Protestant Episcopal Church" in the U.S.A. There is a sizable group of licensed lay readers, and the ladies are active in the women's work of the diocese, and some hold or have held important offices. I myself was appointed Dean of our Convocation for two successive years, before finding it necessary to resign due to the pressure of my outside ministry. St. Luke's is regarded by our bishop and other chief ministers as one of the churches that is, as one said to me recently, "going upstream against the current, in a day when many churches are shrinking and dying."

Ten years ago, only a very small group met me at St. Luke's on a Sunday; now five services are held each Sunday, and during the week a large number of people from a variety of denominations come to various other meetings for prayer and instruction, so that our total weekly attendance runs well over two thousand. The vocal gifts of the Spirit, tongues, interpretation, and prophecy, are sometimes manifested at the "family service" on Sunday morning, but there is still a conservative attitude on this, for the people of the parish know that on Sunday morning they are "fishing," rather than "swimming"!

There is plenty of opportunity at other times during the week for more informal sharing in praise and prayer, as for example, on Tuesday night. The several hundred who meet at that time share in enthusiastic gospel singing, praise, prayer, testimony, and teaching, and the tenor of the meeting is relaxed; yet all things are done in "decency and order." Many get together in homes during the week for more times of prayer and praise.

Each Friday evening there is an "information meeting," and in the course of the last ten years, an estimated eight to ten thousand persons have received the Holy Spirit at these meetings. Very few of these have joined St. Luke's, for we have always insisted that they return to their own churches to share what has happened to them. This is why, although the parish has flourished, we have not become a huge congregation. Our membership on the books is still less than a thousand, precisely because we have discouraged people from joining us.

In the last ten years the budget at St. Luke's has increased fourteen times, from $12,000 to $170,000 per annum; yet there are no "drives" for finances. We do not even have an "every-member canvass." No one is approached individually and asked for money, and we do not seek support from those outside the Christian fellowship. We encourage the members of St. Luke's to tithe* their income as a Christian minimum. The people give willingly, because they believe in, and are involved in, the work that their money is supporting. This year the parish will give $24,000 to the support of outside work, missionary and other, through the Diocese of Olympia. There is much additional missionary giving which is hard to assess, because it is given individually, and as the Holy Spirit leads. If a missionary speaks at St. Luke's, and his work commends itself to the listeners, they will support him regardless of his denomination. During the last few years, for example, sub-

---

* *Tithe* means to give ten per cent of one's income to God's work.

stantial backing has been given to a young Korean Presbyterian, who is doing a wonderful work on the front lines in Vietnam.

In these days, both protestant and Roman Catholic bodies are reporting that thousands of ministers and priests are "bailing out" under the discouragement of the times, and going into other businesses and professions. However, wherever the "charismatic renewal" is in progress, the opposite trend is observed. For the first fifty years of St. Luke's existence, not one man had ever gone into the ministry. In the last ten years, three men have been ordained to the ministry from the membership of St. Luke's; three men are in seminary preparing for the ministry, while three others have been accepted as postulants from the diocese to enter seminary as soon as they have finished their college work. One young woman went into the church army and has since married a minister; another became a deaconess-missionary and is now working in Alaska. Hundreds of people, of course, have gone "into the ministry" right where they live. Most of the personal counselling and praying at St. Luke's is done by lay people; indeed, we regard the parish church as a training centre for lay-ministry.

Physical and organizational growth is not an end in itself. The people of this parish know that a big church does not necessarily mean spiritual success. They are aware that the outward form and organization of the Christian fellowship may change drastically within a short time. For these reasons they have not rushed to build an elaborate new church building.

They know God is not interested in blessing any particular denomination or organization as such. The Church is one: God's people, those who have accepted Jesus and have come alive. On the other hand, God isn't against the "old-line" denominations, but uses them for His purpose if they let themselves be used. The Holy Spirit today is reaching into the structures that man has set up, ignoring our labels, and touching and empowering those who are receptive. What will the Church be like when the Holy Spirit really has His way? None of us know the full answer, but we are catching some exciting glimpses!

The beautiful part about the revival and growth at St. Luke's is that it does not centre around any human person. When the Rector is away—which he often is!—the church flourishes just the same as when he is at home; sometimes better! The work has always been shared, not only with other ministers, but most of all with the people. From the very beginning, one of the great marks of the "charismatic renewal," or Pentecostal revival, in the historic churches, has been that it does not centre on an individual or a group, or any particular denomination. Whenever in the history of the Pentecostal movement any individual or group has tried to gain control, that group or individual has "come a cropper."

Do we have people who do not accept the charismatic renewal, but are still active members of the parish? Yes, we have a number of good folk who, while they are pleased with the new vigour of the church, cannot see the experience of the Baptism of the Holy Spirit for themselves. The experience has in no way been forced upon them, and they see the beneficial effect it as had, both on the corporate life of the church, and on the individual lives of their friends, so they are content to stay.

It is much more difficult to give a brief answer to the question so often asked: "What happens to the social attitudes of the people who have been baptized in the Holy Spirit?" So many earnest people today are convinced that if you believe in an individual experience of salvation through Jesus Christ, you can't possibly be "socially concerned." This, of course, isn't true. When people receive Christ, and the Baptism in the

Holy Spirit, one of the most striking effects in their lives is that they become deeply and truly concerned over their fellow-men, and over the condition of society. However, since at the same time they become much more aware of the reality of God in human affairs, their overall attitude may turn out to be quite different from that of the "social activists" who have perhaps despaired of accomplishing anything through spiritual means, or of believing that God, if He exists at all, really takes any active part in those affairs.

"Social concern" in the Christian is a by-product of the "Fruit" of the Holy Spirit, and it takes a while to grow! The Baptism in the Holy Spirit does not bring an instant answer to social problems. It takes time for the Holy Spirit really to change wrong attitudes, prejudices, etc. Again and again we draw back from the things the Lord desires to accomplish. When the Christian draws back, however, he "loses his blessing" for the time being—he grieves the Spirit. How long will it take the Holy Spirit to bring him to terms? That depends on how deeply entrenched the prejudice or wrong attitude is, how much it touches the false security of the psyche, and other factors. Nonetheless, one could write interminably of healed relationships, saved marriages, changed attitudes in business, deeper concern about others, etc., that have come as a result of the love and power of God working in people's lives. You can't get away with trying to love God and hating your fellow-man at the same time—it just doesn't work!

We know that there is plenty of room for these "fired-up" Christians to get more deeply involved in community action, yet the inclination is already there and the willingness is there. For example, Ballard is an old Scandinavian community, by tradition strongly white and protestant. Feeling the need to break out of this pattern, in 1967 we agreed with Primm Tabernacle Church, an African Methodist Episcopal Church in the south part of the city, to exchange leadership for our Vacation Bible School; so it came about that year that the faculty and one third of the student body of our Vacation Bible School was made up of black Americans, while the opposite was true for the A.M.E. Church. Though this may not sound very daring in this day of get-tough social activism, yet it was interesting and unusual enough for our local Seattle *Times* to print the story on the front page with a four-column picture.

Many unsolved problems at St. Luke's? You bet! But they are ones of action, and not of passivity. The pastoral and other problems at this church are concerned with how to control and guide a fast-moving vehicle, not how to get a lumbering and unwieldy one into motion! The people are eager to serve, but need guidance as to how to do it effectively.

At the very end of Acts 28 we find Paul living in his own hired house, and meeting all who come to him. The Jews— his own countrymen—visit him, and listen with great interest to what he has to say, but when he is finished most of them simply spend their time in learned theological discussion. "The Jews departed, and had great reasoning among them-selves." [1]

I was at a meeting in Oregon where one young minister challenged me. He wasn't ungracious; he just didn't agree with my theology. He held a mild debate with me in the presence of others there—mostly businessmen—and then departed, feel-ing that he had made his point. Shortly after he left, a young businessman asked for and received the Baptism in the Holy Spirit. He was so overcome with the joy of the Lord that he, like others on the Day of Pentecost itself, looked as if he was filled with new wine. I could not miss the sad contrast between the young minister departing in intellectual triumph, but still dry and hungry in his soul, and the young businessman, filled with the joy which he had accepted from God in simplicity and trust.

When the power of the Holy Spirit was received at that first Pentecost, the followers of Jesus were suddenly filled with the glory of God. Some onlookers thought that they were drunk, but Peter said:

"They are not drunk, as you suppose, after all, it's only 9 o'clock in the morning! But this is that which the prophet Joel said would happen: 'And it shall come to pass in the last days, saith God, that I will pour out of my Spirit upon all flesh . . .' "

The outpouring which began at Pentecost has continued ever since, and in these days in an ever-increasing flood. We too, like the young minister, can get so tangled in intellectual questionings that we may spend all our time having "great reasonings among ourselves," and miss the glory of God! The Holy Spirit is ready to answer our questions if we're ready to listen. The Book of Acts is open-ended; it's still going on. Your life, and what you allow God to do in it may yet be another chapter!

Chapter References

Chapter References

CHAPTER I

No references

CHAPTER II

1. *The Book of Common Prayer*, The Ordering of Priests, p. 542
2. Acts 2 : 4, 8 : 15–17, 10 : 46, 19 : 6
3. *The Book of Common Prayer*, The Order of Confirmation, p. 297
4. *The Book of Common Prayer*, Offices of Instruction, p. 291
5. *Doctrine in the Church of England*, compiled by the Anglican Church, Society for Promoting Christian Knowledge of the Church of England with approval of the Archbishops, 1922–1937, p. 93

CHAPTER III

1. Mark 16 : 17 (Author's paraphrase)
2. I Corinthians 14 : 5 (Author's paraphrase)
3. I Corinthians 14 : 18 (Literal Greek)
4. Romans 8 : 26 (Author's paraphrase)
5. I Corinthians 14 : 2 (Author's paraphrase)

CHAPTER IV

1. Philippians 4 : 4–7 (Authorized Translation)

CHAPTER V

1. Isaiah 6 : 1–3 (Authorized Translation)
2. Romans 8 : 15 (Authorized Translation)

CHAPTER VI

1. Matthew 10 : 8 (Literal Greek)
2. Mark 16 : 17–18 (Authorized Translation)

CHAPTER VII

No references

CHAPTER VIII

No references

CHAPTER IX

No references

CHAPTER X

1. Acts 2 : 4 (Authorized Translation)

CHAPTER XI

1. I John 4 : 20a (Revised Standard)
2. James 2 : 16a (Revised Standard)

CHAPTER XII

1. Philippians 4 : 19 (Literal Greek)
2. John 14 : 12

CHAPTER XIII

1. Romans 8 : 26 (Author's paraphrase)

CHAPTER XIV

1. Hebrews 6:6 (Authorized Translation)

CHAPTER XV

1. Philippians 4:19 (Authorized Translation)
2. Ezekiel 24:15-18 (Authorized Translation)
3. Isaiah 57:1 (Authorized Translation)
4. Romans 8:11 (Literal Greek)

CHAPTER XVI

No references

CHAPTER XVII

No references

CHAPTER XVIII

1. *The Book of Common Prayer*, Offices of Instruction, p. 291
2. I Corinthians 12:7-11 (Authorized Translation)

CHAPTER XIX

No references

CHAPTER XX

No references

CHAPTER XXI

1. John 14:12 (Authorized Translation)

CHAPTER XXII

1. Acts 28:29 (Authorized Translation)
2. Acts 2:15-17 (Author's paraphrase, first two verses; Authorized Translation, final verse)

The Holy Spirit and You

A Study-Guide
to the Spirit-filled Life

DENNIS AND RITA BENNETT

KINGSWAY PUBLICATIONS
EASTBOURNE

Contents

THIS BOOK IS DEDICATED TO THE GLORY OF
GOD THE FATHER,
GOD THE SON, AND
GOD THE HOLY SPIRIT

Preface

This book shares some insights of a decade of active witnessing, teaching, travelling, and experiencing the work and manifestations of our Lord the Holy Spirit in many places. Much of the material was intended originally to form a second part to Dennis' book, *Nine O'Clock in the Morning,* but it seemed better to leave that volume to deal exclusively with telling the story of the modern renewal of the Faith as it has touched our lives, and leave teaching and explanation for a separate book.

The part on Spiritual Gifts and the Fruit of the Holy Spirit is taken largely from *A Study Guide of the Spirit-Filled Life,* a booklet prepared by Rita to instruct those who receive the baptism in the Holy Spirit. This booklet has enjoyed wide circulation, and many who know it will welcome it in expanded form here.

The last ten years have been a decade of testimony, as the word of the baptism in the Holy Spirit has penetrated the "old-line" churches. Today thousands of ministers and priests of the older denominations have received the Holy Spirit as on the Day of Pentecost, as have millions of lay people. Now, while the testimony goes forward with ever-increasing strength, there is great need for teaching. Someone has pointed out that the return of the appetite to a sick person is one of the first signs of recovery. God's People have been very sick, nigh unto death, but now the Church of God is convalescent and very hungry! We hope this book will help to supply some of the nourishment needed for a full recovery.

We, Dennis and Rita, are Episcopalians (Anglicans), but in

this study it will be evident that we are not pushing any particular brand of Christianity. Our greatest desire is for people to meet the Lord Jesus Christ, and receive the power of the Holy Spirit, regardless of their denomination—if they have one. Occasionally we made references that would apply especially to our own denomination, or those similar, but the information we have given will also help others understand better these particular churches. We have dealt with the things that unite charismatic Christians, and have tried to avoid discussion of issues that have divided Christians through the centuries. The troubled questions are for the Holy Spirit to deal with, not us!

We do not claim or believe that we have all the truth, nor are we sure that in the coming years some of our views may not change, but we have presented these teachings sincerely and in the light we have at this time. During these years we have heard many outstanding speakers and teachers, and read numerous books on our subject. It would be impossible to give credit to all from whom the Lord has brought us knowledge and understanding. We can only thank the Holy Spirit Who has taught all of us. Where direct quotations are given throughout the book, we have, of course, given the source. Our most important written source, needless to say, has been Scripture itself. Also, we have learned many lessons through our own personal experiences.

We hope and pray that this book, *The Holy Spirit and You,* will be a help to many, both those who have been baptized in the Holy Spirit for years, and those just entering or getting ready to enter this area of Christian experience. We close with St. Paul's words:

"Grace be unto you, and peace, from God our Father, and from the Lord Jesus Christ. I thank my God always on your behalf, for the grace of God which is given you by Jesus Christ; That in every thing you are enriched by Him, in all utterance, and in all knowledge . . . So that you come behind in no gift waiting for the coming of our Lord Jesus Christ . . ." (I Cor. 1 : 3–5, 7).

Seattle, Washington
January 25, 1971

In the love of our Lord Jesus,
Dennis and Rita Bennett

I
The First Step

Several years ago, in one of the New England states, the wife of a Christian businessman, a friend of ours, was busy cleaning up the breakfast dishes when a knock came at the door. She opened it, to see her neighbour standing there—with a woe-begone look on her face.

"I've just come over to say good-bye," the visitor announced. "We've been neighbours for quite a while, and although we don't know one another well, I just wanted to let you know we're leaving."

"Why?" asked my friend's wife. "Has your husband got a new job, or what? Sit down. Tell me about it."

The neighbour dropped wearily into a chair. "No," she said, "nothing like that. We're losing the house—can't make the payments. Losing the car, too, for that matter." She opened her hands, lying in her lap, and stared at them. Then she looked up. "Might as well give you the whole story. John and I are getting a divorce."

"But why? What in the world has gone wrong?"

"My husband and I are both hopeless alcoholics," said the woman sadly. "Just can't seem to shake it. Money's all gone, and everything else with it. What gets me most is our child; I don't like to see him the victim of a broken home—and all that." The little woman was nearly in tears.

"But—," said my friend's wife, "don't you know there's an answer?"

The neighbour looked up abruptly: "What do you mean? We've tried everything we know! We just can't seem to stay on the programme with AA. We've tried psychiatry, but even if that were a possible answer, we couldn't afford long-term counselling."

"Why don't you ask Jesus to help you?"

It was the neighbour's turn to look non-plussed. "Jesus? What's *He* got to do with it?"

"Why, He's the Saviour!" exclaimed my friend's wife.

"Oh," said the visiting neighbour, "you mean religion and all that. Yeah, I'm religious. I mean, I believe in God, and I've tried to be a decent person." She laughed wryly. "I guess I haven't done too good a job of it though."

"No, no, that's not what I mean. I mean Jesus is a *saviour*— He saves, rescues people. He'll rescue you from your situation, if you ask Him to take over. You do want to get out of it, don't you? I mean, you want to be different—to get things straightened out?"

The neighbour looked at her companion for a moment or two. "Never heard it put that way before," she said slowly. "You mean it's that simple?—just *ask* Him?"

My friend's wife nodded. 'Uh-huh. He's alive, and He's right here. He'll do it!"

The neighbour sat for a moment or two in silence, then suddenly slipped out of the chair on to her knees and lifted her hands in a gesture of surrender. "I don't know how to say this," she said, "but, Jesus, please help me out of this mess. Please take over!" Then she stood up and without further comment, she went home.

Two days later the husband came over from next door. "What's happened to my wife?" he asked gruffly. "I want it, too!"

This Christian couple told him, and *he* got down on his knees on the kitchen floor and asked Jesus to take over *his* life!

What happened? The alcohol problem disappeared. It was only a symptom of their empty lives. The home was not lost. The marriage did not break up. Jesus *saves*—He saved their home, their marriage, their health, and probably their lives. Jesus isn't hesitant to start with people's immediate needs. Two of His great miracles were performed to provide hungry people with food. Almost all of His miracles were done to meet the physical needs of people. Often the first step in becoming a Christian is just a cry for help (Acts 2:21).

But more than that happened to the onetime alcoholic couple. Their whole way of life changed. They were different. Something happened to them *inside*.

The Greek word translated "save" in our English Bible is *sozo*, which means, according to the lexicon:

"*Sozo* . . . preserve or rescue from natural dangers and afflictions . . . save from death . . . bring out safely from a situation fraught with mortal danger . . . save or free from disease . . . from demonic possession . . . be restored to health, get well . . . keep, preserve in good condition . . . thrive, prosper, get on well . . . save or preserve from eternal death. . . ." [1]

To become a Christian doesn't mean to accept a philosophy, or a set of rules, or to believe a list of abstract principles; to

1. W. F. Arndt and F. W. Gingrich, eds. *A Greek-English Lexicon of the New Testament and Other Early Christian Literature* (Chicago: University of Chicago Press, 1957).

become a Christian means to have God come and *live in you* (Col. 1 : 27).

To become a Christian is to *repent* (Acts 2 : 38; 26 : 18). That means to want to be different, to admit that you're on the wrong road and want to get right. Many come to Jesus, like the desperate couple in our story, because they know they're in a jam; they're heading for destruction. Jesus accepts them and meets their needs, if they are ready to change.

To become a Christian is to be *converted* (Acts 3 : 19; Matt. 18 : 3). This means turning around, and going in the opposite direction—the right direction—with Jesus.

To become a Christian is to be *forgiven* (Ps. 103 : 11–12). That means to have your sins really taken away, as though they had never existed—to have the record swept clean. More than that, it means to be able to be forgiven every day—to *live* forgiven! (I John 1 : 9).

To become a Christian is to be *born again* (John 3 : 1–21; I Peter 1 : 23), and here we get to the heart of the matter. An elderly scholar came to Jesus late one night looking for answers. Jesus said to him:

"Nicodemus, you've got to be born again!"

The old man shook his head. "How can I be born, when I'm grown up? Do I have to go back to my mother's womb and be born over again?"

Jesus answered: "Don't be silly, Nicodemus. You're a better scholar than that! I'm not talking about physical birth—that's already happened. You have to be born of the Spirit."

What did Jesus mean by this?

The Bible tells us that God created man with the ability to know Him and respond to Him. But at the very first, man broke that contact, and when he did, he died spiritually, and handed on that spiritual death to all his descendants. The very inmost part of us is called our "spirit", or *pneuma* in Greek, and this was created for one main purpose, to know God. An animal has a soul and a body, but a human being has a body, a soul, and a spirit (I Thess. 5 : 23). When man broke fellowship with God in the very beginning—what we call the fall of man—this inmost part died, or went out of action, and man ever since then has operated from his soul, and body (Gen. 2 : 17). No wonder we've got into such a mess! The "soul" called *psyche* in Greek, is the psychological part of us—composed of our intellect, our will, and our emotions. This part of us is wonderful, *when* it is under the control of God through the Spirit, but when it is out of control it does terrible things.

This is why human history is the record of hate, bloodshed, cruelty, and confusion; human beings are dead *spiritually*— "dead in trespasses and sins" (Eph. 2 : 1 KJV) and trying to live *soulishly* while being out of touch with God and therefore lost (Luke 19 : 10). "Lost" means we don't know who we are, or where we are going, or what we are for. If this situation isn't corrected, it obviously means hell—it means that the person is going to be eternally lost, in the dark, frightened, rebellious, and hateful, separated from God forever; and not only that, but sharing in the endless destruction of the devil and his angels, for there is no "no-man's land". The great and desperate need, then, is to come alive, to get back in touch with God; and this is exactly what Jesus Christ is offering us. Through Jesus, and through Jesus alone—there is no other way—God's life can come and bring us alive (John 10 : 10).

However, the evil which we committed while we were lost and out of touch with God, created a wall of sin and guilt which would keep us from receiving this new life (Isa. 59 : 2). God is love, but He is also justice. He cannot "let us off", any more than a just and loving human father could "let his son off" if he knew that he was guilty of a crime. The father would have to insist on the boy's "turning himself in" to the authorities. But if the boy was truly repentant, the father might then offer to pay the son's fine, serve his sentence, or even die in his place, supposing such a thing to be possible. Justice and love would then both be satisfied.

This is just what Jesus did. He met the requirements of justice by dying for us. Jesus was God in human flesh—He was the Incarnation of the Second Person of the Godhead, the Creator God, by Whom the Father created the worlds (Eph. 3:9; Heb. 1:2). He was totally free from any sin or guilt. When Jesus died on the Cross, because He was God, and because He was innocent, He infinitely satisfied justice on behalf of all the sins that man had committed, or would ever commit.

In this way Jesus solved the problem of our guilt that was keeping us from the Father, and when He died and rose again, the way was open for the Father to send the Holy Spirit, through Whom God's life was able to come and live in us. The only requirement is for us to see that we've been wrong, and to ask for forgiveness. Then we must ask Jesus to come and live in us and be our Lord and Saviour. By the Holy Spirit, Jesus comes into our lives, our sins are washed away through His poured-out Blood, and we are given a new kind of life. The Holy Spirit having joined Himself to our spirit (I Cor. 6:17) brings it from death to life; it is "born again", and becomes what St. Paul calls a "new creature" (II Cor. 5:17; Rev. 21:4–5).

The new life created by the Holy Spirit in us is what Jesus calls "eternal life". This doesn't just mean "going on and on", but *God's life* in us, the kind of life that never runs down, never gets tired, or bored, but is always joyful and fresh (I John 5:11).

When Jesus said that a little child was the greatest thing in the Kingdom of Heaven, He was making a comment on eternal life. A little child doesn't get tired of doing the same thing over and over. "Read it again, Mummy!" "Do it again, Daddy!" This continually renewed freshness and lack of boredom comes very close to expressing the kind of life God wants to give us. "Behold I make all things new!" Not just once, but continuously, says Jesus. He is the continual Renewer! We are promised that we shall walk in "newness of life", and this is the same thing as eternal life: continual refreshing, continual replenishing. The word "eternal" literally means "ageless"—never getting old.

Isaiah says, "They that wait upon the Lord shall renew their strength; they shall mount up with wings as eagles; they shall run, and not be weary; and they shall walk, and not faint" (Isa. 40:31 KJV).

How do you accept forgiveness and receive this new life?

1. Realize you've been lost and going in the wrong direction, and be willing to go God's way.

2. Admit that you've been wrong, and ask the Father to take away your guilt and sin by the Blood of Jesus.

3. Ask Jesus Christ, God's only begotten Son, to come into your life, and become your Saviour and Lord (Rev. 3:20).

4. Believe He has come the minute you ask Him to. Thank Him for saving you and giving you the new life (I John 5:11–15).

Here is a simple prayer you might say if you have decided to receive Jesus:

"Dear Father, I believe that Jesus Christ is Your only begotten Son, and that He became a human being, shed his Blood and died on the Cross to clean away my guilt and sin that was separating me from You. I believe that He rose from the dead, physically, to give me new life. Lord Jesus, I invite You to come into my heart. I accept You as my Saviour and Lord. I confess my sins, and ask You to wash them away. I believe that You have come and are living in me right now. Thank You, Jesus!"

When you pray this prayer, you may actually feel something happen, or you may not. Your "spirit" which comes alive through Jesus Christ is in a place far deeper than your emotions; therefore, sometimes there will be an emotional reaction, and sometimes not. Whether you feel anything immediately or not, you will find that you are different because Jesus will do what He has promised. Jesus keeps His Word. He said:

"Heaven and earth shall pass away, but my words shall not pass away" (Matt. 24:35 KJV).

2
The Overflow

If you have received Jesus as your Saviour as described in the previous chapter, God is living in you. By the Holy Spirit He has joined Himself to your spirit. Your spirit, the very inmost part of you is alive, and not only alive, but filled with all the wonderful joy, and love, and peace, and glory of God Himself.

"If any man be in Christ," says the Apostle Paul, "he is a new creature!" (II Cor. 5:17 KJV). He also says of Christians that they are seated in heavenly places with Christ (Eph. 2:6).

If you are like many people, you will say at this point:

"Well, I *am* different. Something certainly did happen to me when I invited Jesus into my heart, and for a while I had a deep sense of the love and joy you are talking about. I really wanted to tell everyone about it, too. But somehow, now, I seem to be cooling off. Life isn't all that different any more. I still know that things have changed down inside me somewhere, but most of the time I feel just about as I did before. In the mornings, when I get away by myself and pray, I do sometimes feel God's presence, but I can't keep track of Him during the day!"

Why is this? It's not hard to understand if you will remember and take seriously what we said in the last chapter. In fact, many very difficult problems in Christian experience become understandable if you will accept what the Bible says about the nature of man, that you are a threefold being: spirit, soul, and body (I Thess. 5 : 23). If you are still thinking of yourself as two parts—soul and body—then you will inevitably confuse your psychological reactions with your spiritual life, and this is not only confusing to the understanding, it can actually, in this very psychological age, lead you into false teaching. Many fine Bible teachers today, under the pressure of psychology, are identifying the spirit of man with the "unconscious mind", or the "deep psyche", simply because they do not take seriously the Bible's ability to divide between the soul and the spirit (Heb. 4 : 12). But if you make this division, you will not only be able to grasp what happens in the baptism in the Holy Spirit, but also will find yourself able to account for other things in your Christian life which may have puzzled you.

When you received Jesus as your Saviour, your *spirit* came alive, began to assert its new life and take its rightful place as head over your *soul*—your psychological part (intellect, will, and emotions)—and your *body*, your physical part. Your body and soul, however, were accustomed to "running the show", and it wasn't long before they had pretty much overwhelmed your new life in the spirit, and resumed the driver's seat. When you pray in the morning, the business of your soul and body is quieted; your spirit has a chance to let you know he is there; and at this, and other times, you get an inkling that, deep inside you, the new life is very real. But as soon as the clamour of existence begins again, you automatically start to trust your soul and body rather than your spirit. You were so accustomed to living by your thoughts, feelings, and desires—by your soul, your psychological being—and by the demands of your body, that you soon lost track of the voice of the newly living spirit deep within you. It would seem that something needs to happen to your *soul* and *body* before your *spirit* can gain stronger control.

This "something" that needs to happen is that the Holy Spirit Who is living in your spirit needs to *flow out* to fill your soul and body. This is described in the Scripture in a variety of ways. Just as the experience of accepting Jesus is spoken of throughout the Bible in different ways, so a number of descriptions are given of the next experience: "baptism in (or with) [1] the Holy Spirit", "receiving the Holy Spirit", "Pentecost", "receiving power", the Holy Spirit to "come upon" or "fall upon" a person. All these are expressions of the same truth, viewed from different sides.

There is much difference of opinion over what terminology to use. We don't want to erect any verbal barriers for anyone, so, if using any one of these titles to refer to this second experience disturbs you, why not call it "experience X-2", or something like that? However, we feel on especially safe Scriptural grounds using the term "baptism in the Holy Spirit", since quite an impressive list of Biblical Persons so used it: God the Father (John 1:33), God the Son (Acts 1:5), and God the Holy Spirit, Who is, of course, the Inspirer of the Scriptures in which these expressions are found; there were also John the Baptist (Matt. 3:11, Mark 1:8, Luke 3:16, John 1:33), the four evangelists, Matthew, Mark, Luke, and John, in the places just cited, and the Apostle Peter (Acts 11:16). If you will read these references carefully, and compare them, you will see in each case it is not salvation that is spoken of, but a second experience.

This is called in the Scripture, "the baptism in the Holy Spirit", because it is a baptism, meaning a drenching, an over-

1. The Greek preposition *en*, used in this phrase, may be translated "in", or "with".

flowing, a saturating of your soul and body with the Holy Spirit. When the Bible speaks of Jesus "baptizing" in the Holy Spirit, we immediately visualize something external, somebody being put into something. However, the word *baptize* in Greek means to "completely suffuse"—it is used in classical Greek of a sunken, waterlogged ship—so it does not really make any difference whether Jesus immerses us in the Holy Spirit in an external sense of the word; whether he inundates us from outside; or whether Jesus causes the Spirit to rise and overflow from where He is living *inside* us, to suffuse our souls and bodies. Probably both pictures are true—He "comes upon us" both from outside and inside, but it is important to remember that the Holy Spirit is living in you, and that therefore it is from within that He can flood your soul and body. Jesus says:

"He that believeth on me . . . *out of his belly* shall flow rivers of living water [the Holy Spirit]" (John 7:38),[2] and the Amplified Bible says: "*Out of* his innermost being shall flow . . ." When we receive Jesus as Saviour, the Holy Spirit *comes in*, but as we continue to trust and believe Jesus, the Indwelling Spirit can *pour out* to inundate, or baptize, our soul and body, and refresh the world around.

This, too, is why again and again in Scripture the first normative evidence of this Pentecost experience is an *outpouring*:

"They were all filled with the Holy Ghost, and began to speak in other languages . . ." (Acts 2:4).

Some are puzzled by the term "receiving the Holy Spirit". A Christian may ask the question: "How can I *receive* the Holy Spirit when I already have Him living in me?" This expression can be understood easily if we remember that we are talking about a Person, not a thing or a quantity of something. Some have talked about the Holy Spirit in a quantitative way—as if

2. Italics ours.

you could receive *some* of the Holy Spirit at salvation, and some *more* at a later date. But if the Holy Spirit is a Person, which He is, then He is either living in you or He isn't.

We all know what it means to "receive" a person. Let us imagine the Brown household. It is 5 : 40 p.m., and Mr. Brown has just come home from work, and is taking a shower before supper. Mrs. Brown is putting the finishing touches on an especially nice meal, for the Browns have invited the Joneses over for dinner. Their guests are scheduled to arrive at 6 : 00 p.m., but alas, at 5 : 45 comes a ring at the doorbell. Mrs. Brown flutters a little—she hasn't finished the gravy; she has flour on the end of her nose; and her hair is a mess!

"Susie!" she calls to her daughter, "for goodness' sake will you go and let the Joneses in; give them the evening paper, or talk to them—I'm not ready for them yet!"

Just then the phone rings in the kitchen, and Mrs. Brown answers.

"Hello! Marie?" says the voice on the line. "This is Helen. Do you have the Joneses over there?"

"Yes," replies Mrs. Brown, "we do."

"Well, how are they?" says the voice of the caller.

"I really don't know," says Mrs. Brown, patiently. "I haven't *received* them yet. I'm still out here working in the kitchen."

"You'd better hurry and receive them," says Helen. "I happen to know they have some wonderful news, and that they have brought you some beautiful gifts!"

So Mrs. Brown hangs up the phone, quickly finishes her cooking, straightens her hair and powders her face, and then, together with her husband, receives her friends, hears the news they have, and accepts the gifts they have brought. The Person of the Holy Spirit has been living in your "house" ever since your new birth, but now you fully acknowledge His Presence and receive His gifts.

Let us sum up, then, by saying that the first experience of the Christian life, salvation, is the *incoming* of the Holy Spirit, through Jesus Christ, to give us new life, God's life, eternal life. The second experience, is the *receiving*, or making welcome of the Holy Spirit, so that Jesus can cause Him to pour out this new life from our spirits, to baptize our souls and bodies, and then the world around, with His refreshing and renewing power. "Out of his belly shall flow rivers of living water!" The word used here is *koilia*, which refers quite literally to the "physical body"; it is by means of the physical body and its speech and actions that we contact our environment and the people around us. The world is not going to be helped or challenged until it sees and hears and experiences Jesus' life flowing from us.

Imagine an irrigation canal in Southern California, or some other area that is normally arid most of the year. The canal is dry, and so are the fields around. All the vegetation is dried up and dead. Then the gates from the reservoir are opened, and the canal begins to fill with water. First of all the *canal* itself is refreshed! The cool flow of water carries away debris and slakes the dust. Next, grass and flowers begin to spring up along the banks, and the trees on either side of the canal become fresh and green. But it doesn't stop there; all the way along the canal, farmers open the gates and the life-giving water pours out into the fields to make the "desert blossom as the rose".

So with you and me. The reservoir, the well, is in us when we become Christians. Then, when we allow the indwelling living water of the Spirit to flow out into our souls and bodies, *we* are refreshed first. Our minds come alive in a new way to God's reality. We begin to think of Him, even dream of Him, with a new frequency and joy. Our emotions respond, and we begin to be happy in Him. Our will responds, and we begin to want to do what He wants. Our bodies respond, not only by feelings of well-being, but by actual renewed strength and health and youth. Then the living water begins to pour out to others, and they see the power and love of Jesus in His people. He is now able to use us to refresh the world around us.[3]

3. In the Episcopal, Lutheran, Orthodox, and Roman Catholic Churches the term "confirmation" is used of the traditional rite intended to confer this experience of the baptism in the Holy Ghost. "Confirm" literally means "to strengthen". The Episcopal Prayer Book says: "The Church provides the Laying on of Hands, or Confirmation, wherein . . . I receive the strengthening gifts of the Holy Spirit." This is made doubly clear by the selection from the Acts of the Apostles which is read at the confirmation service, namely, the story in Acts 8:14–17 of how Peter and John laid their hands on Philip's converts in Samaria so that they might "receive the Holy Ghost". Unfortunately, the rite of confirmation, like so many things, tends to become just a formal action, with no real results expected; but in spite of that, one hears from people who at the time of the bishop's laying on of hands were really set free in the Spirit in a new way. One lady in Louisiana said to Dennis:

"I'm so glad that you came down here to tell us about all this. Twenty years ago, when the bishop laid his hands on my head, I just filled up with Something, and I began to speak in a new language! I didn't know what it was, and neither did the bishop!" That great saint of the early Pentecostal movement, Smith Wigglesworth, tells in his memoirs how he was confirmed in the Anglican Church at the age of nine, and how he was filled with the joy and presence of the Lord for days, and could not understand why the other choir boys were not similarly inspired and changed! He also tells how, years later, the wife of an Anglican vicar laid her hands on his head and prayed for him to be baptized in the Holy Spirit, and at that time his experience was completed as he spoke in new languages and magnified God.

3
What Do the Scriptures Say?

This is the all-important question. No matter how cleverly we may work out our theories, if they don't agree with the Scriptures, they are unacceptable. What then was the work of the Holy Spirit among the early Christians in the New Testament?

First let us talk about Jesus Himself. If anyone was indwelt by the Holy Spirit it was the Lord Jesus. He was *conceived* by the Holy Spirit, that is, His physical birth was by the direct action of the Holy Spirit. He was the Incarnation of the Word of God. By the Holy Spirit's action, God's only Son, the Creative Word, Who was from all eternity with the Father, and by Whom the worlds were created, took upon Himself a human Soul and Body. When He did this, however, He set aside His power, that is, He temporarily accepted the limitations of natural humanity (Phil. 2: 7–8).[1] His human body, although perfect, was really and truly human, with all the limitations of a natural body. His Soul, His psychological being, although perfect, was subject to limitations, too. The Bible tells us that "Jesus increased in wisdom [in His Soul] and stature [in His Body], and in favour with God and man" (Luke 2: 52 KJV).

1. Literally: "He emptied Himself."

He subjected Himself to growth and development as a human child. The foolish stories in some of the Apocryphal "Gospels" about Jesus working fantastic miracles as a child—turning clay sparrows into live ones, striking His playmates dead and then bringing them to life again—are just that—foolish stories. The early believers recognized them as such and by the wisdom of the Holy Spirit kept them out of the approved Scriptures. Rather we see from the Scriptures that Jesus lived in Nazareth until He was thirty years old, and no one had any idea that He was God come in the Flesh. Even His mother Mary had only an inkling. How do we know this? Because when He did begin His ministry, His mother was amazed and worried about Him; and His own brothers and sisters did not believe in Him. The people of the village where He was brought up said:

"Who does He think He is? We know *Him*; He's the carpenter's son!" They were so indignant that they actually tried to kill Him (Matt. 13: 54–58; Luke 4: 16–30).

What was it that happened to Jesus between the time that He was living in the village of Nazareth, and functioning as the village carpenter (stonemason and blacksmith, too, probably), and the time when He suddenly went out and began to proclaim: "The Kingdom of Heaven has come near!" and to heal the sick, and cast out devils, and even raise the dead, in proof of His claim to come from God, and to be God's Messiah-King? The answer is plain enough: "He received the power of the Holy Spirit." He was born of the Holy Spirit from the start, but when He began His ministry at the age of thirty, the Holy Spirit came on Him in a new way. You can read in all four of the Gospels, how John the Baptist saw the Holy Spirit descend and remain on Jesus. Jesus was the Father's only begotten Son from all eternity, long before the crowd at Jordan heard the Voice of God as He spoke from Heaven acknowledging His Son. So also the Holy Spirit was in Jesus from the beginning of His life on earth, long before John the Baptist saw the Spirit like a Dove come down upon Him. Nevertheless, following this, the Spirit began to be manifested through Jesus with new power. His ministry began. The Spirit drove Him into the Wilderness to be tempted by the Devil, and after His victory there, we read: "Jesus returned *in the power of the Spirit* into Galilee; and there went out a fame of Him through all the region round about" (Luke 4:14 KJV). Why was the full manifestation of the Holy Spirit held back until this point? One reason was so that Jesus could lead a normal everyday life in Nazareth without being detected as a very special Person. The Father kept His Son concealed, so to speak, until He was ready to reveal Him to the world. It seems likely that the Devil himself was deceived by this. It was not until Jesus was revealed in the full power of the Spirit that Satan confronted him. We may see Herod's attempt on Jesus' life in his infancy as an earlier effort on Satan's part to get rid of the Son of God, but it really seems even more likely that the prince of darkness was not aware of Jesus until He was baptized in the Holy Spirit.

Another reason for the delay was in order that Jesus could show us by His example what was supposed to happen to *us*. The Baptizer in the Holy Spirit was Himself baptized in the Holy Spirit.

John the Baptist had been told by the Father that the One upon Whom he saw the Spirit descend and remain would be the One Who would baptize in the Holy Spirit (John 1:33). It may well be that this is why John said to Jesus: "I need to be baptized by You, and You are coming to me!" (Matt. 3:14). Although he said this before the actual descent of the Spirit upon Jesus, John could well have prophetically perceived that Jesus was to be the Baptizer in the Holy Spirit.

Baptism with water in the Name of the Father, Son and Holy Ghost, or in the Name of Jesus—both are used in the New

Testament—seems to have been universal in the early Church, as the "outward and visible sign" of the "inward and Spiritual grace" of salvation and new life in Christ. It is assumed that you who are reading this book and who accept Christ, will receive or have received baptism with water in the manner of the particular Christian fellowship to which you belong, and in accordance with your understanding of what the Scripture teaches about it. Notice clearly, however, that baptism with water is the outward sign of baptism into Jesus (Salvation) (I Cor. 12:13), but not the baptism *by* Jesus into the Holy Spirit (Pentecost) (Luke 3:16). Perhaps this is the reason that Jesus Himself did not baptize anyone with water during His ministry on earth, although He must have instructed his disciples to do so even before His crucifixion. John 4:1 says: "When therefore the Lord knew how the Pharisees had heard that Jesus made and baptized more disciples than John, (though Jesus Himself baptized not, but His disciples,) He left Judaea, and departed again into Galilee." Perhaps Jesus refrained from performing water baptism Himself in order to make it clear that He had another baptism to bring—that He was to baptize "with the Holy Ghost and with fire".

No doubt one of the reasons John's converts followed Jesus is that they heard that Jesus had another baptism to give them. They must have expected it to be a wonderful experience from the way John spoke about it, and that this experience would be just as clear and positive as their baptism with water had been. They were probably expecting it to happen at any time, but instead, as they followed Jesus, He did miracles, and healed the sick, was crucified, and resurrected from the dead, but still no one was baptized with the Holy Spirit!

After Jesus had died and risen from the dead, He appeared to His disciples the very evening after His resurrection, and conferred on them the *new life in the Spirit* which we talked about in the first chapter (John 20 : 22). The Holy Spirit came to live in them, bringing their spirits to life—they were "born again of the Spirit" just as you have been if you have accepted Jesus as Saviour. This new birth for us corresponds to the fact that Jesus was "conceived by the Holy Ghost", so your spirits are born again of the Holy Spirit. Jesus had not yet finally ascended to take His place "on high" with the Father, so He could not yet pour out the Holy Spirit "upon all flesh", but He could and did confer Him individually to come and dwell in His first chosen ones. He told them that there was a further experience for them, and that they were to wait for it. His final words to them at the Ascension were to remind them of this.

If you were given a chance to say some final words to your friends and family before departing from them for a long time, they would be well-chosen words, we may be sure! Jesus chose His final words well. His most important message had been "You must be born again", but now that His followers had received the new birth, He gave them the next important instruction: "Wait until you receive the Power!" (Luke 24 : 29).

"John baptized you with water," He said, "but you will be baptized with the Holy Ghost not many days hence" (Acts 1 : 5). The believer follows the pattern that Jesus has set. The new birth in the Spirit corresponds to Jesus' being conceived by the Holy Ghost. The believer is baptized with water just as Jesus was. After this, said Jesus, we are to expect to be baptized in the Holy Spirit, receiving the power of the Spirit just as He did.

So these believing, born-again followers of Jesus, 120 of them, waited, as He had told them. They were praising God, praying, going to the Temple; they even had a business meeting and an election! (Acts 1 : 15–26). We do not read, however, that they were telling anyone about Jesus. The power to do that effectively would come on the day of Pentecost.[2] Jesus had told them: "You will receive power, after the Holy Ghost is come upon you, and you will be witnesses of Me, both in Jerusalem, and in all Judaea, and in Samaria, and unto the uttermost parts of the earth" (Act 1:8). A "witness" is not just someone who sees something happen, but someone who is ready and willing to *say* he saw it happen! This is why our English word "martyr" is the Greek word for "witness"!

Ten days after Jesus had left them to return to the Father, on the Feast of Pentecost, the Feast of the First-Fruits, the Power came, with the sound of a "rushing mighty wind", with flames like fire, and the disciples were all "filled with the Holy Ghost and began to speak with other tongues, as the Spirit gave them utterance" (Acts 2:4 KJV). It is important to remember that the Holy Spirit *was already living in them*, ever since Jesus had conferred on them new life in the Spirit on the evening of the resurrection. This new life was the Holy Spirit joined to their spirits. "He that is joined unto the Lord is one Spirit" (I Cor. 6:17 KJV), says Paul, and he also says: "If any man have not the Spirit of Christ, he is none of his" (Rom. 8:9 KJV). Now, on the Feast of Pentecost, the Father, through the ascended Lord Jesus at His right hand, shed forth the Holy Spirit from "on high", *upon all flesh*; that is, the new birth, new life in Christ, is now available to all who call upon Him. The Holy Spirit has come. God has made Himself available to man in a new way. "The Kingdom of Heaven has come near!" But, as the Holy Spirit was poured out upon the whole human

---

2. Without question there are Christians who do not claim a "Pentecost experience" yet witness effectively; but how much more effective they could be if they received the full release of the Spirit. The most characteristic evidence of the revival of Pentecost is a tremendous increase in Christian witness, resulting in a worldwide spiritual renewal that has been gaining momentum continuously for nearly a hundred years.

race, so He was stirred *within* those first followers—He had been dwelling in *them* ever since Jesus had specially conferred Him on the evening after the Resurrection—and He began to pour forth from them in mighty manifestations of power. He overwhelmed them—this is what the Scripture means when it says He "fell upon them", or "came upon them"—baptizing their souls and bodies in the power and glory that was already dwelling in their spirits. This second experience, the *outpouring* of the Holy Spirit, would happen to others who received Jesus, too, but here again the first chosen followers, the one-hundred-and-twenty, were allowed to receive first. He overflowed from them out into the world around, inspiring them to praise and glorify God, not only in their own tongues, but in new languages, and in so doing, tamed their tongues to His use, freed their spirits, renewed their minds, refreshed their bodies, and brought power to witness. A great crowd gathered, baffled by the sound of these Galileans speaking the praises of . God in languages of far-off countries. The listeners were not foreigners, but devout Jews from all over the world (Acts 2 : 5). They had come "home" for the great Feast Day. They were amazed to hear these humble people praising God in languages they knew they could not have learned, languages of the countries where the listeners had been brought up, and other tongues which they did not recognize, "tongues of men and of angels" (I Cor. 13 : 1 KJV).

Some jeered, and said: "They're just drunk, that's all!" but Peter responded: "No, they're not drunk! After all, it's only nine o'clock in the morning! But *this is that* which was prophesied by Joel: . . . In the last days, says God, I will pour out of My Spirit upon all flesh" (Acts 2 : 13-17). So convincing were the signs, that three thousand of those "devout men" accepted Jesus as Messiah, repented of their sins, were baptized, and themselves received the gift of the Holy Ghost that day.

It's funny that even some outstanding Bible scholars will say: "Pentecost happened only once", when very clearly there is a series of "Pentecosts" in the New Testament. The next one takes place in Samaria. The Samaritans were the remnant of the Israelite Northern Kingdom. They and the Jews, the people of the Southern Judaean Kingdom, were still at loggerheads. They hated one another heartily. In Acts 8, however, we read how Philip—not the Apostle, but one of the seven men appointed to help the apostles (Acts 6 : 1–6)—had gone to Samaria, and was telling the Samaritans about Jesus. It was unlikely territory, but the Samaritans listened to Philip, although he was a Jew proclaiming a Jewish Messiah, because they saw him doing the works of power that Jesus had done, and they heard him speaking with authority, just as Jesus had spoken. The Holy Spirit in Philip impressed the Samaritans with the truth and reality of what he was saying, and they accepted Jesus, were born again of the Spirit, and baptized with water (Acts 8 : 5–12).

When the apostles at Jerusalem heard of this new breakthrough in Samaria, they sent Peter and John to see what was taking place. As soon as these two arrived, they saw something lacking. The Holy Spirit wasn't "falling upon" or overwhelming these new believers. Peter and John didn't doubt that the Samaritans had been born again of the Spirit, but they were concerned that the Spirit had not yet "fallen upon" or overwhelmed them; so they "laid . . . their hands on them, and they received the Holy Ghost" (Acts 8 : 14–17 KJV). Notice that Peter and John expected that the Holy Ghost would already have "fallen upon" the Samaritan converts. As a matter of fact, this is the first time we are told of any laying on of hands to receive the Holy Spirit. We are not told of any laying on of hands for the 3000 converted at Pentecost, and of course the first 120 had no laying on of hands. Later in this same chapter, we don't read of Philip laying hands on the Ethiopian Eunuch (Acts 8 : 27–40). We may presume that often the overwhelming or baptism of the Holy Spirit followed spontaneously after salvation, just as it did later to Cornelius at Caesarea Philippi (Acts 10 : 44). But here Peter and John felt that a laying on of hands was necessary to encourage the Samaritans to receive the Holy Spirit. The Holy Spirit was already indwelling these Samaritan believers. He was ready to inundate their souls and bodies, to baptize, to overflow, but they had to respond, to receive. As soon as they did, the Holy Spirit began to pour out from them just as He had with the first believers on the Day of Pentecost. Undoubtedly they gave the same sign, speaking in new languages and glorifying God. The Scripture does not specifically say so, but the major commentators agree that this is what happened. The solid and conservative Matthew Henry says, for example:

"It is said (v. 16), The Holy Ghost was as yet fallen upon none of them, in those extraordinary powers which were conveyed by the descent of the Spirit upon the day of pentecost. They were none of them endued with the gift of tongues, which seems then to have been the most usual immediate effect of the pouring out of the Spirit. . . . This was both an eminent sign to those that believed not, and of excellent service to those that did. This, and other such gifts, they had not, only they were baptized in the name of the Lord Jesus, and so engaged in him and interested in him, which was necessary to salvation, and in this they had joy and satisfaction (v. 8) though they could not speak with tongues. . . .

"They laid their hands on them, to signify that their prayers were answered, and that the gift of the Holy Ghost was conferred upon them; for, upon the use of this sign, they received the Holy Ghost, and spoke with tongues." [3]

One observer, at any rate, was deeply impressed: Simon Magus, the sorcerer, who had been deceiving the people of Samaria with his black magic for many years. He rushed up to Peter with gold in his hand, and said:

"Look here, I'll make you rich, if you'll just tell me how you did that! Give me the power, so that when I lay hands on someone he will receive this Holy Ghost!" (Acts 8: 18–24). Peter of course, told Simon off very firmly—the Gift of God was not to be bought for money—but still the question remains: "What did Simon see?"

On this occasion it says that by "the laying on of the apostles' hand the Holy Ghost was given" (Acts 8: 18 KJV) and this has led some to claim that the Holy Spirit was *distributed* by the apostles: the Samaritans couldn't receive the Holy Spirit until Peter and John arrived from Jerusalem to "give" Him, since Philips, who was not an apostle, could not do so. This, however, does not match the rest of Scripture. We have already pointed out that in some cases of receiving the Holy Spirit we hear of no laying on of hands at all.

Also when Paul received the Holy Spirit, although he did have hands laid on him, they were the hands of an otherwise unknown man of whom the Scripture says only: "There was a certain disciple ... named Ananias" (Act 9: 10 KJV). Although the Scripture does not record at this place that Paul spoke in tongues, we know that he did so from I Corinthians 14: 18 (RSV): "I thank God I speak in tongues more than you all."

The next "Pentecost" in the Acts of the Apostles took place in the town of Caesarea Philippi which was a centre of the Roman occupation forces. Here a devout Roman officer named

3. Matthew Henry, *Commentary on the Whole Bible* (New York: Revell), VI, 100.

Cornelius, who believed in God with all his heart, was told by an angel to send and ask Peter, who was staying at Joppa, an ultra-Jewish community on the seacoast, to come and tell him what he ought to do (Acts 10:6).

Peter naturally would not have wanted to go to tell Roman soldiers about Jesus, and the baptism in the Spirit. Up to this point it was thought that the new birth and the baptism in the Holy Spirit were for Jewish believers only. If a Gentile, a non-Jew, wanted to receive Christ and the Holy Spirit, he must first become a Jew—and come under all the difficult requirements of the Jewish Law. The Holy Spirit, however, made it very clear to Peter, by a series of visions, and by direct instructions, that he was to go with the Romans when they invited him, and he did (Acts 10:9–23). To Peter's amazement, when he arrived at Cornelius' house, and began to tell the Romans gathered there about Jesus, they immediately responded. The first thing Peter and his companions who had come with him saw and heard was these Romans, filled with joy, speaking in tongues, and magnifying God! (Acts 10:24–48). They had opened their hearts to Jesus, He had given them new life in the Spirit, and they immediately allowed that new life to fill them and overflow. Peter and his friends were amazed, but recognized right away that God was "pouring out His Spirit on the Gentiles", first in salvation and next in the baptism in the Holy Spirit. So Peter said: "Who can hinder us from baptizing these people with water, since they have received the Holy Ghost just as we did?" (Acts 10:47). Defending himself when they returned to Jersusalem against the criticism levelled at him for baptizing non-Jews, Peter said:

"In my beginning to speak to them (the Romans), the Holy Ghost overwhelmed them, even as with us at the beginning. And I remembered the word of the Lord, how He said 'John indeed baptized with water, but you shall be baptized with the

Holy Spirit!' If then God gave to them the like gift as also to us, who believed on the Lord Jesus, who was I to be able to withstand God?" (Acts 11:15-17).

Notice Peter speaks of the gift of the Holy Spirit given to *those who believed*, which makes it clear that the Romans first *believed*, and then the Spirit "fell upon" or overwhelmed them.

We must wait thirty years for the next example in the Acts of a "Pentecost". Perhaps the Holy Spirit left just such a gap in order to show that these things did not die out. Paul is making his second visit to Ephesus, when he is greeted by a group of twelve men who claimed to be disciples. He immediately misses something in them, for he asks them:

"Didn't you receive the Holy Ghost since you believed?" (Acts 19:2). Again we see that the experience of salvation was expected to be followed by the baptism in the Spirit, but that the early Christians recognized that there *could* be a delay—otherwise why would Paul have bothered to ask the question? Rather, he would have questioned their *salvation*.

"We haven't even heard if there *is* a Holy Spirit!" (Acts 19:2), replied the Ephesians. Upon investigating further, Paul found that they didn't even know about Jesus, so he led them to accept Jesus, baptized them with water, and then we read: "When Paul had laid his hands upon them, the Holy Ghost came on them, and they spoke with tongues, and prophesied" (Acts 19:6). Here again the distinction is clear. They received Christ, were baptized with water as the outward sign; then, encouraged by Paul's laying on of hands, they responded to the Holy Spirit Who had come to live in them, and began to pour out the praise of God in new languages.

We have tried to show in this chapter the scriptural pattern of what the writer of the Book of Hebrews calls the "doctrine of *baptisms*". The Apostle Paul, in Ephesians 4:5 says there is "one Lord, one faith, one baptism", yet it is clear that in the

New Testament this "one baptism" divides into three. In I Corinthians 12:13, Paul says: "In one Spirit we were all baptized into one Body . . . and were all made to drink into one Spirit." This refers to the spiritual baptism into Christ which takes place as soon as Jesus is received as Saviour. This was followed by the baptism with the Holy Spirit, in which the now indwelling Holy Spirit poured forth to manifest Jesus to the world through the life of the believer. Either before or after the baptism with the Holy Spirit there was the outward sign of baptism with water—symbolic of the inner cleansing by the Blood of Jesus, the death of the "old man", and the resurrection to new life in Christ.[4] To which of these three baptisms is Paul referring as the "one baptism"?

An artist can look at a picture he has been painting in different ways. He may look to make sure is is a balanced composition; he may look again to check lighting effects of the sunlight on the water and the trees; again he may view it from a different point of view as he checks perspective. We have been looking at the different aspects of God's saving work in man. It is necessary to look at these three experiences—salvation, water baptism, and Pentecost—separately, because in our inhibited way of living they have become separated, and the full picture has been lost. In the early church, the three experiences in each life occurred closely together—but this has not often been the case today.

Having viewed the picture in different ways during our study, we now need to step back and see it as a whole. Paul says there is "One Lord"—yet the Godhead is Three in One: Father, Son, and Holy Ghost. Man is one, yet he is a trinity of

---

4. The normative pattern in the New Testament was to accept Jesus, receive water baptism, and be baptized with the Holy Spirit. However, in two of the five accounts in Acts, they accepted Jesus, were baptized with the Holy Spirit, and then baptized with water.

body, soul, and spirit. The Body of Christ on earth is one, yet composed of many members. So when Paul speaks of "one baptism", it would seem he is speaking of the composite action by which Jesus Christ comes to live in us, the outward sign by which this action is sealed, and the overflow of the Holy Spirit through us to minister to the lost world.

We recommend to you that, even though you may have difficulty with these things in your mind, you come and experience God's reality in the fullness of the Spirit. Intellectual understanding will come later. As the great St. Augustine of Hippo put it: *"Credo ut intelligam"*, that is, "I believe in order that I may understand".

4
Preparing to Receive the Baptism in the Holy Spirit

The Holy Spirit comes to live in us when we receive Jesus, and are born again of the Spirit. The baptism in the Holy Spirit is the *pouring out* of the Spirit. We cannot very well expect Him to pour out through us until He is living in us, so before we ask to be baptized in the Holy Spirit, we must first be sure that we have indeed received the Lord Jesus as Saviour, and invited Him to live in us by His Spirit.

Jesus is the Way to God. There isn't any other. He is the only Way by which we can know God or receive His life. Jesus Christ is fully and truly God and fully and truly Man. This is the meaning of the Incarnation—God really and truly became Man in the womb of the Virgin Mary. Thus Jesus is the Meeting-Point of God and Man.

There are other philosophies and religions that attempt to tell about God, and some of the things they say are true, but if you want God Himself to come to you and live in you, you can *meet* Him only through Jesus Christ. *Whatever you do, do not pray to be "baptized in the Holy Spirit" unless you have received Jesus Christ as your Saviour personally, or you may get into serious spiritual confusion.*

Someone will usually say at this point:

"But what about people who have never heard of Jesus? What about the members of other cultures and other religions? Will they all be lost because they have never heard?" We can only reply:

1. No one will be in the Kingdom of Heaven except through Jesus Christ.

2. For those born since Jesus Christ came to this world, the decision is made in this present life. *There is no opportunity to accept Christ after death* (Heb. 9 : 27).

3. God has ways of reaching people in this life that we know nothing about. We can hope that God is able in some way to offer the opportunity to know Jesus to all who would accept Him if they did meet Him. We know that God wants everyone to come to Him, and takes no "pleasure in the death of a sinner" (Ezek. 33 : 11). God, however, although He is all-powerful and all-knowing, has limited Himself in His dealings with men, by *really* giving us free will.

4. The real answer to the person who feels it would be terrible for any human being not to have the opportunity to know Jesus, is that Jesus was concerned about this, too, and gave the answer: "Go all over the world and tell everybody!" (Mark 16 : 5).

Christians have so sadly failed to do this (one responsible survey recently showed that ninety-five percent of all Christians have never told anyone else about the Saviour) that many intelligent and spiritually hungry people are looking for answers in the wrong places. Many have become involved with the beliefs usually called the "cults", while others are investigating the "occult".

In general, the term "cult" is used of religious groups that teach some other way to God than Jesus Christ, and/or whose teachings add to, subtract from, or contradict those of the Holy Scriptures. Most cults teach that Jesus Christ is something less than personally God. Some cults have been around for a long time, and have acquired a lot of status, often being regarded as "churches", but that does not change their situation; it just makes them more dangerous.

We are not going to try to deal with the cults by name; it is wrong *teachings* we are concerned about, not personalities, names, or titles. Adherents of the cults are often fine and well-meaning people, devoted zealously to their cause, for which they are ready to make real sacrifices. Their human attitudes and behaviour are sometimes better than those of many who claim to be orthodox believers.

The first such erroneous teaching we will name is that of several of the best-known cults; we may call it "mind-science". This teaches that God is "universal mind", that "mind" is the only reality, and that we will be "saved" by getting our *thinking* straightened out. Thoughts and ideas are the only real things, they say; matter is not real; sickness is not real; sin is not real; these things are just "error of mortal mind". Jesus of Nazareth, they say, was not a divine Person; He was a human being Who was greatly filled with the "Christ Spirit". We, too, can be filled with the "Christ Spirit" and be like Jesus. (The "Christ Spirit" turns out to be a kind of generalized spirit of love and goodwill between persons.) Jesus is called the "Way-Shower", instead of the Way. Obviously there is no need for forgiveness of sins, just corrected thinking. There is no need for healing, since sickness is not real, and will disappear as soon as the wrong thoughts are corrected.[1]

1. The question is often asked whether the "healings" that allegedly take place as a result of this philosophy are "Christian" healings. The answer is obvious. Christians accept the fact that

One of the strongest of these "mind-science" groups, that puts out a great deal of prayer literature, and has a strong following among church people, also teaches *reincarnation*. This false teaching is also being popularized very widely by another recent cult organized around the doings of a skilful clairvoyant, who claimed a strong ability to diagnose disease by psychic means. *Reincarnation* is the belief that we are born over and over again in other bodies on this earth to continue our spiritual growth, and to expiate our sins. Untold thousands are being deceived by this teaching, again many of them being from the "old-line" churches.

There is no place for a belief in reincarnation among Christians. It is totally unbiblical and anti-Christian. The Scripture says: "It is given to all men *once* to die, and after that the judgment" (Heb. 9:27).

The teaching of the Scripture is that in God's Kingdom we shall meet and know one another, happy forever in a fellowship never again to be broken. For instance, when I meet my mother in heaven, is it to be as someone else, after fifty or so "reincarnations"? How ridiculous!

The teaching of reincarnation is usually accompanied by the so-called law of karma, which says we must be born over and over again to expiate our sins, and to work out our own salvation. It says our troubles in this life are caused by our sins of past lives; sin can be eliminated only by our living over again

---

people get sick. Sickness is the work of Satan. Jesus Christ cures sickness. That is Christian healing, and it leads people to Jesus as Saviour, not only of their bodies, but of their souls and spirits. The "mind-science" groups, on the other hand, believe the person is not sick at all, but just has wrong thoughts. Once these thoughts are corrected, the apparent illness disappears. This has nothing whatsoever to do with Jesus Christ. There was no disease, so there could have been no healing. There certainly was not witness to the Saviourhood of Jesus, nor are people led to acceptance of Jesus as Lord.

and receiving punishment for it. This is a million miles from the good news that Jesus died on the cross to take away our sins.

Another powerful cult, often accepted as a true variety of Christianity, claims to be the only true "church", that all others are false. It teaches that God the Father was, and is, a man, a being of "flesh and bone", who became an "almighty god". It also teaches that men, if they will keep the teachings of the cult, can become "almighty gods", and have their own planets to rule, which they will people with their "spirit children" that they have begotten by their many "spirit wives"! Rather obviously, one of the first requirements for full salvation in this cult is that you get married! Jesus died on the cross, this group tell us, to bring all men to the point where they could save themselves by keeping the teachings of this particular cult. This group, like others, teaches that the Bible is not sufficient to show the way of salvation; it must be supplemented by other books and writings. In fact, the most important teachings of this cult are not drawn from the Bible at all, but from their special books—one of which was supposedly discovered written on "golden plates" and buried, and others written by "prophets" through the years. Many people are drawn to this cult because of a strong social welfare emphasis.

Yet another of the stronger cults, one that distributes its literature on the street corners, and assiduously calls at homes offering "Bible study", denies the threefold nature of God (the Trinity), saying that Jesus was not God come in the flesh, but a kind of "in-between" being, *a* god. This group, like others, has its own translation of the Scriptures, slanted to support its own peculiar doctrines.

Most cults deny the bodily resurrection of Jesus. They say His "resurrection" was the appearance of His "spirit" only. This, of course, is in flat contradiction to Jesus' own statement on the evening of the resurrection when He appeared to His friends: "Touch me and see that it is I Myself! A spirit doesn't have flesh and bones, as you see that I do!" (Luke 24:39).

The cults would naturally deny the real, physical "second coming" of Jesus to the earth.

Another kind of cult is the "eclectic". This teaches that we must accept the "good" in all religions; that Jesus of Nazareth was just one among many "great teachers". Along with this often goes the claim that another "great teacher" has arisen to take Jesus' place. The basic error here is the idea that religion is a "search for truth", and that Jesus was just one among many "teachers of truth". This is the teaching of most "comparative religion" courses in our colleges and universities.) Christianity, however, is not a search for abstract and metaphysical "truth", but an entering into a new relationship with God: new life. Christianity teaches that God is reaching down to man: "The Son of Man is come to seek and to save that which was lost" (Luke 19:10).

You can easily see, from what we have said so far, that the cults either deny that Jesus is divine at all (except in the sense that "all men are divine", and Jesus may be a little ahead of the rest!), or they deny that He is unique—there are other saviours, too. They deny His resurrection, or spiritualize it. They emphasize His role as a "great teacher". They certainly will have nothing to say about the Blood of Jesus washing away our sins.[2] No matter how ethical or moral the teaching

---

2. The cults will sometimes talk about the "Blood of Jesus", but not as a remedy for sin. They will pick up such phrases as "power in the Blood", but to them it means an occult power that can *do* things for them.

The "power of the Blood of Jesus" is not a generalized spiritual "power", but the power to wash away sin. Since the cults do not usually believe in sin, they are not likely to be interested in this!

may be, no matter how loving and beautiful and attractive, no matter how logical, if it does not present Jesus as the divine Son of God become flesh, dying on the cross and shedding His Blood for the forgiveness of sins, rising again physically from the dead, you may be sure that you are dealing with a false cult. If you find much emphasis on the teachings of Jesus, but little on His Person, you may be sure you are dealing with a false cult.

Christianity is not founded on the *teachings* of Jesus, but on the Person of Jesus. It isn't what He taught, but Who He is, that matters most. To quote a popular proverb: "It isn't *what* you know, but *whom* you know, that makes the difference"! Also, if Jesus is hailed as just a "great teacher", what can we do with His own claims to be God, and the Son of God? [3] If His claim is false, He is either not telling the truth, or He is mistaken . . . neither would be in keeping with the role of a "great teacher"!

Usually a cult centres on a strong leader, for whom often is claimed a supernatural authority and power. Sometimes this leader is asserted to be a "messiah" or "avatar of the divine", and sometimes to be literally and personally "god".

Many of the cults draw ideas directly from the pagan religions—Buddhism, and Hinduism, for example. We have mentioned reincarnation, which is in the very fibre of these religions, but there is also the idea of "pantheism"—that God *is* everything: the creation *is* God. God is the good and the bad, the high and the low, the male and the female, love and hate, life and death, the rose and the rattlesnake. [4] There can be

3. For example: Mark 14:61–64; John 5:18, 23, 26, 39; 6:33–35, 38, 46–51; 8:58; 20:28–29.
4. The devil delights in confusion. In general whenever you have a confusion of thinking or definition, you should suspect that the enemy is at work somewhere. Where light is called darkness, up is called down, male confused with female, etc., you may well suspect

no real differentiation between good and evil, for God not only creates both, they say, but He *is* both. The "fulfilment" for these religions is not a personal fulfilment in God, but an utter loss of the person into the "all", or into the nothingness of "Nirvana".[5]

These pagan religions themselves have been experiencing a revival, not only in the Orient, but in the United States. Even the militant faith of Mohammed is being adopted, in a somewhat modified form, by the adherents of some of the "militant" groups.

Some people who are not involved in any particular cult will tell you that they are interested in "metaphysics", and that they are "seekers after truth". Metaphysics is that branch of philosophy which is man's attempt to reach into the unknown. It is understandable that a person who has not yet met God would want to use his inquiring mind to speculate about what's "out there", but this kind of speculation often leads the person directly into some cultic or strange teaching. The metaphysi-

---

that you are dealing with false doctrine. For example, some of the cults speak of the "father-mother god". Several of the false teachers today are saying that Adam, the original human being, was both male and female, and that these two aspects became separated. This usually goes on into a doctrine of "soul mating": everyone has a male or female somewhere who is his or her "other half". This kind of thinking opens the door wide to all kinds of abuses, tragedies, and perversities.

5. Jesus' command that a man should "deny himself" has often been identified with this Hindu-Buddhist concept of self-loss. The whole content of the Holy Scripture is against this interpretation. The Scriptures tell us that God desires us to have fellowship and communion with Him, to be His children, to enjoy Him, even to be His *friends*. All this must mean not loss of identity, but a heightening of identity in Christ. The oriental religions solve the problem of the self by getting rid of it; they solve the problem of life by getting out of it. Christianity directs us to get rid of the *false* self, the "old man", in order that our true nature, the new creature in Christ, can come to fulfilment.

cian confuses the soul and the spirit, thinking that the spiritual is an aspect of the psychological, and that the spirit is really the "deep unconscious", or something of that sort.[6] "Canst thou by searching find out God?" ask the Scriptures, and the answer is "No, not by intellectual and philosophical searching can you find God." You can only seek God by your "heart", that is, by your inner hunger to meet Him, the personal God, not a set of abstract principles. People say: "I'm seeking the truth," but Jesus says: "*I* am the Truth!"

Metaphysics, the attempt of the *mind* to come into contact with God directly, instead of through the spirit, may easily lead a person into the most dangerous area of all, the area of the psychic or occult. When Satan moved in and took over this world after the fall of man, he created a counterfeit spiritual realm, and any human being who tries to find God, or to come into contact with God, or to influence God, by his own psychological efforts, by thinking, willing, or feeling, is likely to come into contact with Satan's "spiritual" world which is more accurately termed the "psychic" world. Today, psychic and occult ideas and practices are flooding the scene, and being accepted

6. Even men of undoubtedly orthodox belief get into trouble when they try to be "metaphysical" and appeal to the so-called intellectual. The before-mentioned identification of the soul with the conscious mind, and the spirit with the "unconscious" or "subliminal" mind, is a good example of this. This identification is quite false, and yet it appeals to the metaphysician, because he desires to make everything understandable and accountable to the intellect, so that all must ultimately be some aspect of "mind", and thus controllable by man's mind and will. Typically, the metaphysically minded person, confronted by God answering prayer, or healing the sick, will say:

"This is taking place in obedience to a 'higher law'." The implication of this is that some day *man* will understand and use that "higher law". Christian healing and answered prayer is not the result of obedience to an imagined "higher law", but the work of a sovereign and omnipotent God, Who is subject to no law except His own. All so-called law is simply a description of the way God chooses to do things, in accord with His own Nature.

by untold thousands of people, many of whom are "good members" of churches. In fact those very people who are the most determined to "find out" about God, in this way are the very ones most likely to be victimized.

We may sum up the "occult" or "psychic" beliefs as follows:

1. *Precognition* or *"fortune-telling"*. The idea that a human being can validly foretell the future by means of visions, crystal balls, playing cards, palm reading, ouija boards,[7] meditations, drugs, etc. Lurking behind this concept of "precognition" is the idea of a fixed "fate", an unchanging future that is already laid out and cannot be changed. This is in itself a totally unscriptural notion. Christians don't believe in "fate" or "destiny",

---

7. We feel led to give special "dishonourable mention" to the ouija board. This little gadget is a polished board with the alphabet imprinted on it, and numbers from one to ten, with the words "yes" and "no". Over this board slides a little heart-shaped piece of wood, with a felt backing, called a "planchette". The person or persons using the board place their hands on the planchette, and it moves to spell out messages by indicating the letters of the alphabet. Again, this device is treated like a game, but it is not a game. It works, and can bring the users under deep bondage and oppression of the enemy. Sadly, it is sold every year by the millions as a game for children. If you have a ouija board in your home, burn it immediately, claim the protection of the Blood of Jesus, and ask the Holy Spirit to drive out whatever evil has been let in by the use of the board. Be very careful where and what your children are involved in when they visit other homes. Many young people's and even children's parties these days involve some kind of occult or psychic game or activity. Many a "slumber party" ends up as an amateur seance, or with the ouija board being brought out. We have heard of cases where teachers encourage their students to bring a ouija board to class with them and use it. We have even heard of cases where a Sunday-school teacher did the same thing! Explain these things to your children, so that they will be intelligently warned. Remember that their best protection, of course, is that they have met the Lord Jesus and accepted Him as their own Saviour, and have received the baptism in the Holy Spirit. Until they have received the Holy Spirit, most Christians are unaware of the danger of such things, which makes your task more awkward, but God will give you wisdom.

but in a living God, Who guides all things. God is "the Eternal" —meaning the "ageless" or timeless—outside of time. Time is His *creation*. God knows the future, not because He *foresees* it, but because He *sees* it; He is already *there*, just as He is in the present and the past. He gave His Name to Moses as "I AM". The future is dependent on the free actions of free beings, and of God. If Satan is able to deceive people into thinking they can know the future, he can also make them believe that "what will be, will be", and adopt a fatalistic attitude towards life. The strange contradiction is that actually people want to know the future in order to try to change it; yet if the future were a fixed "fate", it would be useless to try to change or avoid it!

Fortune-telling or precognition is often confused with Biblical *prophecy*. One of the most popular fortune-tellers of our day, a woman whose life is the subject of a best-selling book, has been consulted for guidance by high government officials. Her skill with a crystal ball and the other paraphernalia of fortune-telling has made headlines, and she is hailed even by some presumably Christian leaders as a "prophet in the Old Testament tradition", in spite of the obviously occult nature of her activities. The fact is that fortune-telling is strongly condemned and forbidden in the Bible (Deut. 18: 10–13). Biblical prophecy is not *fore*telling, but *forth*telling. The fortune-teller says: "I have the power to peer into the future, and I will tell you what I see!" The Biblical prophet says: "I was talking to God, and *He* told me to tell you . . . !" If a prophet of God foretells the future, he does so because God has chosen to share with him something that He, God, is going to do. There is usually a condition: "If you don't do such-and-such, I will do such-and-such." The scriptural prophet claims no special powers of precognition; he claims that God has spoken to him.

2. *Extrasensory perception: telepathy, clairvoyance,* etc. *Telepathy* or *mind reading* is the idea that a human being can

detect and read the thoughts of another person, or can project his own thoughts to another person.

Not long ago, in Montreal, Canada, Dennis chatted with a young lady who was very active in Christian work—a "fundamental" believer.

"I'm studying telepathy," she said, a little defiantly. "Why do you say it's wrong? There's nothing about it in the Bible!"

"You mean you're learning to read minds?" he inquired.

She nodded her head.

"Tell me," he said. "After you have learned to read minds, how long will your marriage last?" She looked startled, and he followed his advantage: "How many friends will you have, when they know you can read their minds?"

"I see what you mean," she said slowly.

Telepathy or mind reading is one of the psychic practices that is forbidden by God. Nothing could more quickly destroy human community and fellowship than the supposed ability to read another person's thoughts.

Clairvoyance is the idea that a human being can obtain information from beyond his physical senses by "occult" or psychic means.

As we mentioned above, clairvoyance has gained a good deal of publicity lately through the rise of a new cult that centres on the life and doings of a famous clairvoyant. This man claimed to be able to diagnose diseases and prescribe cures by means of his occult powers.

So-called water witching, or dowsing, must be included in this category. This refers to the use of a forked stick, or similar device, that allegedly bends down to indicate the presence of water, or of other things. (There is a report that men in the armed forces overseas are being taught the technique of "dowsing" for the location of land mines!). Those who do this are rarely trying to engage in psychic or occult practices, but think of it as the utilizing of some obscure "scientific" principle, e.g., "rays". It is, however, a subtle form of clairvoyance, and like other psychic practices, will bring oppression to the people who do it. Some well-diggers or drillers will not work on a "witched" well, experience having taught them that trouble usually follows when water is located in this way. The very name "water witching" shows recognition of the true nature of this practice.

Another popular parlour game, that is really clairvoyance, is the "pendulum," in which an object on a string or chain is hung over a person's hand, and questions are asked. The swinging of the pendulum allegedly indicates the answers. This could also be categorized as a fortune-telling device. It should be left alone, and if you have engaged in any such practice, pray to renounce it, and cast out any spirit of oppression associated with it.

Satan, our spiritual enemy, would love to have us try to learn to do these things. Actually, it is likely that there is no such power, but that all so-called extrasensory perception (ESP) is the direct action of the powers of darkness—Satan and his angels and demons—bringing the information to the person who is foolish enough to seek it. If you attempt to read someone's mind, or to foresee the future, or to gain information from a distance by clairvoyance, Satan is overjoyed. He has access to the information that you are seeking, and he can bring it to your mind, knowing that you will think that you have acquired the power to do it yourself. This way he accomplishes several things: (a) He causes you to become more proud and self-centred, and even though you may be "doing good" with your supposed abilities, you yourself are becoming more and more self-important; (b) He is setting you, and all who are believing you, up for a mighty letdown. In Shakespeare's *Macbeth*, Banquo says, referring to Macbeth's experience with the three witches:

" 'Tis strange, yet oftentimes the instruments of darkness tell us truths. Win us with honest trifles, to betray us in the deepest consequence!"[8]

3 *Astrology*. The belief that the stars, planets, sun, and moon have a mysterious influence over human beings, establishing their personalities and characteristics, and affecting the events of their lives. The advertising market today is flooded with "astrological" gobbledygook. One soda-pop company is actually offering "computerized" horoscopes! The popular singers croon about the "Age of Aquarius". Young people are encouraged to select their wives or husbands by their astrological sign, and there are actual cases of marriages breaking up and the parties marrying other people whose horoscopes are more favourable! Many people regard astrology as a kind of game, and read their daily horoscope "just for fun". It is far from a laughing matter, however, for astrology is really a carefully concealed form of idol worship—what the Bible calls the "worship of the hosts of heaven". It ascribes personality and power to the heavenly bodies, often under the very names of the ancient gods and goddesses who were and are themselves fallen angels who have been working for the destruction of mankind for millennia. You can read your horoscope day after day and treat it as a joke, but the day will come when it will get your attention by coming true, or working out, causing you to take it a little more seriously. It will not be long—if you are as unfortunate as many have been—before you are reduced to almost total dependence on the little column in the paper, being terrified to leave the house until the daily paper arrives! Leave astrology *alone!*

The Bible says that God put the stars and the other celestial bodies in the sky for "signs", and sometimes this will be quoted to you as an excuse for believing in astrology. But astrology does not claim that these things are just "signs"—which they

8. *Macbeth*, Act 1, scene 3.

are—but that they have power to influence human lives.[9]

4. *Techniques of so-called mind expansion* by *drugs, hypnotism, transcendental meditation,* etc. The idea here is that the mind can be opened to receive a wider understanding of the nature of things by these methods. What actually happens is that the mind is rendered passive and vulnerable to the enemy, who is only too glad to provide pretty lights while he is taking the opportunity to implant his own evil influences. It is no coincidence that the so-called hippie culture, based on drug use, is directly associated with occult practices of all kinds, and is also associated with many kinds of degrading and degenerate activity, especially sexual promiscuity and perversity. Satan loves to mock and ridicule mankind, and surely nothing could be more of a mockery of the beauty and fittingness of man as God made him, or woman as God made her, than the ridiculous outfit of the typical "hippie"—the effort on the part of the male

9. Do not confuse astrology with astronomy. Astronomy is the scientific study of the heavens, naming and identifying objects in outer space, and trying to understand their nature.

Another confusion arises from the fact that the Bible clearly says that God put these objects in the heavens for "signs" (Gen. 1:14). It is not wrong, therefore, to believe that God may use unusual activity or manifestations in the heavens to convey a message to man. The Wise Men who came to visit the Child Jesus were not necessarily astrologers. They were "Magi", the nearest thing to scientists in that day. They detected from their study of the heavens that God was about to perform some great Action upon the earth. This is *not* astrology. The Star of Bethlehem did not *cause* the birth of the Saviour, nor have any influence on His life. It was a *sign* only. Daniel the Prophet was considered by the Persians to be a "Mage", or Wise Man (Dan. 2:10–13; 5:11). We have no indication, however, that he practised astrology.

Notice that the Bible is saying that God may, for His purposes, cause there to be a *correlation* between events in the heavens and events upon the earth. Astrology is erroneously saying that the activity in the heavens *influences* and *causes* the events upon the earth.

to look grotesque, and often effeminate; the similar attempt on the part of the girls to appear ugly, bedraggled, and dirty; the confusion of the sexes in dress and behaviour.

Hypnotism is particularly dangerous because it is thought of as a valid form of therapy in psychology and psychiatry, or as an alternative to anaesthesia in medicine and dentistry. The fact is that hypnotism, too, by placing the soul in a passively receptive state, even when the hypnotist has no such intention, opens the door to morbid spiritual influences that may bring oppression that last for years, until the person is delivered through prayer and exorcism.

At a recent conference, a Christian leader who works with disturbed young people told of dealing with a teen-age girl, the daughter of a Methodist minister, who had been hypnotized, at the age of eleven, at a Christmas programme in her father's church. This was just a "for fun" thing—an amateur hypnotist at a party—and certainly no harm was intended. The girl, however, behaved abnormally from that point. Her whole personality changed; her parents were unable to reach her. She became involved in some serious misbehaviour, including car theft. At the age of fourteen, she was ministered to for deliverance, and was set free from the spirit that had moved into her personality when she innocently submitted to hypnotism.

Do not allow yourself to be hypnotized for any reason whatsoever.

5. *Sorcery or witchcraft.* In one sense, everything we are talking about in this part of the book is a form of sorcery or witchcraft, for we may define sorcery or witchcraft (also called "magic") as the effort to gain power and control in the "spiritual" world so as to get information, influence other people, get wealth and power, or other material advantages. Much so-called religion is really *magic*. If the main purpose in your "religion" is to learn to *control* God, your religion is really

a form of "white magic", even if it is good things you are seeking for yourself and others. The purpose of the believer is to get to know and love God. Fortunately for us, God desires to bless us in every way, and therefore we find, as we get to know Him, that he wants us to ask and claim good things for ourselves and others. He delights to give them, as we believe for them, but he Himself is always the greatest Good and the greatest Gift. "Seek first the Kingdom (Kingship) of God, and His righteousness, and all these things shall be added to you . . ." (Matt. 6: 33).

In the narrower sense, *sorcery* and *witchcraft* comprise such things as "hexing", or influencing or harassing others by psychic and occult means. The news stands are now blossoming out in an evil cluster of books on how to hex your enemies. Even "witchcraft do-it-yourself kits" are being sold, with complete instructions on how to make a wax doll to stick pins into!

6. *Certain physical phenomena: telekinesis, levitation, astral projection. Telekinesis* is the attempt to control the movement of matter by thought, e.g., the throw of dice, or the fall of cards. *Levitation* is the attempt to neutralize gravity by psychic means, so as to lift objects off the ground, tip tables, or raise oneself from the ground. *Astral projection* is the attempt to project the so-called "astral body" to a distance by psychic means. These things actually can happen, and the power behind them is demonic.

7. *Spiritism or spiritualism.*[10] This is the attempt of human beings to get into contact with the "spirit world", and especially

---

10. *Spiritism* is the general name for the practice of attempting to contact the departed. *Spiritualism* generally is used of the *religion* built around this belief. *Spiritualists* have "churches", and often claim to be Christian. *Spiritists*, however, are sometimes atheists—believing in the existence of the "spirit world", but not in God. The Bible term for *Spiritism* is "necromancy", or "having familiar spirits".

with their departed relatives and friends, through the help of "spirit guides" and mediums. This is the cruellest of all Satan's deceptions, and the one that is peculiarly abominable to God. Human spirits do not remain in this world after death, but are either with God in His Kingdom, or are in Hell awaiting judgment. The person who seeks to get in touch with a dead friend or relative by spiritualism, if he or she contacts a genuine medium, will be put in touch, not with the human spirit of that relative or friend, but with a demonic spirit masquerading as the human person. All the details of dress, physical appearance, etc., are available to the enemy, as are secret thoughts and knowledge. A person will say: "But I know it must have been my grandfather, for he spoke of things that only he and I knew about. He called me by a pet name that only he and I used. . . ." But Satan and his helpers know about these things. Spiritualism may make its way into the life of Christian believers in very subtle ways. You should not accept as true any story of a person who has died appearing spiritually on this earth, whether it be the blessed mother of Jesus, one of the great saints, or some person in your own family whom you love, and who is with the Lord.[11] You should not address prayers to them.

11. There are three seeming exceptions to this in the Scriptures. The first is the return of Samuel's spirit, in I Samuel 28. This is, however, a special act of God, and Saul is specifically condemned for instigating it. The other two are the appearances of Elijah and Moses in the Transfiguration (Matt. 17:1ff., Mark 9:2ff., Luke 9:28ff). But Elijah had never died, but was taken directly up to heaven (II Kings 2:11); and although it is said of Moses that he died (Deut. 34:5), there was something unusual about it, for we are told that the Lord Himself buried him, and that his sepulchre was unknown (Deut. 34:6), and in Jude 9 we have a mysterious reference to some kind of altercation between Michael and the Devil over the body of Moses. It would seem that Moses' body was in some way preserved, in order that he and Elijah might appear *physically*, not spiritually, with Jesus, in the Transfiguration. There is, of course, no prohibition against the appearance of a revived physical person, such

The "communion of saints" means that all believers are in Jesus Christ, but any kind of direct communication between those living on this earth and the faithful departed is strictly forbidden, and whenever it seems to occur, you may be sure that Satan is up to his tricks.

No seeming visitation of a departed person to this earth should be accepted as valid, no matter in what guise it may be presented.[12]

This detailed warning about the psychic and occult is desperately needed today, because the world is being flooded with this kind of thing. Serious-minded but misguided scientists are investigating these phenomena. One leading scientific laboratory has been investigating telepathy as a serious means of communication for years. Word now comes that Russian scientists have been studying these psychic "powers" with the purpose of using them in espionage. In almost all our colleges and universities throughout the nation there are classes in "parapsychology", which are studying such things as psychic phenomena, hauntings, witchcraft, reincarnation, etc.

People often say, and perhaps you may be saying at this point:

"But in this and other books about the work of the Holy Spirit we are reading of wonderful Spiritual gifts and experiences, and now you seem to be telling us that they are wrong!"

No, we are telling you that there are two kinds of experi-

---

as Lazarus, on the earth after his death, nor a resurrected person, such as Jesus after His death and rising again, or those saints that were raised with Him (Matt. 27:52–3). The injunction is against the manifestation of *spirits* of the departed.

12. Note that we are speaking of real *visitations*, not *dreams*, or *visions*. God may permit you to dream about a departed person in order to bring something to your remembrance. He may give you a vision of that person in Heaven, in order to reassure you of his happiness. It is the alleged return of the departed to this world that is to be rejected.

ences, those that come from God, and those that the devil sends as counterfeits, and that it is of the utmost importance for you to be able to tell the difference. The great difficulty today is to distinguish the work of God from the work of Satan. The problem is that many do not believe in spiritual evil at all, but think that anything that seems "spiritual" must naturally be "good". This is why we have such a flood of weird doings. Our only safe guide is the Word of God illuminated by the Holy Spirit (Matt. 24:24; II Cor. 11:14).

We have made what may seem to some a long digression, but it is of great importance. Even though you yourself may not have been involved with any of the cults or the false teachings listed above, or others like them, you will be praying and counselling with other people, so we repeat this solemn warning: Do not encourage anyone to pray to receive the Holy Spirit unless you are sure that, first, he has received Jesus as his Saviour; and, second, that he has renounced any involvement or relationship with any of the wrong beliefs or teachings listed in this chapter. These wrong beliefs carry with them demonic power, and if a person prays to receive "the Spirit", if he is not a Christian, and not indwelt by the Holy Spirit, or if he is a Christian, but has permitted a spirit of error to enter his mind, that wrong spirit may be the one expressed, and the wrong spirit may gain a deeper hold on his mind and body, instead of the Holy Spirit. The result can be spiritual and psychological confusion that may take years to overcome. The Apostle Paul had good reason to command: "Lay hands suddenly on no man!" It is incautious praying with people for the baptism in the Holy Spirit that leads to strange manifestations, that brings discredit to the work of the Lord, and sometimes drives seekers away.

What to do? As specifically as possible, if you have been in any way involved in these false cults or teachings, renounce them in the Name of Jesus. Ask God to forgive you; bind and cast out any spirit connected with the wrong teaching. Claim the protection of the Blood of Jesus, and ask the Holy Spirit to fill every area where any false beliefs have been.[13]

Here is a prayer for you to use:

"Dear Father, if I have believed, studied, or practised anything that is displeasing to You, or contrary to Your Word, I am truly sorry. I ask You to forgive me for being involved in these things, and I promise You that I will not have anything more to do with them, and if I have any books or equipment connected with them, I promise You that I will burn them right away.

"I renounce (here name the cult or false teaching) in the Name of Jesus Christ. Spirit of (here name again the cult or false teaching), I bind you under the Blood of Jesus Christ, and cast you into outer darkness, never to return, in Jesus' Name! Thank You, Jesus!"

Repeat this second paragraph for each cult or false teaching with which you have been involved.

After you have prayed to renounce and cast out these things, immediately pray, or have someone pray with you, that you may be filled with the Holy Spirit in every area where the false teachings have been. If you have not yet received the baptism in the Holy Spirit, proceed immediately to accept the full work of the Holy Spirit in your life, as described in the next chapter.

If you have any doubt about what we have been saying in this

---

13. Several cases have come to our attention in recent years of people with psychic and occult ability trying to bring these abilities to God to be used for Him. The desire is understandable, but God doesn't need Satan's secondhand goods! If you have such "powers", you must get rid of them, renounce them and cast them away from you completely, and let God give you His gifts. Nothing but confusion can follow the attempt to bring these demonic practices into the service of the Lord.

chapter, or if you do not agree with what we have said, *do not pray to receive the Holy Spirit* until you have received further counsel, and can accept freely what has been told here. You will find it helpful to read such books as, *The Kingdom of the Cults* by Walter Martin, *Angels of Light?* by Hobart Freeman, *Spiritual Warfare* by Michael Harper, *The Challenging Counterfeit* by Raphael Gasson.[14] The first three books deal with a number of the better-known cults; the last one deals specifically with spiritualism and spiritism.

14. W. R. Martin, *The Kingdom of the Cults* (Minneapolis: Bethany, 1965). Hobart Freeman, *Angels of Light?* (Plainfield, N.J.: Logos, 1969). Raphael Gasson, *The Challenging Counterfeit* (Plainfield, N.J.: Logos, 1966). Michael Harper, *Spiritual Warfare* (Plainfield, N.J.: Logos, 1970).

5
How to Receive the Baptism in the Holy Spirit

You have received Jesus as your Saviour, you have renounced any false teachings that might hold you back or confuse you, and now you're ready to pray to be baptized in the Holy Spirit. Who is going to baptize you in the Holy Spirit? *Jesus* is going to do it! This being so, you can receive the Holy Spirit anywhere, anytime, can you not?

"But I thought someone had to lay hands on me to 'give' me the Holy Spirit." No, we have already settled that. Because you have received Jesus, you already have the Holy Spirit, so no one needs to "give" Him to you, even if they could! Jesus is living in you, and He is ready to baptize you in the Holy Spirit as soon as you are ready to respond. Having someone lay hands on you may be a help, and it is certainly scriptural, but not absolutely necessary. We have already shown that on three occasions in the Acts of the Apostles, hands were imposed, but in two other cases they were not. Many people have received the Holy Spirit in recent years without anyone being near them except Jesus! You can receive the baptism with the Holy

Spirit in church, at the altar rail, sitting or kneeling in the pew, driving your car down the freeway, vacuuming the rug, doing the dishes, or mowing the lawn. It will happen the moment you ask and believe.

"But do I have to speak in tongues?"

When Dennis was seeking to receive the Holy Spirit, he said:

"I'm not interested in this 'tongues' thing you are talking about!" He thought speaking in tongues was some kind of wild emotionalism, and his English upbringing caused him to be very wary of such things! [1] The Episcopalians who had been telling him about their experience laughed.

"Oh," they said. "All we can tell you is that it came with the package—just like in the Bible!"

We have shown that speaking in tongues is indeed a common denominator in examples of the baptism in the Holy Spirit given in the Scriptures. It seems obvious also that the early believers had a way of telling immediately whether or not their converts had received the Holy Spirit. Some say that we are supposed to tell when a person has received the Holy Spirit by the change in his life—by the "fruit of the Spirit". We certainly should be more "fruitful" Christians after receiving the baptism with the Holy Spirit, but "bearing fruit" is not the scriptural *sign* of this experience. The apostles knew right on the spot when a person had received the baptism with the Holy Spirit. If they had had to wait until they observed fruit or change of character in the person's life, it would have taken months and years to evaluate. Apparently the early Christians had a simpler way, and it isn't hard to see what it was.

What was it that drew the great crowd of "Jews, devout men, from every country under heaven" at Pentecost, three thousand

1. Dennis Bennett, *Nine O'Clock in the Morning* (Plainfield, N.J.: Logos, 1970), p. 18.

of whom were converted that very day and hour? They weren't there long enough to find out what kind of lives the people were living before and after! What was it that immediately convinced Simon Magus that his neighbours had received something that would be so highly saleable that he tried to purchase it? On the other hand, how did the apostles Peter and John know immediately that Philip's converts had not received the Holy Spirit? It certainly wasn't a lack of joy, for the record says: "There was much joy in that city" (Acts 8:8 RSV). What was it that completely convinced Peter at the house of Cornelius that the Romans had received the Holy Spirit, so that he dared, contrary to all previous practice or belief, to baptize these Gentiles? The case of the Ephesians we cited in Acts 19 is a little different, for these people had not received Jesus. Paul undoubtedly missed the presence of the Holy Spirit in them at all; but after they had received Jesus and been baptized in water, what was it that let Paul know, right after he had laid his hand on them, that they had received the Holy Spirit?

"We do hear them speak in our tongues the wonderful works of God" (Acts 2:11 KJV). "They heard them speak with tongues and magnify God" (Acts 10:46 KJV). "They spoke with tongues and prophesied" (Acts 19:6 RSV).

Anyone who takes the Scriptures seriously can scarcely avoid coming to the conclusion that speaking in tongues is important. Jesus Himself said: "These signs shall follow them that believe, they shall speak in new languages" (Mark 16:17).[2]

2. We are quite aware that this passage at the end of Mark has been questioned by scholars, and put down by many as a "later addition". In some popular modern translations it has been "demoted" to a footnote at the bottom of the page. A friend of ours, Mr. George Gillies, a capable leader in small-group ministry, says of this: "Even in a footnote, it still *works!*"

It doesn't take any great scholarship to see that there is a break between the 8th and 9th verses of Mark 16—but whoever supplied the "lost ending" of the Gospel of Mark, whether it was Mark him-

The Apostle Paul said plainly to the Corinthians:
"I want you all to speak in tongues!" (I Cor. 14:5 RSV).
The Greek original here:

$$\theta\acute{\varepsilon}\lambda\omega\ \delta\acute{\varepsilon}\ \pi\acute{\alpha}\nu\tau\alpha\varsigma\ \acute{\upsilon}\mu\tilde{\alpha}\varsigma\ \lambda\alpha\lambda\varepsilon\tilde{\imath}\nu\ \gamma\lambda\acute{\omega}\sigma\sigma\alpha\iota\varsigma$$

"*Thelo de pantas humas lalein glossais,*" can be translated
either as simple present indicative, or in the subjunctive—the
form is the same. Most English translations, including the King
James Version, choose the subjunctive: from "I would that ye
all spake with tongues" all the way to the farfetched "I might
wish that you all spoke with strange sounds" of *Good News for
Modern Man!* The reason is easy to see. The translators of these
versions presumably did not know what speaking in tongues
might be, and therefore did not feel easy in adopting the most
straightforward translation of Paul's words. The Revised
Standard Version, however, has no such hesitation, but selects
the present indicative as the most likely translation: "I want
you all to speak in tongues." The literal translation of Bagster's
Englishman's Greek New Testament is also direct: "Now I
desire you all to speak with tongues."

After all, it is the same Apostle Paul who says later to the
Corinthians: "I thank my God I speak in tongues more than
any of you!" or, as it may be perhaps more accurately translated:

---

self or someone else, it came from the earliest period, and was
accepted in the early days of the Church. It became a part of the
canonical Scripture. While this "lost ending" is missing from the
two earliest extant documents we have, it is present in many others.
Everything in it is confirmed elsewhere by other incidents of Scripture. We say of this passage: "It may have been a 'lost ending', but
somebody found it and stuck it back in our Bible! Apparently the
Holy Spirit wanted it there!" We must be very careful about following the teaching and textual criticism of those scholars of the
liberal-modernist tradition, who would like to "desupernaturalize"
the Scripture as much as possible.

"I thank my God, speaking in tongues, more than any of you" (I Cor. 14:18).

Paul goes on to say: ". . . if I pray in a tongue, my spirit prays, but my understanding is unfruitful. What is it then? I will pray with the spirit, and I will pray with the understanding also: I will sing with the spirit, and I will sing with the understanding also" (I Cor. 14:14–15).

And here we have an answer to what speaking in tongues is, and why God should have chosen such a seemingly strange evidence to accompany the baptism with the Holy Spirit. Speaking in tongues is prayer *with* or *in* the Spirit: it is our spirit speaking to God, inspired by the Holy Spirit. It takes place when a Christian believer speaks to God, but instead of speaking in a language that he knows with his intellect, he just speaks in childlike faith, and trusts God to provide the form of the words. The regenerated human spirit, which is joined to the Holy Spirit, is praying directly to the Father, in Christ, without having to accept the limitations of the intellect. As the new life in the Spirit is expressed, or exercised, if you like, the spiritual life is built up or edified.

"He that speaks in a tongue edifies himself" (I Cor. 14:4). "Edifies" is the translation of the Greek word *oikodoméo* which means quite literally to "build up". Here it means to build oneself spiritually. A related word is used by the Apostle Jude when he says: "Building yourselves up on your most holy faith, praying in the Holy Spirit" (Jude 20). (Quite clearly in this passage Jude is referring to speaking in tongues.) The intellect, on the other hand, not understanding the language, is humbled; the soul (psychological being) is put in its place, which is subject to the spirit. Prayer is said to God in freedom. The prayer comes just as the Holy Spirit intends it to come, therefore it is a perfect prayer, from the perfectness of the new creature, and perfectly inspired by the Spirit.[3] Therefore it is also *effective* prayer. The Father can receive it wholly, for it comes not from our still-messed-up souls, but from the Holy Spirit through our spirit, offered by our volition and co-operation.

Our voice, our speech, or as the Bible calls it, our *tongue*, is our chief means of expression, and it is no coincidence that it is here that the Holy Spirit chooses to flow out first. Spiritually, psychologically, and physiologically, our ability to speak is central. In Proverbs we read: "A man's belly shall be satisfied with the fruit of his mouth; and with the increase of his lips shall he be filled. Death and life are in the power of the tongue: and they that love it shall eat the fruit thereof" (Prov. 18: 20–21 KJV). Our ability to communicate with one another in rational speech is a fundamental part of being human. The King James Bible speaks of the faculty of speech as the "glory" of the body. The Psalmist says:

"Awake up, my glory; awake, psaltery and harp: I myself will awake early" (Psalm 57: 8 KJV). And in another place: "Therefore my heart is glad, and my glory rejoiceth: my flesh also shall rest in hope" (Ps. 16: 9 KJV). In each case the margin explains that "glory" is a metaphor for the *voice*.

In the third chapter of James, he compares the tongue to the

3. A fascinating proof of this is that people who are totally deaf, and have never spoken a word, when receiving the Holy Spirit will speak fluently in tongues! Mrs. Wendell Mason of LaVerne, California, who works with the deaf, says: "I have seen and prayed with at least twenty deaf persons to receive the Holy Spirit, and heard them begin to speak fluently in a heavenly language to God, then return to their sign language when communicating with me. I have seen two deaf-mute persons receive the Holy Spirit and speak in tongues." Similar testimony comes from many others who work with the deaf. It would be absolutely impossible for these handicapped people to imitate a language, or to be speaking words remembered from their "unconscious" mind (as some sceptics have said in trying to explain away speaking in tongues) since they have never heard a word in their lives!

rudder of a big ship, able to control the whole vessel with very little movement, or to the bit in the mouth of a horse, a small object that controls the whole animal. However, James goes on to say that the tongue is an "unruly evil, full of deadly poison" (Jas. 3:8 KJV). He says that the tongue, being set on fire with the fire of hell, can defile the whole body (Jas. 3:6). Psalm 12:4 (KJV) says: "With our tongue will we prevail; our lips are our own: who is lord over us?" It would seem that the same faculty of speech which is so great a thing, is also the main thing that obstructs the freedom of the Holy Spirit in the believer's life. It is a focus of our intellectual pride. A neurosurgeon friend made this interesting comment one day: "I understand why God uses speaking in tongues. The speech centres dominate the brain. I don't see how God Himself could do much about the physical brain unless He got hold of the speech centres!"

"Who can tame the tongue?" asks James, and the answer is: "The Holy Spirit!" and speaking in tongues is the main part of the process. The Spirit says: "I want to inspire and rule the most important means of expression you have—the ability to speak. I also want to tame and purify that with which you *sin* the most, your tongue!"

Speaking in tongues has nothing to do with emotion! Speaking in tongues *cannot* be emotion, for the emotions are part of the soul, the psychological nature, while speaking in tongues is speaking from or in the spirit (I Cor. 14:14). This fact may surprise people who have heard a highly emotional manifestation which was actually a misuse of the *gift* of tongues (public ministry in tongues) and perhaps have been frightened or repelled by it.

The passages in several modern versions of the Scripture that speak of "tongues of ecstasy", or "ecstatic speech", are paraphrases rather than translations. There is nothing in the Greek original to imply that speaking in tongues had anything to do with excitement, ecstasy, frenzy, etc. The phrase is always just *lalein glossais*, meaning simply, "to speak in languages". Speaking in tongues may stir the emotions, just as it may sharpen the intellect, and order the will, and we hope it does these things; but you do not have to become emotional in order to speak in tongues. As a matter of fact one of the greatest blocks to the receiving of the Holy Spirit is the highly charged emotional atmosphere that is thought by some to be helpful or even necessary. When people are seeking to receive the baptism in the Holy Spirit and speak in tongues for the first time, we try to keep their emotions as "calm" as possible. Many begin to speak in tongues rather quietly. Later they will speak more strongly as faith grows and fear is overcome. Actually, excited emotions get in the way of the Holy Spirit just as much as an overactive intellect or an overdetermined will!

There is nothing wrong with *emotion*. We need to learn to express and enjoy our emotions much more than we do, especially in regard to our fellowship with God. What could be more wonderful, or more emotionally stirring, than feeling the presence of God? Emotion, however, is a *response*, an expression, not a *cause*. *Emotionalism* is the expression of emotion for its own sake, without any roots or reason.

You will not be in some "strange" frame of mind when you speak in tongues. It has no relationship with the weird, the occult, the "way-out", as we hope we have made very clear to you in the last chapter. It isn't hysteria or any form of suggestion. You don't go into a trance, or make your mind a blank. When you are speaking in tongues your mind should be actively thinking about the Lord! Blankness or passivity of mind are dangerous things in any circumstances, and should not be encouraged.

There is no *compulsion* involved in speaking in tongues. God does not *compel*. His people to do things, He *inspires* them. It is the enemy who "possesses" and compels people against their will. Whenever anyone says: "I do this because God *makes* me do it!" referring to any physical manifestation, it is likely that it is not God at all, but either his own soulish (psychological) nature that is acting, or worse yet, an alien spirit that is oppressing him.[4] God can and does do unexpected and unusual things, but does not make His children behave in bizarre and grotesque ways that would frighten others (II Tim. 1:7).

In the same vein, many are afraid to speak in tongues because they think they may pop up in church and interrupt the preacher, or suddenly speak in tongues on the golf course! Nonsense! The "spirit of the prophet is subject to the prophet" (I Cor. 14:32). Some say: "But if this is the Holy Spirit speaking, how can I dare to refuse Him?" Ah, but you see this *isn't* the Holy Spirit speaking. Speaking in tongues is *your* spirit speaking, *inspired* by the Holy Spirit, and your spirit is

4. We are not denying that the Holy Spirit can sovereignly cause physical sensations. It is not uncommon for a person to feel a supernatural movement upon cheeks, lips, or tongue, or a stammering tongue, or trembling of the body, when praying for the baptism of the Holy Spirit, and this can happen even to a person who is not only actively desiring to pray for the receiving of the Holy Spirit, but who perhaps does not understand the matter. There are cases of people experiencing a weakness of muscles, even to the point of not being able to stand up. On the day of Pentecost itself they were accused of drunkenness! At Caesarea Philippi the Romans were overwhelmed by the Holy Ghost seemingly without expecting such a thing to happen. Certainly Peter had not mentioned any such manifestation, and did not expect it to take place. Nonetheless, no matter how overwhelming the inspiration may be, and whether it is spiritual, psychological, or even physical in nature, the spirit of the prophet is still subject to the prophet. The consent and co-operation of the individual is always required. No matter how powerful the inspiration, it is never *compulsion*. Notice, however, that the Spirit can and does compel *unbelievers*. Those who came out to arrest Jesus were thrown to the ground. Paul was knocked off his donkey and temporarily blinded. One can think of many other examples.

under your control. Your consent is always needed before you manifest any gift of the Spirit. Sometimes you may be so strongly inspired by the joy and power of the Lord that you *want* very much to speak out in a situation where your mind tells you it would be wrong. That's all right to feel that way; you learn to control yourself just as you learn not to laugh at the wrong time, even though something strikes you as very funny, and you are much inspired to laugh! Indeed, this is a good comparison, for the inspiration of the Holy Spirit is much like joyful laughter.

"I thought the Bible said that there must be no speaking in tongues without interpreting?" This rule applies to speaking in tongues in a public meeting, and will be discussed in more detail in a later chapter on the *gift* of tongues, but here we will only say that private speaking in tongues needs no interpretation. The believer is "speaking to God in a mystery", praying with his spirit, not his intellect.

"What if I don't speak in tongues? Can I receive the Holy Spirit without speaking in tongues?"

"It comes with the package!" Speaking in tongues is not the baptism in the Holy Spirit, but it is what happens when and as you are baptized in the Spirit, and it becomes an important resource to help you continue, as Paul says, to "be being (or keep on being) filled with the Holy Spirit" (Eph. 5 : 18). You *don't* have to speak in tongues in order to be saved. You *don't* have to speak in tongues in order to have the Holy Spirit in you. You *don't* have to speak in tongues to have times of feeling filled with the Holy Spirit, but if you want the free and full outpouring that is the baptism in the Holy Spirit, you must expect it to happen as in the Scripture, and to do what Peter, James, John, Paul, Mary, Mary Magdalen, Barnabas, and all the rest did! If you want to understand the New Testament you need the same experience that all its writers had. A man said to Dennis one day:

"I would like to receive the Holy Spirit, but after a *Wesleyan* manner!"

Dennis' answer was: "There's only one way to receive the Holy Spirit, and that's in a *New Testament* manner!" (John Wesley would certainly have agreed!)

People will say: "But what about the great Christians of history? They didn't speak in tongues!" Are you sure? There is probably not a time in church history when there were not some who knew the fullness of the Holy Spirit and spoke in tongues. Whenever there has been a strong revival of the faith, the gifts of the Spirit have made their appearance. St. Patrick of Ireland, St. Francis of Assis, St. Teresa of Avila, St. Francis Xavier, probably Martin Luther, the early Quakers, the Waldensians, the early Methodists are a few examples of those in earlier days who spoke in tongues. In more recent times the great Charles Finney did. It seems very likely that D. L. Moody did.[5] Many Christian leaders today speak in tongues but do not admit to it because they fear prejudice. Yet there are many who are more bold. There are thousands of ministers and priests in virtually all the denominations who testify that they have received the baptism in the Holy Spirit and spoken in tongues, and the number is growing all the time. An organisation of charismatic Presbyterian ministers alone numbers around four hundred. Five years ago, an American Baptist leader told us that there were at that time five hundred American Baptist ministers who had received the Holy Spirit and spoken in tongues.

There are a number of people who have spoken in tongues, but don't know it! Every now and then when talking about this

5. Carl Brumback *What Meaneth This?* (Gospel Publishing House, 1949) chap. 6.

manifestation someone will say: "Oh, you mean that funny little language I have spoken ever since I was a child—is that it? It makes me feel happy and close to God!"[6]

A pleasant little Dutch lady, perhaps thirty-five years of age, was talking with Dennis after a meeting recently.

"I spoke in tongues once, about eight months ago," she said, a bit wistfully, "and I'd like to do it again!"

"Why don't you?"

"Oh, I wouldn't dare to try. You see, I have a little play language that I talk for my children when we're having fun together. They think it's funny, and we have a good time. I'm afraid that if I tried to speak in tongues, that little play language would come!"

By this time Dennis was smiling: "That's your tongue!" he said.

The little lady was startled: "Oh no," she said, shaking her head firmly, "that's just a play language!"

After several more minutes of discussion, Dennis said to her:

"Would you be willing to speak this little 'play language' as you call it, to God? Talk to God in it?"

It took a little more persuasion, but finally she bowed her head and began to talk quietly in a beautiful language. In not more than thirty seconds, she was in joyful tears: "That's it! That's it!" she said.

A young couple from England who were touring the United States stopped at St. Luke's some seven years ago. They were curious to find out more about the baptism in the Holy Spirit. As they talked, we tried to explain to them what speaking in tongues meant. A half-amused, half-puzzled smile came on the face of the young man:

6. Obviously, for such a thing to be valid, the child would have had to receive Jesus Christ first.

"Could this be something I've been doing in my prayers ever since I was three years old?" he asked. His wife also smiled: "Me, too!" she said. Unknown to one another, they had both been speaking in tongues from time to time in their prayers ever since they were very young children.

Perhaps this is a good time to mention that quite often people first speak in tongues in their dreams! The week before writing this chapter, we spent some time with an airline's jet pilot who was seeking to find out more about the Holy Spirit. He said:

"The other night I dreamed I spoke in tongues. When I woke up, I felt so wonderful!" When a person speaks in tongues in his dreams he will soon begin to speak in tongues in his waking hours if he yields. It is hard sometimes to convince people of this! A young man from a nearby Lutheran school attended the St. Luke's Friday Night Information Meeting together with some other students. He came by the church the next week and said: "Oh, I was so disappointed. You know I wanted to stay and receive the Holy Spirit the other night, but the others had to go home. But that night I dreamed I came to the altar rail in your church and received the Holy Spirit. It was so great! I spoke in tongues, and was just overjoyed!"

"Hm-m-m," said Dennis. "The meeting was in the parish hall, wasn't it?"

"Yes," replied the young man. "I've never been in your church auditorium itself, but in my dream that's where I was!"

"Would you mind describing it to me?" Dennis asked.

"Well, I noticed that the altar itself was in an unusual position. It was so far out from the wall I could have reached out and touched it as I knelt at the side of the altar rail." (This was about seven years ago, when freestanding altars were not so common.) "The church was painted brown—it was all wood —" and the young man proceeded to give a pretty good description of the inside of St. Luke's Episcopal Church, Seattle! It seemed the Lord had not only baptized this man in the Holy Spirit in the dream, but had given him a very recognizable picture of the inside of St. Luke's! (This last would have been a manifestation of the gift of knowledge.)

"Congratulations!" said Dennis. "You've received the Holy Spirit!"

"Oh, no," said the boy, "it was just a dream!"

It took a while to convince him, but at the end of that time, he consented to pray, and immediately began to speak fluently in a new language.

"That's the same one I spoke in my dream!" he said happily.

Before praying to receive the Holy Spirit, we suggest that you first pray to the Father in Jesus' Name, reaffirming your faith in Christ, thanking Him for the new life He has given you in Jesus, and for the Holy Spirit living in you. Continue praying, saying whatever you have on your heart. If you can remember anything that would keep you from coming closer to God, any unconfessed wrong action or wrong attitude, a grudge against someone, for example, or a dishonest deal in business, tell God about it, confess, and then promise Him that you'll straighten it out. If you feel so led, leave your prayer for a time, go and put the thing right, and then return (Matt. 5:23-24), but don't let any notion of some "hidden" or unknown sin keep you from claiming the baptism in the Holy Spirit. "I'm not worthy," some people say, and the answer is: "Of course you're not worthy!" Jesus alone is worthy, and He'll provide the worthiness. Would there ever be a time when you would come to the Lord and say: "Now I'm worthy. So please give me what I have coming to me!" Better not do that—you might get it!

When you ask Jesus to baptize you in the Spirit, you must receive. Receiving is something *you* do. Rita likes to speak of the "ABC's" of receiving:

A. *Ask* Jesus to baptize you in the Holy Spirit. The Book of James says: "You have not, because you ask not" (Jas. 4:2). God gave you a free will and never will take it away. He won't force His blessings upon you, as this is not the way of Love. You must ask.

B. *Believe* you receive the moment you ask. "Ask, and you shall receive that your joy may be full" (John 16:24). Faith is present-tense belief. "*Now* faith is . . ." says the writer of Hebrews (Heb. 11:1). Faith is also active and not passive, which means you must take the first step.

C. *Confess* with your lips. When you received Jesus as Saviour, you believed in your heart and confessed Him with your lips. Now confess with your lips, but in the new language that the Lord is ready to give you. Open your mouth and show that you believe the Lord has baptized you in the Spirit by *beginning to speak*. Don't speak English, or any other language you know, for God can't guide you to speak in tongues if you are speaking in a language known to you. You can't speak two languages at once! Trust God to give you the words, just as Peter trusted Jesus to let him walk on the water. Speaking in tongues is a childlike act of faith. It involves no ability, but rather the setting aside of ability. It is simply speaking, using your voice, but instead of saying what your mind wants you to say, you trust the Holy Spirit to guide your voice directly to say what He wants you to say.

"But that would just be *me* speaking!" Exactly! *God* does not speak in tongues—*people* speak in tongues, as the Spirit gives the words. On the day of Pentecost we read: "They began to speak—in other languages—as the Spirit gave them utterance." So you must *begin to speak, in other languages*—not your own language or languages—as the Spirit gives the utterance, or the form of the words, to you—and He will! Just like a child learning to talk for the first time, open your mouth and speak out the first syllables and expressions that come to your lips. You must *begin to speak*, just as Peter had to get out of the boat. God will guide you when you dare to trust Him by stepping out in faith.

When praying to receive the Holy Spirit, people will sometimes experience such things as, involuntary trembling, stammering lips, or chattering teeth. These are physical reactions to the Holy Spirit that are in themselves without meaning, except that they may indicate His presence. They probably arise out of our resistance to Him. Some have waited for years for the "stammering lips" to become a language, but in vain. The believer must always begin to speak—speaking in tongues is *not* involuntary.

"But I don't want to be told how to speak in tongues! I want God to do it! Otherwise it might be 'in the flesh'!"

No one can possibly tell you "how to" speak in tongues. All we are trying to do is to get you to begin to do it! It is true that many people begin to speak quite spontaneously without any urging at all. In the Bible apparently most of them did. If we were all living in simple faith, we would do so too, but unfortunately many of us tend to be sophisticated and inhibited, fearful of simpleness. Today still, many adults and children with childlike faith receive easily and often spontaneously; mainly our instruction here is for those who have "hang-ups" at this point. All we are saying to you is that it is up to you to get out of the boat if you want to walk on the water. We can't tell you how to walk on the water, Jesus will take care of that, but we can urge you to get out of the ship—to take the first step on top of the waves! As far as "in the flesh" is concerned, a leading Bible teacher says:

"When Peter got out and walked on the water, the 'flesh' were all sitting in the boat!"

The "flesh" is the opposite of faith—it is the "old man",

rebellious and sinful. It is far more "fleshly" to wait for God to take you over, and *make* you do something, than to trust Him in simple faith to honour you as you begin to utter sounds of speech. You may have fear about speaking out in this way because you were taught that speaking in tongues was a sign of the baptism in the Holy Spirit, but that most people did not speak in tongues again except under a "special annointing", that only certain privileged persons were enabled to pray in tongues whenever they chose, because they had received the "Gift of Tongues". Thus, if a person made a few sounds, someone might say: "Praise God, he's got the Baptism!" and let it go at that! If it were true that most believers only prayed in tongues once, at the time of receiving the Holy Spirit, and perhaps never again, or very rarely, it would be of paramount importance to be sure that those first "utterances" were totally inspired by the Spirit, and not human effort. We are teaching, however, what we know to be true, that these first efforts at obeying the Spirit are only the beginning. It doesn't matter if the first sounds are just "priming the pump", for the real flow will assuredly come.

The Psalmist David said, by the inspiration of the Holy Spirit:

"Open your mouth wide, and I will fill it!" (Ps. 81:10) and, "Make a joyful noise unto the Lord!" (Ps. 81:1).

A joyful noise may not yet be speaking in tongues, but even this is pleasing to the Lord. It won't be long before it will be your Holy Spirit language, as God will honour your simple faith.

Several things may happen at this point: you may not succeed in beginning to speak, due to self-consciousness and inhibition. That's all right—you haven't "flunked" the test! You simply have to keep on until you do decide to make that first sound. It is like the parachutist jumping out of the aeroplane for the first time. If he wants to be a parachute jumper, he's got to jump! There's no other way! Don't back off at this point as some do, and say:

"I guess God doesn't want me to have it!" It's you who are holding back!

You may begin to speak, but only get out a few halting sounds. That's wonderful! You've broken the "sound barrier"! Keep in with those sounds. Offer them to God. Tell Jesus you love Him in those "joyful noises"! As you do, they will develop and grow into a fully developed language. It may take days, or even weeks—not because of God, but again, because of you. In a very real sense, any sound you make, offering your tongue to God in simple faith, may be the beginning of speaking in tongues. We have seen lives visibly changed by the release of the Spirit brought through one sound—one little syllable! If you have ever uttered one such sound while trusting God the Holy Spirit to guide you, from then on don't say: "I haven't spoken in tongues yet," but rather: "I'm beginning to speak in tongues!" Remember the manifestations of the Spirit are always God and us working together. "The Lord working with them . . . with signs following" (Mark 16: 20 KJV).

Then again you may begin to speak immediately in a beautiful language. That's wonderful, too, but it doesn't mean you're any holier than the others! It just means that you are a little freer in your spirit, and less inhibited. In any case, the thing to do is to keep on speaking—or keep on trying to speak.

Now and then a person will have some new words in his mind before he begins to speak in tongues. Speak them out! Others will follow.

Occasionally someone will see words written down, as if on "ticker tape", or as if projected on the wall. One woman saw the words in her "tongue", as if they had been written on the wall, complete with pronunciation and accent marks! She "read" them as she saw them, and began to speak in tongues! Why should such things happen? Because the Holy Spirit enjoys variety! Most people don't get these little "helps", so if you do, just praise the Lord. Some are more able to sing than to speak, and that is fine. You can just as well begin by singing in the Spirit as by speaking in the Spirit! Just allow the Spirit to give you the tune as well as the words. At first it will probably come as a little chant, perhaps on one or two tones, but it may help you to get free. We know people who can't sing a note "in the natural", but who sing beautifully in the Spirit!

What am I supposed to *feel* when I speak in tongues? At first, you may feel nothing at all. Remember, this is not an emotional experience. You are trying to let your spirit have freedom to praise God as the Holy Spirit inspires. It may be a little while before your spirit can begin to break through to your feelings, giving you a new awareness of God within you. On the other hand, you may experience a sudden breakthrough and feel as if you were carried right up into the heavenlies! Praise the Lord! It's wonderful to do that—to become suddenly aware of the fullness of Christ in you, and be carried up by it. Many people just sense a lightness and reality down in their spirit as they begin to speak, and the awareness grows.

One thing is sure, though: if you don't accept the experience as real, you won't be aware of its reality! The Christian life is built on faith—trust and acceptance. Inevitably many will say: "That was just me!" Of course it was you—who did you expect it would be, somebody else? It was you speaking, while the Holy Spirit provided the words! But until you accept that it is the Holy Spirit, and that the experience is real, you are obviously not going to get the blessing you are looking for! So believe and accept, and praise the Lord for what He is doing in you and through you!

One day Dennis was asked to give his testimony at a nearby

church. After the meeting many stayed to pray to receive the Holy Spirit. The pastor said to Dennis:

"There is a pastor here who is having a difficult time. Can you help him?" It was a young minister from one of the very stiff liturgical churches. He was determined to receive the Holy Spirit, but obviously very far out of his element in this rather uninhibited setting! The more the well-meaning pray-ers exhorted him, the more he froze!

Dennis asked him to come to his office at St. Luke's, and there, after some reassurance, they quietly prayed that he would receive the fullness he was seeking. After a short time, he began to tremble violently, and then to speak beautifully in a new language. He continued to speak for perhaps two or three minutes, then stopped, looked at Dennis rather glumly, and said:

"Well, thank you very much," and took his leave!

The next evening he telephoned:

"Dennis," he said, very sadly, "I'm really grateful to you for trying to help me, but you know, I didn't receive anything!"

Dennis was on the verge of saying: "Too bad. Better luck next time!" when the Lord's wisdom showed him how foolish that would have been. Instead he said:

"Look here, my friend! I saw you tremble under the power of the Holy Spirit, and I heard you speak beautifully in a language you do not know! I know you know the Lord Jesus as your Saviour, so I know this must have been the Holy Spirit! Stop doubting! Start thanking the Lord for baptizing you in the Holy Spirit!"

The man hung up, but he called back in about an hour. He was "riding high"! "Oh," he said, "when you told me to do that, I began to thank the Lord for baptizing me in the Spirit, and, wow! The joy of the Lord hit me, and I'm really on cloud nine!" It wasn't long before we heard that revival was starting in his little church.

If you have just come through a period of great strain or grief, in which you have been required to keep a firm hold on yourself and your emotions, you may have difficulty in letting go to permit the Lord Jesus to baptize you in the Spirit. You have been hanging on, and you are afraid that if you let go, you will really "go to pieces". It is very likely, if this is your circumstance, that as you attempt to release your voice to the Lord, you may begin to weep. Go ahead and weep! The Holy Spirit knows just how to untie those knots! Sometimes people will weep when they receive the Holy Spirit, sometimes they will laugh! We prayed with a young Episcopal priest and his wife some eight years ago, and as they received the Spirit, the young man roared with laughter, while the wife wept copiously, and both were filled with the joy of the Lord! Our Lord knows what you need, and He will meet you in the way that is the most helpful to you.

There are some believers who have asked to be baptized in the Holy Spirit, but have been unable to begin to speak in tongues. They consider this to be because God doesn't want them to do so; it isn't for them. We find, however, that with proper explanation, and answering of questions, and instruction, such persons often will break through their inhibitions and begin to speak in the Spirit.

With others we find, after counselling with them, that they have been involved in the past with cults, or occult practices— as explained in detail in chapter four. They have discontinued these practices, but have never *renounced* them. After being led to renounce them, they begin to speak in tongues right away.

We are convinced, from the Scriptures and after praying with thousands of people to receive the baptism in the Holy Spirit over the past ten years and more, that there is no be-

*liever who cannot speak in tongues, if he or she is properly
prepared, and really ready to trust the Lord.*

If you are by yourself praying to receive the Holy Spirit,
say this prayer, or if someone else is praying with you, they
will say a similar prayer for you:

"Heavenly Father, I thank You that that I am under the
protection of the precious Blood of Jesus which has cleansed
me from all sin. Dear Lord Jesus, please baptize me in the
Holy Spirit, and let me praise God in a new language beyond
the limitations of my intellect. Thank you, Lord, I believe
that You're doing this right now! In Jesus' Name I pray."

After Jesus has baptized you in the Holy Spirit, your life
will begin to have real power. It's like a soldier getting ammu-
nition for his rifle, and consequently Satan, the enemy, will not
be pleased. Many Christians do not believe there is a real
enemy, a personal devil; that's why they spend their lives sitting in his prisoner-of-war camp! The moment you receive
the fullness of the Holy Spirit, that is, the minute you begin to
allow the power of God to overflow from your spirit into your
soul and body, and into the world around, Satan becomes
painfully aware of you, and you will begin to be aware of his
work. He will give his attention to "shutting you down" if possible.

Jesus' ministry of miracles and power did not begin until
after He had received the power of the Holy Spirit, and immediately following this He was tempted by Satan in the
wilderness (Matt. 3:14-17; 4:1-10). Our new lives in the
Spirit are patterned after Jesus.[7] When we receive the power

7. Some say: "That's right! And Jesus didn't speak in tongues
when He was empowered by the Holy Spirit, so why should we?" It
is true that Jesus did not speak in tongues, but He said that we

of the Holy Spirit, we will also be put to the test. Because Jesus was victorious, we too will be!

The Book of James says: "Submit yourselves therefore to God. Resist the Devil, and he will flee from you."

"Submit yourselves therefore to God" means that the first and most important defence is to stay in fellowship with God; keep on praising Him, enjoying His presence, actively believing and trusting Him. Don't let anything quench your new freedom in fellowship with the Lord.

The next thing is: "Resist the devil and he will flee from you" (Jas. 4:7 KJV). Jesus' way of resisting was to use the Scriptures: "It is written ... it is written." The Scripture is the Sword of the Spirit. Find some swordlike Scriptures and memorize them so that they will always be with you.

"Behold, I give unto you power ... over all the power of the enemy: and nothing shall by any means hurt you" (Luke 10:19 KJV).

"Greater is he (Jesus) that is in you, than he (the enemy) that is in the world" (I John 4:4 KJV).

"For the weapons of our warfare are not carnal, but mighty through God to the pulling down of strongholds" (II Cor. 10:4 KJV).

You will be wanting to tell others what has happened to you,

would do so. Jesus did not need the edification of speaking in tongues, and there were no barriers in His soul that made it necessary for His Spirit to speak to the Father in a language His mind did not understand. Indeed it is impossible to imagine Him doing so. Moreover speaking in tongues is the manifestation that was to come at Pentecost, in "the fullness of time". (John 14:12) We have already seen that it was when Jesus went back to be with His Father in Heaven, that the Holy Ghost could then be given to His fullness, which in turn made speaking in tongues possible. Jesus had said: "The things that I do, you will also do, and you will do greater things, because I am going to My Father." The ability to speak in languages we have never learned, then, is part of the "greater things" that Jesus said we would do after He had gone back to Heaven.

but be sure to wait until the Holy Spirit directs you. Not everyone will be ready for your witness when you think they should be, so share only as the Holy Spirit opens the doors. Prepare yourself to be an effective witness by seriously studying the Scriptures mentioned in this book.

When a person receives the baptism with the Holy Spirit it doesn't mean he's "arrived" spiritually, as we're sure you understand having read this far. Don't ever yield to the enemy's temptation to cause you to feel superior; pray for the fruit of humility; it is a good antidote. The baptism with the Holy Spirit is just the *beginning* of a new dimension of your Christian life, and it is still up to you whether you will grow or regress. If you continue to choose to put the Lord first in your life, then you are on the road to glorious adventures in our Lord Jesus Christ!

6
Introduction to the Gifts of the Holy Spirit

If you have been baptized in the Holy Spirit, you are now becoming more aware of the gifts of the Spirit. Two words are used commonly in speaking of the gifts: one is *charisma* (or plural, *charismata*), gift of God's love; the other is *phanerosis*, manifestation.

The simple word "gift" is a good word, as it serves to remind us that these blessings cannot be earned but that they are freely given by God to His children. A gift is not a reward for good behaviour, but a sign of relationship. You give your children birthday presents because they are your children, not because they have been "good". The word "manifestation" means a showing forth, a making visible, or making known. This word shows the gifts of the Spirit to be the ministry of Jesus shown through His people today. The words, "gifts" and "manifestations" together, give us a fuller picture of the work of the Holy Spirit.

We, the members of the body of Christ, should believe that God will show His love through us as needs present themselves day by day. When a person needs healing we should expect God to manifest the gift of healing through us to the needy person. The gifts aren't owned by us. The person *ministered* to receives the gift. We should not claim to have any certain gifts, but let us remember that Jesus, the Gift of God, lives in us, and within Him are all good gifts.

There have been two extreme ideas about manifesting the gifts of the Holy Spirit in the Church. The most prevalent has been that God permanently gives a particular gift or several gifts to certain individuals and they therefore become, for example, the official "speakers in tongues", "interpreters", or "healers". In support of this way of thinking some may quote the Scripture which says: "To one is given by the Spirit the word of wisdom; to another the word of knowledge by the same Spirit ..." (I Cor. 12:8 KJV) and so forth, not seeing that this chapter is speaking of a church meeting where the Holy Spirit is inspiring one person and then another to manifest various gifts. It doesn't mean that one individual is given one or more permanent gifts. This mistake—claiming to have permanent gifts—leads to pride, to stagnation, and tends to limit God's other gifts in that person. Another result is a focusing down on a few people to express the gifts while the majority of the congregation sit by as spectators with no expectation that God may want to work through them.

The other extreme has been the idea that *everyone* baptized in the Holy Spirit has all nine gifts of the Spirit to manifest whenever *he* chooses, sort of an independent "one man band"! While it is true that the gifts reside within Christ in us, yet the Scripture clearly teaches that they are manifested only at the Holy Spirit's discretion (I Cor. 12:11). God is trying to show us that we need one another, that we can't get along all by ourselves. The body of Christ is made up of *many members*, and God has purposely planned the release of the gifts "as He wills" so that Christians would need one another in order to function effectively for Him. We must "discern the Lord's body", by looking for Christ in other Christians or we will greatly hinder and limit what God desires to do.[1] We should be praying for God's glory to be shown in the lives of others as well as in ourselves.

It is true, however, that as Christians mature, certain gifts may be expressed more frequently and effectively through them. It is then said that they have a *ministry* in those gifts. The person with such a ministry should encourage those who are new to enter into the gifts also and should be careful himself not to get so focused in his particular ministry that he stops expecting God to work through him in other ways. God is a God of variety!

As two Christians were talking one day one said: "Well you can *have* the gifts, I'll take the *fruit!*"[2] The gifts of the Holy Spirit are various ways in which the power of God works through the life of the believer. The fruit of the Holy Spirit is the character and nature of Jesus Christ being shown in the life of the believer. Jesus didn't only say to the sick who came to Him: "I love you," but He said, "Be healed!" One of the saddest things to experience is loving people and not being able to help them! Both the fruit and the gifts are vitally important. To date, however, there has been much more teaching and encouragement about the fruit of the Spirit in Christendom than about the gifts[3] of the Spirit.

1. This does not mean that we should condone what others are doing when they are openly proclaiming false doctrine (Eph. 5:11), but minor differences should not be allowed to break our fellowship.

2. The fruit of the Spirit, according to Galatians 5:22–23 is "love, joy, peace, patience, gentleness, kindness, faith, humility, discipline."

3. I Cor. 12:8–10: "the word of wisdom, the word of knowledge, discerning of spirits, gift of faith, working of miracles, gifts of healing, prophecy, various kinds of tongues, interpretation of tongues."

The Holy Spirit inspired Paul to admonish us to learn about the spiritual gifts: "Now concerning spiritual *gifts* brethren, I would not have you ignorant" (I Cor. 12:1). In this book we will define each gift, give New Testament examples in the life of Christ and others, some references to Old Testament usage, and what we may expect for the Church today. It will show how seven gifts were manifested in the Old Testament and Gospels from time to time as people were moved upon by the Holy Spirit.

These seven are:

1. The "Word of Wisdom".
2. The "Word of Knowledge".
3. The Gift of Faith.
4. The Gifts of Healings.
5. The Working of Miracles.
6. The Gift of Prophecy.
7. The Discerning of Spirits.

It will not require too much thought on the reader's part to remember incidents in the Old Testament and Gospels where these were manifested.

To these seven were added two more since the Day of Pentecost.

8. The Gift of Tongues.
9. The Interpretation of Tongues.

thus making up the total of nine Gifts as listed by the Apostle Paul in I Corinthians 12. Thus believers who have not yet experienced Pentecost may manifest any of these seven gifts occasionally, much of the time not even recognizing them as such. However, after the fullness and overflow of the Spirit, any or all nine gifts may be manifested frequently and in power through the life of the believer.

Do not confuse the first seven Gifts listed above with the "Seven-Fold Gifts of Grace" mentioned many places in Christian literature and liturgy—for example, in the Confirmation rite of several of our denominations, or in the widely known Latin hymn: *Veni Creator Spiritus*:

> "The sevenfold gifts of grace are thine,
> O Finger of the Hand Divine!" [4]

This refers to Isaiah 11:2, which says, speaking of the coming Messiah: "And the spirit of the Lord shall rest upon him, the spirit of wisdom and understanding, the spirit of counsel and might, the spirit of knowledge, and of the fear of the Lord". You will see that these are not Spiritual gifts at all, but characteristics of the Holy Spirit in His sevenfold Nature, referred to in Revelation 1:4 as the "seven spirits" which are before God's Throne, the sevenfold Spirit of God. Nevertheless, we can see a direct relationship between these last six characteristics of the Holy Spirit (the first one being "The Spirit of the Lord" Himself), and the ninefold Gifts.

Those who are willing to be used in the gifts of the Holy Spirit must learn to listen to God. Too much of the time we do all the talking. The beginner is bound to make some mistakes. A child learning arithmetic is not expected to learn without making errors! Rest assured that even mistakes will be turned to God's glory as we trust and rely completely on Him.

"Every good gift and every perfect gift is from above, and comes down from the Father ..." says James (Jas. 1:17). It is obvious that God's gifts are perfect, but we need to be reminded that the mortal channels through whom they are expressed are not. Just because a person manifests the gifts does not mean that he is walking closely with the Lord. As the word

4. *Book of Common Prayer*, p. 544.

"gift" implies, the gifts are not earned or retained—even by living a good life. The Book of Romans tells us: "The gifts and calling of God are without repentance" (Rom. 11:29 KJV). Don't follow a person just because he has a "gift ministry". Instead, look for the fruit in his life, for honesty and purity brought about by the Spirit of Truth—the *Holy* Spirit —and a hunger for and appreciation of God's Word. Look for balanced teaching between literal and spiritual meanings of the Scripture, look for fellowship with other brethren; and then receive only that which is quickened to you by the Holy Spirit, and which agrees with the Scripture. Remember, *Christians don't follow signs, signs follow Christians.*

The gifts of God, when expressed as the Lord intended them to be, are beautiful, and needful in order that the body of Christ may grow and develop. They are not merely to be tolerated, but are greatly to be desired. We should be forewarned against two mistakes frequently made in the past: misuse of the gifts by a lack of scriptural order, and rejecting or quenching the gifts of the Spirit. The second mistake is often a reaction against the first one.

In Christ you have been given all good things freely (Rom. 8:32); however, the promises of God must be appropriated by faith. The gifts will be manifested according to your faith: "According to your faith be it unto you" (Matt. 9:29 KJV; Rom. 12:6). Let us manifest His gifts in faith, love, and obedience, that God's people may be strengthened and prepared for their difficult but glorious tasks ahead.

We are not going to study the Gifts in the same order they are presented in I Corinthians 12, but will group them into three classes, as follows:

A. Inspirational or Fellowship Gifts. (The power to *say*.)

    1. The Gift of Tongues.
    2. The Gift of Interpretation.
    3. The Gift of Prophecy.

B. Gifts of Power. (The power to *do*.)

    4. Gifts of Healings.
    5. The Working of Miracles.
    6. The Gift of Faith.

C. Gifts of Revelation. (The power to *know*.)

    7. Discerning of Spirits.
    8. The "Word of Knowledge".
    9. The "Word of Wisdom".

The order in which the Gifts are listed here has no reference
to their relative importance, any more than it does in the Scripture itself, but it will help us to see the relationship of the manifestations with one another.

7
The Gifts of Tongues and Interpretation

The Gifts of utterance—tongues, interpretation, and prophecy —are not to guide our lives by, but to help unfold God to us, and to help us in our response to Him. They are to turn us God-ward and to give us a healthy fear (awe) of the Lord.

We will look at the gifts of tongues and interpretation together, since they should always be manifested together in a public meeting. Some have said that speaking in tongues and interpretation of tongues are the least of the gifts, because they are the last gifts listed in I Corinthians 12:7–11. If there were any special reason why these gifts are last in the list, a more logical one would be because they were given to the Church last! The first seven gifts in the list are found in the Old Testament and the Gospels, but these two were not given until Pentecost.

There are two ways speaking in tongues may be manifested. The most common is as a devotional language for private edification, needing no interpretation (I Cor. 14:2). This has already been discussed in detail. What we will be talking about now is the public manifestation of tongues, which should be interpreted. We will term *this* the "gift of tongues." When a baptized-in-the-Holy-Spirit Christian is inspired to speak in tongues aloud in the presence of others, with interpretation of tongues usually following, this is the *gift* of tongues (I Cor. 14:27–28; 12:10). The gift of tongues is delivered or given to the listeners, and they are edified by the gift of interpretation which follows.[1] It is preferable that tongues and interpretation should not be used in groups of unbelievers or even uninstructed believers, without an explanation of what they are—either before or after the manifestations.

There are two main ways the gift of tongues may be expressed in the gathered church:

1. Through the gift of tongues and interpretation God may be speaking to the unbeliever and/or to believers.

Although God Himself doesn't speak in tongues (how could there be a language unknown to Him?), yet, He does guide the yielded Christian to do so, and through tongues and interpretation does speak to His people today. Both the Old and New Testaments give joint witness that God does speak to His people through these gifts. Isaiah says:

"For with stammering lips and another tongue will he speak to this people" (Isa. 28:11 KJV). St. Paul quotes this as he explains speaking in tongues and interpretation: "It is written, 'With men of other tongues and other lips will I speak unto this people . . .'" (I Cor. 14:21 KJV), or the literal Greek translation reads: "In other tongues and in lips of others I will speak to this people . . ." Also the Scripture implies that the gift of tongues plus interpretation is equal to prophecy, which is always God speaking to the people (I Cor. 14:3).

The gift of tongues is not a sign to the believer since he doesn't need a sign, but it may be a sign to the unbeliever

1. The gift of tongues may also be prayer or praise to God.

(usually unsought for), causing him to accept the Lord Jesus Christ. "Wherefore tongues are for a sign, not to them that believe, but to them that believe not . . ." (I Cor. 14:22 KJV).

How the gift of tongues can be a sign to the unbeliever:

a) The tongue may be a language known to the unbeliever with God speaking directly to him.

b) The tongue may not be a known language, but the powerful impact of the message in tongues, normally accompanied by interpretation, may speak to the unbeliever, and be a sign to him.

When tongues are a message from God, coming to the unbeliever either by his knowing the language (a translation), by the inspired interpretation through a believer, or in some rare cases even without benefit of interpretation or translation, they are a sign to the unbeliever that God is real, alive, and concerned about him.

In a Full Gospel church in Oregon, there was a young man who married a Japanese girl while stationed in Japan with the armed forces. The young couple returned to the United States, and were doing well, except that the young lady flatly resisted her husband's Christian faith and held steadfastly to her Buddhism. One night, after the evening service, the couple was at the altar, he praying to God through Jesus Christ, and she praying her Buddhist prayers. Next to them was kneeling a middle-aged woman, a housewife from the community. As this woman began to pray out loud in tongues, suddenly the Japanese bride seized her husband's arm:

"Listen!" she whispered in excitement. "This woman speak to me in Japanese! She say to me: 'You have tried Buddha, and he does you no good; why don't you try Jesus Christ?' She does not speak to me in ordinary Japanese language, she speak temple Japanese, and use my whole Japanese name which no one in this country knows!" It is not surprising that the young lady became a Christian!

We have known of many similar cases. What actually happened in this situation is that as the American housewife was yielded to God in *praying in tongues,* the Holy Ghost chose to change the language from prayer *to* God—to a message *from* God—through the *gift* of tongues.

Ruth Lascelle (then Specter)[2] had been brought up in an Orthodox Jewish home. When in her early adult life, her mother accepted Jesus as her Messiah, Ruth thought her mother had lost her mind. She went to her mother's Full Gospel church to try to disprove their beliefs. At one meeting there was a message in tongues which, although uninterpreted, had such a great impact on Ruth that she knew in that moment that Jesus was real, and she too accepted Him as her Messiah.

Here is an example of the gift of tongues, although neither understood nor interpreted, yet bearing a sign of such strength that Ruth was converted on the spot. Ruth says: "I asked God to give me a sign to show if the Christian faith was really true. At the time of course, I had never heard of the New Testament Scripture: 'The Jews required a sign' "[3] (I Cor. 1 : 22 KJV).

Another interesting scene took place in 1964 in Northern California at a charismatic Episcopal church service. A college student had come to the meeting with her father, an important ecclesiastical official. This young lady had known Jesus in her childhood, but had grown further and further away from Him during her college years. Her faith had been pretty much smashed and she was under psychiatric care. Near the close of the meeting the gifts of tongues and interpretation were mani-

---

2. R. R. Specter, *The Bud and the Flower of Judaism* (Springfield, Mo.: Gospel Publishing House, 1955).

3. An uninterpreted gift of tongues in a meeting is of course irregular, but in this case God used it.

fested in love and with power. Tears began to pour down her face as she made her way to the altar for prayer. She told the person counselling with her:

"When I heard speaking in tongues for the first time tonight, and the message that followed, I knew once again without a doubt that God is real and He loves me!"

This last is an example of these gifts as a sign, not to an unbeliever, as previously recorded, but rather to a temporarily unbelieving believer.

The gifts of tongues and interpretation may also be a message from God to bless and exhort faithful people. Examples are numerous; we will take time to give only one. One Friday night about a year after Rita was renewed in her experience of the baptism in the Holy Spirit she was attending a prayer meeting. She prayed for a friend who was working as a missionary nurse in Africa, and was having some difficult trials. As she finished praying for Dorothy, there was a gift of tongues and interpretation, which said in effect: "If you, yourself, are willing to go and help your friend, your prayer will be answered much more quickly." Then the Lord asked Rita three times, just as Peter had been asked: "Do you love Me?" She had been walking closely with Him, and had been an active witness for Him ever since her renewal; it was such a surprise to be asked if she loved Him, that she began to weep. Rita told God, then and there, that she loved Him so much that she was willing to go wherever He wanted her to go. So convincing was the message the Holy Spirit had given that at the end of the meeting her friends gathered round to bid her farewell! As it turned out, although she was willing to go to Africa, two months later the Lord sent her instead—to Texas!

2. The gift of tongues may also be public prayer to God.

Most of us would rather hear from heaven than from earth; we would rather hear God speak to us, than hear man speak to

God. Yet in reading the Scripture, we see the gift of tongues used as prayer in a public meeting and needing interpretation so that other believers can be in agreement (I Cor. 14: 13–16). Therefore, the gift of tongues plus interpretation may also be prayer, thanksgiving, or praise to God, which encourages the congregation. The gift of tongues as prayer or praise may be in a language known by unbelievers, as happened on the day of Pentecost: "We do hear them speak in our tongues the wonderful works of God." Paul also says that someone in the meeting may *sing* praise to God using the gift of tongues; the interpretation may also be given in song, which can be most inspiring.

Any baptized-in-the-Holy-Spirit believer can "sing in the Spirit". This means allowing the Holy Spirit not only to guide one's speech, but to sing as He guides the words *and* the tune. In a group of instructed believers a number of persons may pray or praise God, speaking or singing in tongues all together without interpretation being required. At times when an entire group joins in "singing in the Spirit", allowing the Holy Spirit not only to guide individual voices, but to blend them together, such harmony is produced that it sometimes sounds like the angelic choir itself! If singing in the Spirit or praying in the Spirit occurs in a large group, and all are not instructed believers, a scriptural explanation should be given by the leader as soon as possible. Many unbelievers have been touched by God in such situations—when the meeting was guided with wisdom and according to the scriptural pattern.

Some have been puzzled when a brief utterance in tongues is followed by a long response in English. There are several reasons for this. It may be that the language the Holy Spirit gave was more concise than the more elaborate language of the interpreter. Then too, the interpretation itself may have been followed by words in prophecy. A further explanation may be that the speaking in tongues was really private prayer, and the presumed interpretation actually prophecy.

Though all baptized-in-the-Holy-Spirit believers can and should speak in tongues daily in their prayers, not all will minister the gift of tongues in a public meeting (I Cor. 12: 30). You will know that God is prompting you to manifest the gift of tongues when you have a definite quickening or witness of the Holy Spirit within. This doesn't mean that you have to do anything impulsively. Talk to the Lord quietly and tell Him if He wants to use you in this way to make an opportunity in the service for you to minister. Never interrupt when another person is speaking. As David duPlessis says, "The Holy Spirit is a Gentleman!" Ask the Lord if this is the particular gift He wants for the group. When bringing any of the oral gifts of the Holy Spirit—tongues, interpretation, or prophecy—be sure to speak loudly enough to be heard by all, but don't be unnecessarily noisy or use an affected tone of voice. Either of the latter will frighten some people and make them wonder about the validity of the gift. It will keep them from hearing what God desires to say to them. Speak with the utmost concern for the welfare of all, and in the love of God. If you believe that God wants you to manifest the gift of tongues, be prepared to pray also for the gift of interpretation in case there is no other person present yielded enough to do so (I Cor. 14: 13).

The *interpretation of tongues* is bringing the meaning of what has been said through the gift of tongues at a public meeting. A person feels moved to speak or sing in tongues, and either he or another is given by the Holy Spirit the *meaning* of what has been said. He or she cannot *understand* the tongue. It is not a *translation* but an *interpretation,* giving the general meaning of what was said. The gift of interpretation may come directly into the person's mind, *in toto,* or just a few beginning words may be given, and as the interpreter trusts the Lord and begins to speak, the rest of the message comes. In this way it resembles speaking in tongues—"You speak, the Lord gives the words." Interpretation may also come in pictures or symbols, or by an inspired thought, or the interpreter may hear the speaking in tongues, or part of it, as though the person were speaking directly in English. Interpretation will have the same result as a prophetic utterance, that of: "edification, exhortation, or comfort" (I Cor. 14: 3–5). Remember, the gifts are not to guide your life by, but rather to confirm what God is already saying to you in your spirit and through the Scriptures.

God moves as He wills, but He does have a general pattern for us to follow. Some have called I Corinthians 14 the charismatic Christian's *Robert's Rules of Order*. For example, I Corinthians 14: 27 says, "If some speak in a . . . tongue, let the number be limited to two or at the most three, and each one [taking his] turn, and let one interpret and explain [what is said]" (Amplified Bible). This Scripture gives specific rules. It limits the number of utterances in tongues and interpretation to two or three times in any one meeting. Some think the next verse means that after two or three gifts of tongues an "official interpreter" should bring only one interpretation for the two or three utterances in tongues, but verse thirteen indicates that *anyone* who is used to manifest the gift of tongues may also pray to interpret. This is important to realize since others in the meeting may not be yielded enough at that moment to bring the needed interpretation. To keep from having tongues without interpretation causing confusion to unbelievers and uninstructed believers (v. 23, 33), it seems scriptural that each utterance in tongues should be interpreted singly. Also it would be difficult to retain an interpretation for any considerable length of time.

More speaking in tongues would no doubt be recognized as known languages if there were someone present who knew the language and could translate. It is also possible that some speakings in tongues are "languages of angels" (I Cor. 13 : 1). There are about three thousand languages and dialects in the world, so it is not surprising that few languages are recognized in any particular locality; indeed it is surprising that so many are. On the day of Pentecost there were about one hundred and twenty speaking in tongues, but only fourteen languages were recognized (Acts 1 : 15; 2 : 1, 4, 7–11), even though "devout Jews" were present from all over the then known world. This is about the percentage of known languages identified today. In praying with people for the blessing of Pentecost and being in numerous charismatic meetings in many parts of the world during the last ten years, we have known people to have spoken in tongues in Latin, Spanish, French, Hebrew, Old Basque, Japanese, Aramaic, Mandarin Chinese, German, Indonesian, Chinese Foochow dialect, N. T. Greek, English (by a non-English speaker), and Polish.

At times those who have received the Pentecost experience are challenged by some who do not understand the purposes of speaking in tongues with such questions as:

"If you really have been given a new language, why don't you have it analysed, find out what country it is from, and then go there as a missionary teaching the Gospel in that tongue?" Others challenge:

"If Pentecost is so great, how come missionaries with this experience still have to study language in school?"

These people don't realize that the gift of tongues is manifested to the unbeliever only as the Holy Spirit directs, and even though a person may be used once to speak a certain language, thereby reaching someone for Christ, he has no way of knowing that that specific language will ever be given to him again. Although a baptized-in-the-Holy-Spirit believer can speak in his private devotional tongue at will, yet in this and in the gift of tongues the choice of language he will speak cannot be regulated by the individual. God brings these vocal miracles to pass as He chooses and for His own purposes.

Then too some people mistakenly say the Gospel was proclaimed through the gift of tongues on the day of Pentecost and therefore this would be the only valid purpose for speaking in tongues today. This again is erroneous. Though some were heard speaking known languages by the power of the Holy Spirit on the day of Pentecost—yet they did not proclaim the Gospel in tongues but were instead heard praising God. The one who did the evangelizing that day was Peter. Though prior to his speaking to the people, he too had been edified by speaking in tongues, yet when he brought the message of salvation he spoke a language he understood, in a language all the listeners could understand.

There is a very common, but mistaken idea that the hearers on the Day of Pentecost were "foreigners" who did not understand the Aramaic dialect of Hebrew which was the common language and so had to have the Gospel presented to them in the languages of the countries from which they came. A more careful inspection of the record will correct this. The second chapter of Acts says:

"There were dwelling at Jerusalem *Jews*, devout men, from every nation under heaven" (Acts 2:5).

The people who heard the 120 first believers speaking in tongues on the Day of Pentecost were faithful Jews from the "Dispersion" or *diaspora*, which was the term used to describe the fact that already in those days the Jewish people were scattered all over the world. But just as they have done today, they kept their identity and brought their children up as good Jews. Even though they were born in foreign parts, and perhaps were brought up speaking another language, they were all taught the Hebrew tongue, and no doubt looked forward eagerly to the day when they would visit Jerusalem. The Day of Pentecost scene would be just as if English people from all over the world were to come to London for some great national event, say, the coronation of Queen Elizabeth II. Here are people from New Zealand, and Jamaica, and India—English in nationality, raised in English homes in faraway places, knowing and speaking the English language, yet never having seen "home". In their everyday lives they would often speak a "foreign" tongue. Imagine a group of such people coming to London for the coronation and suddenly hearing a group of cockney Londoners speaking beautifully in the language of the far-off countries from which they came!

"Are not all these which speak cockneys? How hear we then every man in the language of the country where we were born? . . ."

"Oh," say some, "you see they all *heard* in their own language. The disciples were speaking in a mysterious 'tongue' that miraculously sounded to each one like his own language." An interesting theory, but not scriptural! The Bible says: "They began to speak in *other languages* as the Spirit gave them utterance" (Acts 2:4).

When Peter addressed the crowd, he said to them:

"Men and *brethren* . . ." They were not foreigners, but "brethren," a term that the Jew did not use lightly! Besides, it is clear that when Peter stood up to tell them what was going on, he was not speaking in tongues. Fourteen nations and languages are mentioned—did Peter then speak in each of these fourteen languages in succession? Of course not; he spoke in a language which all understood. What would they have been doing in Jerusalem for the great feast day, if they were not able to understand what was going on? The record says that there were a few *proselytes,* that is, converts from the Gentiles, but these, too, would have been instructed in the Hebrew language.

Having made this general point that tongues are not normally used to proclaim the Gospel and were not used this way on the Day of Pentecost, let us also recognize, as always, there are exceptions to the rule. There are examples scattered through Christian history, of those who were given by the Holy Spirit the ability both to speak and understand a new language, this ability remaining with them. The great missionary to the Orient, Francis Xavier, according to his biographers, received the Chinese language in this way. Stanley Frodsham, in his book, *With Signs Following,* gives several similar examples in the modern Pentecostal movement.

John Sherrill, in the book, *They Speak With Other Tongues,*[4] tells of a missionary who in 1922 was used to bring the message of salvation to a tribe of cannibals through the gift of tongues. The missionary, H. B. Garlock, being captured and put on trial by the natives, spoke for some twenty minutes in what to him was an unknown language, but which the cannibals obviously understood and responded to by setting him free, and later turning to Christ. It is significant that Garlock then returned to his own mission station, and continued ministering to Liberian people whose language he had no doubt taken much time and effort to learn. The cannibals' language was not given him permanently by the Spirit, but "loaned" to him for the emergency.

A young woman from St. Luke's Church, Seattle, some eight years ago stopped to talk with an unknown Asiatic woman while making a hospital call. The woman spoke very little English, but was able to say, in response to a gesture by the St. Luke's visitor indicating that she would like to pray with her: "I, Buddha! I Buddha," meaning of course that she was a

4. John L. Sherrill, *They Speak With Other Tongues* (New York: McGraw-Hill, 1964), pp. 107–111.

Buddhist. The girl from St. Luke's felt led to speak to the woman as the Spirit gave her the words, and for several minutes talked to the woman in a language unknown to the speaker. As the lady from St. Luke's took her leave, the other said, with a joyful face: "I! Jesus! I! Jesus!" Obviously the girl from St. Luke's had been witnessing to the Asiatic woman in her own language, and she had responded by receiving Jesus as her Saviour!

Another unscriptural notion is that the Corinthians were the "Peck's Bad Boys" of the early Church! They did disorderly things like speaking in tongues, because they were only half-converted from their paganism! Paul had to lecture them on their emotionalism. He went along with them on their speaking in tongues but he didn't like it!

How wrong this is can be seen quickly, again, by really reading the New Testament. When Paul went to Corinth, God said to him: "I have much people in this city" (Acts 18:10 KJV). It was at Corinth that Paul met two of his greatest helpers, Aquila and Priscilla, and it was to Corinth that they brought Apollos, one of the most effective of the early evangelists. There is no implication that the Corinthians were in any way a second-rate bunch! Indeed, it is a popular misconception that a great church is a church without problems. Just the opposite is true—the greater and stronger the work, the more problems Satan will try to stir up. The Corinthians had troubles because God was doing a great work among them, and it was being challenged by the enemy.

Paul did not remonstrate with the Corinthians because they were speaking in tongues, he did so because they were letting pride and party spirit come into their group. His great concern was their divisions—their sectarianism, which in turn led to a misuse of the gifts. Far from trying to get them to stop using the gifts, he urges them repeatedly: "covet the gifts", "earnestly desire them" (I Cor. 12: 31; 14: 1); "I want you to come behind in no gift" . . . "I want you to be enriched in all knowledge and all utterance . . ." he says to them; but also, "Let all things be done decently and in order" (I Cor 1: 7, 5; 14: 40 KJV).

If Paul were to arrive on the scene today he would undoubtedly deal with us as he did with the Corinthians.

"My brothers and sisters, I hear there are divisions among you . . . for I hear some of you saying you are of Luther, and others of Calvin, still others that you are of Peter, or of Wesley! Is Christ divided? Was Wesley crucified for you? Or were you baptized in the name of the Episcopal church?" Then Paul would turn to the charismatic groups—some of them, anyway—and say something like this:

"My dear brethren, I am so delighted to hear and see the wonderful gifts of the Spirit manifested among you. I couldn't understand where they had gone when I was with those other churches—but please! Did that brother have to shout quite so loudly? I saw someone walk out of the meeting when he did! You had a public meeting and invited unbelievers, and then all of you spoke in tongues at the same time with no explanation! Did that show love and concern for your visitors? I am sure some of the people you were trying to reach thought you were crazy! Remember that the spirit of the prophet is subject to the prophet, won't you?"

Can speaking in tongues be counterfeited? Of course. All the Gifts have their Satanic counterfeit, and there are certainly strange utterances and sounds made by those who worship other gods, or are involved in other religions or cults, that are a counterfeit of speaking in tongues. In a large public meeting, where it is difficult properly to control the situation, it might be possible for such a person to manifest a counterfeit. This is where the gift of discerning spirits is needed. No Christian, however, who is walking in the Spirit, under the protection of the Blood of Jesus, need fear that he or she might produce a counterfeit of speaking in tongues. The Scripture reminds us of our safety in Christ:

"If a son shall ask bread of any of you that is a father, will he give him a stone? or if he ask a fish, will he for a fish give him a serpent? If you then, being evil, know how to give good gifts unto your children; how much more shall your heavenly Father give the Holy Spirit to them that ask him?" (Luke 11: 11, 13). ". . . . No man speaking by the Spirit of God (this can mean a Christian speaking in tongues) calls Jesus accursed" (I Cor. 12: 3).

In summary, the gift of tongues and interpretation of tongues is first of all a sign to unbelievers (I Cor. 14: 22), *when manifested according to scriptural instructions*. Secondly, these two gifts have the same benefit as prophecy and therefore are also for the edification of the Church (I Cor. 14: 5, 26–27).

Ask God to use you in these two gifts; both are needed. The Apostle Paul, in I Corinthians 12, compares the publicly manifested gifts of the Spirit with the various members and senses of the body, each having its place, and each being necessary in its own way. In the light of this Scripture, it is hard to see how any of the gifts could be categorized as less or more significant than any other, since Paul emphasizes that each member of the body is important. Unless all the gifts are manifested, the Body of Christ on earth will be handicapped.

Each should examine his or her life, and make things right with God before manifesting God's gifts. If people are helped, be sure to give God the glory! Pray that God's glory will be manifested through other members in the Body of Christ also (John 17: 22).

8
The Gift of Prophecy

The gift of prophecy is manifested when believers speak the mind of God, by the inspiration of the Holy Spirit, and not from their own thoughts. It is supernatural speech in a known language. Prophecy is not a "private" gift, but is always brought to a group of believers although it may be for one or more individuals who are present. In this way it may be "judged", that is, evaluated by the Church.

Although prophecy is sixth on the list in I Corinthians 12, yet Paul puts it at the top in the fourteenth chapter, as being of the greatest benefit to the Church. He says:

"Follow after charity, and desire spiritual gifts, but rather that you may prophesy . . . he that prophesies edifies (builds up) the Church." The thirty-ninth verse is even more emphatic:

"*Covet* to prophesy!"

In the last chapter we saw that the gifts of tongues and interpretation together were first of all a sign to unbelievers, and secondly, to build up the Church—the believers. Prophecy is just the reverse, being first for the edification of the believers, and secondly for unbelievers. ". . . Prophecy serves not for them that believe not, but for those who believe" (I Cor. 14:22).

There are three ways, the Scripture tells us, in which prophecy ministers to believers: edification, exhortation, and comfort; or building up, urging on, and consoling (I Cor. 14:3). Obviously then, most prophecy to the Church is of an encouraging nature, but not all. If an earthly father never corrected his children, it would be harmful and unloving. They wouldn't grow up and mature normally. On the other hand, if the father were always telling them they were wrong, and never told them that he loved and appreciated them, love wouldn't grow between the parent and the children. We may say that there is a healthy ratio here: one-third exhortation and two-thirds comfort! Thus in a meeting you may expect to hear many prophecies that are frankly the Father comforting, and fewer that are of the "get with it" variety! Valid prophecy will not be harshly condemnatory of believers, but it may strongly counsel them.

Up to the present, in most charismatic meetings there has been more ministry to believers through the gifts of tongues and interpretation than through the gift of prophecy. One reason for this is that it seems to require more faith to speak out directly in prophecy, than for one person to speak in tongues and another to interpret. Speaking in tongues is an easier gift to bring than prophecy precisely because the language is unknown to the speaker and so he or she does not fear saying the wrong thing, and the interpretation is usually brought by another person. The person prophesying, however, has to carry the whole responsibility!

The first purpose of prophecy, thus, is to speak to believers, but this gift can also bring unbelievers to God. The Scripture says: "But if all prophesy, and there comes in one that does not believe, or one that is uninstructed, he is convinced of all, he is judged of all: and thus are the secrets of his heart made manifest; and so falling down on his face he will worship God, and report that God is in you of a truth" (I Cor. 14: 24–25). This indicates the use of the gift of prophecy together with the gift of knowledge. This latter is briefly the divine revelation of facts not learned through the natural mind. We will talk about this gift in more detail in a later chapter. As these intimate facts are revealed about the condition of the unbeliever's heart, he is convinced of God's reality and immediately converted. The "unlearned" or uninstructed believer, on the other hand, who does not fully understand the gifts of the Spirit, not having received the baptism in the Holy Spirit, is often at this point convinced that these things are real. (This last is happening quite frequently today, of course. Many "uninstructed" believers are coming to receive the baptism in the Holy Spirit because they have seen the gifts in operation which they had been told were "not for today".)

In the Old Testament there were men who were moved of God to prophesy. These prophets were especially chosen of God to speak His word to the people, usually ministering the combined gifts of prophecy and knowledge, and often doing other "mighty acts" by the power of God. Many times God's will and intention were given through them. Usually any prophecy concerning the future had an "if" connected with it:

"In forty days Nineveh shall be overthrown" (Jonah 3: 4), Jonah was commanded to announce. But the people of Nineveh repented in sackcloth and ashes. What would have been the point of bothering to send Jonah if there was no chance for them to repent? So Nineveh wasn't overthrown—at least, not at that time—and Jonah was very upset!

Jeremiah was a prophet of old who warned the cities of Judah to turn from the error of their ways. This was a "conditional" prophecy, too. After hearing him speak these words from the

Lord, the priest, the other prophets, and the people wanted to kill Jeremiah. The role of the prophet was often unpopular, and sometimes very dangerous. "Which of the prophets have not your fathers persecuted?" Stephen challenged the Sanhedrin. Jesus cried: "O Jerusalem, Jerusalem, you who kill the prophets . . . !" (Matt. 23: 37, Acts 7: 52).

There are also many *un*conditional prophesies concerning God's definite plans, especially concerning the coming of Christ. Isaiah 53 is a perfect example—it is one of the greatest prophecies in the Old Testament concerning the Lord Jesus. Moses prophesied about Christ: "The Lord thy God will raise up unto thee a Prophet from the midst of thee, of thy brethren, like unto me; unto him ye shall hearken" (Deut. 18: 15 KJV). And indeed Jesus Christ Himself was a "prophet mighty in deed and word" (Luke 24: 19 KJV). He was *the* Prophet,[1] just as He was *the* Priest, and *the* King. We have many prophetic utterances by Jesus Christ in the New Testament. Mark 13 and Matthew 24, are strong prophecies of coming things. John 16 is almost entirely prophecy through Jesus to His closest disciples:

"These things have I spoken unto you, that ye should not be offended. They shall put you out of the synagogues: yea, the time cometh, that whosoever killeth you will think he doeth God service. And these things will they do unto you, because they have not known the Father, nor me. But these things I have told you, that when the time shall come, you may remember that I told you of them" (John 16: 1-4). (Read the rest of the chapter, too.)

These "unconditional" prophecies are mainly given for guide-posts to believers, so that we may discern the "signs of

1. Just seeing Jesus as a Prophet does not make one a Christian; He must be recognized to be the divine Son of God, God made flesh!

the times". Jesus said: "I tell you before it come to pass, that, when it is come to pass, you may believe" (John 14:29). We are not supposed to be arguing over the prophecies, but simply noting them as they come to pass, so that we know where we are in God's time plan.

In Old Testament times God could not yet, by His Spirit, come to *dwell* in His people, but the Holy Spirit did come down to anoint certain people as they were yielded to God. The Spirit rested on them. In one instance, Moses as a prophet and a leader of the Children of Israel found his work too heavy a load to carry alone, so God took of the Holy Spirit resting upon him and put the Spirit also upon seventy other men; when this happened, they too began to prophesy. Then a problem arose as two of the brethren, Eldad and Medad, who were not with the rest of the seventy in the Tabernacle, also were inspired by the Spirit and began to prophesy in the open camp. Some of the others complained and wanted to forbid the two men to minister. Moses' answer was in itself a prophecy:

"Are you envious for my sake? would God that all the Lord's people were prophets, and that the Lord would put his spirit upon them!" (Num. 11:29).

These words were fulfilled on the day of Pentecost. On that day Peter quoted the words of Joel which were similar: "This is that which was spoken by the prophet Joel; And it shall come to pass in the last days, says God, I will pour out of my Spirit upon all flesh: and your sons and your daughters shall prophesy, and your young men shall see visions, and your old men shall dream dreams: And on my servants and on my handmaidens I will pour out in those days of My Spirit; and they shall prophesy." (Acts 2:16–18).

At Ephesus, when Paul laid hands on the twelve men and they received their "Pentecost", they "spoke with tongues and prophesied" (Acts 19:6). The Scripture tells us that ever since the day of Pentecost and the outpouring of the Holy Spirit, any yielded child of God may be moved by the Spirit to prophesy. Paul at Corinth, after urging them all to seek to prophesy, even refers to all those used this way as prophets: "Let the prophets speak two or three, and let the other (Greek —others) judge. If any thing be revealed to another that sitteth by, let the first hold his peace. For you may all prophesy one by one, that all may learn, and all may be comforted. And the spirits of the prophets are subject to the prophets" (I Cor. 14: 29–32).

These verses also tell us the "rules" for the use of prophecy in a meeting. The prophets are to be limited to speaking two or three times—the same as for tongues and interpretation. As wonderful as the vocal gifts are, they must not take over the meeting. Plenty of room must be given to inspired teaching from the Word of God, to praise and prayer, to sharing of testimony, to singing God's praises, etc.

As we have said earlier, prophecy is always to the community: the people of God. It should always be brought in the presence of others, because prophecy is always to be judged or evaluated by the Church, in terms of the witness of the Spirit in the hearts of the other brethren, and in terms of the written Word of God, with which the prophecy must always agree. This provides the control too, from an individual claiming too much for him or herself. The leader of the meeting must especially be sensitive to correct wherever it is needed. Good manners and consideration for others is also mentioned. "The spirits of the prophets are subject to the prophets" reminds us that the gifts of the Spirit are inspiration, not compulsion, and provide no excuse for erratic behaviour. If the Holy Spirit is truly being followed, the meeting will be peaceful, loving, and orderly: "in decency and order", as Paul puts it. The word "decency" for us might be better translated "fittingly", or "becomingly".

Women are permitted to minister in prayer and prophecy as long as they are under "headship", that is, submitted to male leadership. We have found a sort of "semi-Pauline rule" to be effective, asking that two women do not minister one after another, but wait for a man to alternate, e.g., if a woman has spoken in tongues, to expect and wait for a man to bring the interpretation; if a woman brings a testimony or prophecy, to ask the other woman to wait until a man has ministered before another woman does so. This kind of practice encourages both men and women, since there are very few ladies who don't want to see the men take the lead.

If a woman is in doubt as to her right to prophesy, let her remember the beautiful prophecy brought by Mary the mother of Jesus:

"My soul doth magnify the Lord, And my spirit has rejoiced in God my Saviour. For he hath regarded the low estate of his handmaiden: for behold, from henceforth all generations shall call me blessèd. For he that is mighty hath done to me great things; and holy is his name. And his mercy is on them that fear him from generation to generation. He hath shewed strength with his arm; he hath scattered the proud in the imagination of their hearts. He hat put down the mighty from their seats, and exalted them of low degree. He hath filled the hungry with good things; and the rich he hath sent empty away" (Luke 1: 46–53 KJV).

We have been talking about the gift of prophecy for all members of the Body, but now we need to talk about those who have a *ministry* in prophecy. Just as the Apostolic Age has not ended, and the ministry of the apostle is still going on today, so there are still those with the ministry of the prophet today.

Because the Old Testament prophets often spoke out against social and political abuses, and against priestcraft and the hierarchy of that day—the "establishment!"—an erroneous idea has sprung up that every protester and militant campaigner for social justice is a "prophet", and that "prophecy" mainly consists in denouncing human evil. As we have seen, however, it isn't what a man says in the natural realm that makes him a prophet; it is the fact that he is moved by the Spirit of God to speak the words *God* gives him.

The real prophet will not find it necessary to announce to others that he is a prophet; he will be known by his ministry. Moses is a strong example of a prophet, yet the Bible says of him: "Moses was very meek (humble, gentle), above all the men which were upon the face of the earth" (Num. 12: 3 KJV). This is a good test for the prophet today. A prophet of God will naturally minister in the gift of prophecy often, and it will very likely be conjoined to the gift of knowledge—it is often hard to distinguish between the two—declaring God's will and God's mind. When Jesus told the woman at the well about her personal life in detail, she immediately said:

"Sir, I perceive that you are a prophet" (John 4: 19).

A true prophet of God will be a mature Christian, as his ministry is listed as one of the offices to be used to bring the Church to maturity (Eph. 4: 8, 11–16). No person should be allowed to minister as an established prophet in the Church unless he is thoroughly known by the brethren as to his doctrine and his manner of life. A true prophet will speak out against things that are wrong, whether it makes him unpopular or not. He will draw people to God and not to himself.

The ministry of the prophet must be even more carefully judged than that of the brethren in general who prophesy in the meeting. A man may be strongly used in the prophetic office, and yet may be completely wrong from time to time. His words must never be accepted because of his ministry, but tested by the Word and the Spirit; this does not mean at all that he is a false prophet, but that he is still not perfected and therefore liable to error. "We prophesy in part" (I Cor. 13:9 KJV).

The enemy has counterfeits of all the true gifts, and there are plenty of false prophets in the world. A false prophet is a most dangerous person, as he will use his supposed authority to gain wrong influence over people, and keep them in bondage to himself through fear. He will separate them from others in the family of Christ lest he be challenged and found out, using as an excuse that they are a very special and elite group. Recently in our own city a small group of earnest Christians was taken over by a man from another city. He came in and told them that he was to be their "shepherd". They were to have no contact even with relatives and friends who did not approve of the group, and were to read no other literature than that which he permitted them to read—most of which he had written himself! They were, of course, to listen to no other teachers but himself. If anyone separated himself from the group, he would be lost, they were told. There are many such "grievous wolves", as Paul called them, preying upon God's people today, so be warned.

"Thus saith the LORD of Hosts. Hearken not unto the words of the prophets that prophesy unto you: *they make you vain:* they speak a vision of their own heart, and not out of the mouth of the LORD" (Jer. 23:16 KJV). The deceiving prophet will not warn the people to turn from that which is wrong (Jer. 23: 17–22), and usually immorality springs up where there is false prophecy.

We should also be careful of personal, directive prophecy, especially outside the ministry of a mature and submitted man of God. Unrestrained "personal prophecy" did much to undermine the movement of the Holy Spirit which began at the turn of the century. It is still present today. Christians are certainly given words for one another "in the Lord", of knowledge or wisdom, and such words can be most refreshing and helpful, but there must be a witness of the Spirit on the part of the person receiving the words, and extreme caution should be used in receiving any alleged directive or predictive prophecy. Never undertake any project simply because you were told to by presumed prophetic utterances or interpretation of tongues, or by a presumed word of wisdom, or knowledge. Never do something just because a friend comes to you and says: "The Lord told me to tell you to do thus and thus!" If the Lord has instructions for you, He will give you a witness in your own heart, in which case the words coming from a friend, or through the gifts of the Holy Spirit in a meeting, will be confirmation to what God *has already been* showing you. Your guidance must also agree with Scripture. Speaking of the Scriptures, Peter says:

"We have a more sure Word of Prophecy; whereunto you do well that you take heed, as unto a light that shines in a dark place, until the day dawn, and the day star arise in your hearts . . ." (II Peter 1 : 19). The written Word of God is our guidebook, which we must study well, and is the test of all spoken words. There is an old saying which bears repeating: "If you have the Spirit without the Word, you'll blow up; if you have the Word without the Spirit, you'll dry up; but if you have the Spirit and the Word, you'll grow up!"

Note the caution of the prophet Jeremiah. He was told by the Lord to buy a piece of property from his cousin Hanameel. He took no action, however, until his cousin came and offered to sell him the property, having no idea what the Lord had already said to Jeremiah. "Then," said Jeremiah, "I knew it was the word of the Lord." If the prophet Jeremiah, that great man of God, was so cautious, not even believing his own prophecy until it was confirmed, we should be all the more (Jer. 32:6–9).

Prophecy isn't fortune-telling! Prophecy isn't looking into a crystal ball, or reading cards or supposedly predicting the future by any other method. As we have already said in detail in a previous chapter, God strictly forbids any attempt to pry into the future—He has always forbidden it. If men attempt to do this, they will be fed information from the enemy for his own purposes, and if they persist, it will be to their destruction. As we have seen, it is true that the Scripture shows that through the utterances of His prophets God sometimes tells us what is going to happen; however, this has nothing whatsoever to do with fortune-telling; God has simply shared His intentions with His faithful children. The true prophet was not *trying to get* information about the present or the future, but he was having fellowship with the Lord, when God chose to share the knowledge. True prophecy is *forth*telling not *fore*telling.

Prophecy is not *"inspired preaching"*. Preaching which means "proclaiming the Gospel", should indeed be inspired by the Holy Spirit, but in preaching, the intellect, training, skill, background, and education are involved and inspired by the Holy Spirit. The sermon may be written down ahead of time, or given on the spot, but it comes from the inspired intellect. Prophecy, on the other hand, means that the person is bringing the words the Lord gives directly; it is from the spirit, not the intellect. A person can bring prophetic words that he does not even understand himself. In the course of an inspired sermon, the preacher may also prophesy, or manifest the gifts of wisdom and knowledge, but they are to be distinguished from *preaching*.

Prophecy is not *witnessing*. Some, trying to justify the lack of prophecy in the Church today, say that it is. They quote the Scripture: "The testimony of Jesus is the spirit of prophecy." Although it is true that the Holy Spirit wants us to witness to unbelievers and has given us the power to do so, yet how could this be "prophecy", when prophecy is the greatest gift to edify the *Church?*

Paul, in his first letter to the Thessalonians, says: "Don't despise prophesying. Prove all things; hold fast that which is good" (I Thess. 5:20–21). Just because there is misuse of God's gifts, and the enemy has counterfeits, doesn't mean we should reject what God has for us. That's exactly what the enemy would want. When the children of Israel came out of the wilderness into the promised land, they found the fruit to be much bigger, but the enemy was, too! There were giants in the land, along with grapes of Eschol, and we may find this true as we enter this new walk in the Spirit—but the fruit is worth the effort required!

Jesus is Prophet, Priest, and King. We today, through Him, can also have these ministries as prophets, priests, and kings (Rev. 1:6). A prophet speaks the words of God to the people; a priest speaks to God on behalf of the people, in praise and prayer; and a king rules, taking authority by his words over the works of the enemy. In all three ministries the *voice* is extremely important, and gives us further insight into why the *voice* must be yielded at Pentecost. If we desire to bring the gifts of utterance, let us keep our lips from speaking evil, for God says of those who do: "You shall be as my mouth" (Jer. 15:19 RSV).

Expect to prophesy. Ask Jesus to edify His Body on earth through you. As you have fellowship with the Lord and with your brothers and sisters in the Lord, you may find thoughts and words of inspiration coming into your mind that you have not heard, and did not compose. If they are according to Scripture, then share them with the Church. As with interpretation, you may just receive a few words, and as you start to speak, more may come. You may see a picture in your "mind's eye", and as you start to talk about that picture, the words will come. As with tongues and interpretation, the Spirit may bring you the words in a variety of ways. Some also have seen the words as if written down, and just read them *verbatim*.

The gifts are manifested through God's ability, not ours. He will give the faith that is needed, if He has given you some words to speak (Rom. 12:6). Don't be afraid to bring a prophecy, nor feel sensitive about the fact that the Church must evaluate it. Don't quench the Spirit. The prophet Amos asks: "The Lord God hath spoken, who can but prophesy?" (Amos 3:8 KJV). Forget your pride, and testify to Jesus!

9
Gifts of Healing

The gifts of power are healing, miracles, and faith. They are the continuation of Jesus' compassionate ministry to those in need. Almost everyone is interested in the gifts of healing since the need is so widespread. This is one of the most obviously beneficial gifts to man in this life. It is the most widely accepted of the nine gifts of the Holy Spirit in Christendom today. The Lord Jesus brought this gift into prominence in that ninety percent of His recorded ministry on earth was spent healing the sick. His first instruction to His disciples was:

"Heal the sick!" (Matt. 10:8).

Yet after His Resurrection and before His Ascension there is no record of His healing anyone. During this forty days He spent much time teaching and preparing His disciples further to carry on the ministry He had begun. So immediately after Pentecost we find the first believers continuing the ministry of Jesus in healing the sick, raising the dead, and casting out evil spirits. Jesus' healing ministry has been going on now for nearly two thousand years, and will continue until He Himself returns to this earth. Jesus gave us this great promise: "He that believes in me, the works that I do he shall do also; and greater

works than these shall he do; because I go unto my Father!"
(John 14:12).

The gifts of healing are for the supernatural curing of injuries, handicaps, and diseases without the aid of natural means or human skills. They are manifestations of the Holy Spirit working through compassionate human channels to the person in need. Those who are used as channels of God's healing should not claim to "have" these gifts, nor should they claim to be "healers", but rather should realize that any of the nine gifts could be manifested through them as the Holy Spirit moves to meet the needs around them. There is a real interdependence between God and man in the gifts of the Spirit. For instance, if you felt God wanted you to pray for a friend, you would get in the car, drive to your friend's house, go in and tell how Jesus heals today, pray with your friend, and Jesus would do the healing. Some onlooker could say: "It looks as though you were doing the whole thing." Actually you were a "witness" first, telling what Jesus would do; then you were a "delivery boy", bringing the gift from Jesus, through the Holy Spirit in you. God guides us and uses our work, but He is the Healer. We are privileged to be co-workers together with the Lord Jesus. After the Ascension and Pentecost, the Scripture says that the disciples: "Went forth, and preached everywhere, *the Lord working with them, and confirming the word with signs following*" (Mark 16:20 KJV).

A Christian does not have to have the baptism with the Holy Spirit in order to pray for the sick, nor is the fact that a person has prayed effectively for the sick a sign that he or she has received the baptism with the Holy Spirit. Jesus said: "These signs shall follow them that *believe* . . . they shall lay hands on the sick, and they shall recover" (Mark 16:17–18 KJV). Any *believer* can pray for the sick and see them healed by the power of Jesus. Generally speaking, however, it is after the baptism in the Holy Spirit that increased faith for healing comes, and the Christian begins to minister to the sick. Like the other gifts, healing seems to be released with a far greater intensity and reality after the receiving of the Holy Spirit.

The "laying on of hands" usually means touching the sick person's head with one or both hands as you pray. Laying on of hands is not magic, but it is scriptural. It provides a "point of contact" for the sick person to "release his faith" as Oral Roberts puts it. It also can be a channel for real Spiritual power. The Bible says that we may lay hands on the sick, and so we do. However, notice also the great variety of ways in which the Lord Jesus prayed for the sick. Sometimes He laid hands on them, at times on their eyes or ears; sometimes He breathed on them; sometimes He made no outward gesture, but just spoke the word and they were healed. Often He commanded *them* to do something as an act of faith. Once He put mud on a blind man's eyes, and told him to go wash it off! Another time He simply said to some lepers: "Go and show yourselves to the priests" (the health department), and as they turned to go they were healed! This, by the way, should be noted by those who are suffering from diseases that need to be controlled with medication. We do not encourage people to discontinue such medication (for epilepsy, diabetes, heart trouble, etc., for example) until they have "gone and showed themselves to the priests"—the doctors—and their cure has been verified. The same would apply to a person suffering from tuberculosis, or other communicable disease, who is healed by Jesus through the gift of healing.

In the Epistle of James we read of healing in conjunction with "anointing with oil" (Jas. 5:14-15) in answer to believing prayer. The elders, the leaders of the congregation, are to anoint with oil as they pray for the sick of that particular congregation. The disciples anointed with oil as they prayed for the sick (Mark 6:13). Oil is one of the symbols of the Holy Spirit in the Bible. "Anointing" meant to pour oil (usually olive oil) on the sick person as prayer was said. Today the usual custom is to touch the forehead of the sick person with the oil. The Epistle of James goes on to say: "The prayer of faith *shall* save (heal) the sick, and the Lord *shall* raise him up . . ." (Jas. 5:15 KJC). Note the unconditional nature of the promise! We have no scriptural warrant to end a healing prayer with the faith-destroying phrase, "If it be Thy will"! God has made it perfectly clear in His Word that it *is* His will to heal the sick—full stop! Jesus never prayed for the sick in a conditional manner. He tells us that we must believe that we have received the answer to our prayer even before we pray! (Mark 11:24). Some remind us that Jesus prayed in Gethsemane "If it be Thy will"—or rather, "Not My will but Thine". This is an entirely different situation. Jesus knew the Father's will. He had come to earth for just that purpose, that He should die for our sins, and be raised for our justification. He was praying about His own unwillingness to be separated from loving fellowship with His Father as would occur during those painful hours on the Cross when He took the sins of the world upon Himself.

In the case of healing, we know the Father's will: "I am the Lord Jehovah thy God that healeth thee!" (Exod. 15:26). "Who healeth all thy diseases" (Ps. 103:3 KJV). "I will take sickness away from the midst of thee!" (Exod. 23:25 KJV).

Some people feel that Jesus would heal, but they are not sure about the Father! Dennis was asked to call on a woman who was very seriously ill—the doctors said she was dying and there was nothing to be done.

Entering the room, he could see that she was very ill indeed. She was pale and emaciated, yet she had a beautiful glow in her face. She said to him, with a smile: "It's all right. I'm reconciled to the fact that this is God's will!"

What could he say? Here he had been sent to pray for her recovery, and she was sure that God wanted her to die! He said to her:

"I can't argue with you at a time like this, but please answer me one question—if Jesus Himself were to walk into this room what would He do?"

With scarely a moment's hesitation, she replied:

"Why, He'd *heal* me!"

Dennis nodded. "You don't have any doubt of that, do you?"

She shook her head. "No."

"Well," he said, "Jesus said that He only did the things He saw His Father do—that He did nothing of Himself (John 5:9). He also said that He and His Father were so close, as to be like One—that if we had seen Him, we had seen His Father. How can you tell me that Jesus would heal you, but the Father wills that you die of this disease?"

She thought a moment, then her face brightened even more.

"I see what you mean!" she said. Then they could pray for healing.

A woman shared this story with us: "When I was seriously ill quite a few people prayed with me, but they always added the words: 'If it be Thy will, Lord.' And each time, my heart would sink when I heard this phrase. The day I was healed was when someone prayed with real faith. I kept waiting to see *if* they too would say 'If it be Thy will,' but praise God, they didn't!" if we can't pray with assurance and faith for the sick, we should wait until we can, or pray that God will send someone else who can.

We do not need to make long prayers for the sick. When we have the faith to say it, a word of command can be effective: "Be healed, in Jesus' Name!" Jesus healed with a touch, or a word—most often with a command: "Be thou clean!" He said to the leper. To the "sick of the palsy" He said: "Get up, pick up your mat, and go to your house!" To the deaf man's ears He commanded: "Be opened!" To the man with the withered hand He said: "Stretch forth your hand!" and it was instantly healed.

Note that in the list in I Corinthians 12:9 Paul speaks of "gifts" of healing, not just "the gift" of healing. Three times in this chapter it is mentioned, and each time the two nouns are plural in the Greek. The words are actually translated "gifts of cures". This is logical. Since there are many diseases, many gifts of healing are needed. One of the most wonderful of the healing promises concerning Jesus our Healer is this: "He was wounded for our transgressions, he was bruised for our iniquities: the chastisement of our peace was upon him; and with his stripes we are healed" (Isa. 53:5 KJV). Or, as Peter says, looking back at the crucifixion, and we say it with him: "By whose stripes ye *were* healed" (I Pet. 2:24 KJV). Thirty-nine stripes were laid on Jesus' back, and they represent healing for *all* our diseases.

As with the other gifts, some Christians are given a *ministry* of healing—being used often in this way. It is not unusual for this ministry to be stronger in praying successfully for one type of ailment than another. For example, one friend of ours has a strong ministry to arthritics, another for dental problems, etc. Perhaps this is what Paul means by "gifts of healing". Some have developed large and well-known ministries in this area, and thousands have been, and are being, healed and helped. We are deeply thankful for these dedicated and yielded people. It will be even more wonderful, though, when large numbers of God's children begin to move out for Him, and obey the command to "heal the sick". In every local congregation where the baptism in the Holy Spirit is being received, there are people with undeveloped ministries of healing.

A person can be healed through another's faith when he is too ill and weak to exercise his own faith (Mark 2:3-5), though he may be unconscious or in a coma. Healing can come through the faith (in Jesus) of the sick person alone (Matt. 9:22, 29), or with the combined faith of the sick person and the one ministering (Mark 5:25-34). This last of course is the most desirable situation. It is important to take time to build the faith of the sick person, when at all possible, before laying on hands for healing. This may be done by sharing with him or her the Scripture about healing, and by sharing personal testimonies. As the Apostle Paul tells the Romans, "Faith comes by hearing, and hearing by the Word of God" (Rom. 10:17). Impress the fact that we need not even depend on the faith of others, but stand squarely on God's Word.

Rita was sharing her testimony with a group of women in a private home in Spokane, Washington, in 1965, when her hostess' telephone rang. It was a lady by the name of Juanita Beeman. Rita was introduced to her over the phone, and was informed of her need. Juanita had a rapid heart which had required the installation of an electronic "pacemaker" so that it would beat normally. Although it was some months after the surgery to implant this device, she was still flat in bed. Her heart was enlarged, and every two weeks the fluid which collected around the heart had to be removed. She asked if Rita would come and pray for her. The next morning Rita went to hear a visiting evangelist preach on faith. He shared the Scriptures one after the other with real conviction and her own faith was greatly built up. Following this she went to the Beeman's home, and when she met the couple she could tell they were real believers. After sharing the Scripture on healing and talking about different healings she had seen, they prayed. God's presence was so strong that all of them were moved to tears. Several days later, when Juanita *walked* into the doctor's office (she had previously had to be taken in a wheelchair because of her weakness), the doctor asked in surprise: "What's happened to you?" She replied happily: "God answers prayer, doctor!" He tested and examined her, and found that her heart had returned to normal size, and that there was no fluid to be removed. Juanita has been leading a joyful and active life ever since.

When you pray for the sick, both you and the sick person should be edified. Smith Wigglesworth said that he never felt God's power more strongly than when he was praying for the sick. He often had a vision of Jesus in the course of an earnest healing prayer. He found that the atmosphere and surroundings in which the prayer is said are important.

We are sure we have watched a patient literally "murdered" by television, when he had his eyes glued to it and could scarcely be persuaded to turn the device off in order to receive prayer for healing! If you have control over the situation, insist that all possible distraction be removed, not only during the time of prayer, but especially *afterwards*, and if possible, before. Wigglesworth, again, would ask all unbelievers to leave, if he possibly could, before praying for healing. Note that Jesus did this at the raising of Jairus' daughter (Mark 5:38–40). Of course all these things should be done with charity. (We recommend strongly that you read the life of Smith Wigglesworth in the books *Ever Increasing Faith*, and *Smith Wigglesworth, Apostle of Faith*. They are good faith-builders for healing. There are many others.)

The one who feels led to pray for the sick should take time to ask God how He would have him proceed. Other gifts of the Spirit such as the word of knowledge and the word of wisdom should be expected to be manifested in conjunction with the gifts of healing. There may be something in the sick person's life that is stopping the healing, and that could be revealed by the word of knowledge.

The gift of the word of knowledge can be a great faith-builder. At times the Lord will show to one Christian that another has a certain physical need. As this is shared, it will give the sick person tremendous assurance and faith to reach out and receive his healing. Several healing evangelists depend heavily on the word of knowledge to build faith, and as the Lord reveals the needs, people are healed right where they are sitting or standing with no need of any to minister to them individually but the Lord Himself.

Faith is of course the most important of the gifts for the healing ministry. There are times when the gift of faith will be so strong that you will *know*, before you pray, that the person is to be healed.

It is important to explain to the sick person that as hands are laid on him, he should release his faith and receive his healing. As we have said, God's healing can come by a touch, a word, or any other action of faith. Some people have been healed by touching the radio when an evangelist is speaking about healing. This happened recently in the course of our own radio broadcast in Seattle, even though we had never suggested it. A listener touched her radio, released her faith, and was healed! People who are far away have been healed through the prayers of friends (Matt. 8:8), even though they did not know the friends were praying! One day a group of Episcopalians in Van Nuys, California, was praying for a friend who had a terribly abscessed tooth. As they prayed, the telephone range.

"What's going on over there?" the woman asked. "My jaw was just instantly healed!" The Scripture records other unusual cases of healing by the passing of a person's shadow over the sick (Acts 5:15)—or by handkerchiefs or aprons being brought that had been touched by the person God was using in a ministry of healing (Acts 19:11-12). Needless to say, any of these things can be abused or misused, but they certainly are real and valid. Again, they are occasions for the release of faith. We know of cases today where someone has brought a blessed handkerchief and placed it in contact with a sick person—unbeknown to him—and he has been healed! Here it is the faith of the person bringing the blessed object that provides the channel for God's healing.

We know from the Scripture that God wants His people to be whole in spirit, soul, and body. As wonderful as physical healing, is, we still know that our life on this planet, as we know it, is but a drop in the ocean of eternity. The most important healing is, of course, the healing of soul and spirit, for this has eternal value. Many times, however, when the inner man is touched by God in salvation, there is a chain reaction in which God's wholeness touches the soul and body with health. The Book of Romans says: "If you confess with your mouth the Lord Jesus and believe in your heart that God has raised Him from the dead, you shall be saved" (Rom. 10:9). The Greek word here translated "saved" is *sozo*, which means to be healed, saved from danger, kept in safety, or saved from eternal death. It is an all-encompassing word, that applies not only to the spirit, but to the soul and body also. When Ananias prayed for Paul, he was healed and baptized in the Holy Spirit almost simultaneously (Acts 9:17-18). This has been known to happen today. Praying in the language the Holy Spirit gives (speaking in tongues) can also bring healing, as the Spirit guides us to pray for our infirmities and ailments, or for the needs of others (Rom. 8:26).

We have quoted from James 5 the directions to anoint the sick with oil and to pray the prayer of faith. We also note that

James says: "If he has committed sins, they shall be forgiven him" (Jas. 5:15). Sickness, like death, came as a result of the fall of man. But the Lord Jesus made it very clear that not all sickness is the direct result of sin in the individual's life. The disciples asked him about the blind man, in John 9: "Who did sin, this man or his parents, that he was born blind?" Jesus' answer is definite: "Neither has this man sinned, nor his parents: but that the works of God should be shown in him" (John 9:3).

On other occasions, however, Jesus makes a direct connection between the individual's sin and his sickness, and begins His healing by forgiving the sin. In Luke 18 we read how a paralysed man was brought by four friends to Jesus. Jesus' first action is to say: "Man, your sins are forgiven you!" He then commands him to get up and walk.

In John 5, Jesus heals another paralytic, and this time warns him: "Sin no more, lest a worse thing come upon you!" (John 5:14).

In praying for the sick we must be aware that unrepented sin, a deep-held resentment, or a seriously wrong attitude, can prevent healing. The *Book of Common Prayer*, in the service for the visitation of the sick, directs:

"Then shall the sick person be moved to make a special confession of his sins, if he feel his conscience troubled with any matter, after which confession, on evidence of his repentance, the Minister shall assure him of God's mercy and forgiveness." [1] It is always a good policy, before praying with a sick person, to inquire of him whether his "conscience is troubled with any matter", and if so, to help him to come to repentance, and to confess his sin, in the manner to which he is accustomed. [2]

1. *Book of Common Prayer*, p. 313.
2. There is, of course, a great difference of opinion among various

Wherever the Holy Spirit moves, there will be healing. God is not glorified in the sickness of His people, as is sometimes erroneously taught, but in their healing. When Paul tells us that he "glories in his infirmities" (which does not necessarily mean physical weakness or sickness) he means that his weakness is an occasion to show God's strength. Men are led to Jesus through seeing His healing today just as they were in New Testament days. Physical healing of the unbeliever should bring him to Jesus as his Saviour. Because through the years, and still today, so many Christian churches have failed to proclaim the truth that Jesus still heals today, false cults have sprung up around an unbiblical kind of healing that does not glorify Jesus. Someone has called these groups the "unpaid

---

Christian groups as to how confession should be handled. Some feel that it is to be made to God alone, others believe that confession must be made in the presence of a priest. It is our belief that confession to an elder (presbyter, priest) was substituted for confession to the whole church, and that it concerned sins that affected the whole community—that is, open scandal—in which the elder could speak God's forgiveness on behalf of the whole church in a matter that would not be fitting to confess openly. We believe that the command "confess your faults one to another" is sound practice, and that the authority to declare God's forgiveness belongs to the ministry of every believer. Therefore if the person you are praying with has no pastoral relationship with any church, and no custom concerning confession, we suggest that you either direct him to your own minister or priest, or that you assist him in offering his sins to God, and then give him assurance of God's forgiveness in some such words as these: "I have heard you confess your sins to God, and I know you are truly repentant. I assure you by the Word of God, that God has forgiven you your sins, for He says: 'If we confess our sins, he is faithful and just to forgive us our sins, and to cleanse us from all unrighteousness' " (I John 1:9 KJV).

Anything said in your hearing during this time of confession is to be kept in *absolute* confidence, under the "seal of the confessional", which forbids even your speaking to the person himself about anything he has confessed, unless you have his permission. Simply forget what you have heard. God has taken care of it.

bills of the Church"! We have discussed them at length in chapter four.

On the other hand, many churches of all denominations who are moving in the charismatic dimension are seeing more and more healing. Blind eyes are opened; cataracts dissolved (yes, and even empty eye sockets filled!); deaf ears are made to hear; tumours disappear; broken bones are instantly mended; damaged hearts restored; multiple sclerosis, tuberculosis, cancer, paralysis, arthritis, and all the ills the flesh is heir to can be and are being healed by the touch of the Master's Hand. Some of these healings have been instantaneous, some progressive, some partial. In situations where we have desired to see healing, and we have not seen it, the fault is not with God, but with man. We are quick to say: "God didn't do it. I guess He isn't ready to heal me." Yet the Word of God says that He is, and right now.[3]

People say: "I'd believe in healing if I saw a case where the doctor took an X-ray, prayer was said, then a second X-ray was taken and healing proved!" There are many such cases on record, where the healing is completely proven by medical evidence, with all the X-rays, tests, etc., on file.[4] Alas, those who say they demand such evidence never seem to go and look at it! Jesus said: "If they believe not Moses and the Prophets (who certainly bore witness to God's healing), neither

3. The Scriptures promise health for the believer. On the other hand, for a variety of reasons, believers sometimes get sick. The promise, however, is that if we become ill, God will heal us. People say: "You're not going to live forever. You've got to die sometime!" True. But long life is promised to God's people, and when we do go home to our Father, it is not necessary that we go in disease and pain. We read in Genesis 25:8, that: "Then Abraham gave up the ghost, and died in a good old age, an old man, and full of years; and was gathered to his people."

4. Bennett, *op. cit.*, p. 199.

will they believe, though one rose from the dead" (Luke
16:31).

The best way to learn about healing is to begin to pray for
the sick. Ask God to use you in this way, then step out in faith.
Some know when they are to pray for the sick by an inner
witness; others may feel a warmth in their hands; still others
may have an overwhelming compassion. We should not depend only on these outward signs, however, but if they confirm that inner knowing in your spirit, you have double
witness to claim God's healing, especially if circumstances
make it possible for you to pray for the needy one. When
healing takes place, be sure to give God the glory, and lead
the healed one to Jesus if he or she hasn't already met Him.
As you continue to look to our Lord Jesus and stay in loving
fellowship with Him, the signs will follow.

10
The Working of Miracles

Miracles are events that seem to override or contradict the so-called laws of nature. There aren't any "laws of nature", actually. The concept of physical "laws" has been discarded by the modern physicist, who defines natural events in terms of "probability". For example, the old Newtonian physics said:

"There is a *law* that, neglecting air resistance, all objects fall with an acceleration of thirty-two feet per second, per second." Modern science would state it: "it is *probable* that all falling objects will accelerate at the rate of thirty-two feet per second, per second. This seems to be the way it happens!" And this comes very close to what the Christian says: "The so-called laws of nature codified by human science are simply God's usual way of doing things." He keeps things regular for our convenience. How awkward it would be to live in a universe where nothing happened twice the same way! It would be an Alice-in-Wonderland world, indeed, and very confusing! God, however, for His believing people, will change His accustomed ways of doing things, to meet their needs, and thus, too, show them that He is sovereign, and has all power. The great miracles of the Old and New Testaments were done to meet the needs of people, and to show them that God is real, and in full control of the situation.

It is not always easy to draw a sharp line between the gift of miracles and the gifts of healing. It would seem that "healing" should include those acts of power that involve the curing of a condition in the living human body (or animal body, for healing also can take place in animals by prayer). Other events would come under the heading of miracles.

Some of the typical miracles of the Old Testament are: the dividing of the Red Sea for the escape of the children of Israel (Exod. 14: 21–31); the sun and moon standing still for Joshua (Josh. 10: 12–14); the widow's cruse of oil and barrel of meal that did not run out through the time of famine (I Kings 17: 8–16); the descent of the fire on Mt. Carmel to consume Elijah's sacrifice and reveal the true God (I Kings 18: 17–39); the sun going backward ten degrees on Hezekiah's sundial in response to Isaiah's prayer (II Kings 20: 8–11); the miraculous plagues of Egypt (Exod. 7–12); the pot of poisonous soup which was made harmless through Elisha's act of faith (II Kings 4: 38–41). The greatest number of miracles in the Old Testament are recorded in the lives of Moses, Elijah, and Elisha.

The record of Elijah and his disciple, Elisha, speaks to us today. Elisha asked that he might have a "double portion" of the Holy Spirit that rested upon Elijah. As Elijah was caught up into heaven, his mantle—symbolic of his anointing—fell upon Elisha (II Kings 2: 9–14). Sure enough, the Scripture records that Elisha did twice as many miracles as Elijah! This is symbolic of what happened to believers after Jesus' ascension, although Jesus did not bequeath just a "double portion" of His Spirit—He set no limit. He simply said:

"Greater works than these shall ye do, because I go to My Father!" (John 14: 12).

The gift of miracles is one of the gifts which brings much glory to God, and one which should be seen today more than ever before—according to Jesus' promise. God delights in doing miracles, and in using His children in this gift. The power to do *greater* works comes from the fact that Jesus ascended into heaven, and the full power of the Holy Spirit was sent at Pentecost, and has been available to Christians ever since.

Jesus, of course, performed more miracles than anyone else in the Bible, and apparently not all of them are recorded. As John said: "And there are also many other things . . . Jesus did . . . which, if they should be written every one, I suppose that even the world itself could not contain the books that should be written" (John 21: 25 KJV). Some examples of His miracles found in the Scriptures include: turning water into wine (John 2: 1–11), walking on water (Matt. 14: 25–33), the miraculous feeding of the multitude (Mark 6: 38–44; Matt. 16: 8–10), causing the storms to cease (Mark 6: 45–52), directing the disciples to catch fish where there had been none (John 21: 5–12), and sending Peter to find money in the fish's mouth (Matt. 17: 27).

Jesus' first miracle was turning water into wine: "This beginning of miracles did Jesus in Cana of Galilee, and manifested forth his glory; and his disciples believed on him" (John 2: 11 KJV). Jesus' miracles were performed primarily out of His compassion to meet human needs, and for practical purposes. When He walked on water, He wanted to comfort His disciples; He needed to get there in a hurry. When He miraculously fed the multitudes, it was because food was not available otherwise. When He turned water into wine, it was because there was a need at the wedding reception. It is well to note, too, that the miracles were not done to force or frighten unbelievers into believing—they were done to encourage those who already believed or wanted to believe. Jesus said: "A wicked and adulterous generation seeketh after a sign, and no sign shall be given it, but the sign of the prophet Jonah (referring to His death and resurrection)" (Matt. 12:39–40). People say: "There you are! You're not supposed to have signs!" overlooking the fact that Jesus is talking to the "wicked and adulterous generation". On the other hand Jesus said:

"These signs *shall* follow them that *believe* . . ." (Mark 16:17 KJV).

Following Pentecost many signs of power were done by or for the apostles and others: several times believers were set free from prison by angelic power (Acts 12:1–17; 16:25–40; 5:17–25); the Evangelist Philip was transported bodily from Gaza to Azotus by the power of the Holy Spirit (Acts 8:39–40). (Please note! This was not "astral projection", or "astral" anything else. Philip was *physically* and *bodily* picked up by the Holy Spirit and carried from Gaza to Azotus, a distance of twenty-four miles!) Paul miraculously struck Elymas the Sorcerer with a temporary blindness in order to keep him from opposing the Gospel (Acts 13:8–12). Paul was bitten by a deadly snake, but took no harm from it (Acts 28:3–6).

Peter and Paul have the greatest number of miracles recorded in the Acts of the Apostles, but Stephen and Philip also performed miracles, and of course in I Corinthians 12 the gift of miracles is spoken of as one of the nine gifts that were regularly manifested by believers.

What did Jesus mean when He said that those who believe in Him would do "greater things"? Some think it means that there will be many *more* miracles due to the greater number of people who are filled with the Holy Spirit today. Others think it could also mean new miracles will be done in addition to, and even greater than, those recorded in the Bible. One thing is sure, that if Jesus meant that believers would do new miarcles, they would be according to the pattern already set by the Lord, and would be according to the Scripture. There are plenty of weird events taking place these days, as men and women experiment with the occult and the psychic, that is to say with the powers of Satan, and the Christian must not be deceived by them. The Scripture tells us that the followers of the enemy will do "great signs and wonders; insomuch that, if it were possible, they shall deceive the very elect" (Matt. 24 : 24 KJV; Mark 13 : 22).

However, miracles are happening today according to the pattern of the Scriptures. In the book, *Nine O'Clock in the Morning*, we cited several cases in which God strikingly altered the weather in response to believing prayer.[1] There are present-day examples of persons being transported physically in the Spirit as Philip the Evangelist was in Acts 8 : 39–40. David duPlessis, perhaps the best-known witness in the charismatic renewal, tells of such a miracle in his earlier ministry. He and some other men were gathered in the garden outside a friend's home, praying for another man who was lying in bed, seriously ill, about a mile away.

"As we prayed," says David, "the Lord said to me: 'You are needed at that man's bedside *right away*!' I snatched up my hat and rushed round the house and out the front gate, but as I took one step out of the gate, my next step fell on the front steps of the house a mile away, where our sick friend was! It startled me greatly of course. I know that I was carried that mile instantly, because some fifteen minutes later the rest of the men I had been praying with came puffing down the

1. Bennett, *op. cit.*, pp. 101–3.

road. They asked me: 'How did you get here so fast?'"

David needed to get there immediately so God simply provided his transportation!

In the last few years, what is perhaps the most powerful revival of New Testament Christianity the world has ever seen is taking place in Indonesia. Well-documented reports have been coming from there of miraculous events of the same nature and magnitude as in the Bible.[2] Thousands have been miraculously fed on provisions for a few hundred, water has been turned to wine for the purpose of Holy Communion, groups of Christians have walked on water in order to cross rivers to proclaim the good news of Christ, to say nothing of thousands healed, and many even raised from the dead.[3] One might dismiss these reports as fanciful, except they are confirmed by reliable witnesses, and often by Christians who did not previously believe that such New Testament miracles could or would take place today. Perhaps the strongest indirect evidence of the truth of these signs, is that over two and one-half million Moslems have accepted Christ, as well as thousands of Communists. The Moslem press recently admitted to the conversion of two million Mohammedans to the Christian faith! One of the big reasons undoubtedly is that they are seeing the power of God manifested, not only in the miracle of changed lives, but in the literal miracle of the Bible. Why should such amazing events be taking place? It is because people in Indonesia have never been told that certain parts of the Bible are "not for today"; therefore they are putting it into practice in simple faith. It works. God is alive!

God takes real chances when He shares His supernatural

2. "South Pacific. Scene of Miracles Today", *Christian Life Magazine*, April, 1968.

3. "Indonesia: The Greatest Work of God in the World Today", *Acts Magazine* I, no. 3. 1967. (We are saving the topic of the raising of the dead for the following chapter.)

works with His people. He would no doubt work more miracles among His people but knows that unless we are spiritually prepared it may be harmful to us. We heard the true story of an evangelist who had been mightily used of God, until one evening the power and glory of God lifted this person several feet off the ground, in full view of the congregation! The experience was so impressive, that from that night on, that particular servant of God could talk only of how some day Christians would be carried from place to place in the Spirit all over the world to proclaim the Gospel! It became that evangelist's one theme, to the serious hindrance of preaching the Gospel, and a good ministry was rendered almost useless.

It is worthwhile to stop and analyse this particular example. What was the purpose of this miracle? We might say at once: "Oh, it was to prove to the onlookers that what the evangelist was saying was true!" No, that won't quite do; because, you see, Satan can also lift people off the ground in the phenomenon called "levitation". Among those who dabble in the occult today, some are experimenting with this very thing, trying to learn how to float off the ground, or how to lift heavy objects by the aid of "spiritual" powers. So-called table tipping, a familiar party-game variety of spiritism, is a form of levitation. The fact that someone is lifted off the ground in no way proves him to be of God, any more than the fact that he might heal the sick would prove him to be of God.

In this case, there was no need of a miracle to prove that the evangelist was of God—that was clear from what was being said; the Gospel of Jesus Christ was being proclaimed. What then was the purpose of the miracle? It was simply to rejoice the heart of the people who were listening by showing again how real God is! It was just God expressing His love to the speaker and the hearers in an extraordinary way. Our evangelist friend made the mistake of getting ahead of God, and ahead of the Scriptures, in speculating about something God may perhaps do in the future, and building a doctrine on it. Though it is possible that as the battle waxes hotter there will be more instances of persons being transported in the Spirit, yet we have no scriptural precedent for saying that God is going to establish it as a "ministry". If ever anyone could have used such an "airline", it would have been St. Paul, but we have no record of his ever having been transported in this manner. Although God worked in his life through other miracles, he *travelled* the hard way!

Right after the baptism with the Holy Spirit, people experience a greater release of the miraculous in their lives. Then often comes a slackening of these experiences, because the old ways of thinking and living creep back in, and God has to enrol us in the school of the Holy Spirit. He has things to teach us before He can trust us more fully in this area, in case pride and other sins should get in, causing us to exalt ourselves, and then fall with a resounding thud! (I Tim. 2:6). The wise Christian, however, once having tasted of the wonderful works of the Lord, is encouraged to yield to God's dealings and lessons so he can *go on*, and not regress into the way things were before. It is the Father's will for us to remain in this new dimension.

We have already warned in detail in a previous chapter and earlier in this chapter that for every gift of God, there will be a demonic counterfeit. A mushroom and a toadstool look almost exactly alike, but one is delicious food and the other deadly poison. Only the Scripture can teach us to detect spiritual "toadstools". God's true miracles come only through those who have received His divine Son, Jesus. Christians do not expect miracles for the sake of miracles, but because God promised that they would follow in the lives of His children, and because they meet human needs and lead others to Jesus.

The New Testament recounts more miraculous events in the life of St. Paul than in any of the original twelve apostles. If we think that the first apostles had a special "in" because they walked and talked with Jesus during His earthly life, we should be encouraged by Paul, who did not know Jesus "after the flesh" (II Cor. 5:16). Also, Paul's power in the Holy Spirit did not decrease as he grew older. We find him manifesting God's miraculous keeping and healing power more strongly, if anything, in the last chapter of Acts, than in the earlier times (Acts 27–28). Paul never slowed down even in his old age.

Many times God's miracles are done in such a "supernaturally natural" way that you may miss them if you are not on the alert! Look with expectancy for God's miracles to be manifested in you and through your life. Pray that God's power will be manifested also through the rest of the body of Christ. Expect a miracle, and keep your eyes on Jesus.

II
The Gift of Faith

The Bible talks about faith from Genesis to Revelation but there's only one definition given. It is found in the Book of Hebrews: "Now faith is the substance of things hoped for, the evidence of things not seen" (Heb. 11:1 KJV). We learn several things from this verse. Faith is *now* or it's not faith at all. Faith is present tense; hope is future tense. Faith is believing before seeing, but it will eventually bring substance to what you have believed. Faith is not passive but active.

Everyone, believers and nonbelievers alike, can understand *natural human faith.* People have faith in the things of this world through the experience of the five senses. It takes natural faith to turn on the television set, and to believe we will see and hear something of interest. Even though the average person doesn't understand the electronics of television, he still has faith enough to turn it on. It takes natural faith to sit down in a chair. If a person could see the molecular structure of that chair, and the large amount of space represented in something that looks so solid, he might sit down more gingerly! It takes natural faith to turn on a light, ride in an aeroplane, drive a car, and just to live! A person can have this kind of faith and not believe in God at all. Natural faith is trust in something or someone you can see, hear, or touch. "Seeing is believing."

True faith that comes from God is *super*natural, or above the natural senses. There are three kinds of supernatural faith.

The first is "*saving faith*." The Bible tells us that without faith it is impossible to please God (Heb. 11:6). Salvation does not come from our good deeds but from our faith in Jesus Christ. "Believe (have faith in) the Lord Jesus Christ and you will be saved . . ." (Acts 16:31). The key to Christian faith is not "seeing is believing," but "believing before seeing." "Faith," says the writer to the Hebrews, "is the substance of things hoped for, the evidence of things *not seen*" (Heb. 11:1). Jesus is not evident to our physical senses, but by the Holy Spirit we are able to experience His love and fellowship here and now. This saving faith itself is a gift of God, and not something we manufacture (Eph. 2:8–9). Saving faith comes to man by the proclamation of God's Word. "Faith comes by hearing, and hearing by the Word of God" (Rom. 10:17).

Once we have received Jesus, the Scripture says that each Christian has been given "the measure of faith" (Rom. 12:3). We all start out with an equal measure yet some continue to grow in faith and some don't, but the choice is ours. God always has more in store for His children; His supply is unlimited.

The second kind is faith as a "*fruit of the Spirit*" (Gal. 5:22). This comes as result of our salvation: union with Christ. Jesus says: "I am the Vine, and you are the branches. He that abideth in Me, and I in Him, the same brings forth much fruit" (John 15:5). From the time of our union with Him (the Vine) we have the potential of bearing fruit.

Our faith (trust, belief) in Jesus is the work of God the Holy Spirit, and it is He Who supplies the faith as we go along in the Christian life. Our part is to respond to Him. Faith in Jesus, both initial faith and continuing faith, is the basis for all the other fruit and gifts of the Spirit. Its importance cannot be overestimated. "According to your faith be it unto you," says Jesus; and in another place, "All things are possible to him that believes" (Matt. 9:29); Mark 9:23).

Faith the fruit is brought about through the process of time. One doesn't plant a tree, and the next day pick fruit. The tree must be cultivated, fed, and watered. The word "abide" means to take up permanent residence. The result of abiding is the fruit of a Godly Christian character. Our growth in the fruit of faith depends on a consistent walk with Jesus, daily food from the Scriptures, and fellowship in the Holy Spirit.

The *gift of faith* is potential in the believer from the time of receiving Jesus, but like the other gifts, it becomes much more active after the Baptism in the Holy Spirit. Unlike the fruit, it is given instantaneously. It is a sudden surge of faith, usually in a crisis, to confidently believe without a doubt that as we act or speak in Jesus' Name it shall come to pass.

The word "confession" comes from the two root words in Greek, *homo logos*, which means to speak the same thing as the Word of God. The spoken gift of faith is confessing what God says, as led by the Holy Spirit. One of the best Scriptures describing this is recorded in Matthew:

"And Jesus answering saith unto them, Have faith in God." The literal translation of the Greek is: "Have the faith of God." For verily I say unto you, that whosoever shall say unto this mountain, be thou removed, and be thou cast into the sea; and shall not doubt in his heart, but shall believe that those things which he saith shall come to pass; he shall have whatever he saith" (Matt. 17:20).

Elijah is a stirring example of this gift in the Old Testament. He suddenly appears on the scene in I Kings 17:1 (KJV) and announces to Ahab, the most wicked king Israel ever had: "As the Lord God of Israel liveth, before Whom I stand, there shall not be dew nor rain these years, but according to my word!" And sure enough, there wasn't! The prophet Elijah must have lived at a very high level of faith, even though we know that there were times when his faith collapsed almost completely for the time being, as in I Kings 19: 3, when he just plain lost his nerve and ran away! It would seem that to meet crises such as the one we have mentioned, or the tremendous test on Mt. Carmel: "If the Lord be God, serve Him, but if Ba'al be god, serve him!" (I Kings 18: 21) when the fire came down from Heaven to confirm Elijah's God as the true one to serve, there must have been mighty surges of faith, special gifts of faith.

On the other hand, an example of an acted gift of faith is found in the familiar incident in the life of the prophet Daniel. Daniel was "framed" by some jealous associates, and sentenced to be thrown into a den of hungry lions. Daniel said no word, but simply trusted God, and the lions did not hurt him. Even for as great a man as Daniel, it probably took a special surge of faith for him to go through this frightful experience (Dan. 6: 17–28).

In the Lord Jesus Christ, the fruit and the gift merge completely as He was living always at the peak of the fullness of faith in His Father. The Gospels are full of examples of His great faith. One day Jesus and His disciples set out to go across the lake in a small boat. Jesus was tired, and had gone to sleep in the stern on a cushion. Suddenly a squall arose and the waves began to break over the boat, filling it with water. The disciples were terrified, and awakened Jesus. He simply spoke to the storm and it immediately quieted down. Obviously, even awakening from a sound sleep, he needed no special infusion of faith to perform the miracle. The disciples, on the other hand, failed to exercise faith but had to be reassured by a miracle (Mark 4: 35–41).

The gift of faith is distinct from the working of miracles, which we have studied in the last chapter, though it may produce miracles. If the disciples in the storm-tossed boat had remained calm and assured in spite of their dangerous situation, they would have been manifesting the gift of faith. As it was, Jesus had to still the storm by a miracle. If Daniel in the lion's den had slain the dangerous animals with but a gesture it would have been the gift of miracles. As it was, he rested unharmed in the presence of the fully active lions, showing an even greater amount of *faith*. In the New Testament believers, we can see the same sort of thing going on. Who was more "wobbly" than Peter? After Pentecost, the Holy Spirit steadied him down considerably, but, just like us, he had his ups and downs. He had his eyes so much on what people would think, that Paul had to "withstand him to his face" (Gal. 2: 11). Yet when word was brought to him that Dorcas, or Tabitha, the beloved woman disciple in Joppa, had died, he went without hesitation and spoke the word of faith: "Tabitha, get up!" (Acts 9: 40).

We may see the example of acted faith in Acts 12. Peter was arrested by Herod Agrippa I and thrown into prison, with the expressed intention that he be executed the very next morning, as had already been done with James bar Zebedee. We read:

"Peter was sleeping between two soldiers, bound with two chains: and the keepers before the door kept the prison. And suddenly an angel of the Lord appeared and a light shone in the prison; and he struck Peter on the side, and woke him, saying, 'Quick! get up!' And the chains fell off his hands." The angel brought Peter out of the prison before he even knew that he was awake! (Acts 12: 11).

Now the word that is used for "struck" in the above passage means a "blow," not a love pat! Peter was sleeping so soundly, that even when he was awake, it took him a while to "come to", to realize what had happened! This is *acted* faith, in a sense very like Daniel's. You or I might have been lying awake worrying about what was going to happen to us, or perhaps planning a way to escape, but not Peter! He was sleeping soundly, leaving it all in God's hands, and his faith was rewarded.

The Gift of Faith Today.

We've already mentioned the great events which have been taking place in Indonesia today as millions of Moslems and Communists are accepting Christ. Accompanying this revival have been miracles of New Testament magnitude. Three years ago there were already thirty-three thoroughly documented cases of the raising of the dead on the Island of Timor. When David duPlessis visited Indonesia this year he told us that when he asked how many dead had been raised to date, they replied: "We've lost count—besides no one believes us, anyway!"

A friend, Sherwin McCurdy of Dallas, Texas, was used to raise a man from the dead. The story was told in *Christian Life* magazine for October 1969.[1] McCurdy was waiting for a taxi outside the Amarillo airport early in the morning, when a frightened nine-year-old boy came running up, pleading for help: "My daddy's dying!" he gasped. Following the boy, McCurdy found a car in the ditch, the driver a man in middle years, was obviously dead. An older son explained that his father had had a heart attack about forty-five minutes before. He had been giving him mouth-to-mouth resuscitation, but to no avail. The rest of the family was in near hysteria. The Lord gave a gift of faith to McCurdy, instructing him to lay hands on the corpse, commanding the spirit of death to depart, and the spirit of life to return. Sherwin did so. "It was like putting my hands on a piece of melting ice!" he said, but when he laid his

1. S. W. McCurdy as told to Jamie Buckingham, "In Time for God's Appointment", *Christian Life Magazine*, October, 1969, p. 40.

palms on that cold forehead (the corpse was already rigid, and cyanotic in death), and did as God told him, the man instantly returned not only to life, but to normalcy, and he and his whole family accepted Jesus as Lord and Saviour.

A dramatic and true example of the gift of faith coupled with the gift of miracles comes from an Elim missionary in Tanzania. A native congregation had gathered for Easter services, when suddenly an enraged lioness in a wild mood dashed out of the jungle, attacking everything in her path. She killed several domestic animals, then a woman and a child and headed directly for the assembled believers. Bud Sickler, the Elim missionary who received the report from the native pastor, says:

"The congregation suddenly saw the lioness. She had stopped only a few yards from them, snarling ferociously. The people trembled with shock! The preacher shouted, 'Don't be afraid—the God who saved Daniel from the lions is here—the risen Christ of Easter is here.' He turned to the lioness and cried, 'You lion, I curse you in the name of Jesus Christ!'

"Then the most amazing thing happened. From the scattered clouds, without a sign of rain, a bolt of lightning struck the lioness and she dropped dead. The preacher then jumped on the carcass and used it as a platform to preach!" The final punch of the story is that not only were the people's lives saved, but the whole village was stirred, and seventeen gave their lives to the Lord Jesus.[2]

The level of faith in which we are living may ebb and flow. Sometimes we find that we are strong in faith; the Holy Spirit in our spirit is allowed to work, and wonderful things happen in our lives. At other times the "hang-ups," doubts, fears, and the "debris" in our souls that the Holy Spirit is working to remove get in the way, and we are not able to function as well.

Some believers consistently operate at a high level of faith while others often have difficulty "getting of the ground". Though the gift of faith may be active from time to time in our lives, it should not surprise us if we also experience times of doubt. This should only serve to remind us of the Scripture: "It is *God* who works in you both to will and to do of his good pleasure" (Phil. 2:13). Expect the Lord to manifest his wonderful gift of faith through you, just as you expect the other gifts.

*　　*　　*

Concluding this section on the gifts of power, we note again that the gifts of the Holy Spirit are often manifested together, interacting with, and enhancing one another.

In the Gospel of Matthew, Jesus gave his apostles this commission: "Heal the sick, cleanse the lepers, raise the dead, cast out devils: freely you have received, freely give" (Matt. 10:8). In order to carry out this command, all three gifts of power would be required: heal the sick and cleanse the lepers (gifts of healing), raise the dead (gifts of faith, miracles, and healing), and cast out demons (gift of faith, plus others in our next section).

12
Discerning of Spirits

We call the last three gifts *revelation* gifts because they consist of information supernaturally revealed from God. We might call them simply the "mind of Christ being manifested through a Spirit-filled believer". Each of these gifts is the God-given ability to receive from Him facts concerning something, anything, about which it is humanly impossible for us to know, revealed to the believer so that he may be protected, pray more effectively, or help someone in need.[1]

1. There are only two ways by which the human mind can receive information other than through the physical senses of seeing, hearing, smelling, tasting, feeling. One is by opening the mind to the "psychic" world, so that information is received directly into the mind from the spirits of Satan. This is what happens in the phenomena of so-called ESP, spiritism, clairvoyance, etc. It is, as we have said previously, totally forbidden by God, and no one should engage in it.

The other way is for information to come to the mind from the renewed spirit, in turn inspired and informed by the Holy Spirit. This kind of supernatural knowledge is acceptable to God—it comes directly from Him—and is safe for us. The Holy Spirit is going to share with us only those things that He knows to be needful for us, and helpful to us and others. We receive this knowledge, not through trying to develop some mysterious occult ability, but by living close to God in Jesus Christ, and allowing His Spirit to work in our lives.

Discernment

Before we talk about spiritual discernment we need to discuss discernment in general. First there is what we may call "*natural discernment*" which Christian and non-Christian alike have. This is the judgment that we pass on people and circumstances, and on our own behaviour, and is derived from teachings received in our homes, and the effect of our environment and culture. Our natural "consciences" are composed of this kind of material, and therefore are very unreliable. The mind, and that part of it called the conscience, is a mixture of good and evil, truth and error. Its discernment and moral judgments have no absolute value. It is a truism that standards of human morality vary from culture to culture, and from generation to generation, and all the natural mind can tell is what agrees with or is acceptable or unacceptable to the time and place in which we are living. This is what the world in general uses as a basis for decisions. There is no stability in it.

True intellectual discernment comes not from the fallen natural mind but from the mind that is being renewed in Christ. This discernment grows as we meet and receive Christ and get to know Him better, through fellowship and through the study of the Word of God. As the Book of Hebrews tells us: "Every one that uses milk is unskilful in the word of righteousness, for he is a babe. But strong meat belongs to them that are of full age, even those who by reason of use have their senses (Greek: *perceptions, judgment*) exercised to *discern* both good and evil" (Heb. 5:13–14). As we grow in the Christian life, the Holy Spirit sorts through our minds and consciences, discarding the wrong, and adding what is right. If God has been permitted to work in this way, as time goes on, our minds and consciences will become more and more in agreement with the Scriptures and with the Holy Spirit living in us. We become so imbued with the "flavour" of what Jesus Christ is like, and how God works, that we immediately recognize *intellectually* something that is different. It is very important for believers to develop this kind of discernment. It is a strong defence against false doctrine. We should be able to say immediately: "That doesn't sound like God! God doesn't *act* that way!" if we hear a strange new teaching that is not in keeping with the truth.

Our own behaviour towards God and our fellowman will of course be affected by our growth in intellectual discernment. Before Paul accepted Jesus personally, he thought it a matter of good conscience to persecute Christians. After his conversion, and after many years of walking with the Lord, Paul says:

"I have lived in all good conscience before God until this day" (Acts 23:1 KJV). "I do my utmost always to have a clear conscience before God and toward men" (Acts 24:16). We should pray that our minds and consciences will be so renewed by the Spirit that we can say this too.

False Supernatural Discernment

A young woman from St. Luke's Church was going along the street in downtown Seattle one day, minding her own business, when suddenly an elderly lady rushed at her, screaming obscenities and threats, and waving her stick angrily. The Christian girl was startled, but not frightened, as she recognized what was happening. The old woman was demonically possessed and the evil spirit detected the presence of the Holy Spirit in the young lady, and immediately was aroused to angry protest.

Such incidents are not uncommon, although not usually as dramatic and unexpected as this one. If a person has been serving Satan, and got himself thoroughly oppressed or possessed by enemy power and influence, he will be repelled by the presence of anyone who is walking in the Spirit. This is the devil's counterfeit of the discerning of spirits.

One of the most striking examples of this is the great resentment shown by spiritualists to those who have received the baptism in the Holy Spirit. Dennis was sitting at the head table at a Full Gospel Businessmen's banquet one day, when the man next to him, a well-known physician who had received the Holy Spirit, showed him a letter from an acquaintance scurrilously and savagely attacking and condemning the good doctor for his Pentecostal activities. Dennis said:

"That man is a spiritualist, isn't he?"

The doctor nodded: "I'm afraid he is," he concurred.

Do not be surprised if you receive attack and persecution out of all proportion from associates who not only do not know the Lord but are actively engaged in unscriptural and forbidden practices.

Discerning of Spirits

We come now to the spiritual gift. Like all the gifts this does not come through training but is given in a moment when and as it is needed. Any Christian may manifest this gift, but like the others, it is intensified after the baptism in the Holy Spirit. Believers who have not been baptized in the Spirit are not likely to be aware enough of the activities of Satan to be concerned about discerning of spirits, although of course, there are exceptions.

By the gift of discerning of spirits the believer is enabled to know immediately what is motivating a person or situation. A believer may be operating under the inspiration of the Holy Spirit, he may be expressing his own thoughts, feelings, and desires from his soul, it is even possible that he may be allowing an alien spirit to oppress him, and be bringing thoughts from that wrong spirit. An unbeliever, of course, may be completely possessed by the wrong spirit. The gift of discerning of spirits immediately reveals what is taking place.

It may help us to understand the gift of discerning of spirits if we recognize what it is like to discern the Holy Spirit. The gospel song says: "There's a sweet, sweet Spirit in this place and I know that It's the Spirit of the Lord!" Believers know that joyful sense of, or witness to, the presence of the Holy Spirit in another person, or in a meeting. When we say: "I really felt the presence of God," we are speaking of the discerning of the Holy Spirit. We experienced a rather amusing example of this kind of discernment after we came to Seattle.

Dennis had been invited to attend a choir concert in a nearby church. The choral director was a baptized-in-the-Holy-Spirit Christian, who had many friends at St. Luke's. Dennis knew that some twenty or thirty of the people from the church who had received the Holy Spirit were planning to go to the concert, too. He arrived a little late, and was seated in the balcony. He was surprised, at looking over the congregation on the main floor, to see no sign of any of his friends. Dennis enjoyed the programme, but all the way through he was puzzled by a little inner "lift" of joy, a definite witness of the Holy Spirit that kept "nudging" him all the way through the concert. It was great, but he couldn't understand what it meant. The choir was good, but not *that* good! The explanation came as he left the church at the end of the evening, when he was greeted by some thirty "Spirit-filled" Episcopalians who had been sitting right under him—right beneath the balcony. They were out of sight, but Dennis' spirit had discerned their presence!

Reports from those who work behind the Iron Curtain reveal that this gift becomes very important as persecution increases. There are many cases of Christians recognizing Christian, each "in the Spirit" without having to use words. In one place, Christian meetings were continuously being interfered with, so the brethren simply stopped announcing any time or place for their fellowship, but depended upon the Holy Spirit to tell those who should be there! Everyone was present and accounted for just the same. This was probably a combination of the gift of knowledge and the gift of discernment.

We may understand the discerning of wrong spirits by seeing it as the opposite of all this. The sense of the presence of the Holy Spirit brings joy and love and peace; the discerning of wrong spirits brings a sense of heaviness and unrest.

Some years ago, when we were very "green" in all these matters, a person visited St. Luke's Church and spoke to our local prayer meeting. He came with good recommendations, and seemed to be "on the level". Says Dennis: "I had handed over the meeting to our visitor, and he seemed to me to be saying acceptable things, yet as I looked at the faces of the listeners it was obvious that something was wrong. They looked distressed, unhappy, uncomfortable. One woman even got up from her place and left the room, excusing herself as she passed by me by saying that she felt nauseated. I did not have the sense to stop the speaker and say: 'Excuse me, but you are making the people feel sick—what is wrong?' The man went on his way the next day to another town, but as he spoke there, the chairman stopped him and said: 'Your words are fine, but I discern a wrong spirit in your life.[2] What is it?' The man, thus challenged, confessed that he was an impostor, living in open sin." Obviously the purpose of such a gift was not only to protect the

2. Please note that "wrong spirits" are not, and cannot be, the spirits of people who have died. Discerning of spirits has nothing to do with spiritism or spiritualism. The spirits of departed human beings are *not* on this earth, and to attempt to contact them is forbidden! The "wrong spirits" we are talking about are spoken of in the Scriptures as "the rulers of the darkness of this world", that is, fallen angels or else "demons" (Eph. 6:12, Matt. 10:8).

people from the enemy's deception, but also to bring this man to repentance and deliverance.

Sometimes the disturbing influence will not be from the person who is speaking or ministering, but from one who is simply present in the meeting. An individual who is actively engaged in something like spiritism can throw a coldness over a Holy Spirit prayer meeting just by his presence. If there seems to be a deadness in the meeting, it is well to stop and pray that the Spirit will reveal the trouble. If there is someone present who is under oppression he may be helped and delivered.

Thus discerning of spirits is a kind of "police" gift, to keep the enemy's influence from causing serious problems in the fellowship. Unfortunately when people receive this kind of discernment, they often hesitate to use it for fear of seeming hard or unloving. If you have spiritual discernment that something is wrong in a meeting, and you are not the leader, quietly and as unobtrusively as possible let the leader know, so that there can be prayer for the gifts of knowledge from the Lord to show what is wrong, and wisdom to know how it should be dealt with. There will probably be others with the same discernment, as it is usually given to more than one—for confirmation.

Discerning of spirits is especially needful when the other gifts are exercised in a meeting. We are not expected to accept every word spoken through the gifts of utterance, nor in any other manifestation or even in preaching, but we are only to accept what is quickened to us by the Holy Spirit and is in agreement with the Bible. "Let the prophets speak two or three, and let the other judge (discern)" (I Cor 14 : 29 KJV). The gifts of the Holy Spirit are pure, but the channels they come through are at varying degrees of yieldedness and sanctification. One manifestation may be seventy-five per cent God, but twenty-five per cent the person's own thoughts. We must discern between the two.

Then too, the enemy may send people into a meeting expressly to disturb it with counterfeit manifestations. In Acts 16 a woman possessed with a spirit of divination, for several days continued to interrupt Paul with a word which sounded something like prophecy: "These men are the servants of the most high God, which show us the way of salvation" (Acts 16:17). What she was saying was true enough, but she was speaking under the influence of the enemy. When Paul discerned this wrong spirit the Scripture says he was grieved within; he then commanded the evil spirit to leave her and she was set free. This example shows that counterfeit manifestations should be dealt with, if possible, at the time they happen.

The story of Elisha and his servant Gehazi is an Old Testament example of the gifts of discerning of spirits and knowledge. Naaman, a captain in the Syrian army, was a leper. In obedience to the prophet Elisha's instructions he washed in Jordan seven times and was healed. Naaman offered Elisha gifts to show his gratitude but Elisha would not accept them. Elisha's servant Gehazi, however, secretly followed Naaman, and lied to him, telling him that Elisha had just received two unexpected guests, and would Naaman please give two changes of clothing and some money—all of which Gehazi, of course, kept for himself. When Gehazi returned to his master, Elisha discerned his dishonest spirit and then knew by the gift of knowledge exactly what had been done (II Kings 5).

There are many examples of Jesus' discerning spirits. He had not previously met Nathanael, but discerned immediately that he was "an Israelite indeed, in whom there was no guile" (John 1:47 KJV). When Peter made his great confession about Jesus: "Thou art the Christ, the Son of the living God!" Jesus commended him. When Jesus began to tell his followers, however, that He was to die, Peter would not accept His words. He began to rebuke Jesus, saying, "Be it far from thee, Lord: this shall not be unto thee!" Jesus discerned that Peter was speaking in a wrong spirit, and said: "Get thee behind me, Satan: you are an offence to me: for you savour not the things that be of God, but those that be of men" (Matt 16: 15–23). When Jesus was not received in the village of the Samaritans, James and John were so angry that they asked Jesus whether they should command fire to come down from heaven and consume the people. But Jesus said: "You know not what manner of spirit you are of" (Luke 9: 54–55). We see by these last two examples, that even close followers of Jesus can be temporarily misled.

Fulfilled prophecy and other Biblical signs indicate that we may be living in the final part of the Last Days. Scripture teaches that before Jesus Christ returns to earth, there will be many more deceiving spirits unleashed, so to be able to discern between the counterfeit and the true will be increasingly needful (Matt. 24; Rev. 13: 11–14).

Another important use of the gift of discerning of spirits is in bringing deliverance [3] to those bound by the enemy. One of the first signs that Jesus said would follow believers is that they would cast out demons in His (Jesus') Name. About twenty-five percent of Jesus' ministry was spent in delivering captives from Satan, and we too should expect to be used in this way. Jesus said: "The Spirit of the Lord God is upon me; because the Lord has anointed me to preach good tidings unto the meek; he has sent me to bind up the brokenhearted, to proclaim liberty to the captives, and the opening of the prison to them that are bound . . ." (Isa. 61: 1). In this Scripture Isaiah was speaking specifically of Jesus, but now since Calvary, with Christ living in us, we too are anointed with the Holy Spirit, and it also applies to us. This does not mean we are to go and

---

3. Exorcism is the ancient name used for this kind of ministry of casting out evil spirits.

look specifically for those in need of deliverance or to develop an unhealthy fascination with the subject, but we do need to know how to pray for people with such needs. If we are yielded to God and properly prepared, He will bring those in need of deliverance across our pathway.

The Epistle of James tells us how to prepare to pray for those who need to be set free: "Submit yourselves therefore to God. Resist the devil, and he will flee from you" (Jas 4 : 7 KJV). The first step then is to "submit yourself to God". You may do this by praying, and asking Him to show areas in your own life that need correction. All known sin must be dealt with, and made right.

It is also important to establish yourself in the authority you have in Jesus by studying the Scriptures on this subject.[4] Realize that through the Name of Jesus you have authority to bind evil spirits and cast them out. Some people have been taught that in dealing with an evil spirit one must say, "The Lord rebuke you," instead of confronting the enemy directly. They quote Jude 9 and Zechariah 3 : 2 where an angel dealing with Satan says, "The Lord rebuke you." Holy angels, though sinless creatures of God, must deal with the enemy in this way. However, we Christians are not only creatures of God but *children* of God, with Christ in us. Jesus told us to deal with the enemy directly: ". . . In my name shall *they* cast out devils . . ." (Mark 16 : 17 KJV),[5] and throughout the New Testament it is never done in any other way.

Unless the person with whom you are praying is a close friend or relative, *always* have a third person with you when praying for deliverance. This third person may be just sitting or kneeling and agreeing in prayer. If the person needing deliverance wants to talk confidentially, the third person can retire

4. See Eph. 1 : 1–23; 2 : 1–10; Luke 10 : 19; Gal. 2 : 20; II Cor. 5 : 17; I John 4 : 4.
5. See also II Cor. 10 : 4–5.

into the next room while you talk, but always have him present when any deliverance prayers are said. It is not wise for a man to pray in private for deliverance for a woman, or *vice versa* (it is always better for the same sexes to minster to each other, in all areas of ministry). If it is inevitable that a man should be praying for deliverance for a woman or girl, be sure that another *woman* is present.

A Christian cannot be possessed in his spirit (where the Holy Spirit dwells), but his mind, emotions, or will (the three parts of the soul) may be depressed, oppressed, obsessed, or even possessed if he has let the enemy in by choosing to walk in known sin rather than with the Lord Jesus. A non-Christian, of course, may be possessed, spirit, soul, and body. It follows, then, that the most important first step in helping a person to be delivered from the enemy is to make sure that he or she knows the Lord Jesus as Saviour.

If the person you are ministering to is not a Christian, lead Him to accept Jesus. We suggest a re-reading of chapter one to help you at this point. You may find it a great help to have a definite "plan of salvation" in mind, with appropriate Scriptures. A typical series might be:

1. Rom. 3:23: "For all have sinned, and come short of the glory of God."
2. Rom. 6:23a: "For the wages of sin is death."
3. Rom. 5:8: "But God commendeth His love toward us, in that, while we were yet sinners, Christ died for us."
4. Rom. 6:23b: "But the gift of God is eternal life through Jesus Christ our Lord."
5. John 1:12: "But as many as received Him, to them gave He power to become the sons of God, even to them that believe on His Name."
6. Rev. 3:20: "Behold, I stand at the door, and knock; if

any man hear my voice, and open the door, I will come in to him, and will sup with him, and he with me."

Read these verses and explain them, and then lead the person to pray a prayer such as the one given at the end of the first chapter of this book—or a similar prayer in his own words.

Now that you are both Christians, and protected by the Blood of Jesus, make an open confession of this: "Thank you, Jesus, for the protection of Your precious Blood, over us and around us." Ask the person you are praying with if he feels assured that God has forgiven him his sins. If he has any doubt about it, emphasize the Scripture to him: "If we confess our sins, He is faithful and just to forgive us our sins, and to cleanse us from all unrighteousness" (I John 1 : 9 KJV). It may help for him to confess his sins to God in your hearing and presence.[6] If so, listen quietly and prayerfully to what he has to say, and when he is finished, declare God's forgiveness to him. Say something like this:

"I have heard you confess your sins to God, and I know you are truly repentant. God says: 'As far as the east is from the west, so far have I removed your sin from you'" (Ps. 103 : 12). If the person still has difficulty, you may need to call on a trained pastor to give further counsel in order to convince him, and set his mind at rest.

Be sure, of course, that you have confessed and asked forgiveness for known sin in your own life, and that you have forgiven others. A Christian should daily be living in this state of forgiveness and forgivenness.

6. If you do listen to someone else's confession of sin to God, remember that you must never, under any circumstances, reveal what you have heard to anyone—not even to your closest and dearest friend. You must forget what you have heard. It is a very serious sin to wilfully reveal what has been told you in the confidence of a person confessing his sins to God.

Try, if possible, to find out the exact nature of the spirit or spirits you are dealing with. Let the Holy Spirit lead you in this, as in everything else. Don't get into an interminable "counselling" session, which can waste much time, but do try to find out what kind of thing is troubling the person: is it fear, hate, lust, perverse ideas, feelings of persecution, fear of animals, anger, etc.? Now have the person name the things that are troubling him. Treat each problem as a spiritual entity, and *address it directly* as such. The devil is very clever at this point, and he will try to get the person to pray like this: "I cast out this anxiety neurosis!" or "I rebuke this spirit of anxiety." No. Have him say rather: "Spirit of Anxiety, I bind you in the Name of Jesus, under His precious Blood, and cast you into outer darkness, never to return, in Jesus' Name!" You may need to have him or her repeat this prayer (a phrase at a time) after you at first, but then try to get the person to say the prayer himself. After he has said it, you repeat it, rebuking and casting out the spirit from him, agreeing with him in the prayer. It is important to have the person in need of deliverance learn to pray his own prayer, as in this way he gains confidence in using his authority over the enemy, and can pray for himself, if the enemy seeks to return.

You will find that as the person gets the idea, he will often continue to pray for other problems which were not named at first, as the Holy Spirit brings them to mind. Some spirits may create more emotional reaction in the oppressed person than others. Some may create nausea, or exaggerated coughing, yawning, sneezing, etc. There may from time to time be a more violent reaction, even to being thrown down on the floor. If such things happen, don't allow yourself or the other persons to be put off by them. Praise the Lord, claim the protection of Jesus' Blood, and go on. On the other hand, don't feel that because such reactions *don't* take place, nothing has happened.

Do not think, either, that the fact that a person has a physical reaction means that he has been delivered. These manifestations are side effects of the deliverance.

If the person needing prayer is unable to co-operate, or has no insight into his problems, you alone will need to bind the spirits and cast them out in the name of Jesus and under His Blood just as the Apostle Paul did in Acts 16:16–18. If on the other hand a person is perfectly in control of his senses and will-power and does not want help, you are probably wasting your time minstering to him, until he himself wants help and asks for it. Some people really enjoy their problems! Through them, Satan delights in wasting the time and energy of Christians!

In praying for deliverance you may have to be very forceful. The spirit must obey you when you command it by faith, in the Name of Jesus. If the spirit detects any hesitancy on your part, it will evade your command. Insist! (It is well to explain quickly and simply to the "patient" that you are not talking to him when you are rebuking the evil spirit. Just say something like: "I'm not talking to you, but to the spirit that is troubling you.")

There is no example in Scripture of the laying on of hands for casting out spirits, and most agree that it should not be done. We don't believe the person ministering, if he is a Christian, and protected by the Blood of Christ, can be harmed, but the person in need of deliverance will often react strongly and even violently to being touched. It is better to avoid physical contact while offering prayer for deliverance.

When the deliverance has been accomplished, praise the Lord and give Him glory! *Now* lay your hands on the person's head and pray that every empty space left by the spirits that have been driven out will be filled with the Holy Spirit. If the person has not been baptized in the Holy Spirit, this is an excellent time to explain to him how to receive, and to help him receive. It is imperative that his house be filled to overflowing with the Holy Spirit and His power.

Emphasize to the person the importance of daily feeding on the Word of God, prayer, praise, and fellowship with others in the Lord. The last chapter of this book, entitled "The Narrow Way", will provide detailed suggestions in this area.

These are only some brief guidelines on the subject, but before leaving the subject, let us point out that this casting out of spirits is by no means limited to those who are seriously and deeply oppressed or possessed. Any time you feel that a spirit from the enemy is harassing you and you cannot seem to get freedom through your own prayers, never hesitate to call on a friend in the Lord to pray with you and agree to cast out the evil. Any time you are having a struggle with a besetting sin— anger, lust, fear—even though it is only a mild problem, if you can't get it under control, treat it as an oppressing spirit, bind it and cast it out; and if you can't get real freedom by yourself, call for help! It may be advisable to have a qualified Christian counsellor talk and pray with you.

Let us pray that our discernment of the work of the enemy in our own and other's lives will be quickened, so that we may see the captives set completely free. Let us remember, too, that after Jesus gave seventy of His followers power over the enemy and sent them out, they returned with joy, saying that the devils were subject to them through Jesus' Name. But Jesus, Who was obviously rejoicing along with them, still brought them back into perspective: "Rejoice not, that the spirits are subject unto you; but rather rejoice, because your names are written in heaven." As we pray for people to be set free from bondage, let us remember to rejoice most of all that our names are written in the Lamb's Book of Life!

13
The Word of Knowledge and the Word of Wisdom

The eighth gift in our study is the *"word of knowledge"*. It is the supernatural revelation of facts past, present, or future which were *not learned through the efforts of the natural mind*. It may be described as the Mind of Christ being manifested to the mind of the believer, and is given when needed in a flash of time (I Cor. 2 : 16). This gift is used to protect the Christian, to show how to pray more effectively, or to show him how to help others.

The ninth gift, the *"word of wisdom"*, is the supernatural application of knowledge. It is knowing what to do with the natural or supernatural knowledge God has given you—proper judgment for action. The "word of knowledge" is supernaturally revealed information, but the "word of wisdom" tells how to *apply* the information.

The "word of wisdom" is usually given with the "word of knowledge". It is well patiently to wait for it, and not rush off "half-cocked" if you receive supernatural knowledge. Wait until God tells you what to do with it! The "word of wisdom" will show how to do what God has shown you needs doing, how to solve problems that arise, or what and how to speak in a given situation, especially when challenged about your faith. The gifts of the "word of knowledge", and "word of wisdom", may be manifested through a sudden inspiration which remains with you, a knowing deep within your spirit, through the interpretation of a dream,[1] vision, or parable, through the vocal gifts of the Holy Spirit, and though rare, may come through hearing the audible Voice of God, or an angelic visitation.

The Authorized Version of the Scripture speaks of "word" of knowledge and "word" of wisdom. "Word" translated from the Greek in both cases is λόγος (logos), which can mean "word", "matter", or "concern", and is not confined just to a spoken word. This is to say that if the gifts of knowledge or wisdom are received, whether they are spoken aloud or not, they are still the gifts of "*word* of knowledge" or "*word* of wisdom". They are not necessarily vocal gifts. These gifts are often referred to as "the word of knowledge", or "the word of wisdom". The Greek, however, does not use any article, but simply calls them "word of wisdom" and "word of knowledge". To supply any article subtly changes the meaning. We do not even have the right to use the indefinite article: "a word of knowledge", as some modern versions do, for here again the meaning is subtly changed. Nevertheless, to read smoothly in English, we have mostly used the definite article (as the Author-

---

1. Although God sometimes chooses to speak to a person through a dream, this does not mean that one should keep a diary of every dream! The psychologist may be interested in dream data as a clue to what is going on in the subconscious, but this has little to do with our present topic. Many dreams are just a result of eating too much before going to bed! Some dreams are purely from the enemy; why waste your time paying attention to the confusion he has to bring? If God has spoken to you in a dream, and He wants you to recall it, you *will!* He says that the Holy Spirit will: "Bring all things to your remembrance, whatsoever I have said unto you" (John 14:26 KJV).

ized and Revised Standard Versions, and the New English Bible do), but have put it outside the quotation marks, so as to show that the article refers to the gift in general, and not to the specific "word". Perhaps the absence of the article in the Greek is to remind us that these "words" are only fragments of God's wisdom and knowledge.

We May Distinguish Four Kinds of Knowledge:

First: Natural human knowledge which certainly is on the increase. The Book of Daniel says of the end times: ". . . Many shall run to and fro, and knowledge shall be increased (Dan. 12:4 KJV). Just recently a college professor friend stated, for example, that the increase of knowledge in the area of higher mathematics is so great that in some instances researchers in two different maths fields cannot even communicate with one another. Electronic brains or computers have become a necessity in an attempt to relate and process the tremendous stockpile of facts, since it has gone beyond the human mind to do so in any reasonable length of time. As important as the knowledge of this world is, yet it often creates so much pride that some people are kept from entering into the knowledge of the Lord. The Epistle to the Corinthians says: "But the natural man receiveth not the things of the Spirit of God: for they are foolishness unto him: neither can he know them, because they are spiritually discerned" (I Cor 2:14 KJV). Again the Scripture says: "Knowledge puffeth up, but love edifieth" (I Cor. 8:1).

Second: This fallen world's supernatural knowledge which we have mentioned previously is the natural mind's attempt to gain information by supernatural means other than through the Holy Spirit. It includes the occult, the psychic, and the "metaphysical" investigations which Satan is using to ensnare an increasing number of people today. So-called religious experiences through drugs, cults, psychic, and occult phenomena are growing in numbers—all one has to do is look at the latest books on public display to see the level of interest in such things. The fallen knowledge of this world is outside the limit of God's permission. Do not touch it!

Our third category is true intellectual knowledge, which comes by knowing God personally through Jesus Christ (John 17:3; Phil. 3:10), being filled with the Holy Spirit, and through studying the Word of God, which brings the knowledge of God's will and His ways, for which there is no substitute (Ps. 103:7; Exod. 33:13). With the natural knowledge of this world so intriguing and so much on the increase, it is even more exiting to realize that the knowledge of the Lord is increasing in His people as never before. Isaiah tells us that ". . . The earth shall be full of the knowledge of the LORD, as the waters cover the sea" (Isa. 11:9 KJV). Even the Book of Daniel and the companion Book of Revelation have been sealed up from man's full understanding until the time of the end (Dan. 12:4, 9). There is much in God's Word which is ready to be revealed to us in the last times. What glorious days we live in! Man's knowledge will pass away, but the Knowledge of the Lord is permanent and will last through Eternity (Matt. 24:35–36; I Pet. 1:25).

The fourth is the gift of "word of knowledge". In looking at this gift, let us first say what it is *not*. It is not a psychic phenomenon or extrasensory perception such as telepathy (the supposed ability to read minds), clairvoyance (the supposed ability to know things that are happening elsewhere), or precognition (the supposed ability to know the future). These "abilities" are forbidden in God's Word (I Chron. 10:13; Deut. 18:9–12). We are not to reach out for such things—or we will open the door to Satan. All activities of this nature are dangerous and wrong. Experimentation with such psychic phenomena is toying with the *fallen powers of this world* which are controlled by Satan. There are two sources of spiritual power in the world: God and Satan. Just because something is "supernatural" does not mean that it is good, or from God.

The gift of the "word of knowledge" is not a human "ability" at all, but the sheer gift of God. It is not "developed" as the demonic manifestations may be, but is manifested as a result of staying close to the Lord. The Christian has something infinitely better than the counterfeit gifts of this world, for he is tasting the *powers of the world to come,* through Jesus, and the gifts of the Holy Spirit (Heb. 6 : 5). The Epistle of James says: "Every good gift and every perfect gift is *from above,* and *comes down* from the Father . . ." (Jas. 1 : 17). God's gifts are from above, from heavenly places in Christ Jesus, where the Christian lives in His Spirit. Paul says to the Ephesians: God "hath raised us up together, and made us sit together in heavenly places in Christ Jesus . . ." (Eph. 2 : 6 KJV). The Christian should not use the terminology of the world to describe supernatural experiences. If a believer suddenly became aware, without receiving the knowledge through any natural channels that a friend was in trouble, and needed his prayers and help, that would not be "extrasensory perception", but rather God manifesting the gift of the "word of knowledge". The gifts of the Holy Spirit come from and through the Holy Spirit to our *spirit,* and not from or through the soul or physical senses.

Paul says to the Christians at Corinth: "But the manifestation of the Spirit is given to every man *to profit withal*" (I. Cor. 12 : 7 KJV). These gifts are given to profit and benefit one another. They must not be misused. When God chooses to share His knowledge with us, it is for a purpose. It is not given just to make us feel "spiritual", or clever!

Some examples of a "word of knowledge" as given in the Bible:

It was used to recover lost persons or property, as in the case of Saul and the lost donkeys (I Sam. 9: 15–20; 10: 21–23). (Note that the "word of knowledge" can give information in seemingly very prosaic matters. God is concerned about every human need.)

A "word of knowledge" was given to Nathan regarding the affair between King David and Bathsheba. Nathan was also given wisdom to deal with the King (II Sam. 12: 7–13).

It was used to expose a hypocrite, Gehazi (II Kings 5: 20–27.)

Elisha, by miraculous revelation, knew the location of the Syrian army camp, thereby saving Israel from battle (II Kings 6: 8–23).

The Lord Jesus used the gift of the "word of knowledge". When He laid aside his glory, He accepted the limitations of a human intellect. While on earth He was not omniscient—"all-knowing"—but all the knowledge He needed to meet any given situation was available to Him through the Holy Spirit, just as, in Him, such knowledge is available to us today.

When Jesus healed the man sick of the palsy, he also forgave his sins. This made the scribes think evil in their hearts against Him. Jesus knew by a "word of knowledge" (not by "mind reading") the condition of their hearts and openly said so (Matt. 9: 2–6).

By this gift of revelation (not by "clairvoyance") Jesus "saw" Nathanael long before He met him, standing under the fig tree, and Jesus also knew what kind of person he was. We see that a "word of knowledge" may reveal the whereabouts of a man and the nature of his heart or thoughts (John 1: 47–50).

It was used to convince the woman at the well of her sin, and of the need to accept Jesus as Messiah. "Come see a man, which told me all things that ever I did . . ." (John 4: 17–18, 29 KJV).

We see the continuing manifestation of this supernatural knowledge in the days of the early Church.

It was used to reveal corruption in the Church—Ananias and Sapphira (Acts 5:3).

A different Ananias, an otherwise unknown Christian, received in a vision the knowledge of Saul's conversion, the name of the street (Straight), and the name of the man in whose house he was staying (Judas), whom he was to look for (Saul of Tarsus), what Saul was doing (praying), his attitude (he was repentant), and his needs (healing and the baptism with the Holy Spirit) (Acts 9:11–12:17).

The Holy Spirit revealed to Peter by the "word of knowledge" that three men were at the gate of his house in Joppa looking for him, and that he was to go with them without having any doubts (Acts 10:17–23).

For a present-day example, we'll share something that happened in Spokane, while Rita was teaching a class on the gifts of the Holy Spirit. They were not only studying this subject intellectually, but praying and expecting that the gifts would be manifested. Faith grows by hearing God's Word, and as the class studied the Scriptures the atmosphere of faith increased to a point in which the miraculous could happen. At the end of the class, as they prayed, Rita had a strong impression, an unusual feeling in her right ear. Not knowing at first where the impression was coming from she asked God's protection. Then the thought came to her, "Maybe God is trying to show me that someone here has something wrong with his right ear!" Being among friends, she decided to ask. A young woman named Fran responded immediately, and said she had been deaf in her right ear for over twenty years. Of late her deafness had begun to trouble her so much, that she had been praying earnestly for God to heal her. "The 'word of knowledge' had never come to me in this way before," said Rita, "and I knew without a doubt that God was going to heal her." The prayer group gathered around as they laid hands on Fran, but petitionary prayer wasn't necessary, for God had already revealed what He was going to do; in simple faith Rita commanded Fran's ear to be healed in Jesus' Name. Fran said that she knew something happened, but did not fully testify to her healing until she had been examined by her doctor. Later she said that when she was prayed for, her ear "popped", and her hearing was restored. The doctor confirmed that the ear had been completely healed. It has remained so ever since. This account shows a combination of three gifts beginning with a "word of knowledge", which brought a gift of faith, which in turn brought a gift of healing.

As wonderful as it is to have God speak and tell us what He is going to do and what part we will play in His plans (knowledge), yet it is equally important to have Him show us how to do our tasks (wisdom). If a mother showed and instructed a child about all the ingredients and measurements that go into making a cake, but didn't share wisdom as to how they were to be put together—the knowledge would be to no avail. In fact, the result would be a mess. So we see that knowledge and wisdom are companion gifts; it is important to have both. The Book of Proverbs tells us: "The tongue of the wise useth knowledge aright" (Prov. 15 : 2 KJV).

We May Also See Four Kinds of Wisdom

Natural human wisdom is naturally applied knowledge. This kind of wisdom is obviously on the increase, since knowledge is so much on the increase. Knowledge without wisdom would be futile. Of course, compared to God's wisdom, man's wisdom is but foolishness. It may also be a stumbling block to keep man from God. The wisdom of the natural man will one day pass away: "For it is written, I will destroy the wisdom of the wise, and will bring to nothing the understanding of the prudent" (I Cor. 1: 19 KJV).

This fallen world's supernatural wisdom and knowledge were the very things which were used to tempt the first man and woman to disobey God's commandment. "A tree to be desired to make one *wise*," we read (Gen. 3: 6 KJV). This kind of wisdom was, and continues to be, forbidden by God. Man already had natural wisdom, which was good, but now he opened himself up to supernatural evil knowledge, and the application of it, evil wisdom, which until then existed only among the fallen angels. Astrology is an example of counterfeit wisdom today (Dan. 2: 27–28).

True intellectual wisdom. The Books of Proverbs and King Solomon's wisdom are good examples of this. We are told to get this kind of wisdom. It comes by respecting the Lord and the Word of God (Job 28: 28; Prov. 9: 10), and also by studying God's Word which can be understood only as it is revealed by the Holy Spirit. In order to do this we must first receive Jesus Christ, Who is the wisdom of God (I Cor. 1: 24), and obviously, it is important to have received the baptism with the Holy Spirit.

The Scripture says: "If any of you lack wisdom, let him ask of God, that giveth to all men liberally, and upbraideth not; and it shall be given him" (Jas. 1: 5 KJV). Paul also prayed without ceasing for the Church that: "You might be filled with the knowledge of his will in all wisdom and spiritual understanding" (Col. 1: 9). We should ask and believe that God will give us liberally the wisdom needed to do the best job possible for Him.

The supernatural gift of the "word of wisdom" is the sudden and miraculous giving of wisdom to meet a particular situation, or answer a particular question, or utilize a particular piece of knowledge, natural or supernatural. Like the "word of knowledge" it is not a human ability at all, but the sheer gift of God. It would be difficult to say whether wisdom or knowledge is the more important. It would be rather like trying to decide which is the more important, the paint, or the painter, for whereas the artist can't paint a picture without the materials, the materials without the person who knows how to use them can be a source of damage and ugliness. So if a person has knowledge—either in the natural or the supernatural—and has no wisdom to use it properly, much damage may be done.

Let us look at some examples of the gift of the "word of wisdom" in the Old Testament Scripture:

When Joseph interpreted Pharoah's dream, this was not natural wisdom, or wisdom through study and preparation, but Joseph was given an immediate supernatural answer. Joseph was "on the spot"! He had been let out of prison just long enough to be given a chance to interpret this dream. Later, Joseph gave wise counsel in such matters as: the need of appointing a wise leader and officers, and how to store the needed food for the time of famine. This latter, however, was not by a "word of wisdom", but by the true intellectual wisdom that God had given Joseph, and which he used continually. This led to Pharoah to call Joseph "discreet and wise", and he placed him over all Egypt as second only to the King (Gen 41).

God called to Moses out of a burning bush, asking him to deliver Israel from the bondage of Egypt (knowledge), and he needed the word of wisdom many times as he was faced with a rebellious people (Exod. 3).

God gave knowledge of the plans of construction of the Tabernacle in the Wilderness to Moses and told him that He had called Bezaleel and filled him with wisdom and knowledge (which he didn't have naturally) to work with the gold, silver, brass, stones, timber, and to do the principal work of the building of the Tabernacle (Exod 31).

One of the great "faith" stories in the Old Testament is also a remarkable example of the Spiritual gifts of prophecy, wisdom, and knowledge. King Jehoshaphat was beset by an alliance of three powerful enemies. Knowing that he did not have the resources to defend his kingdom, he put the whole matter before the Lord. All the people of Judah "stood before the Lord", waiting for an answer. The answer came when "upon Jahaziel . . . came the Spirit of the Lord in the midst of the congregation", and Jahaziel first began to prophesy:

"Be not afraid nor dismayed by reason of this great multitude, for the battle is not yours, but God's." This was "edification, exhortation, and comfort". Then followed the "word of knowledge", as Jahaziel told the King and the people exactly where the enemy would be, and where they would find them. Again, he brought a "word of wisdom", telling them they wouldn't have to fight, but just stand still and watch what God would do. Jehoshaphat then is given a "word of wisdom" from the Lord, and instead of going out with his best warriors in the front rank, he sends out men to sing and praise the Lord —and lo and behold, the enemies proceed to ambush each other! (II Chron. 20: 12–23).

Daniel had wisdom and knowledge in the intellectual realm, and therefore was chosen to teach in the King's palace. However, even greater was the supernatural word of wisdom which God gave him from time to time, so that when he was called in to Nebuchadnezzar to reveal the dream the King had forgotten and the interpretation of it (wisdom), he was able to do so. These secrets were revealed to Daniel in a "night vision". Daniel said, "Blessed be the name of God for ever and ever: for wisdom and might are His . . . He gives wisdom unto the wise, and knowledge to them that know understanding. He reveals the deep and secret things . . ." (Dan. 2: 20-22). Consequently the King made Daniel ruler over Babylon and chief of the governors. In the fourth chapter of Daniel we read where Daniel again interprets Nebuchadnezzar's dream, this time telling him of the departure of his Kingdom. Later, under Belshazzar's reign, he was called in to interpret the handwriting on the wall. Daniel's life and the lives of others were spared many times through this God-given gift.

As our Example in all things, the Lord Jesus displays again and again the "word of wisdom" to meet especially challenging circumstances. The chief priests and elders of the people asked Jesus by what authority He made such great claims. Jesus' answer in the form of a question was a "word of wisdom" (Matt. 21:23-27).

The Pharisees tried to entangle Jesus in His words by asking if men should pay tribute to Caesar or not. Jesus answered with a "word of wisdom": "Render therefore unto Caesar the things which are Caesar's; and unto God the things that are God's" (Matt. 22:15-22 KJV).

A lawyer and Pharisee tempted Jesus with a question to find out which He thought was the greatest commandment in the law. Jesus answered this with wisdom. Then Jesus asked the Pharisees who they believed Him to be. When they answered, "The son of David", Jesus' reply from the Psalms was so profound that the Gospel of Matthew says from that day on they dared not ask Him any more questions (Matt. 22:34-46).

Even as Jesus had great wisdom, we are promised that in the midst of persecution He will give us "a mouth and wisdom" which our adversaries will not be able to deny or resist. This gift will be needed more in the days ahead. The Gospel of Matthew says: "But beware of men: for they will deliver you up to the councils ... synagogues ... governors and kings for my sake ... But when they deliver you up, *take no thought* how or what you shall speak: for it shall be given you in that same hour what you shall speak ..." (Matt. 10:17-19).

This passage of Scripture shows the wisdom Peter and John applied when they were threatened by the rulers of the Jews because of the healing of the lame man (Acts 4 : 7–21). Later when they were arrested because of this healing we read: "When they saw the boldness of Peter and John, and perceived that they were unlearned and ignorant men, they marvelled; and they took knowledge of them, that they had been with Jesus" (Acts 4 : 13 KJV).

It was said of those disputing with Stephen, who was a man full of faith and power: "They were not able to resist the wisdom and the spirit by which he spoke" (Acts 6 : 8–10).

The Apostle Paul was certainly not trained in seamanship, yet when he was involved in a shipwreck, he so took command of the situation that even though he was a prisoner being taken to Rome, the Roman officer listened to him with respect (Acts 27 : 21–35).

We must set our thinking aright, get rid of our old habit of limiting God in our lives, and begin to live with expectancy. In Christ are hidden "all the treasures of wisdom and knowledge" (Col. 2 : 3 KJV). Since Jesus Christ lives within us, the tremendous fact is that His wisdom and knowledge are there also— ready to be revealed to us by the quickening of the Holy Spirit. With this wonderful treasure of Jesus Christ living in us, let us rest assured that the Holy Spirit will draw from the treasury that which is needed as we believe God for these gifts. Take time to thank Him right now that divine wisdom and knowledge will be manifested in your life, at God's bidding, when the need arises. Praise God for his unspeakable riches!

*　　*　　*

In this study of the gifts of the Spirit we began with the gifts of *inspired speech,* because they are mostly easily observed, and most frequently manifested; then the gifts of *power;* and lastly the gifts of *revelation*. Every supernatural happening in the Bible (excluding counterfeits, of course), can be indentified with one or the other of these nine gifts of the Holy Spirit listed in I Corinthians 12:7–11.

There are three other lists in the New Testament that are termed "gifts", but one of them, in Ephesians, is a list of offices or ministries in the Church: apostles, prophets, evangelists, pastors, and teachers (Eph. 4:8, 11). In this place, too, a different word is used in the Greek: *domata*, rather than *charismata*. Another "list" is found in Romans but it is really not an attempt to list the gifts at all, but rather a series of illustrations given to instruct in Christian living (Rom. 12:4–21). It mixes a few of the gifts and ministries with other functions—some of which, according to Paul's rationale elsewhere, would be called "fruit" of the Spirit. In I Corinthians 12, the very same chapter in which the clear-cut list of the gifts appears, the Apostle again cites, at the end of the chapter, a number of the gifts and ministries for illustrative purposes.[2] It seems most in keeping with the general pattern of Scripture, though, to say that I Corinthians 12:7–11 is the list of the gifts, while Ephesians 4:11 lists the "official" ministries in the Church. Similarly the fruit of the Spirit is listed in Galatians 5:22–23, but in Ephesians 5:9 (KJV), Paul uses the term in illustrative style: "The fruit of the Spirit is in all goodness and righteousness and truth."

Any person who has been baptized with the Holy Spirit may exercise any of the nine spiritual gifts as the need arises, and as the Holy Spirit chooses. We know many Christians who have during a period of years been used in all of the nine gifts of the Spirit. This doesn't mean that they're more spiritual than

2. Any of the gifts of the Spirit may develop into a ministry as we have stated before, but those at the end of this list are specifically listed as such.

the rest but merely that they have been perhaps more available and expectant.

We pray that this study will help to bring greater understanding so that the gifts of power and revelation will be manifested in the body of Christ much more than in the past, and that the better known gifts of inspired speech will be expressed in greater beauty and edification in the Church.

It is our opinion that God wants the gifts to be active in the Christian's life to increase our own edification and joy, and also to make it clear to the world that Jesus is alive and real. The Holy Spirit divides the gifts to every man severally as He wills, and the Holy Spirit wills that we live an abundant life in Christ.

"Now unto Him that is able to do exceedingly abundantly above all that we ask or think, according to the power that worketh in us, unto Him be glory in the Church by Christ Jesus throughout all ages, world without end" (Eph. 3:20 KJV).

14
The Excellent Way

In Exodus 28 we read a description of the vestments of the high priest, worn when he served in the tabernacle in worship of God. The high priest had a garment called an *ephod*. It was blue, and around the hem had a very special decoration:

"And beneath upon the hem of it thou shalt make pomegranates of blue, and of purple, and of scarlet, round about the hem thereof; and bells of gold between them round about: a golden bell and a pomegranate, a golden bell and a pomegranate, upon the hem of the robe round about" (Exod. 28: 33 KJV).

The golden bells may be taken to symbolize the gifts of the Holy Spirit. The gifts are seen and heard, and they are beautiful. The bells sounded as the high priest moved in the Holy Place, invisible to the worshippers outside, but they knew he was praying for them. So the gifts show us that Jesus, although invisible to our earthly eyes, is alive and ministering for us in the Holy Place.

The pomegranates represent the fruit of the Spirit. They are sweet in flavour and attractive in colour, and are loaded with seeds, and thus not only remind us of fruit, but of *fruitfulness*. We have made quite an extensive study of the gifts of the Holy

Spirit, the golden bells, and now we must be careful to remind you that the gifts of the Spirit are balanced by the fruit of the Spirit.

The gifts of the Spirit (I Cor. 12: 7–11 KJV), again, are: wisdom, knowledge, discerning of spirits, faith, miracles, healing, prophecy, tongues, and interpretation of tongues; the fruit of the Spirit (Gal. 5: 22–23) is: love, joy, peace, patience, gentleness, kindness, faith, humility, and discipline. Believer-priests today should check the hem of their robes, that is, their lives, to see what is there.

In order for there to be a "golden bell and a pomegranate, a golden bell and a pomegranate" as the Scripture says, around the robe of the priest, there would have to be an equal number of each. It is interesting to see in the preceding lists that there are exactly nine gifts and nine fruits of the Spirit. In order for the golden bells to ring clearly, harmoniously, without clashing into one another, there must be fruit between each one.

Gifts brought through lives that are lacking in fruit, and motivated by a desire for self-esteem and a wish to be noticed, will be about as uplifting as so many clanging tin cans. The gifts of the Spirit are given "without repentance"—that is, God does not take them back because they are misused—and so they may function through lives that are unconsecrated, and through persons who need to make restitution to God and man; but these would be nothing more than ear-shattering brass bells to those who have discernment. This is what the Apostle means when he speaks of "sounding brass" and "clanging cymbals." Our bells should not be brass or tin, but pure gold. Golden bells represent lives that are in tune with the Lord and the brethren, and whose central desire is to lift up Jesus Christ, as they manifest the gifts.

'It's significant that this pattern of the alternate bells and pomegranates carries into the New Testament, since between

the two great chapters on the gifts, I Corinthians 12 and 14, is
found the beautiful chapter on the central fruit of the Spirit—
love—in I Corinthians 13:

"If I have the gift of being able to speak in languages
of men and of angels, without having learned them, but
have not love,

  I am like noisy brass bells,
  Or clanging cymbals.

And though I have been used in the gift of prophecy,
and understand all mysteries, and all knowledge;
And though I have the fullest measure of faith,
so that I could remove mountains,

    And have not love,
    I am nothing.

Though I give away all I have to the poor, and
give my body to be burned, and have not God's
love shining through me,

    It profits me nothing.

  Love is patient and kind;
  Love is not envious;

Love is not puffed up with pride,
Does not behave itself unmannerly or out of order,

  Seeks not her own way,
  Is not easily irritated,
  Entertains no evil thoughts;

Rejoices not at injustice and unrighteousness,
but rejoices when right and truth win;

    Love is consistent,

Love is always ready to trust,
Expects the best, in everything

    Endures as a good soldier.
    Love never ends;

As for prophecies, they will pass away; as for tongues,
they will cease; as for knowledge, it too will one day
    pass away.
For our knowledge is fragmentary and our prophecy is limited.
But when the Perfect comes, the imperfect will no longer be
    needed.
When I was a child, I spoke as a child, I reasoned as a child;
but when I became a man, I gave up childish ways.
For now we are looking in a mirror which gives a dim reflection,
but then we will see face to face!
    Now I understand in part,
but then will know fully, even as I have been known.
    So faith, hope, and love abide,
        these three;
but the greatest of these is love."

Love is the most important fruit of the Spirit; without it the
other eight fruit could not exist. They are called "fruit" instead
of "fruits" because the others are like sections of an orange con-
tained within the fruit of love.

What kind of love is this which is described as being greater
than faith, which is the key to the Bible, and without which we
can receive nothing from God? This love is spoken of as being
greater than knowledge, which is a gift of the Spirit, and one
greatly desired by Christians. It is greater than martyrdom for
our trust in Jesus! It is greater than giving to the poor, though
this is certainly a good thing to do. This love is greater than the
gift of prophecy, which Paul said all Christians should desire
as it is the greatest gift with which to edify the Church. It is
greater than speaking in unknown languages. It is greater than
hope.

This must be speaking of a different kind of love from ordinary human love, which is inconsistent and limited. In English

we have only one word for "love", whereas the Greek language has seven! Only two of these are used in the New Testament, however: *philia*, which means affection or fondness for another as in friendship—a limited kind of love; and *agape*, which means God's perfect love—unconditional love—as expressed in the love of God for man, or Christian brotherly love in its highest manifestation coming as a result of God living in man.

A third word for love in the Greek tongue is the familiar *eros*, which means physical or sensual love. Thus we have a trinity of words for "love": *agape*—spirit; *philia*—soul; *eros*—body.

The fruit of the Spirit we are talking about in this chapter is *agape*. God's love for man was shown to us through the birth, life, and death of Jesus Christ. "Greater love has no man than this, that a man lay down his life for his friends" (John 15: 13 RSV)—and even His enemies (Rom. 5: 7-10). God's love in man comes as a result of salvation. The baptism with the Holy Spirit causes a greater outflow of God's love, as long as the person is abiding in Christ and walking in the Spirit. "The love of God is shed abroad in our hearts by the Holy Ghost which is given unto us" (Rom. 5: 5 KJV). First Corinthians 13 is speaking of *agape*, self-sacrificial love, love without reservation.

Love is not only the central fruit of the Spirit but a commandment from Jesus:

"Thou shalt love the Lord thy God with all thy heart, and with all thy soul, and with all thy mind. This is the first and great commandment. And the second is like unto it, Thou shalt love thy neighbour as thyself. On these two commandments hang all the law and the prophets" (Matt. 22: 37-39 KJV).

Jesus also said: "A new commandment I give unto you, That you love one another; as I have loved you . . ." (John 13: 34).

Love is also given in the New Testament as one of the things that "edifies" us spiritually. "Knowledge puffs up, but love edifies."

The beginning stage of love is when we can only love the one who loved us first. "We love him (God) because he first loved us" (I John 4:19 KJV). It is a necessary beginning, but a mixed love. With pure love comes a forgetting of self and a greater desire to give than to receive. As we do this we find ourselves loving God not for what He has done or is doing for us but loving Him for Himself alone.

Only after we have made connections with that heavenly resource of love, can we be expected to love our neighbours. The first and great commandment, to love God, had to come before the second, to love our neighbour, because without tapping into God's love it is impossible for us to love our fellowman.

God wouldn't have made this requirement if it were impossible for us. Some people say that loving God takes up all their time so that they have none left over to give to anyone else! Jesus commanded His disciples to love one another in the same manner as He had loved them, as a sign to the world that they were His followers. When we love the brethren we are loving Christ because the Bible says we are all the body of Christ, flesh of His flesh and bone of His bones (Eph. 5:29-30; I Cor. 12:27). God receives love from us *as we love* the brethren in Christ, as well as in our devotion to Him in prayer and praise. As we mature in love we will also be able to reach out and love the unbeliever, and even love and forgive our enemies (Matt. 5:43-48).

Love on an earthly plane, however, is impossible without loving yourself first, as the Scripture says: "Love your neighbour *as yourself*." If you hate yourself you will not be able to truly love God, the brethren, the unbeliever, or your enemy. Only through knowing who you are in Christ, and that the essential you is a new creature where God dwells, can you ever love yourself. Only through Jesus is there anything worth loving in ourselves. It is a sin *not* to love ourselves. How can we help but love all that God has created?

Paul says at the end of the twelfth chapter: "Covet earnestly the best gifts: and yet I show unto you a more excellent way" (I Cor. 12:31). The more excellent way is not "instead of the gifts" but instead of "coveting the gifts": loving so much that the gifts flow forth in such beauty that they are as a refreshing river blessing all in their pathway.

Agape never fails, says Paul; but prophecy, tongues, knowledge, and the other gifts will vanish away when Jesus the Perfect One returns for His Church. The gifts are mainly for the edification and protection of the Church on earth, but when the Church is with the Edifier, the gifts will no longer be needed. But they are needed today.

A young man enlists in the army. We can expect that he will develop "fruit" in his life—courage, stamina, perseverance, reliability, etc. The fruit are most important and are being established permanently in his character. What if this young man was sent to a war zone and told: "Now, son, you have the most important things; the fruit have really been developed in your life, and you don't need anything else:" He would probably reply:

"Sir, that sounds very good, but I've heard rumours that there's an enemy around here, and the casualties coming in confirm the rumours. If you don't mind I'd like some weapons (gifts) to protect myself with; there's a war on!" If he were then told that the weapons had passed away because they were no longer needed by the army, he would be hard to convince!

Yes, there is a war on; and as long as we live in this fallen world, we will need the gifts. The gifts have not passed away yet; in fact Scripture indicates that before Jesus returns for His

Church there will be an even greater moving of the Holy Spirit to combat the increased work of the enemy, and the gifts will obviously be included (Joel 2 : 23–24, 28–31; Hag. 2 : 9). One glorious day when the battle is over and won, the gifts will no longer be needed.

Faith and hope as we know it in this life shall also pass away. "Hope that is seen is not hope . . . but if we hope for that we see not, then do we with patience wait for it" (Rom 8 : 24–25 KJV). "Now faith is the substance of things hoped for, the evidence of things not seen" (Heb. 11 : 1 KJV). Seeing the evidence of our faith will bring us into a different kind of faith relationship from what we have now. When we see Our Lord face to face, all these things shall pass away as the Scripture tells us. That which remains for Eternity will be love—*agape*—for "God is Love".

We have tried to show that there needs to be a balance and an interplay between the gifts and fruit of the Holy Spirit. The gifts, the golden bells, need to be ringing, to proclaim to the world that our great high priest is alive for evermore, and still doing His saving, healing work on earth through the ministry of His people. The fruit needs to be seen, in order to show people what Jesus is like and that He loves them. The world must see the love of God active in His people.

15
Consecration

We have talked about two basic Christian experiences: the most important being salvation and next, the baptism with the Holy Spirit. These are given freely to anyone who asks, and nothing can be done to earn them.

There is also a vital step we may call *consecration*.[1] The first two steps God offers to us for our simple acceptance, whereas in consecration we give ourselves back to God:

"I beseech you therefore, brethren . . . that you present your bodies a living sacrifice, holy [consecrated], acceptable unto God which is your reasonable service" (Rom. 12:1).

Paul is here speaking to the "brethren"—to believers who are saved and no doubt baptized in the Holy Spirit. Consecration is something that *we* do, but we can only do it because God gives us the ability. It is yielding our self-will to God to the fullest possible measure, so that His perfect will may be done in and through us. This step is a response to the prayer:

"Thy kingdom come, Thy will be done *in* earth [in earthen

1. Other terms often used are: commitment, discipleship, or dedication.

vessels (II Cor. 4:7)], as it is in heaven . . ." (Matt. 6:10 KJV).

It means really allowing Jesus to be King and Lord of our lives.

"Who . . . is willing to consecrate his service this day unto the Lord?" King David asked the people (I Chron. 29:5 KJV). The children of Israel responded willingly and with a "perfect heart"; they gave of themselves and their substance for the building of the Temple of the Lord. Then David prayed a beautiful prayer ending with the familiar words:

"All things come of thee, and of thine own have we given thee" (I Chron. 29:14 KJV).

We, and all we have, belong to God, but having given us free will, He must wait for us to give all back to Him willingly.

Just as we are saved when we first receive Jesus, and yet our salvation continues, day by day; just as we receive the Holy Spirit, once and for all at a particular time, and yet must allow Him to fill us day by day; so we need to make an initial act of consecration which must be renewed also day by day, as we gather up the parts of our lives that seem to have grown away from Him, and bring them back where they belong. There are many who have been born again and baptized in the Holy Spirit who don't realize the need for consecration. Yet consecration is the only way to a full and victorious Christian life.

Consecration then, is *choosing* to walk with Jesus every day; it means putting Jesus first in your life and going His way. "Seek first the kingdom of God, and His righteousness; and all these things shall be added unto you" (Matt. 6:33). Jesus promises always to be with you, but the unconsecrated believer makes Jesus accompany him where he wants to go, while the consecrated person follows Jesus where *He* wants to go. Jesus said: "If any man will come after me, let him deny himself, and take up his cross daily [yield his self-will daily] and follow me" (Luke 9: 23 KJV).

Some may say at this point: "This all sounds very good but how can I learn to do it?" One of the best helps found is the discovery of the difference between soul and spirit. "We've mentioned before the importance of seeing that we are not two parts, soul and body, like the animals; but three parts: Spirit, soul, and body.

The spirit (*pneuma*) is the innermost part of us which was created to have fellowship with God. It was dead in "trespasses and sins," and came alive when we became Christians, and God came to live there. Within our spirit is that place of an inner knowing or witness to the will of God. The Book of Colossians says: "For in Him [Jesus] dwelleth all the fullness of the God-head [Trinity] bodily. And you [the Christian] are complete in him" (Col. 2: 9–10). In the Gospel of John, Jesus says: "If a man love me, he will keep my words: and my Father will love him, and we will come unto him, and make our abode with him" (John 14: 23 KJV), and "I will pray the Father, and he shall give you another Comforter, that he may abide with you for ever" (John 14: 16 KJV). With the Father, Son, and Holy Spirit living in our spirit, what more can we ask for? This is the part of us called the "new creature" where our spirit and the Holy Spirit have been joined together and have become one (I Cor. 6: 17). This is too often the most neglected part of our being; yet it is the most important.

The soul (*psyche*) is the part of man that has ruled him ever since the fall. It has three parts: intellect, will, and emotions. The soul in the Christian is in the state of being straightened out; it is still a mixture of good and evil. When the soul is yielded to God it is wonderful—when it is not, it can seriously block what God wants to do in and through us. Although the "old man" was crucified with Christ, the mess he left from the time he was in charge is still in our soul; the clean-up job in scriptural language is called sanctification. This area is a real battleground! It is the area of the "self" which Jesus calls us to deny.

The body (*soma*) is the area of the five senses: tasting, touching, smelling, seeing, and hearing. The body is the house of the soul and spirit, and the Christian's body becomes the temple of the *Holy* Spirit (I Cor. 6 : 19). With the baptism in the Holy Spirit it is filled to overflowing with the glory of God. As long as our bodies—which still have fallen tendencies—do not control our lives, but rather are controlled by the Holy Spirit and our "new creature" life, they will express the beauty and joy of the Lord. God has a plan for our physical bodies, and will bring it to pass as we are obedient to the promptings of the Holy Spirit and His Word concerning His temple. God wants you to prosper and be in health even as your soul prospers" (III John 1 : 2).

Our situation in life might be compared to a great ocean liner. The captain has been critically ill, and unable to command the ship for a long time. The crew know very well how to work the ship, and so they have taken over. Unfortunately, they really do not know where they are going, or what the voyage is all about, so they have been sailing aimlessly over the ocean. They have been quarrelling among themselves, and the ship is nearly out of fuel. Since they don't know how to navigate or how to get to port, they can't refuel. Things are in pretty bad shape! Miraculously, the captain recovers, but he finds it is going to take him a while to gain control of the ship again. Now and then the crew listen to him, but most of the time they say: "Now, sir, we have been sailing this vessel around for a long time without your help, and we know how to do it. Just let us alone!"

Your spirit in union with the Holy Spirit is supposed to be

the ruler of your soul, and your submitted soul is supposed to direct your body. For a long time, however, ever since you were born, your spirit has been out of action, and your soul and body have been running things for themselves. How is the captain of the ship going to get his position back? What the crew doesn't know is that there will be true happiness only when the captain with his charts and compass and knowledge of the sea is allowed to take complete command. The captain also knows how the radio works and can call for help and instructions, for fuel, and other needed supplies. Only with the captain in charge will peace and joy reign on the ship!

For the Christian, right after his baptism in the Holy Spirit, God's Presence is so real that it is no effort to put God first. He's first on his mind in the morning, the favourite topic of conversation through the day, and last on his mind before retiring at night. His renewed spirit (the captain) is on top and his soul (the crew) and the body (the ship) are functioning according to the captain's directions. In some, this peace and order lasts longer than in others, but soon the soul begins to contend for its former place of control. To keep things in the right order the Christian needs to understand the difference between his *soul* and his *spirit*. He can know this through study and application of the Scriptures.

"The word of God is quick, and powerful, and sharper than any two-edged sword, piercing even to the dividing asunder of soul and spirit, and of the joints and marrow, and is a discerner of the thoughts and intents of the heart" (Heb. 4: 12 KJV).

Why does the Scripture tell us of the need to divide or separate between the soul and spirit? The soul, as we've said, is still a mixture of good and evil. The Bible never tells us to walk in the soul or live in the soul, but it does say over and over again, "walk in the spirit", "live in the spirit", "pray in the spirit", "sing in the spirit"! Only as we learn to walk in the spirit, with

our souls in a place of submission to God's Spirit, can our souls
be cleansed, healed, restored, and used to His glory. The Psalmist David's words are appropriate here:

"He leads me beside still waters; he restores my soul" (Ps.
23:2–3 RSV).

Just as we are three parts: spirit, soul, and body, our souls
also have three parts: intellect, will, and emotions. Our *intellect* is one of the most difficult areas of our soul to yield to the
work of the Holy Spirit. It seems to have fallen the farthest in
original sin, as it was through the reaching out of the intellect
into areas forbidden by God that sin entered the world. The
tempter said:

"For God knows that in the day you eat thereof, then your
eyes will be opened, and you will be as gods, knowing good and
evil" (Gen. 3:5).

Man has lived by the reasonings of his fallen intellect ever
since. We're taught from the first grade that the intellect is the
greatest part of our lives, but education isn't the complete
answer to change our world. (Dennis' mother used to say: "If
you educate a devil, you just get a clever devil!") Satan is
slicker than the world's greatest criminal lawyer; he certainly
will fool our intellect if that's strictly what we're going by. Our
mind has accumulated good and bad, true and false information, and even after conversion and the baptism with the Holy
Spirit, it takes time to be changed. The intellect is wonderful,
though, when submitted to God and renewed by the Holy
Spirit.

"And be not conformed to this world: but be transformed
[transformed and transfigured come from the same Greek
word *metamorpha*—where we get the word metamorphosis]
by the renewing of your mind, that you may prove what is the
. . . perfect, will of God" (Rom. 12:2). The Scripture also
says:

"Let this mind be in you, which was also in Christ Jesus" (Phil. 2 : 5 KJV).

Don't accept every thought that pops into your mind as yours. Check to be sure of its origin by asking yourself: Did this come from God? Did this come from my new life in Christ? Or did this come from the enemy? The enemy's fiery darts and evil imaginations need to be cast out of your life immediately. Temptation is not sin, but entertaining temptation is, and it will eventually lead to wrong actions. The Bible says:

"Casting down imaginations, and every high thing that exalteth itself against the knowledge of God, and bringing into captivity every thought to the obedience of Christ" (II Cor. 10: 5 KJV).

The "knowledge of God" is that the believer is a new creature, and so his thoughts will be healthy and good. All other thoughts come from the enemy or from the soul life and should be resisted. The believer must continuously oppose these wrong thoughts (it will get easier as he goes along), or he may return to many of his old ways. Watchman Nee,[2] the great Chinese spiritual leader, says that there are many of God's children who have new hearts but old heads.

The words "casting down" in the preceding passage indicate that our co-operation is needed, and here's where our will comes in. The *will* is the central part of the soul, where choices and decisions are made. It is the essential self, and has been used for self-will instead of God's will. God gave man a free will so that he could freely choose to love Him, but man's wrong use of free will, to reject God, cost the death of Jesus. Free will was purchased by Jesus' death. God never takes free will away

2. We recommend many of Watchman Nee's books to you: *Sit, Walk, Stand, Release of the Spirit,* and *Changed Into His Likeness* to name but a few.

from us, but each day we show Him our love by freely giving
our will back to Him. This is what consecration is all about.

God is not interested in having us "automatically" obey
Him because we have no will of our own. This would be a
travesty of scriptural teaching. It is what the so-called peren-
nial philosophy, the intellectual mysticism which man concocts,
comes up with, but it is entirely foreign to the Judaeo-Christian
way of thinking. Those who accept God's revealing of Himself
in the Scripture, and especially in Jesus Christ, know that God
wants creatures who willingly want what He desires for them.
They do not lose their wills; they consciously, actively, and
with joy, bring their wills into conformity with His, because
they feel and know His love, and because they are responding
to His love. God gave us free will, the power to choose, so that
we could freely love and freely obey Him. God wants children,
not robots. The Father longs for His children's obedience, because He loves them and wants to bring them to the very best.
The children desire to obey the Father, because they love Him.

Jesus, whose will was sinless and thus different from ours, set
an example for us. He said:

"I seek not my own will, but the will of the Father who sent
me" (John 5 : 30).

You may have been afraid to yield your will to God because
the enemy has scared you by saying such things as: "God will
surely make you leave your family and will send you to some
far-off country," or "God will make you stand on a street corner in your hometown and preach to the passers-by!" Don't
listen to him!"

Settle in your mind once and for all that God loves you and
wants only the best for you; only in going according to His plan
will you bear the most fruitful life now and through eternity!
We must let nothing hold us back from God's best!

The will also controls that third part of our soul: our

emotions. Emotions are the "feelings" of the soul. Some Christians have emotions much like a Yo Yo! Today they feel "saved"; tomorrow they feel "unsaved". Today they feel God is really guiding them; tomorrow they're not sure if He knows they exist. The novelist George Macdonald describes it thus:

"They had a feeling, or a feeling had them, till another feeling came and took its place. When a feeling was there, they felt as if it would never go; when it was gone they felt as if it had never been; when it returned, they felt as if it had never gone." [3]

Obviously our emotions are undependable, and if we try to guide our lives by them it will lead to confusion. In the past we have misused our emotions: letting our temper fly, giving way to self-pity, etc. Our lives can't be directed by our feelings; they too are a mixture of good and evil. We must go by that inner knowing in our spirits which is in agreement with God's Word. "Feelings aren't facts." This doesn't mean that a Christian's life should be devoid of emotion, but that God has a work of healing and renewing in this part of our lives to perform also.

The step of consecration—greatly assisted by learning to divide between soul and spirit—needs to be taken if it's not yet a reality in our lives. It's something we must consent to, and when we do, it deepens and establishes the rest in our souls. It is no accident that the fourth chapter of Hebrews speaks of entering God's rest just before telling of the need to divide or distinguish between soul and spirit. Choosing to live in the spirit instead of in the soul brings this rest, but many Christians have yet to learn the difference. Salvation is a rest in the spirit of man: "Repent therefore, and be converted, that your sins may be blotted out, when the times of refreshing shall come

3. George Macdonald, *What's Mine's Mine* (New York: McKay, 1886), chap. 16.

from the presence of the Lord" (Acts 3:19). Jesus said: "Come to Me, all you that labour and are heavy laden, and I will give you rest" (Matt. 11:28). The baptism with the Holy Spirit is an outflowing of that rest bringing a rest in the soul. Isaiah puts it this way: "For with stammering lips and another tongue will he speak to this people. To whom he said, This is the rest wherewith you may cause the weary to rest; and this is the refreshing . . ." (Isa. 28:11-12). The intellect comes into rest as it is yielded to God, and praying in tongues is one important means of letting the Holy Spirit renew and refresh our minds and souls. As we learn to deny our souls the right to rule us and walk in that rest with our souls and spirits submitted to the Lord, then God can get rid of the "wood, hay, and stubble" and establish those things of permanent value in our lives (I Cor. 3:12-13). Jesus said:

"Take my yoke upon you, and learn of me; for I am meek and lowly in heart: and you shall find rest unto your souls" (Matt. 11:29).

"Take My yoke upon you." Even as one oxen (you) is led by the other (Jesus), the two being yoked together—both are servants and burden bearers—the one in the lead guides the other in the way, and bears the heaviest load. When we begin to feel the weight of the load, we can be sure that we're taking the lead away from Our Lord and need to get back into our place —one step behind Him. The heaviness of the load is like a spiritual thermometer to warn us that the soul is taking the lead and not the Spirit. The heaviness reveals that our souls are not resting in Christ.

Let's be careful not to revert back to functioning out of the fallen intellect, emotions, and self-will, but instead continue that flow which began at our Pentecost: the mind of Christ manifesting in us, His emotions flowing through us, and His will being done by us.

Here is a prayer you might like to use, or you may want to pray using your own words:

Dear Heavenly Father,

Thank you so much for the wonderful gifts of salvation and the baptism in the Holy Spirit. Words are inadequate to express my gratitude! I know these gifts were free, given to me, on no merit of my own, but just because You love me. Now I want to give You the only thing I have to give . . . myself. I know Your will for my life is marvellous and so I ask that Your perfect will be done in and through me, from this day on. Help my will to yield to Yours until they blend together as one. I ask Your Son, Jesus Christ, to come and take the throne of my life and reign as Lord.

I know I can't do this in my own strength, but I'm relying on Your daily guidance and strength to help me. Thank You, Father, for hearing my prayer. Praise Your Name!

In Jesus' Name I pray,
Amen

16
The Narrow Way

Jesus said: "Narrow is the way which leadeth unto life" (Matt. 7:14 KJV). He didn't say: "Hard is the way," He said it was *narrow*. On the other hand He also said: "My yoke is easy, and my burden is light" (Matt. 11:30 KJV); and "Fear not, little flock; for it is your Father's good pleasure to *give* you the kingdom!" (Luke 12:32 KJV). Nothing could be more delightful than walking the King's Highway. One of the great Christians of the Middle ages said: "God gives us a little bit of heaven to go to heaven in!" The road to heaven is glorious—illuminated by the love of God, and the fellowship of friends in Jesus. The Scripture says: "If we walk in the light, as he is in the light, we have fellowship one with another, and the blood of Jesus Christ cleanseth us from all sin" (I John 1:7 KJV). The Christian way isn't difficult in itself, it is made difficult by the attacks of the enemy, who wants to push us off the track. Jesus said: "In the world you will have trouble, but be of good cheer I have conquered the world!" (John 16:33). The difficult things don't come from God, but the challenges of the world, the flesh, and the devil. If we stay on the "narrow way" and are not frightened by the attacks, if we don't listen to the lies of the enemy, we will have no difficulty in applying Jesus' victory to the situation, and walking on in triumph and joy, no matter what happens. God doesn't want us defeated, but victorious.

When Jesus speaks of the "narrow way", He means that the true path is a very thin line between extremes. Think of it in terms of navigation. When a big airliner is flying across the Pacific to the Hawaiian Islands, it is flying a narrow way. There is a certain compass heading which, according to the charts, will take that aircraft to the destination, but if the captain were to take up that heading—say 225°—and simply hold to it all the way across the water, he would almost certainly miss his destination. His instruments aren't that accurate, for one thing, and for another, winds and turbulent air would combine to throw him off course. What actually happens is that the navigator is busy correcting the course all the way along, and instead of flying by "dead reckoning", the course is being checked all the time by other means. It takes effort to stay on that "narrow way", that tiny thin line across the trackless waters that leads to the Honolulu airport! This is the sort of thing Jesus is talking about when He speaks of the "narrow way"—it is that one correct road, that one correct heading that leads to heaven. In order to stay on that heading, we have to be continually correcting our course by the chart, that is, by the Word of God, and by the sightings we take, that is, by our experience of God.

Satan has many devices to delay us if he can. Most people are on the alert for the obvious ones. They can see the danger in out-and-out temptations—violations of the moral law: murder, theft, adultery, etc. But the more subtle ones are the dangerous ones. If someone wanted to stop you from getting on a horse and riding, say, to a town ten miles away, there are several ways he might accomplish his purpose. First of all, he might try to persuade you that horses are not safe. 'I once had an uncle who was kicked by a horse, and spent three weeks in the hospital!" he might say. So Satan tries to persuade people that religion in general is dangerous. "Leave it alone—you'll go off the deep end!" he'll say. "Why, look at so-and-so! You don't want to get like him, do you?"

If he fails in this, and sees that you are going to get "on the horse" anyway, then he changes his tune completely: "I'll help you!" he says, and tries to give you such a boost into the saddle, that you fall off the other side and bump your head! In other words, he sees that you are going to try God, so he arranges for you to encounter some peculiar things at the very beginning that will frighten you. He tries to get you to a meeting where people are not observing decency and order, or where there are obvious false teachings, and "strange" people, so as to cause you to "bump your head" right from the start. Some people are backed off for years by one bad experience, when they thought they would like to find out about God, and encountered some "wayout" people.[1]

If, however, you get firmly seated in the saddle, his next gambit is to send you in the wrong direction! Especially when people are new in their journey on the "narrow way", the

---

1. We quite often meet folk who, when confronted by the "charismatic renewal" will say:

"Oh, forty years ago I went to a 'Holy Roller' meeting across the tracks in the little town where I was brought up. They were really carrying on. I don't want anything to do with *that!*" This is just as if a person might say:

"Oh, I had a ride in a 1917 Model T Ford back in 1923. It was awful. We broke down five times in twenty miles. It was dusty, and bumpy. I certainly don't want anything to do with automobiles, if they're like that! I'll walk, thank you!" On the other hand, if the same people encounter "Model T" practices today, one cannot blame them if they get discouraged!

enemy tries to get them involved in "new gospels",[2] and strange doctrines. He loves to say: "Look at the people in your church, in your prayer group—they are just 'milk and water Christians'! They're just 'babes in Christ'. You'd better go and join Brother X's organization. They are teaching some new doctrines. The Lord's given them a special word. They're special people. They're going to get to heaven first, and get a higher seat than anyone!"

If he can't get you involved with strange doctrines, if he can't get you to "come out" and join some separated brethren, then he'll send you some "Judaizers"—that is, some folk who are like the Jewish Christians who troubled the Gentile converts: "We're glad that you have met Jesus Christ, and received the Holy Spirit. You realize, however, that Jesus was the Messiah of the *Jews,* and you Gentiles must now keep the Jewish laws!" So these good souls say:

"Now, we're really happy that you got into the kingdom so easily, but now that you're in, you've got to start keeping the law, just like the rest of us! You haven't been properly baptized, for a start! Then you must change your manner of dress; take off your lipstick—or your loud neckties, let your hair grow —or, if you are a man, cut your hair—and be like us!"

Or the "dispensationalists" may make a "pass" at you: "We're really glad you have had this wonderful experience which *you* call the baptism in the Holy Spirit," they may say. "What really happened was that you finally got *saved!* Speaking in tongues, and all those things are not for today. We'll come and give you Bible lessons and explain it all away for you!"

But if you insist on riding the right way, then Satan's last at-

2. Paul says: Though we, or an angel from heaven, preach any other gospel unto you than that which we have preached unto you, let him be accursed" (Gal. 1:8).

tempt will be to stampede you! He says: "Good! You're going in the right direction. Now you'd better not waste any time! Hurry up!" And so he tries to get you to go overboard. "Speaking in tongues? By all means!" says he. "As often as possible! Interrupt the preacher at your church on Sunday morning. He doesn't believe in speaking in tongues—so you *show* him! Witness? By all means! Tell everybody! Bend everyone's ear at all times! Don't ever talk about anything else! Buttonhole all your friends! Ask them if they're saved, and the more you embarrass them the better! It'll show how fearless you are!" If you repel this attack, he'll just trot along beside you on the journey and renew his various attempts. But if you resist him and pay no attention to his lies, he has no further power over you. Satan's power lies mainly in his lying tongue. It is through this that he gains power, first over your mind, and then over your body. Shut him out!

The "narrow way" is, then, a true course between extremes. In II Timothy 2:15 we read: "Study to show yourself approved unto God, a workman that needs not to be ashamed, rightly dividing the word of truth." The original Greek on this reads:

"Be diligent to present yourself approved unto God, a workman not ashamed, cutting the word of truth correctly." The word "correctly cutting"—*orthotomeo*—does not mean to cut the truth up into sections or pieces, as some dispensational teachers have used it, but it means to cut a straight or correct path to a goal. It would be used of pioneers cutting a track through a forest, or across an unexplored wilderness, and thus agrees exactly with the idea of the "narrow way".

The narrow way is not a compromise, as some will try to tell you. Being in balance between extremes doesn't limit how far you can go. A railroad train stays on the "narrow way"—on the track, that is—and can go for thousands of miles, and at very high speeds. If it got off the track, it would soon stop, and very drastically! A building that is kept in balance over its foundations can be built as high as you like. So there is no limit to how far you can go and still remain at the right distance from the extremes.

What are some of the extremes through which we are called to cut a balanced path? Well, to begin with, there is the balance between freedom and legalism. Jesus expressed the "narrow way" perfectly Himself when he warned His followers to "beware of the leaven of the Pharisees, and of the leaven of Herod." The Pharisees were the legalists, who insisted that a man would be saved by keeping every detail of the law. Herod, on the other hand, stood for compromise and "anything goes" —libertinism. So today there are those who want to be completely free of all restraint. "We are the children of God," say they. "All things are ours! We can do as we please!" On the other hand, there are the legalists who would like to take all freedom away from the Christian, and put him under interminable "thou shalts", and "thou shalt nots". The middle way here was well expressed by St. Augustine, in his memorable saying: "*Habe caritatem, et fac quod vis.*" "Have the love of God in you (*agape*), and do what you will!" When you are guided by God's love you will want to do what pleases Him.

There is the narrow way between those who emphasize the need for Christians to share Christ's suffering and death, and those who emphasize His risen life. St. Paul holds these in balance beautifully when he says: "That I may know him, and the power of his resurrection, and the fellowship of his sufferings, being made conformable unto his death; If by any means I might attain unto the resurrection of the dead" (Phil. 3: 10–11 KJV).

The narrow way cuts between those who say that a Christian should possess nothing, and those who seem to feel that he should be a millionaire! Here again it is the Apostle Paul who points out the "narrow way": "I know both how to be abased, and I know how to abound: every where and in all things I am instructed both to be full and to be hungry, both to abound and to suffer need. I can do all things through Christ who strengthens me" (Phil. 4: 12–13).

The way goes between those who want to emphasize the humanity of Jesus, and those who want to see only His divinity. The true path shows us God Who is Man, and Man Who is God.

It cuts between those who would present the Christian life as a matter of individual salvation only—concerned only with the individual's relationship with God—and those who focus entirely on the "group", as though God dealt with people only in "bunches".

It cuts between those who emphasize *religious experience* and those who emphasize *objective truth*. The *Spirit* and the *Word* must go together, and of that we want to talk in detail in the next chapter.

17
The Charts

To travel any distance you need a chart—a map that clearly shows you where you are going, and what lies along the way. The believer's "chart" is the Holy Scriptures. The Anglican *Book of Common Prayer* says, speaking of the Scriptures, that we are to "read, learn, mark, and inwardly digest" them [1]—one of the most important pieces of advice for a believer who wants to move steadily along the King's Highway.

Read the Scriptures. Let the Bible be your main Book. Some great men and women of God have read little else! Equip yourself with several different versions and translations. If you read, even with difficulty, another language, be sure to get a copy of the Bible in that language. Every version or translation reflects the attitude of the reviser or translator, but if you compare several, you begin to get a picture "in depth" of the real meaning of a passage. Of course, the ideal would be to be able to read the original in Hebrew and Greek. You may not have time to learn these languages, but if you are serious about your New Testament study you should get an *Interlinear Greek-English New Testament*, which has the literal translation of the

1. *Book of Common Prayer*, p. 92.

Greek words immediately under them. Even if you know no Greek at all, you will find this book interesting and informative; with a very little effort you can learn the Greek letters; and with the help of a Greek-English lexicon, a Greek concordance, and a minimum of grammar, you can learn a lot. If this sounds formidable, how much effort and expense would you put into learning, say, to play golf, or to ski? Should you not be prepared to spend at least that much on learning God's Word?

Don't read little "snatches" of Scripture! Read it in big chunks—at least several chapters a day. How much time do you spend reading the newspaper? Watching TV? Reading the latest magazine? Reading the latest best seller? How does your time reading the Bible compare?

It isn't a good idea to begin at the beginning of the Bible and read straight through to end, as if it were a novel. The name of the Holy Scriptures in Greek is *Ta Biblia,* which means *The Books.* The Bible is a symposium of writings, different, and yet all on the same theme, because they were all inspired by the same Holy Spirit. Each book in the Bible supports and enhances the others, and yet each one is a unit in itself. Some books, of course, are like a serial story—I and II Kings, I and II Chronicles, Luke and Acts, the first five books (the Pentateuch), etc. Some of the most difficult parts of the Bible to understand are the very first books; so if you are reading the Bible seriously for the first time, you should begin with the Gospels, which tell of the life, death, and rising again of the Lord Jesus Christ. Then go on to the Acts of the Apostles, which tell of the doings of some of the earliest Christians. As you read the Acts, you can read the letters of Paul (Epistles) that he wrote to the places he visited. You will want to explore the Epistles written by others besides Paul. Now you can start at Genesis and read of the beginnings, then follow with the story of the patriarchs and the rise and fall of God's people of the Old Testament. Here you can read the books of the Prophets and the histories of Job, Esther, and Ruth. You will find that Psalms and Proverbs make excellent daily reading. Finally, you may want to dip into the very difficult Book of Revelation, which tells of the "last things".

As a Christian baptized in the Holy Spirit, you will find the Bible speaking to you all the way through, even though you do not always understand the background of what you are reading. This is the most important use of the Scriptures, to let the Holy Spirit speak to you, and of this we'll have more to say a little later.

There are lots of books available that will help you to set up a plan of Bible-reading and study. You will need some commentaries, that is, books written to help you understand, verse by verse, what the Bible is talking about. Be very careful in your selection of these commentaries—just as careful as you would be in picking a live teacher to help you. Avoid those that are the work of modernist scholars, many of whom do not believe in the divinity of Jesus, or in His saving work. Use the older commentaries, unless you are sure that the modern one you have is written by a person sound in the faith.

If possible, get into a good Bible class, with a believing teacher. We strongly recommend that you find a teacher who has received the baptism in the Holy Spirit. If you can't get a "live" teacher, records and tapes provide an excellent resource. They are a good supplement to class teaching, too. There are some good radio ministries. In all things you must be selective and discerning.

Watch out for "proof texts". It is not what a particular verse in the Bible teaches that we must focus on, but what the *whole* Bible teaches. Most false teachings are built on an isolated verse or verses of the Scripture, taken out of context, and blown up out of proportion. The better you know the whole Book, the better you will be able to deal with the person who uses isolated "proof texts". For example, those misled people who deny the threefold nature of God (the Trinity) quote Jesus saying: "I and My Father are One!" or, "He that hath seen Me, hath seen the Father!" in an attempt to prove that Jesus and the Father are one Person, but Christians don't believe in the threefold nature of God because of proof texts, but because the Trinity is presented in the Bible from start to finish—even though the word "Trinity" is not used. The Bible instead uses the word "Godhead" when speaking of the threefold God: Father, Son, and Holy Ghost. On the very first page of the Scriptures we read: "In the beginning, God created the heaven and earth . . . and the Spirit of God moved upon the face of the waters" (Gen. I: 1-2 KJV). In the first chapter of the Gospel according to John we are told: "In the beginning was the Word, and the Word was with God, and the Word was God. The same was in the beginning with God. All things were made by him [the Word] and without him was not any thing made that was made. In Him was life; and the life was the light of men . . . (John 1: 1-4 KJV). And Who is the "Word"? We read on: "And the Word was made flesh, and dwelt among us, (and we beheld his glory, the glory as of the only begotten of the Father,) full of grace and truth" (John 1: 14). So the Word which was in the very beginning with the Father, is none other than Jesus Christ—the "Word made flesh". Thus we see the Father, Son, and Holy Ghost at the creation. Are there other Scriptures to back up the fact that the Father created all things through Jesus Christ? Yes, for the Apostle Paul says it in so many words in Ephesians 3: 9 (KJV): "And to make all men see what is the fellowship of the mystery, which from the beginning of the world hath been hid in God, who created all things by Jesus Christ." Then in the first chapter of Hebrews we read: "God . . . has in these last days spoken unto us by His Son . . . by whom also He made the worlds" (Heb. 1: 1–2). In the Gospels we are presented with the record of the baptism of Jesus, and are shown the Son of God standing in Jordan, the Father speaking from heaven, and the Holy Ghost descending upon Jesus. Many times in the Gospels Jesus speaks of His Father in heaven, and He promises to send the Holy Spirit to take His, Jesus', place, after He has gone back to the Father. In Acts 7: 55 we read: "But he (Stephen), being full of the Holy Ghost, looked up . . . and saw . . . Jesus standing on the right hand of God." Here again, the three Persons of the Trinity are clearly distinguished. In II Corinthians 13: 14, Paul says: "The grace of the Lord Jesus Christ, and the love of God, and the communion of the Holy Ghost, be with you all . . ." Thus all the way through the Bible, we find reference after reference that keeps pointing us to the fact that God is Father, Son, and Holy Ghost—three distinct Persons in one Godhead. This should be our test with any doctrine—not what does one verse say, but what is the teaching of the *Scripture*.

Inspiration. Intellectual understanding and training in the faith is very important, but the most important ministry of the Bible to you will be *inspiration*. You need to let God speak to you personally through His Word. The Christian life must be an interplay of *experience* and *truth*. To return to our original illustration: if you set out to find the Hawaiian Islands without a chart, you may have many exciting experiences, but you won't get where you want to go! So if you simply set out, as many do, to have "spiritual experiences", you may have an exciting time, but you will almost certain to end in confusion. Indeed, you will be in far greater danger than if you were navigating the ocean without a map, because there at least you are confronted only with the impersonal forces of wind and wave, but in the spiritual realm you are surrounded by enemies whose chief design is to lead you astray, and destroy you. However, if someone handed you a chart of the Pacific Ocean, pointed out the route to Hawaii and said: "There you are! You've got the chart; now you don't need to make the trip!" you would not be satisfied. The purpose of the chart is that you might see and enjoy the Islands; it is not an end in itself. So the purpose of reading the Bible is that we might come to a deeper personal experience of God; then for every wonderful experience of God in our lives, there must come a scriptural understanding of what it means, which prepares us for further experience. The *Spirit* and the *Word* must be in continual interplay in order to keep the balance. In Heaven we will finally know the complete blending of the two, as God grants us full experience of Him, with full understanding.

Therefore, spend part of your time reading the Bible just waiting for the Holy Spirit to speak to you from its pages. When you do this, be prepared for some surprising insights, and some unexpected interpretations! The Holy Spirit can use the Scripture very freely and allegorically when He chooses. You may see a profound spiritual truth for your life in very unlikely places. A factual description of some aspect of the Temple, or an unlikely spot in a long list of names, may suddenly strike you with spiritual significance. When you try to share it with someone else, they may look at you blankly—but don't be disheartened by that. *That* little morsel was for you! The Rev. J. A. Dennis, of Austin, Texas, tells in his testimony how he was healed by laying hold of a promise for him from the Scripture. He was suffering from stomach trouble, and the Holy Spirit showed him the text: "I will take sickness away from the *midst* of thee!" (Exod. 23:25 KJV). "That's for me!" said J. A. Dennis. "In the midst of me, in my stomach, I've got trouble. God will take it away!" And God did take it away, and healed him completely. Later on, the Rev. Mr.

Dennis told this to a well-trained Bible scholar, who laughed and said: "But *that* isn't what that verse means!" J. A. Dennis was healed, just the same, because the Holy Spirit said: "That's what *I* want it to mean to you, to build your faith!" This kind of inspiration is for blessing, not for doctrine.

When you begin to read the Bible, you will find many things you don't understand. Worse yet, you will find things you don't *like!* You will find things that seem contradictory. That's all right; it isn't because the Bible is defective, it's just because you don't yet comprehend. The answer to the seeming contradiction lies beyond your field of vision. Don't reject the thing you don't understand; just put it aside and say: "I don't get it, Lord! I don't even like it! But I'll just wait until You explain it to me. In the meantime I'll thank You for what I *do* understand!"

Mark your Bible! The *Book of Common Prayer* quotation we have been using didn't literally mean to "mark with a pencil or pen", but "pay strict attention to"; nevertheless, we can interpret it to mean: "Underline the words in your Bible that speak to you". Develop your own system of marking. You may want to get a loose-leaf Bible, or a pre-marked Bible, or a wide-margin Bible—check and see the different helps there are to *marking* your Bible.

Learn! Memorize the Scripture. Set out to learn whole passages and even whole books by heart. It's not as hard as you think, and it's a great way to emphasize what is there. Some married couples are memorizing by learning alternate verses —the husband takes one and the wife the next. This is good, because it is shared, and also when you learn this way, both really learn the whole passage. Remember that behind the Iron Curtain in many places Bibles are forbidden. There may come a time when you will wish you had learned more of the Scriptures by heart. The Scripture tells us of the Holy Spirit that He will "bring all things to our remembrance"—but He can't very well do that if you have never put them into your memory! It's true that the Holy Spirit can, if He chooses, give you a passage of Scripture that you have never heard before, but for the most part He works by quickening your memory. Don't be worried if you forget a passage after having once memorized it. You haven't really forgotten it. It's still there, down in your mind. It's just that you have lost track of it for the time being, but the Holy Ghost can fish it out when He wants to! Put it in there—that's the important thing! [1]

Inwardly digest! Let the Word of God become a part of you. Thus you make yourself more sensitive to God, and also more able to recognize that which is not of God. "That doesn't sound like God!" the person who knows his Bible will say, upon hearing false teaching. "That isn't the way God acts in the Bible!"

Carry a Bible with you at all times, but not a great big one; for that will frighten people! Carry a little one, which will fit into your pocket or your handbag. When you have some time during the day, you can read the Word. When you are witnessing, you can use your Bible. The Holy Scripture is the "Sword of the Spirit", so don't go about unarmed!

Theology. Don't be frightened by the word. Theology is simply the *summary* of what the *Bible* teaches about *God.* It might be termed the "truth about the truth about the Truth"! It is true that the Bible is the summary of our belief and practice, but it is also true that we need a summary of what is in

1. We have found a simple 3 × 5 file card a useful aid to memorizing. Take a fairly familiar passage that you would like to memorize. Cover it with the file card, and begin to repeat it, while checking yourself by uncovering a line at a time. If you get "stuck", take as little a peek as you need, to get yourself started again. You will be surprised at how much you *do* know in the familiar chapters of the Bible. Then go back over the passage again, and again. Each time you will find that more has lodged in your memory.

the Bible. You can't very well read the whole Bible to everyone, or take the time to go through the entire Book and give all the references on every occasion. Theology is really such a summary, and the conclusions drawn from it. For example, we showed already how the Bible presents God all the way through as Father, Son, and Holy Ghost—as three Persons in one Godhead. Theology gives to this the title the "doctrine of the Trinity", and points out how it answers some difficult questions. To illustrate, if there were only one Person in the Godhead—if the Father, Son, and Holy Spirit we read about in the Bible were really all the same Person—then it had to be God the Father Himself Who died on the Cross! But what would have happened to the world during the time that God was dead!? Obviously it couldn't have been the *Father* Who was crucified. Our whole salvation, however, depends on the fact that it was *God* Who died on that Cross. If Jesus wasn't really and truly God, or if He didn't truly and really die, we are not saved, and are still in our sins, for only God could make the infinite offering. The only way all this could fit together is that the Father and the Son must be One in Their Godhead, yet distinct in Their Persons. To understand, explain, and interpret such things is the work of theology.

Then, too, the doctrine of the Trinity helps us to see that even in the very Being of the Godhead there is a sharing of mutual love. Love is something you *do*, and it is difficult to see how a God Who was only One Person all by Himself could be *love*, since He would have had no other Being of His own Nature to share with. As one theologian put it: "It is not good for *God* to be alone!" Our God, however, is a divine "Community" in Himself, a Community of shared love and joy—Father, Son, and Holy Ghost: perfectly united, yet perfectly distinct so that They can enjoy and love One Another. This too is a part of theology. Every Christian needs to have a basic theology. If you don't have a true one, you are likely to acquire a false one! A lot of speculation and false teaching goes by the name of "theology" these days, but if we remember that theology is just the attempt to sum up in an orderly and usable way what the Bible is saying about God, we won't go far wrong. As soon as theology becomes human speculation, or an intellectual game, it is worse than useless.

The briefest theological summaries are called the "creeds". Most Christians are familiar with the Apostles' Creed, not so many with the Nicene Creed. Every believer would profit by being familiar with these two statements. They are true because they agree with Scripture. They do not present the complete way of salvation to the unbeliever. They are statements for the *believer* regarding the nature of God, Christ, the Holy Spirit, the Church, etc. A third, called the Athanasian Creed, is far less known; yet it is a magnificent statement about the Trinity that would help every believer. It is true that this statement presents salvation as depending on right intellectual belief, which we know is not true—yet it would not hurt modern Christians to lean a little more in that direction! These three creeds came into existence as defences against false teachings. Each phrase or clause affirms an important fact in the face of Satan's attempts to mislead the people of God. Today, as the Church is being renewed and brought to life in the Holy Spirit, false doctrines are again flourishing as Satan counterattacks. We may need to expand further our statements of belief as useful summaries of right teaching in the face of falsehood.

Longer and more detailed statements of theology are to be found in the confessions of the various churches: the Westminster Confession, the Augsburg Confession, the Thirty-Nine Articles are perhaps the three best known. Then there are the catechisms of the various churches. *Do not scorn or discard* out of hand these products of Christian experience. Remember the saying: "Don't throw the baby out with the bath-water!" Inspect carefully the statements of faith that your particular church has inherited. It may well be that many no longer take the confession and catechism of their churches seriously. That doesn't matter. *You* take it seriously. Study it in the light of the Scriptures, illuminated by the Holy Spirit. You will find gems of understanding that will equip you for battle. *Of course* you will find things you can't accept—that are unscriptural— but those you can reject without throwing away the whole thing. "Submit yourselves one to another in the fear of God" also includes submitting yourself to believers who came before you in history, listening to your forefathers who also knew the Lord!

This is a good time to speak of Christian reading in general. There are some excellent popular books of theology which will help you to be a better-equipped soldier in the Lord's army. Here again you need not necessarily accept everything that is written in a particular book, but if the writer is a believer, you can listen and learn, while discarding that which does not strike you as being right. The books of such men and women as C. S. Lewis, Dorothy Sayers, Andrew Murray, Watchman Nee, and a host of others will help you greatly.

The Ministry. While we are talking of the churches and their confessions, and the need for sound theology, it is a good time to talk about the ordained ministry. It is very popular today to condemn ministers along with the denominations, as if the whole were simply an artificial human organization without divine power or authority. Remember, that while God is certainly not interested in "labels", or in our human divisions, He does call men to the ministry. People grow impatient with the pastors of their dead churches and tend to turn away from them, but be careful. Many of these men were validly called of God to exercise ministry in the Church of God: elders, pastors, evangelists, apostles, prophets, teachers. They may have become entangled in the web of denominationalism, but the Holy Spirit is trying to free them. When God calls a man, He calls him. The "gifts and calling of God are without repentance", and the Scripture says that we are to respect the ministry that the Spirit has established. Listen to your pastor, even though he is not yet open to your witness about the work of the Holy Spirit. Help him, pray for him, and conform to his "Godly admonitions". Your relationship to your pastor, as long as you are a member of the congregation, is to "obey them that have the rule over you", just as the Christian wife is to obey her husband. Obviously she does not obey him in things that would be against the Lord, but she obeys him in everything she can. So with the pastor. You cannot obey him if he tells you something that is against the Word of God, but you can obey him in many things. God will bless you for it, and it may be the means of leading your minister to the baptism in the Holy Spirit.[2] If you find yourself unable to respect a minister at all, or to in any way go along with his leadership, then leave that congregation and find another. Do not be a "troublemaker". (Of course, you may be accused of troublemaking unjustly—you can't help that, but don't really and knowingly be a *rebellious* member.)

The decision whether or not to remain in a church that seems dead is one that you alone can make. Our advice is always to "stay put" if you can, as long as there is anyone listening to you. On the other hand, you can stay in an unbelieving situation only as long as you are able to make it clear that you do

---

2. You may be in a church where the minister has not yet accepted Christ. Don't assume that because he is in the ministry, he must therefore be a believer! With a minister, just as with a lay person, always find out first what the relationship is with the Lord Jesus before going on to pray about receiving the Holy Spirit.

not agree with the wrong teachings. You cannot be put in the position of seeming to be part of it all, or you may lead others astray. If you yourself are strong enough to be uninfluenced by the teaching, you may be able to "stay put". If you have children, however, who are not yet able to protect themselves, you cannot expose them, but must find a fellowship where they can be properly nurtured. As one man put it: "If you can sit on an ice cube and melt it, stay where you are, but if it is freezing you, get off!"

Denomination. God isn't necessarily deserting the denominational churches, either. Most of the leading denominations began in deep Christian belief and fervour. They did not begin in a desire to separate, but to spread the fire of God. The Methodist movement is a good example. Wesley had no desire to separate from the Church of England, and indeed, he himself never did do so. It was the Church of England that forced the early Methodists to construct their own organization. Martin Luther had no desire to separate from Rome, but he was forced to do so by the Roman Catholic leadership of the day. Gradually, as the years went by, much of the original fervour died out, and the denomination is left trying to keep in existence for the sake of existing. "There has always been an Episcopal Church in this town, and we'll see to it that there always will be, even if only two people attend services!" As God reaches into the churches of various denominations, and brings people to life within them, denominational walls are crumbling. We must let the Holy Spirit do His work, which is the real ecumenical movement.

Don't pay attention to the "come-outers". Often with the best intentions in the world, they are simply creating new denominations that further complicate the scene. Each tradition has something to contribute to the fellowship of Christians in the Holy Spirit. Those of us who have been ministering among

Roman Catholics who are receiving the baptism in the Holy Spirit are realizing what a depth of real humility and understanding of devotion is to be found among our Roman brothers and sisters; the Baptists restored to the Church the fuller symbolism of baptism by immersion; the Lutherans remind us of the standing fast in the faith; the Presbyterians, the reality of God's calling and election; the Episcopalians (Anglicans) can claim to have been used to bring the great King James Version of the Bible, for so many years the standard of the English Scriptures, and still unrivalled for literary beauty, and also the *Book of Common Prayer*, a classic of Christian devotion which should be known and loved much more widely than in the confines of one denomination. The Pentecostals, of course, brought the great witness that is reviving the Church today, the knowledge of the baptism in the Holy Spirit. It was the Methodists who reminded the English-speaking church of the most important message of all, personal salvation through Jesus Christ. And we could go on and on. God is drawing these treasures together to become a common heritage for us all.

18
The Compass

The compass. The *charts* are terribly important, but so is the *compass*, because without navigational instruments you can't follow the course line laid out on the chart. Now the compass for the Christian is *not* the Holy Spirit, but our *response* to the Holy Spirit. The compass in a ship or aeroplane responds to the magnetic pole of the earth, but the instrument is not always reliable. Corrections have to be made for variation, deviation, declination, etc. Thus it is important that we give attention to the accuracy of our compass, that is, that we spend much time learning how to respond more accurately to the Holy Spirit. The compass responds to the magnetic pole because it is itself magnetic. So it is the Holy Spirit in you that makes you able to respond to God. It follows that your sensitivity will increase as you allow the Holy Spirit to inspire and move you more from within. This you do through praise and prayer, and closer personal friendship with God and experience of Him. You sensitize your own instruments by using them.

Set yourself a pattern of praise and prayer that will keep you sensitized! God created for you one purpose—that you might get to know Him personally, and have personal fellowship with

Him. Heaven is the state of perfect fellowship with God, and with one another. We can have a foretaste of it here and now!

Lots of people think that God created them only to "serve" Him, in the sense of doing *chores* for Him. Recently, while we were on a "missionary journey" to far-off places, our elder son came over to the house and washed and waxed the car! He didn't *have* to do it. He has a home and family of his own, living some thirty miles away. We didn't ask him to do it, or expect him to do it. He did it because he loves us. When we arrived home, Dennis didn't say to him:

"I'm glad you finally got the message! This is why I begat you—so that you could *serve* me! Now, tomorrow morning why don't you cut the lawn, and then start painting the house?"

Can you imagine us saying to our children: "We've got lots to do around here, so don't let's waste time in foolish chatter. When you come over to *serve* us, don't bother to come in the house. Just wave at us through the window. We know you love us, but the important thing is to get the *work* done!"

That's how a lot of people think about God. They think He chiefly wants them to run errands and do chores for Him, and that *that* is what is meant by "serving" God. But God really doesn't need our help in running this world—in fact, He could do it better without us, for sure. But because He loves us, He lets us share in it, as a mother might let her three-year-old "help" her bake a cake.

God created us for His *pleasure*, the Bible says. He created us because He wanted to share His love with us. Actually, if your son came over, and offered to cut the lawn, you would be more likely to say:

"Come on in, and have a cup of coffee. Let's talk a little bit. What have you been doing lately?" And then, when you were ready, you would probably say:

"I'll come and help you cut the lawn; we can talk some more while we do it together."

This is exactly what God wants us to do: first spend a good deal of time "talking" with Him; then go out and do the things that He lets us share in, in company with Him. "The Lord working with them," the Bible says. "We are fellow-workers together with God."

It is very hard, when we face a busy day, to spend an extra amount of time getting into fellowship with God—praising Him, and praying, and listening to what He has to say to us. It's hard to convince ourselves when we already have more to do than there is time for, that we should spend extra time with God. Yet when we are in fellowship with Him, we can accomplish many times as much; we get things in the right order; we are inspired to say and do the right things at the right time.

Make yourself a time at the beginning of the day to spend with the Lord. Start with a period that you know you can keep —it may be ten or fifteen minutes. Spend much of this time in praising God—just telling Him you love Him, and acknowledging how wonderful He is. We do not praise God because He is conceited! We praise Him because He is worthy of praise, and as we praise Him, our hearts are opened to Him to love Him more. Think of a husband coming home after work to find a delicious supper waiting for him. After the meal he will say to his wife—if he is a wise husband—"Thank you, dear, for that wonderful dinner!" That's fine! But notice that he might have said the same thing to someone he didn't even know. If he had taken his business associates to dine at a restaurant, and the meal was especially good, he might have said to the maître d'hôtel: "Please convey our thanks to the chef!" He has never met the chef, and perhaps never will. You don't have to *know* someone in order to *thank* him. People thank God and are grateful to Him, who have never met Him! He has answered prayer, and in gratefulness they thank Him. It is very important to *thank* God, but it is more important to praise Him.

If the husband we talked about a little while ago really loves and appreciates his wife, he will *praise* her. He will say:

"Honey, you're a wonderful cook! In fact, you're a wonderful girl! I love you very much!" Notice that he could say this even though she had just returned from a two-week trip to visit her mother, and hadn't cooked him anything for two weeks! He isn't thanking her for something she's done, he's praising her what she *is*. You thank someone for what he's *done*, but you praise him for what he is. It follows that in order to *praise* someone you have to *know* him.

When the husband praises his wife, she does not swell up with pride and say: "Well, I'm glad you recognize my worth!" No, she says to him something like: "Well, honey, I think you're pretty wonderful, too!" and love grows between them. Praise is not insincere flattery. The wife knows that her husband is telling the truth—she is a good cook, and she does honestly try to be a wonderful wife.

God rejoices in the love of His children, and we praise Him, our hearts come open, not only to love Him more, but to be able to accept more freely the blessings He is ready to pour upon us. So spend much time in praising God, both privately and publicly, and your love for Him will grow. This is, of course, not separated from your inspirational use of the Bible. You will want to relate your Bible reading to your prayer and praise. Many find it helpful to begin with reading the Scripture, looking for a verse or passage that especially speaks to them, and then moving into praise and prayer.

Spend much time in speaking in tongues—let the Holy Spirit guide you to pray and praise "in the Spirit". This is very important indeed.

Offer your requests to God with confidence. There is nothing wrong with petitionary prayer (asking God for things). Jesus strongly instructed His followers to do it. He said: "Up till now you have not asked anything in My Name. Ask, and you shall receive, that your joy may be full!" (John 16:24). Remember that Jesus said you should thank God ahead of time for the answer to your prayer. Mark 11:24 says: "Whatever you ask when you are praying, believe that you receive it, and you shall have it." Don't just lamely tack "if it be Thy will" on to the end of every prayer. If you are not sure what God wants in a particular situation, then pray first of all that He will show you how to pray. Search the Scriptures to see how God feels about your need. Pray confidently, and you will see results. Confession of sin is, of course, also a part of your daily prayers. Always offer to God immediately anything in your life that has been wrong, ask His forgiveness, and *accept* it! It is as important to say, "I accept Your forgiveness, Lord," as it is to say, "I ask Your forgiveness, Lord." (Refer to pages 121 and 151, and footnotes.) Stop many times during the day and offer God praise and prayer. If you can turn completely away from your work, and get by yourself in a place where you can pray out loud, strongly and firmly, so much the better; if not, pray where you are, under your breath, but stop and praise and pray. The Scripture says: "Seven times a day do I praise Thee" (Ps. 119:164 KJV).

During the course of the day, at work or at play, try to remain sensitive to the leading of the Holy Spirit. Don't be afraid to trust His leadings, if they are in keeping with God's Word, and in "decency and order." You will make mistakes sometimes, but God will take care of you. Actively believe Jesus to open the way for you, to meet your needs, to work miracles in your life. The Scripture says that the greatest sin is not believing in Jesus (John 16:9). This doesn't just refer to our initial belief in Him and acceptance of Him, but to our moment-by-moment trust in Him to preserve us and guide us. Whenever you find yourself dropping into worry or anxiety or upset, reaffirm your active belief in Jesus. Tell Him: "I believe! I believe! I believe that You are meeting my needs and guiding my life, right now!" Jesus said: "All things are possible to him that believeth" (Mark 9: 23 KJV).

Fellowship. The Christian faith is not a solitary thing. When a certain modern philosopher defined religion as what "a man does with his solitariness," as far as Christians are concerned, he couldn't have been farther afield! The aim of God is not only to draw us to enjoy Him, but to show us how great it is to enjoy one another in Him. To enjoy God by oneself is great, but to enjoy Him in company with others is far greater—this is why the early Christians would risk their lives any time to "assemble themselves together," because when they assembled together, the glory of God was so heightened, that sometimes the very room they were meeting in would be shaken as if by an earthquake! This kind of fellowship is still available to you today. When you compare the kind of thing "going to church" has become—a kind of dull, if not unhappy, duty—with what it meant to the early Christians to get together, you will see how much we have lost track of what it is all about, but the baptism in the Holy Spirit has begun to restore this fellowship in the Lord. A "worship service" is supposed to be God's people enjoying a little foretaste of Heaven, as they share their joy in Christ with one another! They meet together to enjoy the Lord and one another in the Lord. Out of this joyful service, the gifts and fruit of the Holy Spirit proceed.

Where will I find this fellowship? If you are in a church where the pastor and perhaps many of the people know about the baptism in the Holy Spirit, there is probably a prayer meeting—or several—at which you can share in praise and prayer in the freedom of the Spirit. If so, praise God! You are very fortunate! But if your church is not like this, that does not mean you should leave. No—but it *does* mean that you need to go elsewhere to get your "spiritual food"! It means that you need to be faithful in attendance at your own church, while going to prayer meetings and Bible study somewhere else to get nourishment so you can show the joy of the Lord to your *own* church. God is not concerned with our labels; He is working in every denomination today to reach His people. He is not rejecting the old-line churches. He is working in them when He is permitted to, and if you leave your old-line church you may be deserting the work God has for you. You may discover that the group to which you go has problems, too.

God is not starting new churches and denominations today, but many human beings *are*, often with the best intentions in the world. The world is being dotted with little groups where a leader has said: "I am your apostle, and we're going to start a *New Testament* Church with *me* at the head!"

In the New Testament we find the churches sharing ministry. We find prophets, apostles, evangelists, and others travelling from church to church, sharing, correcting errors, encouraging, exhorting, rebuking in the Spirit where they found something wrong. We do not find isolated fellowships living under one elder or teacher, and having nothing to do with others. We do not find men claiming absolute authority over one church or another. We find a shared ministry—submitting one to another. No one in the New Testament says: "I just get my word from the Lord." The instruction in the New Testament is: "[Submit] yourselves one to another in the fear of God" (Eph. 5:21 KJV), and we find this going on both at the level of the local assembly, and also among the leaders—even the apostles (Gal. 2).

So the most important thing you must look for when selecting a church or prayer group for fellowship, or when selecting a teacher is their *fellowship* and submission to others on as wide a basis as possible. Jude speaks of those "Who set themselves apart, soulish, not having the Spirit" (Jude 19). Paul, in Romans 16:17 (KJV), says: "Mark them which cause divisions . . . and avoid them." Do not be led astray by having some of these folk quote you: "Come out from among them and be ye separate . . . "If you will examine this verse in context, you will see that it speaks of *believers* coming out from among *unbelievers, not* brethren from brethren (II Cor. 6:17 KJV). The only time we are to separate is from unbelief—false teaching, denial of the faith—or wrong moral behaviour that destroys fellowship with God.

No one can "join the church". When a person meets and receives Jesus, he becomes a part of the Church, the people of God. It is Jesus Who joins us to the Church, and the "local church" is simply all those in a given locality who have received the Lord.

If the fellowship you join, or the teacher you listen to, is submitted to others, then you are sure you will have a "balanced diet", and excesses or errors will be corrected as the Holy Spirit moves among His people. Remember, too, that you must be willing to submit to your brothers and sisters in the Lord. You must be willing to listen, and to learn. The sheep is safe as long as he stays with the flock and the Shepherd. The first thing a wolf wants to do is to get a sheep to leave the flock; then the wolf can easily devour him. There are, as Paul says, "grievous wolves" prowling around the flock of God (Acts 20.29), and the first mark of the wolf is that he wants to separate sheep from the flock and get them to himself. The most vulnerable believer is the dear soul who says, "I don't belong to any church; I just follow the Lord!" It is very hard for a sheep to follow the Shepherd without being part of the flock! If you follow the

Shepherd, you are automatically going to have to be part of the flock!

Christians need fellowship. As we have said, there is nothing greater than enjoying the joy of the Lord in company with others. This is what Heaven is. Remember, though, that you can continue this fellowship with the Lord when you are not able to be with other believers. If you don't get regular fellowship, you will find it harder to keep your own freedom in the Spirit, but you *can* do it. Don't despair because you can't find fellowship, or are in a situation where for the time being you can't have it. This is why Paul tells you:

"Be filled with the Spirit, speaking *to yourselves* in psalms and hymns and spiritual songs, singing and making melody in your heart to the Lord" (Eph. 5: 18–19 KJV). When you can't share fellowship in the Lord with others, you keep the fire burning in your own heart by speaking *to yourself* of the joy and glory of the Lord! Then too, the fellowship will be that much more wonderful if each member has been keeping up his individual fellowship with Jesus while he is apart from the others. Don't let down on this, and expect to get a spiritual "pick-me-up" from the meeting! If everyone comes to a prayer meeting expecting to *get* something, all are likely to go away hungry and frustrated! The blessing of the fellowship is greatest when all come with something to *share*.

Witness. In Isaiah 9:3 (KJV) the Scripture says: "They joy before Thee according to the joy in harvest . . ." and some of the greatest joy of your Christian life will come as you tell someone else about Jesus, helping Him with the harvest. If you don't witness to others about the Lord, you will not be likely to keep your own joy. One of the greatest ways to stimulate your freedom in the Spirit is to make a *personal* witness. A personal witness means telling another person "eyeball to eyeball" what Jesus means to you, personally. Pray that you may have many such opportunities. Pray that God will let you witness every day.

Wait for God to open the doors when you witness. A good witness is not necessarily rushing in and saying: "Are you saved?" or, "Do you know Jesus?" You may so frighten or offend the person that he may run away from God for years. Jesus said we were to be fishermen, and fishing is a delicate skill. So is witnessing! You may spend an hour just in casual conversation with someone, getting acquainted with him, letting them know you are a sensible, normal person, before you can even begin to move in the direction of telling him anything else. You may even have to break off the conversation the first time before getting to the point, but you will have broken the ice, and gained the person's confidence. Don't lecture! Get the other fellow to ask the questions, and don't go on and answer questions he hasn't asked! The minute he shows the least sign of losing interest, you change the subject. If *he* changes it, he's likely to go away shaking his head, saying that you tried to stuff your religion down his throat! But if he or she shows real interest, don't be afraid to move ahead.

You will be surprised how easy it is to get a person to follow right along and accept the Lord, and the baptism in the Holy Spirit, if you are sensitive to the moving of the Spirit. The Holy Spirit will be moving ahead of you, if you are being sensitive to what He is doing—He will be opening the doors, and all you have to do is go through them! It is, after all, the Holy Ghost Who convicts the world of sin. This, by the way, should be the focus of your witness. Don't get off on discussing theology, morality, or politics—get to the point. A person is a sinner, not because of his habits, or his behaviour, but because he doesn't believe in Jesus Christ (John 16 : 7–11).

Relax and enjoy witnessing. Don't get "up tight". Don't be a "scalp collector"! The Apostle Paul said: "I have planted,

Apollos watered, but God gave the increase" (II Cor. 3:6 KJV). You may be used to speak just a few words to someone, to start things going. Someone else may actually reap the crop that you planted. That's just fine—another time you'll get to reap a crop that someone else has planted and watered!

Witness, after all, is simple enough. It's just one human being telling another about something wonderful that he has found, and that he wants to share. Up our way our young people say, "Have you had your spiritual vitamins today?" That means: "Have you told someone about Jesus today?"

Enjoy God yourself—glorify Him in your own heart; then go and tell others about Him! Remember, too, that the gifts of the Holy Spirit are given for witness—so that others can see that Jesus is really alive, and working through you. Expect God to honour you when you step out to manifest the gifts. Is the girl who works at the desk next to you looking sad this morning?

"I've got a terrible headache," she says.

What about trusting Jesus to heal her? Oh, don't pounce on her and frighten, but say something like:

"Would you mind if I prayed for your headache to go away?"

"What do you mean?"

"Oh, we believe that Jesus Christ stills heals people, like He did in the Bible, you know, and we often pray for people who are sick."

"*Jesus* heals people?" your friend might respond. "He lived 2000 years ago!"

"Well, you see, He rose from the dead, and we believe He's still with us, and still doing the sort of thing He did while He was on the earth; only now He works through people who believe in Him."

"Oh. Well, this head is splitting. I don't care what you do!"

Now—watch it! This is the time the Devil will tempt you to go overboard. You've got a fish on the line—*don't* yank it. Don't give her a sermon. Don't jump up and lay hands on her begin to speak in tongues! Play it *cool*. Say something like:

"Well, okay, I'll pray." Be as natural as you know how. Don't even bow your head, and all that—just talk to God, quietly and simply.

"Lord, please heal Jane's head. Thank you very much."

If you feel it's all right, put your hand on her shoulder, but be careful about this. Some people don't like to be touched, you know.

What will Jesus do? He'll *heal* her, if the channel is open at all.

"Say! My head feels better!" Now's the time for lots of "cool" on your part! *Don't* say—"Well, praise the Lord!" Say something like: "That's great!" Let *her* pick up the ball. She may have to think about this quite awhile before she's ready to ask any more questions. If she turns back to her work without asking you anything else, you drop it, too. Don't start volunteering information. Don't pursue her with: "You see— I told you! Now don't you want to know more about it?" Let the Holy Spirit draw her—He will. This is perhaps the most difficult part of witnessing, knowing when *not* to say anything. Remember this is the Holy Spirit's work. You are just following along what He is doing. Without His support, you cannot lead anyone into the Kingdom.

Suppose nothing happens? Leave that to the Lord, too. I have almost never known anyone to resent or reject or react badly to a prayer for healing, whether there was any sign of results or not. Even if there is no apparent healing, because there is a block of some kind in your friend's acceptance, she may still very likely be moved by your concern, and by the fact that you would even ask to pray for her, or that you believe in prayer enough to "stick your neck out". People are so accustomed to the kind of religion in which nothing happens or is expected to happen, that they are startled when someone really believes.

Economics. Giving your money to God's work is a vital part of your life in the Spirit. Don't overlook it. God cannot bless your economic life unless it is open to Him. The Holy Spirit wants to guide and bless your pocketbook and your chequebook, just as He wants to guide and bless and fill every other part of you! We strongly recommend that you adopt the scriptural pattern of "tithing" (Gen. 28:22), that is, returning to God the "top ten percent"—the "firstfruits" of what He gives to you. If you receive one hundred dollars in income, immediately take ten dollars "off the top"; that is, before using the money for anything else, return one-tenth of it to God. This basic tithe should be given to your local congregation—your local family of God—and should not be diverted from there for other purposes. Over and above your basic tithes, you can make special gifts and offerings to the work—a favourite missionary project, or someone in need you are interested in helping. You will find that you can't outgive the Lord, and that the more generous you are with others, the more He can be generous with you.

Manner of living. Your freedom and sensitivity to the Holy Spirit will be affected a great deal by your manner of life. Remember, too, that if you have received the baptism in the Holy Spirit, people will have their eyes on you to see how you are going to behave! Satan will be watching to, for he knows it will be a double victory for him if he can get a baptized-in-the-Holy-Spirit Christian into disgrace. When you received the Holy Spirit, you moved into the "front line" of the Lord's Army. You began to take a more active part in spiritual battle and discovered that you had power and authority over the forces of the enemy. This of course did not make Satan, the enemy, very happy. But don't let that fact bother you; as long as you stick close to Jesus the enemy's pot shots can't touch you (I John 5:18; 4:4). Don't foolishly go wandering away from the Lord's protection! Watch your manner of life, for your own sake, and for the sake of your witness to others. The Apostle Paul said: "Abstain from all appearance of evil" (I Thess. 5:22 KJV), and that's very good advice.

The Holy Spirit does not deal at first with our specific sins and vices and bad habits. He first convicts of unbelief. The basic sin, as we have pointed out, is not believing in Jesus. When we believe in Him, and have received Him, the Holy Spirit moves on to press us to be more and more like Jesus— to change our habits of living so that we are not "conformed to this world" but "transformed by the renewing of [our] mind[s]" (Rom. 12:2 KJV). Some of this change comes quite quickly, some much more slowly. Always, Satan will be tempting us to turn back to old patterns and habits.

Some expect the process of cleanup and change to be automatic and without effort on our part. They say:

"I'll leave my bad habits when God does it for me: when He just takes them away!"

But that isn't the way it is. We have to work *with* the Holy Spirit. He never takes away our free will. We have to help Him as we purify ourselves, even as Jesus is pure (I John 3:3). Therefore it behoves the Christian to be careful of his or her manner of life. The Christian who doesn't pay his bills, who isn't quite honest in his business dealings, who quarrels noisily with his family is not going to help the cause of Christ by his behaviour. The world is also going to be watching to see how you conduct yourself in lesser matters. The Christian who always looks grubby, or whose house is always a mess, to say nothing of the garden, is also making a poor witness for the Lord. The mother who isn't at home to greet her children from school, but lets them run wild in the neighbourhood while she is at church, or at a prayer meeting, is not going to impress her friends with her faith. Most of this is a matter of common sense, and of asking yourself: "How would it appear to me, if I were one of the onlookers?"

Recreation and entertainment. The Bishops of the Church of England recently declared the Realm of England to be a missionary field. They recognized that their country can no longer honestly be called "Christian". It would give us a better sense of perspective if we could realize that our modern culture, worldwide with its literature, art, music, customs, and morality is pagan, not Christian.

This does not mean we have to stay this way. The fires of the Holy Spirit are springing up in many parts of the world. We are delighted with the fact that a number of top-notch entertainers are meeting Jesus and being baptized with the Holy Spirit, and some of their influence is already being seen in the entertainment fields.

All we are saying is, be on the alert. There's no need to make a blanket condemnation of all entertainment—movies, TV, art, music, etc.—but rather there is a need for the Christian to be very careful in selecting what of these things he or she can take part in. Don't leave the television set running all day, dribbling the thinking and attitudes of the world into your home, and into the minds of your family. Don't go to just any movie for a means of escape. Most movies today are spiritual poison. Don't subscribe to all the "regular" magazines. There are still a few left that can safely be brought into your home—select those few. Are your children believers? Do they know Jesus, and the wonderful experience of His Holy Spirit? Then you must explain and point out to them how listening to most modern "teen-age" music will take away their joy in Christ, and fill their minds with erroneous teaching. Provide them with some of the good record albums of Christian folk music and other styles of music being made available for them today.

Don't build your family life around commercial entertainment. Let it be the exception rather than the rule. Develop creative family good times: games, recreation, hobbies, outdoor activities—instead of watching TV, or going to the movies. It's safer, and a lot more fun!

Good works. You know by now that doing good things isn't what makes you a Christian, but the Bible says repeatedly that God will reward us according to what we have done. Loving your neighbour as yourself includes feeding him when he is hungry, clothing him when he is in need, visiting him when he is sick or in prison. And your neighbour isn't just the family next door, as Jesus pointed out, but whatever person in need you may come in contact with. The Apostle James says it is mockery to say to someone who is hungry and cold: "God bless you! Be warmed! Be fed!" unless you actually *do* something to help them.

Christian social action, about which so much is said today, should be simply Christians at work in the world wherever they are. The Church organization is not supposed to be a political pressure group, but Christians are supposed to take an interest in politics, and bring their convictions with them. The church organization is not supposed to be directly involved in disputes between capital and labour, but Christians who are leaders in capital and labour must bring their convictions into their confrontations. The businessman who is in Christ, will treat his employees as Jesus would treat them, and the Christian employee will give the kind of day's work that Jesus would give. "As He is, so are we in this world" (I John 4: 17) is the basis of true "social action".

You and your family should also be taking part in helping

God's work on a broader basis—helping to support people on the mission field, sharing in church community projects, etc. Of course you must wait on the Lord, Who will direct you in all these things, but don't use "waiting on the Lord" for an excuse for not doing them. They are a vital part of your Christian life and witness.

Co-operating with God. The word *co-operate* simply means to "work together", and the Scriptures teach that God wants us to be co-workers with Him (I Cor. 3:9; II Cor. 6:1). This means that although God has created us as free beings, He is depending on our co-operation in bringing His love to the world.

The Lord Jesus didn't write a book, though the most important Book in the world has been written about Him; He didn't travel more than a few miles from His birthplace, yet He had a plan to reach the ends of the earth. After washing away their sins. He filled His first followers with God's love, joy, and power, and sent them to pour out this joy, love, and power to others, and to tell them that they, too, could be forgiven, and filled with the glory and power of God. This is the Good News, the Gospel, and the people who hear and accept become God's people, the Church.

It is a most effective method, for if one person receives Christ today, and a greater power to witness through the baptism in the Holy Spirit, and tomorrow helps two others to receive Him, making sure that they also are baptized in the Holy Spirit, and those two people in turn reach four others on the following day, and those four reach eight, and so forth, then in thirty-one days, *one billion* people would be reached and brought into the Kingdom of God!

This amazing multiplication would be the case if each Christian reached only one other person for God in a life time. Obviously empowered Christians should pray for an opportunity *daily* to witness for Christ, and during their life time to win hundreds to Him.

This is the principle Jesus Christ depended upon to reach the world: each person to tell others, and they in turn to tell others, until millions all over the world are filled with the glory of God. The plan again and again has started up and then has seemed to fail, because of the unfaithfulness and forgetfulness of human beings, and the confusions and sidetracks of the enemy. Mostly it has failed because only a partial message has been transmitted; forgiveness without power. Today, however, the "full Gospel" is once again being proclaimed, not only the essential fact that God forgives and loves His people, but that having done so He empowers them to reach others. God's plan is to have millions of men and women, yes, and children, too, all over the world bringing His love and forgiveness and healing and power to mankind. We are living in the age of the revival of the Church, and it's exciting! All over the world, people are discovering how wonderful it is to tell others about Jesus and the power of the Holy Spirit, and we know God's plan is not going to fail! This may well be the last great renewal before the coming of the Lord Jesus Himself. We hope and pray that this book will help you *co-operate* with God, and that as His child and co-worker, you may continue to be filled to overflowing with His great joy.